Imperial Material

D1604395

Imperial Material

National Symbols in the US Colonial Empire

ALVITA AKIBOH

The University of Chicago Press
Chicago and London

The University of Chicago Press, Chicago 60637
The University of Chicago Press, Ltd., London
© 2023 by The University of Chicago
Published 2023
Printed in the United States of America

32 31 30 29 28 27 26 25 23   1 2 3 4 5

ISBN-13: 978-0-226-82636-3 (cloth)
ISBN-13: 978-0-226-82848-0 (paper)
ISBN-13: 978-0-226-82847-3 (e-book)
DOI: https://doi.org/10.7208/chicago/9780226828473.001.0001

Library of Congress Cataloging-in-Publication Data

Names: Akiboh, Alvita, author.
Title: Imperial material : national symbols in the US colonial empire / Alvita Akiboh.
Other titles: National symbols in the US colonial empire
Description: Chicago : The University of Chicago Press, 2023. |
    Includes bibliographical references and index.
Identifiers: LCCN 2023012191 | ISBN 9780226826363 (cloth) | ISBN 9780226828480
    (paperback) | ISBN 9780226828473 (ebook)
Subjects: LCSH: Emblems, National—United States—Territories and possessions. |
    Money—United States—Territories and possessions. | Signs and symbols—
    Political aspects—United States—Territories and possessions. | Nationalism—
    United States—Territories and possessions.
Classification: LCC F965 .A35 2023 | DDC 929.90973—dc23/eng/20230405
LC record available at https://lccn.loc.gov/2023012191

Contents

Figures

A Note on Terminology:
On Mainlands and Americans

At the heart of this project is the question of how US national identity has been created, challenged, and transformed in the US colonial empire. It rests on the claim that the moment US imperialists planted their flag in overseas colonies, US national identity was no longer confined to the continent. Thus, I do not use the terms "US" or "US American" to refer *only* to people from or places in the continental United States. It is important, however, to differentiate between the places the United States claims sovereignty over on the North American continent, and those overseas in the Caribbean and the Pacific. While the term "mainland" is commonly used in studies of US empire to refer to the parts of the United States on the North American continent, recent scholarship from American studies and Pacific Island studies in particular has noted the ways in which the term "mainland" reinforces the centrality of the continent. Thus, I have opted for the terms "continent" and "continental" to refer to those parts of the United States on the North American continent. It is a shame that there is no mainstream English equivalent of the Spanish *estadounidense* to refer to someone or something from the United States. My historical actors frequently use the term "American" to refer to people or things from the United States. I have not amended their language. However, following a call from scholars of Latin America, I have opted to use the term "US American" rather than "American" when, in my own words, I refer to someone or something from the United States.

The US government has adopted different official spellings over time. You will see "Porto Rico" instead of Puerto Rico and "Hawaii" instead of Hawaiʻi, and "Agana" instead of Hagåtña, when I am quoting actors directly. Many today use the spelling Guåhan, but as that is not yet widespread, I have opted to use the mainstream spelling, Guam.

National Symbols in the US Colonial Empire

At the turn of the twenty-first century, a sixty-six-year-old man born and raised in Puerto Rico told an ethnographer from the continental United States, "[The] American Flag is the only Flag I know." As children, he said, "we learned about the American Flag" and "we had the Pledge of Allegiance." It was "the same thing they have in this country," he added, to clarify his meaning. The ethnographer found it "interesting that this respondent stated that the American Flag was the only Flag he knew considering he was born and raised in Puerto Rico," and commented that his "Puerto Rican accent was still noticeable." Puzzled, the ethnographer noted that the "respondent was conscious of his Puerto Rican-ness but contends that his native land is America." Thus, the ethnographer concluded that, "in explaining his attachment to the Flag," the respondent "downplayed his Puerto Rican-ness, or his Other-ness."[1] To the ethnographer's mind, the respondent's "attachment" to the US flag as a Puerto Rican was a contradiction.

Around the same time, across the Pacific at the other end of the US colonial empire from Puerto Rico, a journalist from the continental United States wrote that "no people recite the pledge of allegiance to the flag with such ardor, nor belt out the 'Star Spangled Banner' with such gusto," as the people of Guam. He speculated that although they were geographically "the Americans most removed from national soil," they "may be the most emotionally attached." The journalist concluded that Guam was "more American than America."[2] But by claiming that Guam was "removed from national soil," and even in the way he called Guam "more American than America," the journalist implied that Guam was not quite part of "America." Thus, like the ethnographer, the journalist found himself confused about reverence for the US flag on Guam.

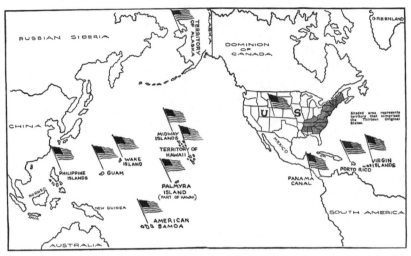

FIGURE 0.1. The continental United States and its overseas colonies—in flags. From James A. Moss, *The Spirit of the American Flag* (Washington: United States Flag Association, 1933), 40–41.

Puerto Rico and Guam were two of several overseas territories the United States claimed sovereignty over around the turn of the twentieth century as the result of a war, a coup, and several interimperial treaties. In the span of just a few short years, as a map by the president of the US Flag Association shows (figure 0.1), the US flag began to fly over a new colonial empire including Puerto Rico, Guam, the Philippines, Hawai'i (in 1898), American Samoa (in 1899), and the US Virgin Islands (in 1917).

In legal and political terms, the relationship between these places and the continental United States was unclear. Not long after the United States claimed these overseas colonies, legal experts posed the question: "Does the Constitution follow the flag?" In other words, would these places and peoples have the same legal status as the continental United States? The answer was decidedly ambiguous: Congress incorporated some territories and deemed others "unincorporated," which meant the US Constitution—the highest law of the land—need not apply there in full. Some inhabitants of overseas territories were US citizens, while others were "US nationals"—a new category created for noncitizens in the colonies who still, according to the government, owed their allegiance to the United States. In a series of cases known as the *Insular Cases*, meant to define the relationship between the United States and its new territories, one Supreme Court justice famously stated—with conscious paradox—that the colonies were "foreign to the United States in a domestic sense."[3] The rulings themselves, as the phrase "foreign in a domestic sense" suggests, did not actually articulate a clear relationship between the United States and its colonies. No wonder the ethnographer and journalist wondered if Puerto Rico and Guam were part of the United States.

In symbolic terms, however, standing in any one of these US colonies, the fact of being on US soil would have been obvious; the Stars and Stripes flew outside every schoolhouse, post office, and government building. School-children recited the Pledge of Allegiance and sang "The Star-Spangled Banner." People conducted their everyday business with money and postage stamps covered with US national iconography, from national heroes like George Washington and Benjamin Franklin to symbols like the American eagle and Lady Liberty. These nationally symbolic objects were an ordinary part of everyday life in US overseas colonies, just as they were in the continental United States. The ethnographer was confused that the Puerto Rican respondent did "not see a divergence between what he experienced as a child in terms of learning American Flag worship and what children are taught on the US mainland."[4] But the respondent, born in the mid-1930s, would likely have attended schools in Puerto Rico that resembled one photographed in 1946 by Jack Delano (figure 0.2).[5] He and millions of other children in Puerto Rico, Guam, American Samoa, Hawai'i, the Philippines, and the US Virgin Islands would have grown up, just like the children in Delano's photograph, routinely pledging their allegiance to the flag of the United States of America.

People from the continental United States tend to imagine their country as a nation of states and citizens. But from its inception, the United States has always been both a nation and an empire, with various groups enjoying different levels of citizenship rights.[6] Even the flag itself—which adds a new star for each state—shows that in the United States, nation and empire have always been layered and intertwined.[7] The acquisition of overseas colonies threw this tension into sharp relief. The existence of colonies and colonial subjects—especially ones like the people the ethnographer and journalist encountered, who claimed attachment to US national symbols and membership in the US national community—disrupted clean divisions between insider and outsider, foreign and domestic, and nation and empire. As people in US colonies began to incorporate these nationally symbolic objects into their everyday lives, the borders of US national identity became unstable.[8] Those who were supposedly unwelcome in the polity as citizens were being brought inside the national community in other ways, interacting with objects that suggested that their national identity was linked to the United States.

This book tells the story of how these objects laden with US symbolism— flags, money, and postage stamps—came to be part of everyday life in the

FIGURE 0.2. Puerto Rican children pledging allegiance to the US flag, Padilla, Corozal, May 1946. Photo by Jack Delano. Instituto de Cultura Puertorriqueña, Archivo General de Puerto Rico, Departamento de Instrucción Pública, Ce42 X2158.

United States' colonial empire.[9] The legal dispensation from the Supreme Court that the colonies were "foreign in a domestic sense" has allowed generations of people, including our ethnographer and journalist—not to mention many historians—to believe that the colonies were "removed from national soil," or separate from the United States. But the Supreme Court did not dictate how US imperialists would approach ruling over new colonies and colonial subjects. Indeed, the rulings provided imperialists with a fuzzy, flexible doctrine that allowed for improvisation and inconsistency in colonial governance.[10] And, more importantly, while Congress and the Supreme Court could dictate official status, they could not dictate how people in the colonies would choose to identify themselves and their national affiliation(s).

So, while Congress and the Court distanced the colonies from the continent, and many in the continental United States began to forget about their country's overseas territories, something different was occurring in the colonies themselves: US imperialists decided to plant the star-spangled banner on every schoolhouse, post office, and government building. They decided that colonial subjects from the Virgin Islands to the Philippines would use money and stamps bearing images of George Washington, Lady Liberty, and other nationally significant iconography. Colonial subjects may have been living under the US flag without full constitutional rights, but they were still living under the US flag. And that meant something—to both US imperialists and US colonial subjects.

Instead of asking whether the Constitution follows the flag, this history follows the flag itself, along with money and postage stamps. In doing so, it shows how the ambiguous rulings of the *Insular Cases* were, in the decades that followed, given concrete meaning by the actions of people administering and living under US rule. Along the way, I ask readers to follow the journey of a US flag from a patriotic organization in New York to the hands of a child in Puerto Rico; to be a fly on the wall as bureaucrats debate which US national heroes to put on Philippine stamps; to witness coins bearing images of the Hawaiian king being shipped to San Francisco, melted down, restamped with the American eagle, and shipped back across the Pacific; to watch Puerto Rican children pledge their allegiance to the US flag and then haul that same flag down in protest; to sit with Hawaiian women as they quilt subversive symbols of the deposed monarchy; and to be with women on Guam as they secretly stitch US flags while under Japanese rule.

Following these symbolic objects opens a new set of questions beyond the letter of the law: Why was it so important to US imperialists that colonial subjects encountered material objects with US national iconography in their daily lives? How did these imperialists—soldiers, colonial officials, federal bureaucrats, teachers, patriotic organizations, businessmen, and more— orchestrate the creation and distribution of these objects throughout a vast colonial empire that spanned the Caribbean and the Pacific? How did the boundaries of the US nation shift and change as these symbolic objects became part of everyday life in the colonies? And how have people in the colonies—excluded from the US national polity, yet surrounded by US national symbols—conceived of their own relationship to the United States?

The narrative that follows reveals how objects with national symbols became an arena in which contests over national identity played out in the US colonial empire. As US imperialists introduced these symbolic objects to people living in US overseas territories, they tried to assign a particular meaning to these symbols. But a lesson taught is not necessarily a lesson learned, and once released into the world, imperialists could not dictate what meanings people would attach to them.[11] People in US colonies have adopted, rejected, and creatively repurposed US national symbols to their own ends, shifting and changing the meaning of these symbolic objects as they have done so.

Imperialists have imagined this process as a one-way street—imperial objects remaking colonial subjects—but colonial subjects have remade imperial objects too.

Flags, stamps, and currency are official markers of sovereignty. For the imperialists who eagerly planted the flag and other nationally symbolic objects in overseas colonies, these objects performed the basic function of letting everyone know that the United States now claimed sovereignty over those spaces. But if the initial goal in deploying these national symbols was to affirm US sovereignty over new territorial possessions, some imperialists hoped that, in the long run, routine encounters with nationally symbolic objects would invite those who were legally and politically excluded from the polity to nevertheless imagine themselves as part of a broader "imagined" community—a community that many preferred to imagine as national but that, partially through the efforts of these imperialists, was becoming undeniably imperial.[12]

These efforts to spread US national symbols throughout the colonies fell under the umbrella of a larger project US imperialists referred to as "Americanization." Americanization was not unique to the colonies. In the continental United States, this was the era of "Indian schools" that sought to rid Native American children of their culture and heritage and impose white US American customs.[13] Americanization in the colonies also coincided with a mass influx of European immigrants who, in the eyes of progressive reformers, also needed to be assimilated into the mainstream.[14] Last, the federal government at the turn of the twentieth century was still dealing with former Confederates, who continued to resist rejoining the US national community.[15] The term "Americanization" has also been used to describe the United States' cultural or political influence on foreign countries around the world.[16]

In US colonies, neither foreign nor domestic, scholars have argued that Americanization was a "hodgepodge of half-baked, poorly articulated, and easily altered notions" that coalesced around the goal of making the lives and cultures of people in US colonies more closely resemble "Anglo-Saxon" (white) US culture.[17] In that way, Americanization can be thought of as the US equivalent of France's "civilizing mission"—the cultural component of a broader imperial mission.[18] But whereas France had a colonial school that attempted to standardize that imperial mission, there was no centralized training in how officials ought to Americanize the colonies—the closest the US government came to codifying it was President William McKinley's proclamation that US troops should approach the military occupation of the Philippines with the goal of "benevolent assimilation." Each proponent of Americanization had their own ideas about what it meant and how to achieve it, whether through education, infrastructure, public health and sanitation, drug control and policing, material culture, or, more specifically in our case, through the spread of nationally symbolic objects.[19]

Proponents of Americanization via nationally symbolic objects believed that there was a link between these objects and people's own sense of their national identity, allegiance, and affiliation. This idea was not unique to actors in the US colonial empire or even in the United States. Scholars of nations and nationalism have emphasized the vital role that national symbols, emblems, iconography, and the rituals and traditions that surround them have played in forming and maintaining national identities all over the world.[20] But objects and symbols do not inherently contain or convey nationalist sentiment. Unless someone imbued these symbolic objects with meaning, a US flag was just a piece of cloth, an American eagle on a coin was just a large bird of prey, and George Washington's likeness on a stamp was just a portrait of an old man.[21] The ability of these emblems and symbols to create and promote national affiliation and patriotic feeling rested on people understanding and accepting their significance. So, in order for US national symbols to work in the colonies, US imperialists felt it was their duty to teach people what the symbols represented, how they should be revered, and why.

It can be tempting to accept that the symbols these imperialists deployed unquestioningly represented the national character, culture, and history of the United States—or, in other words, that everyone understood what it meant for something, someplace, or someone to be "American," and that the imperialists were simply exporting that idea to the colonies. Nations are heterogenous, messy, tenuous formations, and the United States—a multiethnic, multiracial, settler colonial state built largely by the labor of enslaved African people on land stolen from Indigenous people—was no exception. There was no one US nation or universally agreed-upon set of national symbols to be exported to these new territories.[22] For example, at the turn of the twentieth century, George Washington was regarded by many in the United States as a founding father. But many Black Americans knew him as an enslaver, and the Six Nations of the Iroquois Confederacy called him "Town Destroyer."[23] Encouraging colonial subjects (especially those fighting for their own independence from the United States) to revere George Washington complicated his symbolic meaning even further. Indeed, the acquisition of colonies prompted a full-blown identity crisis in the United States. The contradiction between the nation's ostensible anticolonialism—rooted in the founding experience of the Revolutionary War against the British Empire—and its actual colonial practice complicated one of the most cherished ideals of US national character.[24] Rather than assume that imperialists were simply exporting "America" or "Americanness" to the colonies, this history instead shows how, through their efforts to "Americanize" the colonies, the imperialists were actually creating and affirming particular ideas about what "America" was.

Official national iconography—that is, iconography officially sanctioned by and, in the case of money and stamps, produced by the state—seeks to smooth over these rough edges and divisions and to present a coherent vision of a nation and its purportedly shared culture, ideals, and history.[25] While the range of material culture deployed to "Americanize" the colonies was vast, including everything from architecture to food and beyond, this book focuses on flags, stamps, and money as symbolic markers of sovereignty—objects meant to represent not just the imposition of US "culture," but explicitly the presence of the US state.[26]

States circulate these symbolic objects within the boundaries of the nation to reaffirm the boundaries of the nation. The objects themselves are typically not bounded by borders, but their meaning usually is. Official iconography is meant to function in different ways, depending on the national affiliation of the viewer. Officials at the US Bureau of Engraving and Printing have chosen people, places, historic scenes, and symbols they deem nationally significant, and have placed them on paper money and postage stamps. Ideally, when people within the US national community see these designs, they would see a reflection of their US national identity and an affirmation of their place within the US national community.[27] Outside the boundaries of a particular nation, its stamps and currency might hold value as collectibles, but they are likely not considered legal tender. And people from outside that country understand that the symbols on these objects are meant to represent that nation's culture and history, not their own. People outside the US national community viewing US paper money or postage stamps can learn how the United States has conceived of its own national character, but will not feel they are part of the US national community.[28] The same holds for flags. When insiders fly the flag or pledge their allegiance, it affirms their national identity and affiliation. Beyond that country's borders, its national flag is the emblem of a foreign country. There it serves a different function, appearing on foreign embassies, diplomats' limousines, or foreign vessels.[29]

In a world of nation-states, objects with national iconography change meaning at the border.[30] When people enter a foreign country, they exchange their own currency for other currency that carries marks of that foreign country's sovereignty and national iconography. When someone travels from the United States to one of its overseas territories, they continue to use US dollars with US national iconography. Foreign countries have their own flags and their own flag rituals. People in the US colonial empire—like the man who grew up in 1940s Puerto Rico—pledge their allegiance to the US flag.

This blurring of the boundaries of US national identity was a direct result of the actions of US imperialists who spread US national symbols to the colonies. Proponents of this kind of Americanization often flattened the differences between the continent and the colonies, promoting the idea that these US symbols meant the same thing whether they were in Philadelphia or the Philippines. As the United States' global influence expanded throughout the twentieth century, people all over the world were forced to contend with the political and cultural influence of the United States, many even living under direct US occupation, as in Cuba.[31] But it was only in formal US colonies that imperialists told the people living there that the US flag was *their* national flag, that "The Star-Spangled Banner" was *their* national anthem, that people like George Washington and Abraham Lincoln were *their* national heroes, and that when they saw these symbols, they too should think of themselves as "Americans."

Official rhetoric about "Americanization" had an inclusionary element that implied that people in the colonies might actually become "American."[32] Some have argued that in this way, Americanization was different from other empires' civilizing missions.[33] This book hopes to reveal more of the similarities between the United States and other imperial powers, rather than claim any kind of exceptionalism. The British and especially the French also toed a careful line between inviting colonial subjects into the national community and leaving them on the periphery. The French grappled with the same contradictions inherent in being both a republican nation-state and an overseas empire. They also tried to spread a kind of French nationality to their colonies without conferring full citizenship rights.[34] What did it mean for colonized peoples to be told they were part of a nation—not an empire—that both refused them full legal inclusion and obscured the very existence of its colonies? It can be easy to dismiss as a farce the imperialists' inclusive rhetoric promising colonial subjects access to Frenchness or Americanness—a consolation prize meant to paper over the refusal to grant full legal rights and citizenship. But, as historian Gary Wilder has argued in the French case, colonial efforts to "differentiate and primitivize subject populations" did not always stand in contradiction to concurrent efforts to promote ideas about equality and inclusion.[35] This book will show that Americanization, like France's civilizing mission, could also be both "sincerely republican *and* genuinely colonial."[36] It also shows that, like British and French colonial subjects, US colonial subjects had their own ideas about their place within the national-imperial

community that often contradicted official declarations.[37] As colonial subjects grappled with assuming, rejecting, and operationalizing US national
identity in different places at different times, their own distinct histories and
cultures came to reshape what it meant to be "American" as well.[38]

Imperialists promoted this "inclusive" idea—that the colonies and the
people who lived there were part of the US national community—throughout
the US colonies, but no one was doing the same in the continental United
States. Already by the end of the first decade of the twentieth century, the
mainstream continental US public had lost sight of the US colonial empire,
and the prevailing image of the United States became that of a continental
nation stretching from sea to shining sea—and not beyond.[39] While the presence of US iconography became a banal part of everyday life in the colonies,
the Post Office Department, for example, constantly had to remind people,
including its own employees, that overseas colonies used domestic US postage stamps.[40] This history shows how such different ideas developed in the
continent and the colonies about the borders of national identity and about
who could legitimately make claims to "Americanness." It helps us understand how, despite these practices being a routine part of everyday life in
these places for more than a century, the ethnographer and journalist could
be so surprised to find attachment to and veneration of US national symbols
in places like Puerto Rico and Guam.

This book's central goal, however, is not to show why a history of the US
colonial empire matters in the continental United States. Many scholars have
taken up this task, convincingly making the case for the significance of the
US colonies to US history writ large.[41] This book includes many events that
did matter a great deal in the continental United States, including the initial
conquest of overseas territory at the turn of the twentieth century, a world
war fought over maintaining Pacific colonies, and an island revolt that rained
bullets down on the House of Representatives and almost assassinated a president. But it also sits with the utterly mundane moments in between, highlighting them precisely *for* their seeming insignificance. A US flag hanging
limply over a US post office in American Samoa or a coin with George Washington changing hands on St. Croix would likely be of little consequence to
an ordinary person in the continental United States. But, as the scholar Ann
Stoler has argued, " 'minor' histories should not be mistaken for trivial ones."[42]
The spread of national symbols to colonies fundamentally changed the national character of the United States and what it meant to be an "American."
But what happened in the colonies was not just a microcosm of a larger history of "Americanization." This history matters not just for what it can tell us
about the continental United States, but for what it can tell us about the lives

of the millions of people who have lived under the US flag in the colonial empire since the turn of the twentieth century.

In illuminating the shared experience of people who have lived under the US flag, this book does falsely extricate US territories from their surroundings. The Tongan and Fijian scholar Epeli Hauʻofa has argued that colonialism transformed "a once boundless world into the Pacific Island states and territories that we know today. People were confined to their tiny spaces, isolated from each other."[43] This book shows how nationally symbolic objects facilitated this separation and isolation. Imperialists divided the Samoan archipelago, for example, between those living under the US or the German flag. Through these objects, US imperialists asked people in American Samoa, Guam, Hawaiʻi, the Philippines, Puerto Rico, or the US Virgin Islands to feel more connected to a community of people living under the US flag than to people in their neighboring islands. While this book examines the US colonies together because they are under US sovereignty, it does not suggest that people living in the colonies need acknowledge or accept US sovereignty any more than Indigenous people living under US jurisdiction on the North American continent. Referring to the US empire is meant not to reify the political authority the empire has claimed, but rather, as Moon-Ho Jung has argued, to "identify the United States for what it is and what it has always been"—an empire.[44] People living under US jurisdiction have made their own decisions about how they identify themselves, some rejecting US national identity outright, some embracing it as their own, and others claiming Americanness alongside other national, ethnic, or regional identities—a "hyphenated-American" identity.[45] National identities need not be mutually exclusive, nor do they even have to be tied to a sovereign nation, as in the case of Puerto Rican national identity.[46]

My work adds to the growing chorus of scholars who seek to take the US colonial empire as a whole, or multiple places within the empire, as their object of study.[47] But it does not attempt to give equal space to each place. Because I follow the stories of these nationally symbolic objects—flags, stamps, and currency—different locales feature more prominently at different moments. And while there is a wide range of distinctive places and peoples under study, this book cannot offer the same level of detail and specificity that a history of one place alone might. Each of these places can be studied at any number of different scales: local, national, imperial, regional, or global. The history of Puerto Rico, for example, could be told as a national history, as a local history of a particular place in Puerto Rico, or as a history situated within a larger frame such as the greater Caribbean, Latin America, the Atlantic world, the entire globe, or, as in this book, the US colonial empire.

Something different and useful is revealed from each vantage point, and choosing one approach does not negate the importance of the others. Indeed, these histories rely on and inform one another.[48] In the endnotes to this book, readers will see that this research builds on and is informed by scholars in various fields who have conducted careful studies of each US colony, as well as those who have examined similar processes in other nations and empires. My basic approach is more integrative than comparative. The hope is to assemble individual histories into a broader story that reveals something about the nature of US colonial rule and the experiences of the people who have lived with it. And while revealing patterns across the empire, it also seeks to clarify important distinctions between individual colonies.[49]

Importantly, this book offers a history of the US colonial empire from the colonies themselves. When viewed from Washington, the whole enterprise can seem incoherent. The cacophony of legal categories created by Congress and the Supreme Court—incorporated, unincorporated, organized, unorganized—has seemed to differentiate between the colonies.[50] The colonies have also been governed by different entities within different parts of the federal government—the Naval Department, the War Department, or the Department of the Interior—and have been transferred between these entities.[51] From Washington, the United States appears an indifferent colonizer with a haphazard empire. Positioning ourselves in the colonies, however, we see a different story. There, US imperialists who spread nationally symbolic objects have operated with a different logic, one of inclusion—with all the baggage that entails in a colonial context—rather than differentiation.

Following these objects through multiple colonial sites allows us to see the US colonial empire as a tangible entity made up of distinct geographic spaces, rather than as an abstraction or idea. Doing so lets us move beyond the idea that the overseas territories were simply far-flung appendages of the United States, or, in the words of one scholar, mere "geographical crumbs."[52] The US colonial empire does appear to lack the grand scale of the European ventures. But these small island territories gave the United States effective naval control of the Caribbean and most of the Pacific. And at its height, the US colonial empire was relatively large—the fifth largest in the world, on the eve of World War II.[53]

The objects under study, too, can seem small and insignificant compared to other modes of colonization. Nationally symbolic objects are so ubiquitous that, aside from collectors and scholars of semiotics and material culture, many people do not take the time to analyze them.[54] The objects are, however, frequently commented on. People colloquially refer to US colonies as being "under the US flag," without interrogating how that flag got there or what the flag's presence means in tangible terms.[55] And writings about the US colonies are littered with rich vignettes in which people describe the strangeness of finding US national symbols in these places.[56] These moments appear incongruous to the reader, showing US national iconography in places most people do not think of as being within the US nation. Like the surprise expressed by the journalist about flag veneration on Guam, these observations are usually made in passing, on the way to some larger point. But as the scholar and politician Robert Underwood has argued about flag veneration on Guam, "The notion that Chamorros were more American than America needed closer study. This rabid patriotism has roots."[57] Making flag veneration the object of our study, rather than an interesting anecdote, helps us better understand the roots of US patriotism in the colonies, as well as resistance to US rule, and, importantly, the ambivalent space in between.

This book shows that these nationally symbolic objects played an important and distinct role in US imperialism. Once established, they could circulate without requiring anyone's constant attention. So even where the United States did not have boots on the ground, it could have flags in the sky and currency in the pockets of people throughout its colonial empire. In places where there was no cholera and little crime, and for people who did not attend the public schools, these nationally symbolic material objects were the primary tangible connection between a colonial subject and the US government. This book is an effort to understand how officials, activists, and ordinary people have thought (or not thought) about these symbols both during moments of conflict and in banal everyday life.[58]

Indeed, part of the insidiousness of these objects lay in their quotidianness. If at first these objects signaled the arrival of US sovereignty in the colonies, over time they became part and parcel of what the scholar Michael Billig has termed "banal nationalism," or the way in which nationalism is reproduced in mundane, quotidian ways that remind a populace "of their national place in a world of nations." The quintessential embodiment of banal nationalism, Billig argues, "is not a flag which is consciously being waved with fervent passion; it is the flag hanging unnoticed on the public building."[59] Eventually, US imperialists hoped, the US flag would hang unnoticed on public buildings throughout the colonial empire, making the very fact of US colonial rule banal.

This book does not suggest that symbols were more important than other aspects of US colonial rule like education, law, politics, commerce, or the military. Indeed, it shows that nationally symbolic objects were intimately connected to these other aspects of colonial rule.[60] The US military planted the flag in these places. Educators understood the symbols as a crucial part of a broader colonial education. Economic experts managed the introduction of US money in these places. The symbols were inextricably linked to broader colonial processes; and, because of their symbolic nature, for many people they came to *represent* the United States and US colonial rule.[61] Imperialists welcomed this connection between the symbolic objects and people's feelings about US colonial rule when they believed colonial subjects were following the rules and routines laid out for them. In the historian Robin Bernstein's terms, each symbolic object came with a particular kind of "script" or set of actions it invited its users to perform.[62] Sometimes these rituals were pre-scribed in formal procedures; at other times they were conveyed through cus-tom and collective instruction. But in either case they shaped the meaning of these objects and, more importantly, the way users felt about them. Imperial-ists wanted people to raise, lower, fold, salute, and pledge allegiance to the US flag in a particular way. They believed that if used properly, the symbolic object itself could uplift, civilize, and "Americanize" colonized people while inculcating a sense of patriotism and loyalty to the United States.[63]

Many colonial subjects did adopt these objects and the scripts imperialists laid out for using them. Others, however, explicitly "flipped the script" and used their repudiation of these objects and rituals to challenge US sovereignty. People who wanted to express their displeasure with US rule could lower the US flag from a schoolhouse and raise another flag in its place. Both actions, following and subverting the script, rested on a mutual recognition of the sig-nificance of the flag raising ritual. Government officials took these challenges to the supremacy of US symbolic objects very seriously. The colonial officials who imposed these symbolic objects, the colonial subjects who used them as instructed, and those who rejected them all agreed that the symbols and the way people used them mattered. Flags, postage stamps, and currency have at times been mundane items whose iconography people barely noticed in passing. At other times, these symbolic objects have been powerful markers of national identity and affiliation. Throughout this book we will see that they were far from insignificant; people were willing to kill and to die for them. But even when they were not the center of any conflict, the objects were still part and parcel of the violence of colonization writ large.[64]

These objects also reveal the longevity and durability of US colonial rule. Since the first decade of the twentieth century, the colonies have rarely, if ever, been a primary concern of officials in the federal government. Many people living in the continental United States have been blissfully unaware that their country even holds overseas colonies. And yet the objects of empire remain. The US postal service continues to deliver the mail in the territories. US coins, bills, and stamps continue to circulate. And the US flag continues to

fly over the millions of people who live there and encounter these symbols of
the US state every day. The simple presence of these objects undermines any
idea that an "age of US colonial empire" ever ended.

The history that follows highlights the real-world consequences of exclud-
ing colonial subjects from historical narratives. Atrocities that have occurred
in the colonies were often not counted as "American" lives lost. Even though
Hawai'i was also a territory at the time of the Japanese attack on Pearl Harbor,
its eventual statehood has meant that in our national narrative, that attack
receives far more attention than the concurrent bombings of the Philippines
and Guam, which occurred across the international date line.[65] Distancing itself from its colonies allowed the US government to claim on the world stage
that it had no colonies while it displaced colonial subjects—most of them US
citizens at the time—throughout the Caribbean and Pacific to build military
bases during the Cold War.[66] It has allowed the federal government to neglect
to allocate proper resources to the territories during natural disasters.[67] A
sense that these colonial subjects are not really "Americans" has meant that
their suffering has rarely garnered continental attention until it has reached
catastrophic proportions; and even then, attention has often wandered before
that suffering has been alleviated. This book asks those from the continental
United States who have ignored the existence of the empire to examine why
they have been able to do so, while people in the colonies themselves are
forced to grapple with it every day.

While this history is situated in the colonies, it sheds light on the partial
rights and multiple loyalties enjoyed by other groups in the continental United
States. After all, colonial subjects are not the only ones who have pledged
their allegiance to the US flag without enjoying full citizenship rights. They
are also not the only ones who have recognized the importance of nationally
symbolic objects in shaping, affirming, and rejecting US national identity.
Like other groups who have come under US sovereignty unwillingly, colonial
subjects have at certain times accepted US rule, have at other times resisted it
fiercely, and have sometimes ambivalently accepted it as a fact of life. These
banal moments, too, deserve our attention.

Our story begins at the turn of the twentieth century, when the United States
planted its flag on inhabited territory outside of the North American continent for the first time. These flag raising ceremonies were immensely important to colonial officials; they were an opportunity to show new colonial
subjects, US citizens back on the continent, and people around the world
that the United States was now in the business of overseas colonial imperialism. In Washington, the Supreme Court decided that the Constitution would

not follow the flag to the new territories. This raises the question: What did? Chapter 1 traces the range of rituals and practices that followed the flag itself as the object spread throughout the US colonial empire. After performative flag raising ceremonies, patriotic organizations followed, planting the Stars and Stripes throughout the empire. From the Virgin Islands to the Philippines, US flags began appearing on schoolhouses, post offices, government buildings, and people's homes. Children on Guam began their days by pledging their allegiance to the flag, and people in American Samoa learned the words to "The Star-Spangled Banner." The chapter examines the immense effort expended by colonial officials and patriotic organizations to spread the US flag to every corner of the empire, and what it meant for people in the colonies and in the continental United States for the US flag to fly over these spaces.

Chapter 2 recounts US efforts to spread national iconography through two pocket-sized symbolic objects: currency and postage stamps. The government's goal was to have money and stamps decorated with nationally significant symbols circulating throughout the colonial empire in the same quotidian manner they did in the continental United States. This process was incredibly involved. US officials spent a great deal of time thinking about what national symbols to place on currency and postage stamps. Then colonial officials had to convince people living in the colonies, many of whom were not accustomed to using just one national monetary or postal system, that they should now use these objects exclusively. People living in the US colonies had a range of responses to these objects: many used them, some repurposed them, and others rejected them outright. US colonial officials went to great lengths to fully incorporate the colonies into the domestic postal and monetary systems. Once that was accomplished, these networks became an effective way to ensure that colonial subjects were constantly interacting with US national symbols. And as the designs on stamps and currency changed over time, they became a way to trace the colonial state's changing ideas about the colonies themselves.

Chapter 3 deals with how US imperialists responded to challenges, real or perceived, to the supremacy of US symbols in the colonies. Given how crucial these objects were to establishing US dominance, and how often people interacted with them in their everyday lives, it is not surprising that the objects often became tools for resistance to US rule. Women in Hawai'i secretly stitched Hawaiian flag quilts, and people in the Philippines and Puerto Rico carried their national flags in the streets. Chapter 3 examines how US colonial subjects in Hawai'i, the Philippines, and Puerto Rico used their national symbols to resist US rule and how US colonial officials attempted to manage that resistance—particularly in the Philippine flag ban from 1907 to 1919, and in harsh crackdowns in 1920s and 1930s Puerto Rico.

While the United States continued to manage internal challenges to its symbolic supremacy in its colonial empire, an external threat emerged: the Japanese empire. Chapter 4 examines the role of nationally symbolic objects in the conflict between the US and Japanese empires in the Pacific theater of World War II. Japan occupied the Philippines and Guam during the war, and in all places it sought to undo "Americanization," directly dismantling the symbolic systems the United States had established in the early twentieth century. The Rising Sun flag replaced the Stars and Stripes. Japanese officials blacked out the words "United States of America" on US postage stamps. Possession of the US flag suddenly became a crime punishable by death. This chapter deals closely with the experiences of people in the Philippines and Guam who lived under Japanese rule, and of those in Hawai'i who lived under martial rule and the threat of Japanese invasion. It reveals the centrality and significance of the national symbols to the way colonial subjects defined their national identity and allegiance under the extreme conditions of Japanese occupation.

If the first two chapters of this book show US officials engaged in symbolic colonization, chapter 5 shows postwar attempts at symbolic *decolonization*. On July 4, 1946, the US flag came down in the Philippines, and the Philippine flag rose alone in a formal declaration of Philippine independence. It was an extravagant ceremony, not unlike the US flag raising ceremonies at the turn of the century. But where those initial US flag raising ceremonies were meant to signal the beginning of US colonial rule, US officials hoped the Philippine flag raising ceremony would send a different message: that the United States was leading the charge for decolonization by voluntarily granting the Philippines their independence. But while the United States preached decolonization on the international stage, it engaged in brutal repression of the independence movement in Puerto Rico, where a resurgence of Nationalist activities led the government to effectively criminalize the possession of the Puerto Rican flag in 1948. In 1952 the Puerto Rican flag became the official flag of the new Commonwealth of Puerto Rico, and the US government was able to convince other countries to remove it from the United Nations list of "non-self-governing territories." But the flag remained central to Nationalist resistance in this period, from an island-wide uprising to a shooting in the US House of Representatives. The United States' final performance of symbolic decolonization came at the end of the 1950s, with Hawaiian statehood. This chapter examines the centrality of the fifty-star US flag to statehood ceremonies, reflecting on how placing Hawai'i on the flag alongside stars representing every other state naturalized the idea that it had always been destined to become a state. Through each of these events, I show how the United States used national symbols to convince the rest of the world that it was leading global decolonization, even as it maintained most of its colonial empire and even colonized new territory in this period, planting its flag on the hundreds of islands it administered through the UN Trust Territory of the Pacific Islands.

In the colonies, in that tenuous space between foreign and domestic, seemingly mundane symbolic objects have been central to the establishment and maintenance of colonial rule and to performances of identity, making claims to belonging, and resistance to US rule. Tracing the lives of these objects in the colonies reveals how people's relationships to US rule have shifted and changed during a century of colonization, integration, exclusion, world war, and (partial) decolonization. People living in the US colonial empire have suffered legal exclusions, violence, and political disenfranchisement; but they have always had their own understandings of their relationship to the US nation and national community—understandings often formed by and expressed through these symbolic objects.

What Followed the Flag

In late December 1898, Puerto Rican schoolteacher Ines Caparros Soler received her first US flag. She said of the experience, "My heart is filled with untold joy in feeling that in receiving this beautiful emblem, I am becoming baptized as an American."[1] Caparros Soler would have grown up under the Spanish flag—a flag that, in some iteration, had flown over Puerto Rico for more than four centuries. During the recent war, US troops had hauled down the Spanish flag and raised the US flag in its place. Just before Caparros Soler received her first US flag, US and Spanish officials in Paris had signed a treaty ceding Puerto Rico, along with Guam and the Philippines, to the United States. In that moment—with Puerto Rico no longer a Spanish colony, but also not an independent nation—national identity was in flux for many Puerto Ricans. Caparros Soler began to form her new national identity in relation to a new national object: the US flag. Possessing that piece of cloth made her feel, in her own words, like she was "an American."

When the United States acquired most of its colonies around the turn of the twentieth century, it was unclear what the new empire would look like. There appeared to be no grand strategy guiding the governance of these places. Government officials, experts, and ordinary people puzzled over whether the colonies would have the same status as states and territories on the North American continent, or would be thought of differently in legal, political, or cultural terms. It was not even clear whether the Constitution— the supreme law of the land—would apply in the new territories. People often framed these inquiries around the broad question, "Does the Constitution follow the flag?"[2] The question itself assumed that the flag was already there. But it actually took considerable effort to spread the US flag throughout the new colonial empire.

The spread of the US flag was the result of the combined efforts of the US military, US colonial officials, and private patriotic organizations. First, the US military planted the flag. Then, government officials would hold an official flag raising ceremony lowering the flag of the former sovereign and raising the Stars and Stripes. Soon after that, private patriotic organizations would begin sending flags out by the hundreds, hoping they would become a banal part of the landscape throughout the colonial empire. The federal government may have been unclear about the status of these places, and about whether the people there were "Americans." But lack of clarity from the continental United States did not stop imperialists in the colonies from moving forward with plans to, in their words, "Americanize" the colonies—trying to make them more closely resemble their imagined vision of the continental United States. The flag became central to their efforts. The US flag was the first national symbol the United States exported to its new possessions, and this chapter explores the importance of this symbolic object to the early years of US colonial rule.

Caparros Soler's account of "becoming baptized as an American" upon receiving her first US flag was a dream scenario for US imperialists—which is why a patriotic organization called the Grand Army of the Republic included it in a report detailing its efforts to spread the flag to new US colonies.[3] These proponents of Americanization via national symbols wanted people in the colonies to receive a US flag and to feel, like Caparros Soler, that they were becoming "American." But they did not see that such a statement could be both subservient and subversive—subservient in that Caparros followed the script laid out by the patriotic organization giving her the flag, yet subversive in that the federal government would explicitly decide to *not* make Puerto Rico part of the United States and *not* make Puerto Ricans part of the US polity. If receiving a flag made Caparros Soler and other people living in US colonies recognize the sovereignty of the United States and perhaps even feel loyalty or allegiance to it, the object also made them feel they could claim belonging in the US national community, and thus being entitled to the same rights and privileges as any other "American." The manner of the introduction of the US flag in the colonies created an arena in which it would be central to debates over inclusion, exclusion, belonging, and resistance for both imperialists and people living in the colonies for decades to come.

By 1898 it was widely accepted that a rectangular piece of cloth with stars in a blue field in the upper left-hand corner and thirteen red and white stripes represented the United States. However, there is nothing natural about a piece of cloth with a certain design representing a polity—whether that polity be a nation, a republic, an empire, or, in the case of the United States, an uncomfortable combination thereof. While this chapter shows how planting the flag in overseas colonies complicated its meaning, the flag it was not a neutral symbol in the continental United States before 1898.

It is tempting to think that the Stars and Stripes has always been the ultimate national symbol of the United States. That was the story US imperialists told new colonial subjects—that the flag "had been the standard of the Republic since the Revolution."[4] In fact, the "Stars and Stripes" was just one of many banners under which British American colonists fought during that war.[5] And the national myth of Betsy Ross stitching the first US flag was virtually unknown until her grandson started promoting it almost a century later.[6] Indeed, the US flag was not terribly important to most US citizens until the Civil War, when, in the face of a secessionist challenge from the Confederate States of America in the South, people began flying US flags all over the North where they never had done so before: on schoolhouses, public buildings, churches, hotels, shops, and ships.[7] After that war, the US flag became an important part of efforts, largely by white men, to reunite the nation.[8] When US imperialists brought the flag to the colonies at the turn of the twentieth century, there were not even official rules for its design or use. The flag's design was not standardized until 1912. "The Star-Spangled Banner" would not become the national anthem until 1931, and the Pledge of Allegiance would not become official until 1942.[9]

But imperialists planted the US flag in the colonial empire at a particular moment in the life of that object—when private patriotic organizations had just taken a vested interest in making sure the flag was an integral part of everyday life for all people in the United States. In the continental United States this began in schools, as it would in the colonies. In the 1880s people from various sectors of society, including veterans' organizations, philanthropic societies, and teachers' associations, began to push for more flag education in schools. The Grand Army of the Republic, an organization of Union veterans of the Civil War, would lead the charge in the colonies as well. In 1892 a national children's periodical called *The Youth's Companion* began promoting routine recitation of a "pledge of allegiance." The patriotic organizations hoped that routine flag veneration would instill patriotism and national loyalty in various groups they felt were outside the national fold: former Confederates, Indigenous people, and new immigrants who were arriving by the millions.[10] Americanization via flag education was unfinished in the continental United States when US troops began planting the flag in the colonies in 1898.

When the military first planted the flag, it was meant to symbolize a change in sovereignty. People who lived in these new US colonies knew that flags symbolized sovereignty, most having lived under imperial flags before. But proponents of Americanization did not just want colonial subjects to see the flag as the symbolic representation of US sovereignty. They wanted them to believe the US flag symbolized what *they* believed it symbolized, and to revere the object as *they* believed it ought to be revered. "Americanization" happened in a number of ways in the continental United States and its colonial empire. But there was a reason why imperialists were so focused on the flag. First, these efforts were primarily led by veterans who had fought and killed for the flag, believed it sacred, and believed that all who lived under it should venerate it in a certain way. Second, these imperialists realized the Americanizing potential of a material object. Flags could perform a kind of work different from that of educators, missionaries, and others who sought to spread US ideals. Compared to other empires, the US empire lacked manpower. They could not send a teacher from the continental United States to every school, or an official from the continental United States to every town. Imperialists hoped that, even in places where they could not maintain a constant presence, the US flag could serve as a constant reminder of US sovereignty and US national ideals. Once these flags faded into the background of everyday life, they then performed a different kind of work, quietly naturalizing US rule.[11] Ideally, a US flag in St. Croix would be no more noteworthy than a US flag in St. Louis, because people would unquestioningly accept that both places were under US sovereignty. The flag was often the center of attention in debates about allegiance and identity. But the flag has played a powerful role in the US colonial empire even when people have not consciously noticed it.

Proponents of flag veneration in the colonies often flattened differences between the continent and the colonies, promoting the idea that the US flag symbolized the same thing whether it was in Philadelphia or the Philippines. They told colonial subjects that the flag had always represented and would always represent high national ideals like democracy, freedom, liberty, and justice—even though the US government systematically denied colonial subjects those things. Despite their difference in status, people throughout the colonial empire routinely participated in a number of patriotic exercises surrounding the flag: raising it, lowering it, saluting it, singing songs about it, and pledging their allegiance to it. Most importantly, imperialists told colonial subjects that the US flag was *their* flag. And in doing so, I argue, they disrupted the boundaries of the US national community.[12] While Congress and the Supreme Court gave colonial subjects a murky, liminal status, living under the Stars and Stripes was meant to send a clear message, one that Caparros Soler had immediately picked up on: that you are "an American."[13]

The imperialists who spread the US flag in the colonies often spoke of it as though it was a sentient object: a flag could be revered or disrespected, depending on how one treated it. Imperialists also spoke of the flag having agency, claiming that the flag itself protected all who lived under its folds, or that it brought civilization, education, or economic development wherever it was planted. Of course, these conditions were the result of the efforts of specific human actors representing the United States. But by repeatedly instilling in people that these things could be ascribed to the US flag itself, colonial subjects learned that it could be the object of both their praise and their protest.

US imperialists presented the flag as an object with unchanging meaning, but they did not have a monopoly on constructing that meaning. For people in the colonies, the US flag has represented both democracy and inequality, both liberation and oppression, both freedom and the denial of self-determination. Its stars and stripes have sparked righteous anger, fervent patriotism, and dull indifference. For many, when the Stars and Stripes was first raised, the flag was a symbol of violent conquest; for others it meant welcome liberation, and for some it simply signaled a new colonial power on the scene. The meaning people assigned to the flag as the symbolic representation of the United States would shift over time, as people's feelings about the United States and its colonial rule changed. As we will see in subsequent chapters, the same people who warmly welcomed the flag could vehemently reject it later, once they realized the United States did not live up to the national ideals that imperialists claimed the flag represented.

So, if, as legal scholars have established, the Constitution did not "follow the flag" to the colonies, this chapter shows what did follow the flag: a new set of patriotic routines and practices, only recently implemented in parts of the continental United States, that were designed to invite colonial subjects to imagine themselves as part of the US national community. This chapter shows the important role the flag played in the early years of US colonial rule, and lays the groundwork for an account of later events. As the twentieth century wore on, people in the colonies would use flags both to claim Americanness and allegiance to the United States and to challenge US colonial rule and claim distinct national identities. We cannot understand why the flag was so central to these later conflicts without understanding the actions of the government officials and private citizens who spread the flag, and the initial reactions of those who encountered it in these early years of colonization. This complex and contested process started, in most places, with someone—usually the military—planting the US flag.

Planting the Flag

The US flag arrived in each colony under different circumstances: following a coup, during a war, or after a treaty. In some cases, people planted the flag well before they knew whether the US government would approve of the acquisition. In 1893, a group of US citizens overthrew the Hawaiian monarchy, lowered the Hawaiian Kingdom's flag, and raised the US flag in its place, only to have to shamefully lower it after the US government refused to annex the islands.[14] The US flag would not be raised there officially until 1898. That same year, while at war with Spain, the US military planted US flags as it conquered territory in the Caribbean and Pacific. Some stories were triumphant: during the battle for Manila, the capital city of the Philippines, Admiral George Dewey ordered his flag lieutenant and two signal boys to enter the city, lower the Spanish flag, and raise the US flag in its place.[15] The flag lieutenant eagerly took the largest US flag they had on board, carried it through the city (which was still swarming with armed Spanish soldiers), and raised it at Fort Santiago amid "the audible crying of a number of Spanish women and scowls of Spanish soldiers," as he recalled it (figure 1.1). US ships fired a salute while the band played "The Star-Spangled Banner." With the US flag now flying where the Spanish flag had flown for the last three centuries, the flag lieutenant triumphantly proclaimed, "an empire had changed hands."[16]

Other stories revealed the superficiality of the military's flag raisings. On Guam, where there was no resistance from the Spanish garrison, the captain and the lieutenant commander went to great lengths to raise a US flag on Fort Santa Cruz, only to take it down later that day. As a *New York Sun* correspondent traveling with the Navy reported, the captain "hoisted it merely for the purpose of saluting it," with "no intention of leaving one here."[17] No official flag flew over Guam for almost a year until civilian officials returned for an official flag raising in 1899.

Back in the continental United States, the newly formed American Flag Association wrote that because of the war with Spain, "the flag now has a new and expanded meaning." In a letter the association asked newspapers around the country to publish in advance of Flag Day, they argued that the "Spanish-American contest of civilizations" had shifted how people around the country—only recently divided by civil war—related to the US national emblem: "Sectionalism is being blotted out, and the representatives and citizens of forty-five sovereign States are contending with each other in their eagerness to plant the ensign of the Republic where its ample folds shall protect a people struggling for liberty against the iron heel of an oppressor."[18] For imperialists, the spread of the US flag to island colonies in the Caribbean and the Pacific was a point of pride. They believed, on the one hand, that the US flag signaled the coming of "liberty" for those who had lived under Spanish imperialism. But they were also clear that the arrival of the US flag meant

FIGURE 1.1. "Raising the flag over Fort Santiago, Manila, on the evening of August 13, 1898—Drawn by G. W. Peters." From *Harper's Pictorial History of the War with Spain* (New York: Harper & Brothers, 1899), 421.

the beginning of US imperialism. Making use of language that aligned their enterprise with history's greatest empires, they declared that the sun would never set on the US flag.[19] This sentiment was not only expressed by people in the continental United States. In London, six hundred British and US attendees at an "Anglo-American banquet" donned buttons bearing the image of a blended Union Jack and Stars and Stripes, which they called "the flag of the future."[20] The message was clear: the US flag, like the British flag, was now the flag of a global imperial power.

Not everyone was enthusiastic about this transformation; and as the symbol of the nation-cum-empire, the flag quickly became one of the central sites of contestation in the anti-imperialist debate. For their part, anti-imperialists believed that planting the US flag in overseas colonies contaminated the nation's most sacred symbol. William Jennings Bryan, pictured in a political cartoon chopping down the US flag while President William McKinley raises it in the Philippines (figure 1.2), argued in 1898 that there was no place for a colony on the US flag, whose stars "stand for an indissoluble union of indestructible States." Would the flag be redesigned, he wondered, to include "a milky way composed of a multitude of minor stars representing remote and insignificant dependencies?" Perhaps, he suggested, the Philippines could be added as a "blood-star": red, "to indicate that we have entered upon a career

FIGURE 1.2. Cartoon depicting William Jennings Bryan chopping down the US flag as President William McKinley raises it over the Philippines. Victor Gillam, *Judge*, May 12, 1900. Library of Congress Prints and Photographs Division.

of conquest."[21] Mark Twain agreed; if the United States was to be a colonial empire, he wrote, a flag "with the white stripes painted black and the stars replaced by the skull and cross-bones" might be a more fitting national emblem.[22] Bryan proclaimed that the "mission" of the US flag was "to float—not over a conglomeration of commonwealths and colonies—but over 'the land of the free and the home of the brave.'"[23]

Whether they approved or disapproved of the change, imperialists and anti-imperialists agreed that the meaning of the US flag changed in 1898. In reality, the flag had always been an expansionist and imperialist emblem. In fact, it was the *only* national flag whose design explicitly accommodated ongoing territorial expansion, adding a star for each new state added to the Union.[24] And in 1898, the flag already flew over a "conglomeration" of places and peoples with differing status: states, territories, citizens, "wards," and those who technically had citizenship but, because of white supremacist laws and procedures, could not access or enjoy their citizenship rights. If, as scholars have argued, empires are polities in which different people have different kinds of status and are ruled differently, the United States had been an empire long before 1898.[25] But most understood overseas colonial imperialism to be a new endeavor, and the US flag's role in it to be unique.

While the imperialist and anti-imperialist debates continued in the continental United States, the US government decided to keep these new colonies, claiming sovereignty over the Hawaiian Islands, the Philippines, Guam, and Puerto Rico, as well as American Samoa by the beginning of the twentieth century, and the US Virgin Islands soon after. And while the military had prided itself on the initial symbolic conquest of planting the flag, now that these places were to remain under US rule, civilian officials had a different role in mind for the Stars and Stripes.

Making It Official

Once the United States decided to keep these territories, colonial officials believed the meaning of the flag needed to change. With these official flag raising ceremonies, in Hawai'i and Puerto Rico in 1898, Guam in 1899, American Samoa in 1900, and the Virgin Islands in 1917, US officials sought to inaugurate a new era in which the flag would cease to be a symbol of temporary occupation and would instead become the official symbol of permanent US colonial governments. With the flag already flying—having been planted by the military or other US officials months or sometimes years earlier—it might seem that extravagant flag raising ceremonies were an unnecessary undertaking for these new colonial governments. And yet, in every place except the Philippines (where a new war complicated US officials' plans), colonial officials decided to dedicate time, energy, and money to staging official flag raising ceremonies that would officially mark the beginning of US sovereignty. Whether they enthusiastically accepted, staunchly opposed, or ambivalently acknowledged the object, after these ceremonies people living in these places became part of the newly expanded community of people, now stretching from Southeast Asia to the Caribbean, who lived under the US flag. These extravagant ceremonies and the publicity surrounding them ensured that people around the world witnessed this transformation.

In Puerto Rico, US troops had first planted the flag during their initial invasion on July 25, 1898, and continued spreading it as they advanced throughout the island.[26] That October, US officials decided to hold an official flag raising ceremony at the Governor's Palace in San Juan.[27] Even though the US flag had been in Puerto Rico for months, and the United States had not even begun treaty negotiations with Spain, the ceremonies were significant to participants and onlookers. With the official lowering of the Spanish flag and the raising of the US flag, "Puerto Rico Is Now American Soil," as the *New York Times* put it.[28] By all accounts, the flag raising in Puerto Rico was a happy occasion. US officials reported that people "accepted without hesitation the Stars and Stripes in place of the red and yellow bars."[29] Even Pedro Albizu Campos, who would later lead the Puerto Rican Nationalist movement against US colonial rule, wrote that Puerto Ricans "welcomed the American flag in 1898 because we believed it . . . to be a symbol of democracy and justice."[30] But not all flag raising ceremonies were happy affairs.

The official flag raising ceremony in Honolulu was, for the US citizens who had been pushing for annexation since overthrowing the Hawaiian monarchy five years earlier, a day of celebration. The *Chicago Tribune* reported that as the "beloved flag" was raised over 'Iolani Palace—the former home of Hawai'i's last reigning monarch, Queen Lili'uokalani—"cheer upon cheer rent the air" (figure 1.3).[31] But Bernice Piilani Irwin, a close friend of Queen Lili'uokalani, recalled that few Native Hawaiians were actually present at the official ceremony.[32] So, as cheers sounded from the annexationist crowd gathered at 'Iolani Palace, a mourning chant began to rise from about a block away, where Hawaiian women had gathered at the Kawaiahao Church.[33] Adding insult to injury, Irwin remembered that annexationists took the Hawaiian flag that was lowered in the ceremony and cut it into small three-inch strips to be kept as "souvenirs."[34] Queen Lili'uokalani spent the day in seclusion with her shutters drawn. Yet her compatriots reported that she could still hear the ceremony at her former palace, and that "she shuddered and trembled like one in a chill when the first strains of 'Hawaii Ponoi' "—the Hawaiian national anthem—"and the booming of guns warned her that her flag was setting to rise no more."[35]

After the official flag raising, Irwin recalled that the annexation commissioners traveled around the islands holding meetings, "explaining to the people that Hawaii was now part of the United States of America and expatiating upon the great advantages they would now enjoy under the American flag." When the commissioners arrived in Kailua, Irwin and Queen Lili'uokalani happened to be there the same day. The annexationists were only able to draw a "small audience," almost entirely of foreigners. "The people of Kailua had all gone on board to greet the Queen," recalled Irwin. "This fact should have spoken volumes to the Annexation Commissioners," she argued.[36] Indeed, Native Hawaiians did not readily accept the US flag at all. One woman recalled that for months after the official flag raising, "Hawaiians wore a special hat band as a sign of mourning—a band printed with the legend: *Kuu hae aloha*—'My beloved flag' "—in honor of the flag of the Hawaiian Kingdom.[37]

Ceremonies were a bit more complicated in American Samoa, the eastern half of a chain of islands in the South Pacific acquired by the United States

FIGURE 1.3. After the annexation ceremony, ʻIolani Palace, August 12, 1898. Photo by Frederick Jewett Lowrey. Hawaii State Archives.

following an 1899 treaty with Germany and Great Britain. The official flag raising took place on April 17, 1900, in the capital city of Pago Pago on the island of Tutuila. The event was well-attended by Samoans from both the island of Tutuila and the neighboring island of Manuʻa—but not without some coaxing. The US naval governor, Captain Benjamin Franklin Tilley, personally sailed to Manuʻa, accompanied by high chiefs of Tutuila, to convince the high chiefs of Manuʻa to attend the ceremonies. There, Tilley found that the leaders of Manuʻa, particularly the highest-ranking chief—the Tui Manuʻa— had no interest in ceding the sovereignty of their independent nation to the United States or any foreign power.[38] Tilley presented the Tui Manuʻa with a copy of President McKinley's proclamation announcing US sovereignty over all Samoan Islands east of the 171st longitude line, and explained that US officials did not intend to take Samoan land or interfere with their way of life, but that they did intend to raise the US flag at Pago Pago, where it would "be the sign of the authority of the United States of America over the islands of Tutuila and Manuʻa," as stipulated by the treaty with Germany and Great Britain. Tilley told the Manuans he hoped they would attend the ceremonies as "evidence of your friendship and goodwill." But, he warned, "whether you come or not, the authority of the United States is already proclaimed over this island and will be maintained."[39] After an afternoon of deliberations

Tilley was not privy to, the Tui Manuʻa presented him with a letter accepting the sovereignty of the United States. The next morning, Tilley sailed back to Pago Pago with, in his estimation, one hundred Manuans—including the Tui Manuʻa—who had agreed to participate in the flag raising ceremonies.[40]

On April 17, those in attendance received programs of the day's events in English and Samoan, emblazoned with an illustration of the Great Seal of the United States: an eagle with a striped shield, a scroll with the US national motto "E Pluribus Unum" in its beak, and olive branches in one talon and arrows in the other. As he raised the US flag, Tilley declared, "I hoist this American flag as a sign that these islands now form part of the territory of the United States."[41] After Tilley's declaration, pupils and teachers of the London Missionary Society sang "America," followed by national salutes from US and German ships.[42] The press reported that the rest of the day consisted of games, sports, singing, dancing, and general merriment.[43] In addition to Manuans, in attendance were German colonial officials, who had just held their own official German flag raising ceremony in Western Samoa the month before.[44]

Nowhere was cautious ambivalence more evident than at the official flag raising in the US Virgin Islands—a group of Caribbean islands including St. Croix, St. John, and St. Thomas that the United States purchased from Denmark during World War I. March 31, 1917, began "dull and drizzly," a local St. Thomas newspaper wrote, as Danish West Indians, soon to be US Virgin Islanders, watched the Danish flag go up for the last time. One observer noted that the Danish flag "could not open out, there was no breeze, and for all the world it looked as if it were drooping in sorrow, clinging like a last farewell embrace to the pole that had proudly borne it aloft so many years."[45] The occasion, called "Transfer Day," saw the birth of the famous line, still repeated in the US Virgin Islands in the twenty-first century: "We know what we got, but we don't know what we going to get."[46] The US Virgin Islands was the only majority-Black US overseas territory—populated largely by the descendants of enslaved Africans brought to the islands during the period of Danish colonial rule. It is not hard to imagine why, during the heyday of Jim Crow in the US South, people there would have reservations about coming under the US flag.[47]

The way US officials decided to stage the flag raising only confirmed their fears. An all-white detachment of US Marines dressed in all-white uniforms carrying a US flag disembarked from the USS *Olympia*—the same ship Admiral Dewey had sailed into Manila Bay when the United States invaded the Philippines in 1898.[48] One observer later recalled that "the Marines looked so rough and tough . . . that most of us were frightened."[49]

A local St. Thomas newspaper reported that "as the old flag came down tears filled the eyes of our women, and strong robust men shook as the tears rolled down their cheeks—it was a sad sight, cutting to the heart." But it was not all doom and gloom: "Quickly ran up the Starry Banner and again the hearts of the people cheered. . . . With fervent hopes for the future they saw the Stars shine out." New US Virgin Islanders were well aware that, as the newspaper put it, the ceremony "was to change a people's nationality." And, they wrote, "We shall give our loyalty unstintedly to the flag that now floats over us." But Virgin Islanders had their own understanding of what being "taken under the Stars and Stripes" would entail: "From this moment on it is our flag and in every respect we demand every privilege, all the rights and all the protection for which it stands."[50] This was not a simple one-way imposition.

The only US colony where there was not a formal flag raising ceremony was the Philippines, where conflict over which flag should fly over the islands lasted for more than a decade. The US flag had first come to the Philippines as the welcome symbol of an ally. Philippine revolutionaries had been fighting for independence from Spain since 1896, and officially proclaimed their independence in June of 1898.[51] When US troops first arrived that August, they joined Philippine revolutionaries in their efforts to oust Spain from the islands. One month after the arrival of US troops, Philippine revolutionaries celebrated the inauguration of the new independent Philippine Republic and the new president, Emilio Aguinaldo, in elaborate ceremonies surrounded by Philippine flags.

The new nation's flag had been designed and created by Philippine revolutionaries then exiled in Hong Kong.[52] It featured a sun with eight rays, each representing a Philippine province, and three stars, representing the main island groups of Luzon, Visayas, and Mindanao, where their revolution had begun (figure 1.4).[53] The Philippine Proclamation of Independence stated that the choice of red, white, and blue was to honor "the flag of the United States of North America as a manifestation of our profound gratitude towards this Great Nation for its disinterested protection which it lends us, and continues to lend us."[54]

Over the next few months, homemade Philippine flags waved throughout the archipelago: silk embroidered ones in the homes of well-to-do families, and humbler homemade versions in others.[55] People were proud of their national flag and the independence it symbolized. And they thought of the US flag as a symbol of a friendly foreign nation who had helped them achieve their independence. That December, when the United States decided to

FIGURE 1.4. Inaugural session of the Congress of the First Philippine Republic, September 15, 1898. Filipinas Heritage Library.

purchase the Philippines from Spain instead of recognizing Philippine independence, the US flag became the symbol of a new colonial oppressor. In February of 1899, when a new war began between the United States and the Philippine Republic, the US and Philippine flags came to symbolize opposing sides in the war for sovereignty over the Philippines. The new US colonial government never staged an official flag raising ceremony in the Philippines. But despite this ongoing conflict, US imperialists continued spreading the flag throughout the Philippines. These efforts began, as they had in the continental United States, in schools.

A Flag on Every Schoolhouse

On December 4, 1898, at 9 a.m., about 1,200 schoolchildren and their principals gathered in the Plaza de Armas in San Juan, Puerto Rico (figure 1.5). While the principals each received a US flag for their school, the band of the Eleventh US Infantry played patriotic songs, and "flags dotted the sunny, child-crowded square with brilliant bits of color," according to the *New York Times*.[56] In addition to Puerto Rican children and the US press, representatives of Britain, France, and other foreign nations were in attendance.[57]

The person handing out these US flags was a man named Allan C. Bakewell, who had sailed from New York on November 16—just three months after the cessation of hostilities with Spain. Now, on December 4—one week *before* the signing of the Treaty of Paris, which would formally cede Puerto Rico to the United States—he was standing in the formerly Spanish plaza, leading this grandiose event, distributing US flags as a private citizen representing a patriotic organization called the Grand Army of the Republic (GAR).

Bakewell did not just deliver flags that December day in San Juan. He also delivered an address about the meaning of the US flag. Bakewell's address began by explaining the Civil War origins of the GAR: that it was a "fraternal and charitable order" founded on "loyalty to the government of the United States and the flag which is the emblem of its sovereignty and the ensign of freedom."[58] He explained how for the past decade his GAR post in New York had been gifting US flags to educational institutions, hoping to promote patriotism and flag veneration among youth in the continental United States.[59] Now that Puerto Rico had come under US sovereignty, the post was expanding its efforts. Bakewell encouraged teachers in Puerto Rico to view the US flag "as a text-book of freedom," and to "tell these children of its birth, its history, its glorious achievements."[60] But his enthusiastic speech ended with a warning: "Whoever holds up that flag is a benefactor of the human race;

FIGURE 1.5. "The distribution of flags to the school children of Puerto Rico, Dec. 4, 1898." Instituto de Cultura Puertorriqueña, Archivo General de Puerto Rico, Álbum de Puerto Rico de Feliciano Alonso, item 119.

whoever hauls it down is a master of oppression and a curse to his kindred."[61] After Bakewell's ominous conclusion, the address was repeated in Spanish by an interpreter, who concluded by calling for three cheers for the United States, President McKinley, the GAR, and the military government. Bakewell reported that the crowd "heartily responded."[62] As the event ended, the principals, carrying their new US flags, led their students out of the plaza and the band played "The Stars and Stripes Forever."[63]

It might seem surprising that a private organization would oversee the distribution of flags to Puerto Rico's schools. But while the US flag was the official emblem of the government, it was common for private citizens to aid in its creation and distribution. The massive 120 × 43⅓-foot flag created for the US military to raise over Morro Castle after Spain's surrender in Cuba—a flag the press speculated had broken the record for "the largest flag in the world"—had been financed by "a patriotic Wall Street man."[64] And the first US flag raised by the military in Ponce, Puerto Rico, had been donated by a patriotic organization—the Children of the American Revolution.[65]

The GAR was not the only patriotic organization in the United States, but it was the one that took the most vested interest in extending its work to the new colonies. It had a particular vision of patriotism rooted in its history as an organization of Union veterans from the US Civil War. The organization was, in Bakewell's words, open only to those who had served "under the banner of the Stars and Stripes."[66] This attachment to the US flag stemmed from the members' experience of defending it from Confederates. The GAR had been struggling to standardize flag veneration in the continental United States, particularly in the South, and it was eager to have a new audience in the territories. There, its members believed, it had a blank slate on which to teach people about the flag, what it symbolized, and why it ought to be revered.

The GAR was organized on military lines, with departments, posts, commanders, and missions—including Bakewell's mission to Puerto Rico. After the cessation of hostilities in August 1898, the GAR quickly learned through its military connections that there were 548 public schools and 38 private schools in Puerto Rico—all without US flags.[67] The members of Bakewell's GAR post based in New York decided they would purchase and forward, at their own expense, six hundred four-by-six US flags. For every two dollars donated, a GAR member could have his name or that of a loved one inscribed on a flag intended for a Puerto Rican school, "thereby connecting the individual with the work."[68] From the comfort of their own homes in the continental United States, ordinary people could feel personally involved in the Americanization of Puerto Rico. The post decided that Bakewell, as the chief aide in charge of military instruction and patriotic education in schools, would travel to Puerto Rico to deliver the flags personally.[69]

While this was a civilian mission, Bakewell had the full support of the government in Puerto Rico, which was run by the US military at that time. The secretary of war personally instructed military officials in Puerto Rico to "extend to Colonel Bakewell every facility to carry into effect the mission on which he comes."[70] After all the effort that had gone into the official flag raisings, these colonial officials welcomed the help of the GAR in continuing to spread the US flag and patriotic messages about its meaning. The military governor of Puerto Rico agreed to assist Bakewell in his "most praiseworthy and patriotic work." While the governor was following orders from the secretary of war, he added his own thoughts: "I am sure that the raising of these flags on the schools of this beautiful island will add much to the patriotic feeling that exists now, and tend to endear our country more to its people, now a part of our own."[71] The official flag raising in October had not completely stamped out the Spanish flag. Observers still noted that "if a stranger were to judge alone from the flags to be seen displayed from the housetops" of San Juan, "he would surely think he was in a Spanish city"—the ratio of Spanish to US flags being, they estimated, about thirty to one.[72] The colonial governor issued an order requiring the display of the US flag "and no other flag" on all important public buildings, but needed the GAR to actually provide those flags and to teach people throughout the island the rituals for raising, lowering, and venerating them.[73]

With the help of the military, Bakewell spent the next few weeks traveling from San Juan to Ponce on horseback and by boat, delivering flags along the way. With each flag came the same speech, translated by an interpreter, and a certificate the GAR hoped would be framed in the school.[74] The certificate, printed in both English and Spanish with an embossed US flag in the center, explained the GAR's origins and mission, and said that as an organization "it desires that Porto Rican youth should speedily follow our customs to venerate and love this flag."[75] Each school also received a circular of instructions, again printed in English and Spanish, telling educators what exercises ought to accompany the flag. It explained how it should be raised each morning; gave detailed instructions for how children should perform the Pledge of Allegiance, including the particular positions of their hands and even palms during various moments of the pledge; and said that the ritual should conclude with students singing "America," also known as "My Country, 'Tis of Thee."[76] With these detailed instructions, the GAR was enlisting Puerto Rico's teachers in their mission, trusting them to carry it on.

Bakewell recalled his journey fondly, bringing stories back to his fellow GAR members about how eagerly Puerto Ricans seemed to accept the US flag. In various reports he described an experience with a young boy in Fajardo: "I saw a half-naked little Porto Rican standing near me, and I took a small silk flag out of my pocket and gave it to him. With a squeal of delight he dashed toward a tumble-down hut as fast as his little brown legs would carry him." The boy procured a bamboo stick and, "in less time than it takes to tell, the flag was floating over that hut."[77] Bakewell's language, emphasizing the boy's brown skin, lack of clothing, and "tumble-down hut," painted a picture that his readers in New York would have likely found exotic and unfamiliar. But Bakewell emphasized that, though Puerto Ricans had not been granted US citizenship, he viewed them as "fellow-citizens."[78] So, as he traveled around Puerto Rico delivering US flags, Bakewell was also delivering that message.

This sentiment was echoed by Ines Caparros Soler when she spoke of "becoming baptized as an American." In that address—delivered to Yauco's pupils and teachers at an event like the one in San Juan—Caparros Soler promised that the US flag "shall ever stand in the place of honor in our school and that our scholars shall be taught to love and venerate it." The GAR imagined that Puerto Rico's teachers would follow their instructions for flag veneration to the letter, instilling patriotism in generations of Puerto Rican children. But, as the historian Solsiree del Moral has argued, Puerto Rican teachers— and the majority of Puerto Rico's teachers were Puerto Rican, not transplants from the continental United States—had their own goals for "Americanization" in Puerto Rico: to "*hacer patria*," or "build the nation." And importantly, many Puerto Rican teachers did not see this project as incompatible with the continuation of US rule.[79] The Puerto Rican nation could be built under the US flag. As Caparros Soler elaborated on what it meant to "become American," she articulated her own ideas about Puerto Ricans' status within the US national community. She, too, believed that coming under the US flag made Puerto Ricans "fellow-citizens" of the "American people," and "thus becoming in possession of all liberties that our new father country enjoys."[80] It is not surprising that some decades later the US flag, and flags on schools in particular, became a target of resistance once Puerto Ricans began to realize that the flag had not brought the promised rights and liberties US imperialists claimed it represented.

In those early years, however, the GAR's efforts to place a flag on every schoolhouse in Puerto Rico were successful. And because their efforts focused on schools, many people began to form an association between the US flag and the colonial school. As one district supervisor wrote: "Teachers and pupils have come to look upon the flag as a necessary adjunct to the school."[81] Travelers from the continental United States also noted, "Whenever they see a flag, they naturally infer there is a school."[82] US colonial officials crafted narratives about Puerto Rican children beginning to form an attachment to the flag as part of their daily routine. One school supervisor reported, "Ofttimes hungry, half clad, many of our little people trudge through tropical rains, bareheaded, under a burning sun, over roads impassable for vehicles, crossing brooks, fording streams, climbing hills, they go on till the welcome sight of the flag floating over the little palm-thatched hut shows the end of the toilsome journey."[83] His words are less a reflection of what Puerto Rican children actually thought of the US flag, and more a reflection of the positive associations with the Stars and Stripes that US imperialists hoped they were developing.

After personally visiting most of the municipalities in the island, Puerto Rico's director of public instruction boldly claimed, "I have never seen the Flag saluted in the States with more enthusiasm than I have seen it here in the schools in Puerto Rico."[84] Even in Lares, the town where the "Grito de Lares" call for Puerto Rican independence from Spain had begun in 1868, children routinely participated in patriotic US flag exercises.[85] After witnessing students reciting the Pledge of Allegiance and singing "The Red, White and Blue," a missionary visiting from the continental United States proclaimed that "the salutation of the flag by the children of the public school" was "suggestive of the process of Americanization that is going on here."[86] In other words, flag veneration was visible proof of Americanization in Puerto Rico.

These stories of success in Puerto Rico prompted the GAR to embark on a campaign to ensure that there was "a flag on every schoolhouse" throughout the new colonial empire.[87] In 1900 the organization began to expand its efforts across the Pacific to Hawai'i and the Philippines. In Hawai'i, George W. DeLong single-handedly managed what the GAR called the "herculean task" of ensuring safe delivery of 160 flags donated by Bakewell's GAR post in New York to all the schools in Hawai'i.[88] The flags and flag raising ceremonies came with the reading of an address from Colonel Bakewell himself. Native Hawaiians who had mourned the official raising of the US flag would now be told a different story. At every flag raising, they would hear that the US flag came to Hawai'i as "an emblem of their release from the bondage of inhumanity and servility."[89] In a not-so-veiled dig at the Hawaiian monarchy, the audience would be told that "under the government of this Flag all children are of royal birth; all men may become rulers of the nation and all women have an equal heritage and place of honor."[90] The GAR also encouraged inhabitants of the Hawaiian Islands to "observe the patriotic anniversaries of the year which commemorate the brightest pages of American history when Liberty was born, Freedom restored and Inhumanity overthrown"—never mind that the Hawaiian Kingdom had been overthrown by US citizens less than a decade earlier.[91] Wherever a US flag from the GAR was raised in Hawai'i, those who gathered to see it would receive this lesson.

The GAR also expanded its efforts to the Philippines, where US and Philippine troops remained at war, starting with a shipment of two hundred four-by-six-foot flags to fly over schoolhouses, and two hundred smaller salutation flags for individuals to wave. In the Philippines, trying to spread the flag was an even more complicated task, because it had become the symbol of a conquering army, not a civilian colonial ruler. The Stars and Stripes was the flag carried by US troops when they had killed thousands of Filipinos, placed people in concentration camps, tortured suspected independence sympathizers, and destroyed entire towns and villages. The members of the GAR, veterans themselves, understood that the Philippines remained a war zone, with Philippine revolutionaries fighting for independence and US troops attempting to establish US sovereignty. However, they hoped that the introduction of US flags to the area might "giv[e] assistance to our conquering heroes so far from home, who are enlisted in the spread of humanity in the great mission of civilization which the direction of Providence has placed upon this Land of Liberty to perform."[92]

Colonel John W. French represented the GAR in the Philippines. When French arrived in Manila, he found that local colonial officials had planned a whirlwind tour for him that included attending flag raisings at twenty-five different schools over the course of just three days.[93] The flag raisings had to be performed quickly, in order to keep to schedule. First, a chaplain would explain in Spanish what the flag raising ceremony meant, and then in English would read an address from Colonel Bakewell, much like the ones delivered in Puerto Rico and Hawai'i, about the meaning of the flag. Then the school principal, a person either from the continental United States or from the Philippines, would announce, "*Se sube la bandera*," or "Raise the flag," and French would hoist it.[94] Manila's superintendent of public instruction reported that teachers, pupils, parents, continental US Americans and Filipinos alike, gathered to see "'Old Glory' rise and fall for the first time on the Philippine breezes over American Public Schools."[95]

As in Puerto Rico, imperialists in the Philippines showcased stories about the US flag being embraced by people whom those in continental United States would find exotic and unfamiliar. In the Philippines, that was a group Spanish and US imperialists referred to as the Igorot people, from northern Luzon. Most people in the continental United States learned about this group from the "Igorot village" exhibition at the 1904 St. Louis World's Fair. As the historian Paul Kramer has written, this incredibly popular exhibit made a spectacle of the Igorot people, seeking to scandalize audiences with what one booklet described as "the wildest race of savages," and including spectacles like dog eating.[96] US colonial officials viewed Igorots as so different from other Filipinos that they ruled this area, which they called Mountain Province, separately from the rest of the Philippines.[97] The racialized depictions sought to emphasize the difference between Igorots and other groups under the US flag. But in the Philippines themselves, Igorot children raised the US flag and recited the Pledge of Allegiance at their schools just like children anywhere in the continental United States (figure 1.6).[98]

The GAR sent a total of nine hundred US flags to the Philippines by 1901.[99] The US governor of the Philippines wrote to Bakewell that flags had been "in great demand," such that the government was unable to keep up with their requests, and he thanked the GAR for stepping in.[100] Even in Mindanao, a region with fierce resistance to US rule, the US flag soon became an ordinary feature on Philippine schoolhouses.[101] By 1905, imperialists had distributed five thousand US flags to schools throughout the Philippines.[102] And the superintendent of public instruction in the Philippines was proud to report to Bakewell that, insofar as supplies would allow, there was a US flag flying "over every school house in the islands."[103]

Even in smaller territories where the GAR had not been involved, schoolchildren participated in flag veneration. Indeed, Guam, one of the smallest

FIGURE 1.6. "Igorot school house and pupils, Benguet, P.I." 1920s. Bureau of Insular Affairs photo. US National Archives, 350-P-9.

territories, developed the most impressive routine of flag veneration in the entire empire, perhaps including anywhere in the United States. Every single school day, the children in the capital city of Hagåtña—over one thousand of them—would gather in front of the Governor's Palace, raise the US flag, and recite the Pledge of Allegiance.[104] A visitor from the continental United States noted that this display "would dispel any fear that here are people who knew no love of country. They are proud of their connection with the United States."[105] The US governor of Guam called it "the most impressive sight on the island."[106]

Colonial officials were very forthright about the work they believed the flag was doing in and on the schoolhouse. The director of education in Puerto Rico wrote that the flag served as "an object lesson, bringing to the minds of the people, as they learn the facts of American history and sing the songs of liberty, the principles and institutions which are offered to them."[107] Another education official described how this "object lesson" worked in practice: Even in a town that could only be reached by a mountain trail, where the government had little reach, he "found a large and enthusiastic body of children drawn up at the side of the public plaza to take part in the regular morning exercise of flag raising."[108] Yes, children would need to be taught the patriotic stories and songs. But once they were taught, US imperialists hoped the flag itself could serve as a constant reminder of these lessons. The colonial education children received inside the schools was a key part of the Americanization process. The historian Sarah Steinbock-Pratt has argued that US teachers in the Philippines, often the only representatives of the US government in their local communities, were the ones who were "expected to win hearts and minds, and thus local support for the colonial state," and who were responsible for "convincing local populations to 'Americanize.'"[109]

While they were focused on the content of the curriculum in colonial schools, education officials admitted the importance of the flag itself, writing that "the flags on school buildings do more than almost any other agency in assisting the Government in the Americanization of the Island, and in helping us to teach the lessons of patriotism to the people."[110] While Congress and the Supreme Court had decreed inhabitants of the new territories as "foreign in a domestic sense," the prevalence of US flag veneration in the colonies sent a different message. As one official put it, these exercises gave "to the American visitor a feeling that the future of Porto Rico as a part of the United States of America is assured."[111] A school superintendent in the Philippines wrote that "in many schools, as the Flag arose, the children as they rose to salute would break forth in most excellent singing in English of 'Star-Spangled Banner' or more often 'America.'" The superintendent noted that, as Filipinos sang patriotic songs in their "native accent"—to him the lyrics sounded more like "My country, tiss ob dee"—he felt "the veil seemed to lift for us to listen down the corridors of time to the gradual changes of the expression dropping from native lips, into the fully-rounded out 'My Country, 'tis of thee,' with a pure American accent." Watching Filipinos perform US flag veneration, the superintendent believed he "could see the Philippino emerging into the full-rounded, true-hearted, soul-devoted American citizen."[112] This was the GAR's dream for all US American children—immigrants in the Northeast, former Confederates in the South, former Mexicans in the West, Native Americans throughout the continent, and now colonial subjects overseas—to feel, like Caparros Soler, that in coming under the US flag they were becoming "American," regardless of their legal status.

Flag Days

Every person in a community could see the US flag on a schoolhouse. But children were the only ones who directly received the flag education being offered in schools and participated in daily flag routines there. And in many places, school attendance remained low—especially in rural areas.[113] In the minds of US imperialists, patriotic national holidays became important opportunities for extending their efforts beyond the schoolhouse and encouraging colonial subjects of all ages to participate in flag veneration. Indeed, a key part of Americanization in formerly Spanish colonies, as Anne Perez Hattori has argued in the case of Guam, was to replace the Catholic calendar of festivities with US national holidays.[114] And there was no shortage of US national holidays that centered the flag: the Fourth of July, Memorial Day (then known as Decoration Day), Washington's Birthday, and of course Flag Day.

In 1899, US imperialists organized the first formal Fourth of July celebrations in Manila (figure 1.7). The main events took place on the Luneta—Manila's largest urban park. Major William Wheeler recalled that the Luneta was "crowded like a country fair on prize day," with "Filipinos of all shades," as well as Spaniards, Germans, Japanese, Chinese, French, and English people. But Wheeler felt that "the most picturesque feature of the scene" was the "school boys in holiday attire" who had been "trained to sing patriotic songs in English." The "climax" of the whole event, in his estimation, was when the children, after having "struggled through" the songs "America," "Hail Columbia," and "The Red, White and Blue," sang "their masterpiece, 'The Star Spangled Banner.'" Even though the Fourth of July was a "transplanted holiday" in the Philippines, Wheeler suggested that "some of the impromptu choruses at home would have been put to the blush by that performance on the Luneta."[115]

FIGURE 1.7. "Our young Filipinos in holiday attire at the Fourth of July celebration, Manila, P.I." Library of Congress Prints and Photographs Division.

The real celebration, however, Wheeler wrote, took place on Escolta Street, "which might be called the Broadway of Manila" (figure 1.8). The street was "alive with bunting, and if it was not all the Yankee arrangement of red, white, and blue, it was fluttering and floating, moving and dipping in the strong breeze which blew up from the harbor, simply in honor of July Fourth, 1776." The Philippine flag was conspicuously absent, but, Wheeler noted, "if Aguinaldo's standard was missed by any one on the Escolta that day the disappointed individual didn't let his neighbor know it." Despite the military government's curfew, Wheeler estimated that "it took from 8:30 p.m., the curfew hour, until some time in the forenoon of the 5th for Manila to really give over tooting and toasting and gyrating in honor of Uncle Sam's birthday." The holiday was celebrated well in Manila, but Wheeler admitted he did not know how "impressed" people were with the occasion. "The Filipinos are a peculiar people," he concluded. "But they enjoy holidays, the more the better, and they will not be in a hurry to forget the first noisy, blowing, flaring Fourth of July in Manila."[116]

Outside Manila, where the United States held less authority, patriotic celebrations were more tenuous. Alice Condict, a missionary from the continental United States, recalled that for Washington's Birthday in February 1901, Filipinos set about preparing an "Americana Fiesta." For the occasion, US "soldiers on guard said that everyone must put out the American flag." While Old Glory was "very popular," in her estimation, there were not enough US flags in supply. So Filipinas, likely to comply with the soldiers' orders, began stitching their own homemade flags: "Some ingeniously sewed the stripes of doubtful hues of purple and white frequently with the blue field of stars in the lower and wrong corner or possibly the stars are in a crimson field," Condict wrote. But "no matter, it is a flag, the best that can be made."[117] Condict's use of the word "ingeniously" is interesting. She meant to praise the women's resourcefulness in using what they had, even if the flags did not come out quite right. But while people in the town participated in this "Americana fiesta" for Washington's birthday, Condict noted there were still revolutionaries in the mountains "from which raids were frequently made on our soldier boys in the plains below."[118] The Filipinas forced to stitch US flags for Washington's birthday celebration most likely had loved ones among the revolutionaries who continued to fight for independence under the Philippine flag. It did not occur to Condict that perhaps these women may have purposefully, even "ingeniously," stitched the US flags incorrectly. The US soldiers had made it clear

FIGURE 1.8. "Escolta Street on the 4th of July, 1899, Manila, P.I." Library of Congress Prints and Photographs Division.

that every home needed to display the US flag, but they could not control how these women sewed their flags, or whether they did it correctly.

Participation in these events was not always coerced, but colonial governments often took the lead in organizing particularly impressive displays. In Puerto Rico on Flag Day in the early 1900s, thousands of children marched through the streets of San Juan, holding US flags and singing patriotic songs like "The Star-Spangled Banner" and "Yankee Doodle."[119] As the years went on, the displays became more dramatic. In 1908 the US colonial governor of Puerto Rico described how for the Fourth of July, one thousand children all dressed in red, white, and blue marched through San Juan, forming a pennant more than three hundred feet long. Then, upon arriving in the principal plaza, "the pennant was metamorphosed into an American flag of proper proportions, nearly one hundred feet long. The children, while in this formation, sang the 'Star Spangled Banner,' 'America,' and other songs" (figure 1.9).[120]

In addition to these "transplanted" US holidays, colonial officials created new ones celebrating the beginning of US colonial rule. Occupation Day commemorated the anniversary of the first landing of US troops in Puerto

FIGURE 1.9. "School children formed into American flag, San Juan, 4th of July, 1908." Department of Education of Porto Rico photo. US National Archives, RG 126, central files, Puerto Rico box 786, envelope 9-8-8.

Rico and the Philippines—July 25 and August 13, respectively. Other holidays commemorated the first official raising of the US flag: Flag Day on February 1 in Guam and on April 17 in American Samoa, Annexation Day on August 12 in Hawai'i, and Transfer Day on March 31 in the US Virgin Islands.

Participating in US national holidays like the Fourth of July invited colonial subjects to imagine themselves as part of a broader US national community taking part in similar exercises on the same day. But these colony-specific holidays served a different purpose: that of inviting colonial subjects to celebrate their own colonization. These annual exercises reaffirmed US sovereignty, and the supremacy of the US flag in each place. Colonial officials took this opportunity to remind the broader public of the meaning of the US flag. For instance, on Flag Day in American Samoa, the US colonial governor used the occasion to remind and inform those in attendance of the meaning of the US flag: that "red is the symbol of courage," "white is the symbol of purity," and "blue is the symbol of justice." The governor also made the case for the benefits the US flag had brought to the people of American Samoa. He argued that the flag had "insured peace and safety," "prevented designing outsiders from obtaining property belonging to the natives," and had "preserved Samoan customs insofar as this is possible."[121] In doing so, he invited Samoans to attribute any benefits of US colonial rule not directly to the colonial government, but instead to the flag.

But people living in the colonies also spoke effusively about the flag on these occasions. Overall, these speeches were notably patriotic. But, as Hattori has argued, often these holidays were the only time people from the colonies were given a public platform, so they had to perform a certain level of patriotism that colonial officials would expect on these holidays.[122] Sometimes this required a bit of finesse. For example, the CHamoru teacher and minister Joaquin Sablan gave a speech on Guam's "Flag Day"—"a day," he argued, "which should mean as much to us as the Fourth of July to the United States." Sablan's speech on the significance of the American flag was patriotic, but it also obliquely raised an uncomfortable truth about the US flag on Guam. The flag's design recognized, with its stripes, the thirteen original colonies, and with its stars, the US states. Its design did not recognize the existence of territories like Guam. But Sablan argued, "To me this flag represents more than the Thirteen Original Colonies and the forty-eight States. This flag symbolizes the national pride of America—the heart of the American Republic." And with statements such as "Where-ever the American flag goes, the American civilization follows," and "This flag wherever it is hoisted guarantees the life, liberty, and the pursuit of happiness," Sablan argued that Americanness could include anyone who lived under the US flag, regardless of their status.[123]

These celebrations were important. National holidays are a time when normal daily routines halt and people are meant to actively think about celebrating the flag.[124] This does not mean everyone felt patriotism on these occasions. People also participate in holidays because of the leisure and recreation they offer. But however colonial subjects felt about the US flag—positive, negative, or ambivalent—these occasions invited them to publicly perform their allegiance to it, and perhaps to reflect on their own relationship to it as well.

Conclusion

In the early years of US rule in the Philippines, a man from Kansas in Manila, referring to the Supreme Court's decisions in the *Insular Cases*, declared, "I am sorry our Supreme Court said that the Constitution does not follow the flag; but this I *do* know—that patriotism and loyalty will always follow the flag."[125] His comments implied that this was a natural process. But there was nothing inherent in the flag itself that would naturally invoke feelings of patriotic loyalty. Imperialists knew this association would need to be inculcated over time. The GAR had been instrumental in ensuring that the flag would fly on every schoolhouse throughout the US colonial empire. In their speeches and in the materials they passed on to teachers, GAR representatives spread their messages about the meaning of the US flag to schoolchildren. After the GAR's initial flag donations, the federal government took over, supplying thousands of flags annually to the colonial possessions.[126] The Stars and Stripes now flew outside every schoolhouse and government building, and on many private establishments as well.

Thanks to the joint efforts of public and private actors, the US flag did become a banal part of the landscape throughout the colonial empire. What followed was a whole new set of rituals and practices designed to Americanize new colonial subjects by making flag veneration a banal part of their everyday lives. Imperialists began teaching people these lessons as schoolchildren, and hoped they would spread to the general population through public celebrations of national holidays. In this way, the flag served a purpose different from that of other elements of colonial education. Whether the flag was on a schoolhouse, a courthouse, a post office, or some other government building, most people in a US colony could not go about their everyday lives without seeing it. US imperialists sought to teach colonial subjects what the flag symbolized, how it was to be revered, and that it was their flag.

The spread of flag veneration throughout the colonial empire was remarkable in its own right, but especially when compared to the situation in the continental United States. In the first decade of the twentieth century, people

in the continental United States *resisted* legislation that required flag veneration, and in the South many former Confederates refused to revere the US
flag at all.[127] In Texas, the GAR's local representative reported that "even the
women of this city have in the past torn and cast under foot the little Flags
that we use on Decoration Day."[128] Even where there was not outright resistance, the GAR lamented "the indifference of the American people in saluting
the flag" in the continental United States.[129] By contrast, in 1901 the Puerto Rican commissioner of education had already required that all schoolchildren
begin the day by saluting the US flag, reciting the Pledge of Allegiance, and
singing the national anthem.[130] In 1905 the colonial government in Hawai'i
passed a law requiring the display of the US flag on each public school, joining Puerto Rico and thirty-one continental states and territories in having
laws on the books requiring standardized flag display and ritual in public
schools.[131] Fifteen states, almost all former Confederate states, had refused to
pass similar legislation.[132]

Just as lack of flag veneration in the Southern states could indicate a lack
of loyalty to the United States, government officials in the colonies often cited
flag veneration as proof that colonial subjects were loyal to the United States.
The flag brought with it many promises. Living under the "Flag of Freedom"
or "Banner of Liberty," as the GAR called it, meant membership in a community of people who could call on the federal government to provide for
their well-being. "No power may wrest from you the homes and happiness
protected by the Flag," the GAR promised.[133] As people in the colonies began
to make claims on the flag and the nation for which it stood, their relationship
to the object changed. By the 1910s, the Philippine press reported that while
Filipinos had initially celebrated the Fourth of July "with great enthusiasm,"
some took "advantage of the Fourth of July to throw in the faces of Americans
that they have no right to celebrate the independence of their nation while
they deny it to the Filipino people."[134] Recall that Pedro Albizu Campos wrote
that Puerto Ricans "welcomed the American flag in 1898 because we believed
it . . . to be a symbol of democracy and justice."[135] When we meet Albizu
Campos again in the 1920s, he will have discovered that the Stars and Stripes
had not brought democracy and justice to Puerto Rico as promised. By then,
these small symbolic representations of US sovereignty in Puerto Rico had
become, to him, flags "of tyranny."[136]

Pocket-Sized Imperialism

It is difficult to think of a more iconic example of US national currency than the one-dollar bill. Its design is so familiar that the look of the 1903 US-Philippine ten-peso bill seems surprising (figure 2.1). The similarities are uncanny; even with the words "Philippine Islands" and the "pesos," the latter could be easily confused with the US bill. That was precisely what troubled the US treasury secretary in 1928 when he requested the removal of George Washington's portrait (along with that of William McKinley, then on the Philippine five-peso and US ten-dollar bills), from US-Philippine money. The treasury secretary argued that Washington and McKinley's portraits were "a principal distinguishing feature of US currency."[1]

Indeed, this particular image of George Washington—based on Gilbert Stuart's 1796 "Athenaeum Portrait"—had graced the US one-dollar bill since 1869. But until 1928, US paper money was quite large (over three by seven inches), and the one-dollar bill with Washington's portrait had a very different design. There was no concern that the 1903 design of the ten-peso bill might be confused with that of the one-dollar bill until the Treasury Department decided to shrink the size of US money to match US-Philippine money, and to adopt the ten-peso design for the one-dollar bill.

The treasury secretary's request wound its way through the hierarchy of US colonial governance in the Philippines, from the secretary of war to the chief of the Bureau of Insular Affairs—the federal agency tasked with governing the Philippines and some other territories—and, finally, to the US governor-general of the Philippines, who insisted that the portraits stay.[2] To "eliminate the portraits of McKinley and Washington" from Philippine money, he replied, "would be an unwise policy for American interests in the Philippines" and could "give rise to serious misunderstandings and misrepresentations."[3]

FIGURE 2.1. Washington's portrait on the US-Philippine ten-peso bill, 1903. Bureau of Engraving and Printing Historical Resource Center.

The governor-general felt that Washington and McKinley's portraits on money were doing important work in the Philippines—so important that he dared to defy the request of a US Cabinet member to keep them.

Debates about currency were hardly uncommon in the late nineteenth and early twentieth-century United States; this was the era of bimetallism campaigns at home and dollar diplomacy abroad, and scholars like Emily Rosenberg, Yoshiko Nagano, Peter James Hudson, and Allan Lumba have established currency's significance as a financial and political tool in the US colonies.[4] But this particular dispute stands out because it was not about gold or silver standards, exchange rates, or loans. The disagreement over whether Washington and McKinley's portraits should remain on Philippine currency was about design. The same economic experts who conducted currency reform in foreign countries created the US-Philippine peso, but as Emily Rosenberg has argued, the entire purpose of dollar diplomacy was to extend US economic control over foreign countries while explicitly *avoiding* the extension of formal colonial rule.[5] Currency in the Philippines, emblazoned with US iconography and the legend "United States of America," was a symbolic expression of formal colonial rule. Government officials placed the same iconography on US-Philippine coins and postage stamps. Throughout the colonial empire, people used money and postage stamps that bore US national iconography. Imperialists believed that, like US flags, these small symbolic objects could "Americanize" colonial subjects.

Money and postage stamps are inherently different from flags. First, while states often standardize the designs of their flags, they do not have a monopoly on producing flags. But only the US government or a company it officially contracts can make legitimate US money or postage stamps.[6] So, while the spread of flags emphasized the efforts of nonstate actors, this chapter shows the US colonial state at work. Second, like flags, paper money, coins, and stamps are pocket-sized markers of sovereignty. But while flags are purely symbolic objects, money and postage stamps have practical, nonsymbolic uses; money provides a means of exchange for goods and services, and stamps pay for postal material to reach its intended recipient. Beyond the borders of the country that has created them, stamps and money might retain value as collectibles or commemoratives, but usually are not accepted as legal tender.[7] Imperialism complicated this divide by producing spaces that were neither fully internal nor external to the United States—in the Supreme Court's terms, "foreign to the United States in a domestic sense."[8] Despite that ruling, US officials decided that people in the colonies would use US money and stamps—in most cases, the exact same money and stamps used in the continental United States, and in the Philippine case money and stamps that used much of the same US iconography. Just like flags, as these objects formerly only officially used within the continental United States spread throughout the colonial empire, they invited people who were excluded from the polity in legal and political terms to nonetheless imagine themselves as part of the national community. Finally, money and stamps presented more iconographic opportunities than did flags. There is only one US flag, but every denomination of coin, paper note, or postage stamp could have its own intricate design. And whenever government officials felt a certain portrait, vignette, or symbol no longer fit their vision, they could change them. As we will see, government officials used this flexibility to meet the moment, changing the designs of stamps and money to reflect changing conditions throughout the colonial empire.

While US officials did concern themselves with monetary and postal policy, they were just as focused on the symbolic potential of these objects. As the historian Sheila A. Brennan has argued in the case of stamps, these were "not mere instruments of postal operations." They were "designed to be symbolic, and we should interpret them as such."[9] Around the world, government officials have carefully chosen designs for their money and stamps that they have felt best represented their countries' national character and history.[10] The hope is that as these objects circulate, they can affirm national identity for those inside the national community.[11] In the United States, the US Bureau of Engraving and Printing, the US Mint, and the US Post Office Department have been the arbiters of how the United States has been officially represented on these objects. US officials hoped that a person in Puerto Rico or Guam sending or receiving a letter stamped with George Washington or Benjamin Franklin's portrait would feel that these men were *their* national heroes, or that someone in the Philippines or the US Virgin Islands purchasing goods with coins bearing the American eagle and the legend "United States of America" would feel that, despite their status, they too were connected to the United States.

Money and stamps had only recently been standardized in the continental United States when US officials introduced them in the colonies. The United States did not have uniform national currency until the Civil War.[12] In the early to mid-nineteenth century, the silver peso produced in Mexico had been the dominant coin throughout the Americas, the Pacific, East Asia, and even eastern Russia.[13] In the United States even as late as 1845, Mexican money made up 90 percent of the coins in circulation.[14] Making the dollar the exclusive currency used in the United States took considerable effort. The US Mint first introduced uniform coinage in 1853; but even after a four-year campaign from 1857 to 1861 to encourage people to use only US currency, foreign money continued to circulate, especially in rural areas.[15] Money took on a strong political valence during the Civil War, as both the Union and the Confederacy issued massive quantities of paper money imprinted with battling iconographies.[16] In 1863, the US Treasury inaugurated a new national banking system that standardized the design of all paper money in the United States. The hope was that the scenes on banknotes would, in one Treasury clerk's words, "teach the masses the prominent periods in our country's history," reaching people "who would never read them in books" and "imbuing them with a National feeling."[17] During and after the Civil War, people in the United States began to use US coins and paper money exclusively, making every transaction an opportunity for someone in the United States to be imbued with "a National feeling."[18]

The nineteenth-century US post office was perhaps the most well-articulated part of the federal government. As sociologist Theda Skocpol put it, "the early United States may have been not so much a country with a post office as a post office that gave popular reality to a fledgling nation."[19] Every town, no matter how remote, had a US post office.[20] That visible representation of the federal government helped foster a feeling of citizenship, belonging, and national inclusion for people far from Washington, giving them "real assurance," in the words of the postal historian Wayne Fuller, "that Uncle Sam had not forgotten them."[21] But Congress did not grant the postmaster general the authority to "prepare postage stamps" until 1847, and prepayment with official government stamps only became mandatory in 1855.[22] Postal patrons quickly adopted this new method, however, and stamp use became a crucial part of US postal culture in the mid-nineteenth century.[23] By the 1890s, the US Post Office Department began to take an even more vested interest in using stamps to circulate national narratives, as it started to produce commemorative issues.[24]

As these brief histories suggest, money and stamps have served different purposes for the US state and its citizens. Stamps linked users into a communication network of letter writers. Money linked users into a monetary system of global capitalism. The particularities of these systems made the introduction of these symbolic objects in the colonies a complicated endeavor; indeed, the raising of US flags throughout the empire seems a simple task in comparison. The introduction of US money required economic experts to establish colonial currency regimes. The introduction of US stamps required the extension of the US postal service thousands of miles from the continental United States. However, this chapter treats money and stamps together because, once these systems were established, these pocket-sized objects served strikingly similar symbolic functions. The designs on money and stamps indicated which country held sovereignty over a space, and how that country's government wanted to officially represent its own history and culture. Even though they were used for different purposes, money and stamps can be analyzed together to reveal what national symbols and narratives US state actors wanted circulating among people living in their country's colonies.

This chapter recounts the story of how US money and stamps became part of everyday life in the colonies. It first shows the haphazard way both objects first arrived in the colonies, where they were often used alongside money and stamps from previous colonial administrations. Next we see how, though officials extended US monetary and postal networks to the colonies out of practical necessity, they quickly seized on the symbolic potential of these objects and their ability to spread national iconography. As government officials encountered questions of what designs to place on currency and postage stamps for the colonies, they consistently opted for US national iconography in the hope that these objects would have the same effect there that they had in the continental United States: imbuing colonial subjects, too, with "a National feeling."

The US government was able to spread money and stamps with US national symbols throughout its colonial empire, but this transformation did not always occur on the terms that they expected or wanted. Officials struggled to get colonial subjects to communicate via the US postal service. Some people in the colonies melted coins down into bullion, wore them as jewelry, or simply ignored them and continued using old currency.[25] This chapter shows how much effort US officials put into making the US postal service the primary method of communication and US money the sole method of exchange, sometimes using coercive tactics. They persisted because they knew that mundane objects like currency and stamps were never simply a neutral means of exchange. Because of the iconography they carried, every transaction, however banal, could become an opportunity to present a subtle reminder of US sovereignty and national iconography. In these early years of colonization, US officials insisted that the designs of these pocket-sized objects were significant. Later, people in US colonies would both push for inclusion in the national narratives presented on these symbolic objects and, at other times, use the objects to reject US rule altogether.

Stamping Sovereignty

On January 17, 1893, a group of US citizens in the Hawaiian Islands backed by US Marines overthrew the Hawaiian monarchy. The coup plotters formed a "provisional government," hoping the United States would annex the islands, but President Grover Cleveland refused. The Hawaiian stamps in use at the time, printed by the American Banknote Company in New York City, were markers of the Hawaiian Kingdom's sovereignty, with portraits of members of the Hawaiian royal family, including the last reigning monarch, Queen Lili'uokalani. Once they learned annexation was not imminent, the Provisional Government ordered its postmaster general, Joseph M. Oat, to have all Hawaiian Kingdom stamps overprinted with the words "Provisional Govt. 1893" (figure 2.2, left).[26] The Provisional Government overprinted more than two and a half million stamps, most of which sold out by the end of the year, despite Hawai'i having a population of less than a hundred thousand at the time.[27] These overprints became a visible manifestation of the unsettled nature of sovereignty in the Hawaiian Islands in the months after the coup.[28] They sent the message to anyone using the postal system that the coup plotters had sought to stamp out the Hawaiian monarchy and annex the islands to the United States, but had not fully succeeded.

Eager to replace Queen Lili'uokalani's portrait, Postmaster General Oat held a competition for new stamp designs in October of 1893. A US citizen in Honolulu won, and his five stamp designs—including one that would feature a portrait of Sanford Dole, one of the primary coup plotters—went into circulation in early 1894.[29] Interestingly, the design placed Dole's portrait alongside the flag of the Hawaiian Kingdom—which the newly inaugurated "Republic of Hawaii," with Dole as its president, soon decided to co-opt as its own official ensign (figure 2.2, right).[30] The same company that had produced the Hawaiian Kingdom's stamps now printed these new stamps for the government that had overthrown it. Indeed, the consul representing the new Republic of Hawaii personally visited the American Bank Note Company in 1894 to oversee the destruction of all the dies and plates that had been used to print the stamps of the Hawaiian royal family, ensuring that they could never be produced again.[31] The new Hawaiian Republic stamps would remain in circulation until 1900.

The first US stamps used in Puerto Rico, the Philippines, and Guam also reflected unsettled conditions. US postal service arrived in these places in the

FIGURE 2.2. Stamps of the Provisional Government (1893) and the Republic of Hawaii (1894). Author's collection.

crucible of war in 1898. There was no grand strategy for setting up a colonial postal service, but US Postmaster General Charles Emory Smith had made his wartime mission clear: "The mails follow the flag."[32] During the war, the Post Office Department's organizational capacity allowed it to act quickly, establishing US post offices alongside or sometimes even ahead of the military.

US troops invaded Manila, the capital city of the Philippines, on August 13, 1898. While the battle raged, Frank Vaille, a postal worker from Oregon whom Postmaster General Smith had appointed to run postal service in the Philippines, was already at work.[33] In Vaille's telling, "By a combination of circumstances, I was enabled to land and enter Manila an hour or more before any of our soldiers entered the city, and soon thereafter succeeded in finding the Manila post-office. There I was courteously received and shown over the office."[34] Thousands of miles from his superiors in Washington, Vaille had astounding autonomy in the Philippines. As he put it, "no instructions had been issued to govern"; but people, especially merchants, needed postal service, and he did not think it wise to let the Spanish continue operating it. "There was but one thing to be done—assume charge at once of the Manila office and administer its affairs," Vaille singlehandedly decided. Thus the Manila post office became a US post office. It happened so quickly that one newspaper wrote, "Before the Spanish flag had fairly been hauled down from the governor's palace the sign 'U. S. P. O., Manila,' was hung out."[35]

After the cessation of hostilities, postal officials back in Washington publicly expressed restraint. First Assistant Postmaster General Perry S. Heath, Smith's second-in-command, told the press, "We cannot establish a postal system in the Philippines, nor make any aggressive effort in that direction. The peace protocol provides that we shall possess Manila and Manila bay. . . . But beyond that the post office department cannot go for the present."[36] Vaille's report shows otherwise. "Immediately after the cessation of hostilities," he wrote, "I began exchanging mails with those points that were still in possession of Spain, and have kept it up." Furthermore, while the Post Office Department had extended the domestic US postage rates to military personnel, Vaille ordered that those rates would apply to the entire Philippine archipelago. This declaration had its limits, of course; US postal service could only securely expand into areas under US military control.[37] In his first few months on the job, Vaille had established US postal service in the Philippines and extended (in decree, if not in deed) domestic rates throughout the archipelago, all before representatives from the United States and Spain had even convened to begin negotiating the Treaty of Paris, which would officially cede the Philippines to the United States.[38] Vaille had even personally met with Emilio Aguinaldo, president of the independent Philippine Republic, to try and make arrangements for "dispatching mail to the provinces." Among other things, Aguinaldo wanted Vaille to recognize the validity of the Philippine Republic's postage stamps. The United States had not yet claimed sovereignty over the Philippines, but Vaille still felt he "was not in a position to recognize the stamps issued by the Filipinos."[39]

Meanwhile, Smith had appointed a committee to investigate postal service in Puerto Rico. While postal officials knew their authority in the Philippines was murky, Heath argued that Puerto Rico "belongs to us by right of conquest."[40] The chair of the postal committee to Puerto Rico, James Stuart, was no stranger to expansion; newspapers boasted that he had established "not less than 10,000 post offices" in the western United States.[41] When the committee began its work in Ponce, in Stuart's telling, "We followed in the rear of the advancing army. And as a town was captured we evicted the native postmaster, put one of our clerks in charge, introduced a money order and registry system, and there we were." He bragged they "had an up-to-date American post office running like clock work four hours after a town was captured." It soon became clear that this was more vanguard than investigative committee, as postal workers began moving ahead of the military: "Finally we broke away from the army and proceeded to the interior and along to coast towns by ourselves. . . . This enabled us to make even better time in setting up a post office, when the troops finally came along and claimed the town in the name of the United States Government." While Smith proclaimed that the mails followed the flag, in Puerto Rico it was the other way around. Between August and October 1898, this committee established fifteen US post offices in Puerto Rico.[42]

FIGURE 2.3. US stamps overprinted for use in Guam, Puerto Rico, and the Philippines, 1898. National Postal Museum, Smithsonian Institution.

US citizens expected the post office to facilitate communication between soldiers in the colonies and loved ones in the continental United States. Indeed, since the mid-nineteenth century, the public had expected that the post office would facilitate communication with anyone anywhere on US soil.[43] Despite the thousands of miles that separated Minnesota from Manila, the *St. Paul Globe* wrote that as soon as "soldier boys" left for the Philippines, "everybody who has a son, a brother, or a friend among the troops which will occupy the Philippines will be anxious to have a letter go forward by the first and quickest steamer."[44] This anxiety, echoed in newspapers around the country, made it clear: as "US soil" expanded overseas, the public expected that postal service would follow.[45] Even if they were initially motivated by a desire to appease the demands of US soldiers and civilians in the colonies (and their loved ones on the continent), postal officials understood that the US post offices created under military authority would need to "carry on the general postal service of the communities in which they are located."[46] Indeed, Postmaster General Smith argued that postal service had a unique role to play in US imperialism: "American rule and influence will carry blessings and benefits to the new peoples who have come under the flag, and in no feature more distinctly than in an honest, thorough and progressive postal service."[47]

In this interim period, the US Post Office Department overprinted US stamps to be used in these territories (figure 2.3). These overprints stemmed from practical necessity and were intended to be a temporary measure. Nevertheless, they indicated a clear change in sovereignty. After decades of using stamps bearing images of Spanish monarchs like King Alfonso XIII, these overprinted US stamps introduced people in former Spanish colonies to a pantheon of US national heroes: George Washington, Benjamin Franklin, Thomas Jefferson, James Madison, Andrew Jackson, Henry Clay, Daniel Webster, Ulysses S. Grant, David Farragut, William Tecumseh Sherman, and James Garfield.

While these overprints introduced US national iconography in former Spanish colonies, the use of overprints rather than regular US stamps revealed that these places were, for now at least, separate from the rest of the US postal network. And printing the names of places legally not part of the United States *over* the faces of US national heroes shows that this was not just a one-way imposition: the stamps suggest that the acquisition of colonies might also leave their imprint on US national culture.

Between 1899 and 1901, the Post Office Department fully integrated Puerto Rico, Guam, Hawai'i, and American Samoa into the domestic postal network, giving these places the same postal status as the rest of the United States.[48] The Philippine postal service would operate independently of the US Post Office Department and continue issuing US stamps overprinted with the word "PHILIPPINES."[49] But Philippine postal service was not so "independent" in practice. High-level appointments still came from the US Post Office Department, and all Philippine post offices were required to follow the regulations, standards, and practices put forth by the department. The primary difference was financial: the US colonial government in the Philippines, not the US Post Office Department, appropriated funds for the Philippine postal service's operations and paid any postal deficits. Government officials troubled themselves with appropriations and revenues, but users of the post office likely did not dwell on these matters. The stamps they used, bearing the legend "United States Postage," indicated who was in charge.

Regular postage stamps contained portraits of US politicians and military leaders, with Washington's portrait on the most commonly used two-cent stamp. But the Post Office Department had also recently introduced commemorative stamps, which almost exclusively celebrated world's fairs and expositions.[50] One series featuring the 1893 World's Columbian Exposition commemorated Christopher Columbus's 1492 arrival in the Americas. Another set of stamps depicted scenes from US continental expansion, including white settlers enduring the "hardships of emigration," John Fremont planting the US flag in the Rocky Mountains, white settlers "farming in the West," and an "Indian hunting buffalo." These stamps explicitly celebrated imperialism. People from Hawai'i, Puerto Rico, Guam, and American Samoa were not a part of the collective national story promoted on US postage stamps, but neither were many people living in the continental United States.[51] The Post Office Department deployed these images in the colonies for the same reason they deployed them in the continental United States: so that anyone who encountered a stamp would see official narratives of the nation's history and culture.

But postage stamps could only have these intended effects if people were using the postal service. Postmaster General Smith bragged that in the colonies, the "vast improvement of the postal service . . . presents to people the visible evidence, perhaps more universal and palpable than any other exemplification, of the beneficent character of American administration."[52] Postal officials in the colonies were decidedly less optimistic. As the US military pulled troops out of the colonies, postal revenues plummeted.[53] Officials blamed some of this on the Spanish. The director of posts in Puerto Rico described how in Spanish post offices "when a mail arrived it would be dumped on a table and people who could read and cared to call at the office for their mail were at liberty to sort the pile over."[54] Vaille blamed low postal revenue on Filipinos, claiming that "the great number of languages is prohibitive of extensive correspondence between the different provinces."[55] He told the US Post Office Department not to expect revenue from the Philippines to be any more than that from Western states, "the natives not being considered, because their correspondence is as near nil as that of ranchers and plainsmen at our army posts in the States."[56] Vaille argued that "the Philippine races are not a letter-writing people."[57]

The numbers did seem low at first. In 1903, the average annual per capita consumption of postal service in the United States was $1.43. By contrast, it was sixty-six cents in the Hawaiian Islands, seven cents in Puerto Rico, and just over one cent in the Philippines.[58] But these numbers grew steadily. In 1905, annual per capita postal consumption in Puerto Rico was one and a half times what it had been in 1901.[59] Between 1903 and 1905, per capita postal consumption in Guam almost doubled.[60] Officials saw hope in this slow growth. The Philippine Commission wrote hopefully that once "the masses of the people become better educated," they would "learn to better appreciate and understand the value of a regular and frequent mail service," and that "the service will be more extensively patronized."[61] Postal patronage was directly linked to broader civilizing discourses. As a *Harper's Weekly* reporter put it just after the war, "The condition of the postal system of a country is always an indication of the standing of that country, not only in commerce, but in civilization."[62] US officials like Vaille used the fact that Filipinos did not patronize the US post offices as an argument for their lack of civilization. But his reports neglected to mention that Filipinos had another postal service at their disposal: that of the independent Philippine Republic.

Since Vaille's initial meeting with Aguinaldo in late summer 1898, the United States had purchased the Philippines from Spain, and in February of 1899 US soldiers opened fire on Filipino soldiers, beginning a war between the two countries. During this period, both the Philippine Republic and the US colonial government issued their own postage stamps.[63] The Revolutionary Government's stamps contained distinct Philippine iconography, like the

FIGURE 2.4. Philippine Revolutionary Government Stamps, 1898. Author's collection.

Philippine flag's sun and stars, and clearly indicated Philippine sovereignty in their Spanish legends "Philippine Mail" and "Revolutionary Government" (figure 2.4). The US military took these pocket-sized markers of sovereignty seriously, ordering soldiers to confiscate and destroy any stocks of Philippine stamps they encountered. One soldier recalled that in Cavite, US Army troops captured more than three million two-centavo stamps, along with several cases of Philippine paper money, and that superiors ordered them to burn the entire supply.[64] In March of 1900 a US colonel in Negros complained that "there have been considerable letters carried through the mail conveying rebellious matters against the constituted authorities of the United States"— and that most of those letters carried stamps of the Philippine Revolutionary Government. The colonel ordered that whenever soldiers found letters with Philippine stamps, they had to inspect them for "matter rebellious in character." Even if the soldiers deemed the content of the letters acceptable, they were to replace any Philippine stamps with US stamps before delivering the letters to their addressees.[65] While Vaille claimed that "the Philippine races are not a letter-writing people," the military's actions suggested otherwise.

In official reports, Vaille and his successors never mentioned the military's destruction and removal of Philippine stamps. Postal officials in the colonies preferred to present their work as innocuous, writing that they were able to effect "a complete change in a system which deals so directly with the people as does the mail service . . . without the least friction or interruption of business with the public."[66] The same could not be said for the introduction of US money in the colonies.

Mixed-Up Money

The federal government had made US dollars and cents the exclusive currency in the United States during and after the Civil War, but Spain and Denmark had less success regulating currency within their empires. After Mexico declared independence from Spain, Spanish officials tried and failed to remove Mexican money from circulation in their remaining colonies throughout the nineteenth century.[67] In their last efforts to standardize currency, Spanish officials created exclusive currencies for Puerto Rico in 1895 and the Philippines in 1897. Spanish–Puerto Rican and Spanish-Filipino pesos featured a bust of King Alfonso XIII, the Spanish coat of arms, and the legend "Isla de Puerto Rico" or "Islas Filipinas." But Mexican money continued to circulate. Similarly, in the Danish West Indies (the future US Virgin Islands), there was an official Danish West Indian daler, but other national currencies circulated freely.[68] In none of the aforementioned colonies did any sovereign power control the currency as tightly as the federal government had done in the United States since the Civil War. But in their mix of monies, the Philippines, Puerto Rico, and the Danish West Indies were hardly unusual, and did not look that different from the United States just a few decades earlier.[69]

In the Hawaiian Islands, foreign coins from the United States, England, Spain, and France were common in the nineteenth century.[70] In 1883 the Hawaiian Kingdom began issuing its own coins, which were actually produced by the US Mint and designed by its chief engraver, Charles E. Barber (figure 2.5).[71] A bust of the current Hawaiian monarch, Kalākaua, graced the front of the coins, along with the legend "Kalakaua I King of Hawaii." The reverse bore the

FIGURE 2.5. Hawaiian one-dollar silver coin with effigy of King Kalākaua, 1883. National Numismatic Collection, National Museum of American History, Smithsonian Institution.

Hawaiian Kingdom's official motto. "Ua Mau ke Ea o ka Aina i ka Pono" (The life of the land is perpetuated in righteousness), and various symbols of the monarchy, depending on the denomination. The US Mint made these Hawaiian coins in the same denominations and the exact same size, weight, and fineness as US coins.[72] Importantly, with the introduction of the Kalākaua coins, the Hawaiian Kingdom banned all other foreign coins except US coins, which it authorized as legal tender in the Hawaiian Kingdom.[73] After annexation, some US citizens called for the withdrawal of Hawaiian coins; but because those coins had the same denominations and value as US coins, the situation was not as complex as in Puerto Rico and the Philippines. It was, however, an "inconvenience to the business community," Honolulu bankers claimed, because the custom house in Honolulu would not accept Hawaiian coins as payment since they were not legal tender in the continental United States.[74]

When people from the continental United States encountered multiple fluctuating foreign and domestic currencies in their country's colonies, they saw chaos. The *Manila Times* wrote that US citizens spent most of their time "figuring out how many reales there are in a peseta, and how many quartos there are in a cent," and trying to differentiate between coins that looked "more like disorganized trouser buttons than anything else."[75] The Philippine Commission, a governing body of US colonial officials and elite Filipinos appointed by the president, brought in bankers and other financial experts to testify about how this system worked, and Congress sent special commissions to conduct interviews on "the money question" in Puerto Rico and the US Virgin Islands.[76] This system of multiple currencies, though it had prevailed in the United States before the Civil War, appeared mysterious to them. And as long as it remained mysterious, US citizens were never sure how far their dollars would go.

US officials in Puerto Rico and the Philippines established an official two-to-one exchange rate between pesos and dollars. In theory, a person in either place should have been able to take their US dollars and purchase goods or services at half the price listed in pesos, but in practice the exchange rate was not uniformly observed. In San Juan the rate was more like 1.75 pesos to a dollar, and in rural Puerto Rico many people did not accept US dollars at all.[77] In the Philippines the exchange rate fluctuated constantly with the global price of silver. To US officials, disregarding the exchange rate seemed like an act of resistance to US rule.[78] US citizens did not trust Puerto Rican, Filipino, or Chinese methods of valuing money, and their confusion soon turned to racialized suspicion.[79] When the exchange rate was not observed, the *Manila Times* noted, US soldiers were "deprived . . . of a percentage of their pay," and "a few clever Chinese" were able to "juggle with the fluctuations in change and currency legislation so as to score always."[80] During the Civil War, US citizens had learned that faith in the national currency equaled faith in the nation.[81] However, to the people living in Puerto Rico and the Philippines who were accustomed to valuing money on the basis of its bullion content and global market prices, it simply seemed unwise to "accept a fictitious rate based on nothing," as one Puerto Rican banker put it.[82] It was counterintuitive to accept that the Mexican peso coin, which was larger than the US dollar and contained more silver, was worth half as much.

In the early years of US rule in the US Virgin Islands, municipal budgets were still accounted in Danish francs and bits, while the export duty on sugar (the islands' primary export) was accounted in US dollars. Local banks did their business in francs and bits, while businessmen operated with dollars and cents. The system, according to a US congressional commission, was "very confusing to the uninitiated." World War I had only complicated matters, causing local Danish money to depreciate in value—a burden which, officials reported, fell "alike on all classes."[83] The "currency question" in the new US Virgin Islands, the congressional commission wrote in 1920, was "creating a great spirit of unrest, and was absolutely unfair to the population."[84] The Colonial Councils in St. Thomas and St. Croix had submitted formal resolutions to the US governor to end the circulation of Danish money and make US currency the only legal tender in the islands.[85]

US citizens were the loudest voices calling for currency reform in the colonies. In Honolulu, bankers complained that "as a territory of the United States our circulating medium should be uniform with the currency of the mainland," and that in the Philippines "a large proportion of Americans . . . could not see any reason why the American dollar should not at once follow the flag."[86] They believed that wherever their country claimed sovereignty, US currency ought to be legal tender.[87] But officials were aware that if introduced in the colonies, these objects would be used by colonial subjects as well. Thus, currency reforms struck many as a useful tool in the broader project of "Americanization." These efforts were linked to broader colonial discourses of civilization, tutelage, and modernity. As Allan Lumba has argued, US imperialists were eager to turn colonial inhabitants into monetary subjects "forcefully bound to the U.S. dollar."[88]

Congressman Charles N. Fowler of New Jersey put it plainly: "If American civilization is to be the salvation of the Filipino, you will lift him further and faster by the adoption of American money than by any other force. It will teach him the lessons of the flag, and impress upon him the power and glory of the Republic, while the theoretical instruction of the schools is making comparatively slow progress." While many officials and indeed many scholars of Americanization in the US colonies have focused primarily on childhood education, Fowler noted a distinct advantage of currency—that it had the potential to reach much more of the population. He argued that money could quickly educate masses of people about the culture and history of the United States, and could thus "start the Filipino on the sure road to a perfect confidence in the American people and in the justice and honor of our Government."[89] Colonial officials agreed that standardizing currency would "gratify the pride of the natives, and tend to cultivate among them a national spirit and ultimately a feeling of gratitude toward this country."[90] There was a sense that the introduction of US money might allow colonial officials to accomplish two goals at once, linking colonial subjects to the US monetary system and Americanizing them in the process. But once currency reform had been conceived of by experts in Washington, it actually had to be carried out on the ground in the colonies. Much to the surprise of financial experts who believed change would happen easily, US officials encountered great difficulty in implementing currency reform in most of the colonies. And while monetary policy was often front of mind for currency reformers, we will see that iconography mattered a great deal, too.

Dollars and Cents

In 1900, the US Treasury undertook its first experiment with colonial currency reform in Puerto Rico. The 1900 Organic Act that created Puerto Rico's civilian government stipulated that Puerto Ricans would use the same US dollars and cents used in US states and continental territories.[91] Whereas the Treasury had given continental US citizens four years to exchange their foreign currency after the Coinage Act of 1857, it gave Puerto Ricans just three months—from May 1 to August 1, 1900—to redeem their currency. To oversee the exchange, the Treasury Department sent two special agents who traveled around the island trying to convince people of the benefits of redeeming their Spanish and Mexican currency for US money. Unsurprisingly, given the unforgiving timeline, the Treasury agents reported "considerable opposition" to the exchange.[92] At the agents' request, the federal government granted an extension, but only of twenty days. Even with this short timeline, the exchange—or *canje*, as it was known in Puerto Rico—was largely successful. By August 20, 1900, pennies, dimes, and quarters had replaced pesos and centavos. But if the US government had hoped Puerto Ricans would appreciate the introduction of US money, it was sorely mistaken.

Puerto Rico, according to one Puerto Rican in the employ of the US colonial government in 1899, "has been the country of untold changes of coin, whereby she has been vilely victimized."[93] The *canje* in 1900 was no different. The last time the Spanish had attempted to remove Mexican money from circulation in Puerto Rico, they had established more than forty offices throughout the island where people could exchange their currency.[94] The United States had established just three: in San Juan, Ponce, and Mayagüez. Putting the exchange offices in Puerto Rico's largest cities made it easy for urban dwellers—mostly bankers, merchants, and speculators—to convert their money into US currency before the deadline. But US Governor George W. Davis reported that for the majority of Puerto Ricans living outside those cities, some as far as fifty miles from the nearest exchange office, "to get the local money from the interior to these points was not easy, and the expense for transportation was considerable."[95] Davis roundly condemned the *canje*, arguing that "the work of the exchange was controlled from Washington by people unfamiliar with Porto Rican conditions, the force employed to carry on the work was altogether too small, and the length of time allowed for its accomplishment was under the circumstances inadequate."[96] The people who were unable to exchange their currency in time found that their old currency was only worth its bullion value—forty-four or forty-five cents per peso, instead of the established sixty.[97] Poorer rural populations paid the price for the US government's poor planning.[98]

The *canje* also caused an estimated 10 to 15 percent rise in the cost of living in Puerto Rico.[99] Just as many people had not observed the government's two-to-one exchange rate before, many ignored the new exchange rate as well. US coins were not much larger than the pesos Puerto Ricans were accustomed to using, even though the government claimed they were worth much more.[100] Some merchants split the difference, but many simply switched prices from pesos to dollars, leading to an immediate 66.6 percent rise in prices.[101] Again, Governor Davis argued that this hurt poor Puerto Ricans most. A "poor peon," he wrote, would receive six dollars for ten pesos at the exchange office, but merchants inflated the price of goods and landlords inflated their rent. "The dense ignorance of 80 per cent of the inhabitants and their general helplessness was taken advantage of by the merchants, local bankers, and employers of labor."[102] It did not help that the former Spanish Bank of Puerto Rico, whose note-issuing power the United States was treaty bound to honor until 1913, was issuing notes that suggested pesos and dollars were worth the same amount.[103]

Financial experts estimated that the *canje* caused the average agricultural worker to lose approximately 40 percent of his monthly wages.[104] The *canje* also infuriated wealthier Puerto Ricans, because some service workers used the confusion to garner higher real wages. An August editorial in *La Corre-*

spondencia wrote, "The cook refuses to season the *olla* unless we give her in gold what she formerly earned in silver, the washwoman demands the same pay in gold for the washing . . . and since the incomes of most people have not increased, the result is a deficit in the household budget."[105] The *canje* had essentially doubled the cost of labor.

In 1901, the new governor reported success in Puerto Rico: "People have at last realized the fact that one American dollar is as good as another, no matter whether it be composed of silver, paper, or gold, and that the Spanish coins and Mexican dollars are only worth their weight in the corresponding bullion."[106] The colonial government had forced Puerto Ricans to use US money exclusively, but at the cost of conflict between rich and poor, between employers and employees, and between colonial subjects and the United States.

Because Hawaiian currency was already pegged to the US dollar, its replacement with US money did not cause as much disruption in monetary terms. Yet it still took five years for Congress to officially demonetize Hawaiian currency. Hawaiʻi's 1900 Organic Act had ordered people to exchange their Hawaiian stamps for US stamps, but did not do the same for Hawaiian money, even though government officials in the Hawaiian Islands and in the United States had been calling for it since annexation.[107] Since the proposed redemption of Hawaiian coins would remove silver coins from circulation and replace them with gold-backed US coins, advocates of "free silver" in US Congress sought to block the legislation.[108]

The local white press in Honolulu, however, blamed Robert William Wilcox for the bill's failure. Wilcox—a Native Hawaiian politician—had led multiple uprisings in the Hawaiian Islands, first against the Bayonet Constitution, which stripped the monarchy of its power, and then against the coup and the Republic of Hawaii. After annexation, Wilcox was elected as the first delegate from the Territory of Hawaii to the US House of Representatives. While he could not vote, he was assigned to the Committee on Coinage, Weights, and Measures. Wilcox did not object to the redemption bill, telling House representatives in early 1901 that "our country being annexed to the United States, we might as well have the same kind of dollars as the United States."[109] Wilcox wavered, however, on the symbolic value of the Kalākaua coins: "You see, we Hawaiians have nothing left to us to show that we ever were a people, and the native Hawaiians do not want their money with the head of the king taken away from them. . . . We want to keep something to show that we once were a people."[110] The redemption bill did not pass in 1901.

When Congress took up the bill again in 1903, its opponents brought up their pro-silver arguments, and claimed that because Hawaiian coins circulated on par at the same value as US dollars in the Hawaiian Islands, there was no need to demonetize them. One congressman even reminded his colleagues that "in the halcyon days of our Republic, in the days of Jefferson, Monroe, and Jackson, down to 1857," there "circulated in our own Republic foreign coin."[111] Ebenezer Hill of Connecticut, one of the bill's primary supporters, got down to brass tacks: "There seems to be but one argument against the bill and that is that the money is circulating at par, and therefore it is wise not to disturb it." Hill's argument for the bill had less to do with monetary policy and more with the symbolic nature of currency: "I do not think that anywhere in the American Republic money should circulate with the face of any king or queen upon it."[112] His colleague from Alabama put it more bluntly, asking (despite the fact that Queen Liliʻuokalani had never appeared on any official Hawaiian coins), "Why should we continue to have a coinage of a dollar on which we put the likeness of a negro queen?"[113] Hill argued that, monetary questions aside, the bill's purpose was to take Hawaiian coins with "the image and superscription of King Kalakaua," send them to the US Mint in San Francisco, melt them down, and "give back dollar for dollar in American money, with the eagle upon it . . . precisely as they did in Porto Rico."[114]

The bill passed in January of 1903, setting in motion the same process that the Treasury had undertaken in Puerto Rico three years earlier, but with a more forgiving timeline. Hawaiian coins would be accepted as legal tender until January 1, 1904, and paper money until January 1, 1905.[115] Within just two months, one-third of the one million dollars of Hawaiian silver coinage in circulation had already been redeemed by the First National Bank of Hawaii and shipped to San Francisco, and by the end of the exchange period a year later, $815,000 had been redeemed—$15,000 more than the bank had estimated would come in. The cashier in charge of redemption speculated that much of the remaining amount had "been made into jewelry or else are being kept as souvenirs."[116]

The US government took no immediate action on currency reform in the US Virgin Islands, despite a congressional commission's recommendation as early as 1920 that US currency be the only legal tender in the islands, and the Colonial Councils in both St. Thomas and St. Croix voicing their support. The National Bank of the Danish West Indies had been issued a charter in 1904 allowing it to produce currency for the next thirty years.[117] So even after the 1917 transfer of sovereignty, the king of Denmark's portrait still featured prominently on money used in the US Virgin Islands.

The bank's charter expired during a tense time in the US Virgin Islands. Prohibition (which, Virgin Islanders noted with resentment, was not enforced in the Philippines) had stifled the rum trade, and in 1931 President Herbert Hoover had ruined the first presidential visit to the new colony when he insulted the islands by calling them an "effective poorhouse."[118] Currency reform began three years later. Virgin Islanders would receive 96.5 US cents for every five francs in Danish West Indian currency.[119] Despite experience from Puerto Rico and the Hawaiian Islands to draw on, the exchange did not go smoothly. Debates continued about what constituted a fair exchange rate.[120] And while the original proclamation gave Virgin Islanders one year to exchange their currency, the Treasury ended up extending the exchange period by another four years.

The introduction of US money in the colonies was a labor-intensive endeavor for the US government. For people living in the colonies, it was directly linked to disruption and loss—sometimes financial, sometimes symbolic. But eventually the government succeeded in redeeming existing coinage and replacing it with US dollars and cents throughout the colonial empire.

The US Mint melted down redeemed coins that bore images of King Kalākaua, King Alfonso, and King Christian, and the words "Isla de Puerto Rico," "King of Hawaii," and "Dansk Vestindiske"—and recast them into new coins expressing US sovereignty. Most US coins in circulation at this time had been designed by Charles E. Barber, the chief engraver of the US Mint, who had also designed the Kalākaua coins in 1883. Barber nickels, dimes, quarters, and half dollars all featured the "Head of Liberty"—a woman with the word "LIBERTY" inscribed in her headdress—and the legend "United States of America." Different denominations carried additional US iconography, like the heraldic eagle of the US seal, or the unofficial motto "In God we trust." The chief engraver at the Philadelphia Mint, John Barton Longacre, had designed the penny—"the coin in terms of which most people thought and bought" in Puerto Rico, according to economic experts.[121] Longacre's design depicted a woman whose headdress was also inscribed with the word "LIBERTY," but she wore "the feathered tiara" that, in Longacre's explanation, was "characteristic of the primitiveness of our hemisphere."[122] This one-cent coin was colloquially known as the "Indian Head cent" (figure 2.6).

The United States had just colonized the people of Puerto Rico, Hawai'i, Guam, and American Samoa, and would now force them to use coins in their everyday lives that proudly evoked the national memory of another group's colonization. And yet, while continental US citizens often lumped US colonial subjects and Native Americans together as federal wards, many elite colonial subjects were eager to set themselves apart from Indigenous peoples. Puerto Rican elites, for example, preferred to emphasize their Iberian heritage, and balked at being equated with Native Americans.[123] The circulation of this penny as the dominant coin in Puerto Rico demonstrates the complications inherent in extending national iconography to a colony. These coins were not designed with colonial subjects in mind; yet when they circulated

FIGURE 2.6. "Indian Head cent," circulated 1859–1909. National Numismatic Collection, National Museum of American History, Smithsonian Institution.

FIGURE 2.7. William McKinley's portrait on the First National Bank of Hawaii at Honolulu ten-dollar bill, 1902. National Numismatic Collection, National Museum of American History, Smithsonian Institution.

in the colonies, they still presented an opportunity for people in Puerto Rico, Hawai'i, Guam, American Samoa, and the US Virgin Islands to think of themselves as being connected to a nation with a long history of conquest.

Since the advent of the national banking system during the Civil War, all people within the United States had used paper money with identical designs and national symbols. The legend "National Currency, United States of America" appeared on all denominations along with landmarks, figures, and events the Treasury deemed important to US history. Only the name of the bank printed on the front varied from place to place. In the Territory of Hawaii, the First National Bank of Hawaii at Honolulu began issuing paper currency with the same designs as those used in the continental United States in October of 1900. The 1902 ten-dollar bill seen in figure 2.7 commemorated William McKinley. The money had not been designed with Hawaiians in mind; all US national banks circulated ten-dollar bills with this exact same design. Most people in the continental United States using the ten-dollar bill with McKinley's portrait would recognize him as their late president, who had been assassinated the previous year. But in the Hawaiian Islands, McKinley's portrait meant something very different from what it meant in the continental United States. Native Hawaiians knew him as the president who had ignored their protests to retain Hawaiian sovereignty, and who had pushed for the annexation of the Hawaiian Islands to the United States.

All national banknotes used in the United States had the same design, with a blank space on the front where the local bank would print its name. In the continental United States, these bills bore names like "First National Bank in Detroit" or "First National Bank of Denver." But in the colonies, bills with the same design bore names like "First National Bank of Hawaii," or "First National Bank of Porto Rico at San Juan." For people unfamiliar with the status of the Hawaiian Islands or Puerto Rico, seeing these bank names in the same spot where they would usually see a bank name from somewhere in the continental United States suggested that Hawai'i or Puerto Rico had the same status as the rest of the continental United States. These designs obscured the fact that the First National Bank of Hawaii was located in a territory where US citizens had overthrown an independent monarchy to establish colonial rule, or that the First National Bank of Porto Rico at San Juan, named on the front of the bill issued in Puerto Rico, was located in a territory where people lived under US rule without US citizenship. By the time the US Virgin Islands began exclusively using US money in the 1930s, US national banknotes had been replaced by federal reserve notes that did not name a local bank on the front. Then there was no difference between money circulating in the continental United States and money circulating in the colonies, except in the Philippines.

Colonial Currency

In 1900, two years into the US occupation of the Philippine Islands, Clarence R. Edwards, the first chief of the Bureau of Insular Affairs (BIA), posed a simple question: "What is the currency of the Philippines? It should be easy to answer, and it should be American coin; but it is not."[124] In fact, there was nothing "easy" about the currency situation in the Philippines, where economic experts worried that introducing the gold-backed US dollar might stifle trade with the silver-standard countries of Asia. Moreover, officials feared that any disruptions from currency reform like those seen in Puerto Rico would only further exacerbate tensions in the Philippines, where people were still fighting for their country's independence. Faced with this difficult situation, the BIA turned to an expert: Charles A. Conant, a famous proponent of the gold standard.[125]

While Conant and Congress debated whether coins in the Philippines should be backed by silver or by gold, officials in the Philippines concerned themselves with what would appear on the coins themselves. In December of 1901, "in anticipation of legislation providing for a special coinage system," the Philippine Commission created a special committee led by Filipino members T. H. Pardo de Tavera and Benito Legarda "to confer with competent persons and obtain suggestions and designs from native artists, if possible, for the Philippine coins."[126] Pardo de Tavera and Legarda submitted a report with their selections and photographic designs to the governor-general of the Philippines, who forwarded it to Washington. There, the BIA, in consultation with the secretary of war, selected designs by the Filipino artist Melecio Figueroa. As chief of the BIA, Clarence Edwards emphasized Figueroa's European artistic training, but did not mention that Figueroa had been the engraver for the Spanish colonial mint in Manila and, more controversially, had served as a member of the Malalos Congress in Aguinaldo's Philippine Republic.[127]

Because the United States was creating a separate currency for the Philippine Islands, these designs could express distinct national iconography. Much as officials used US stamps and money to circulate narratives about US national identity, they sought to use US-Philippine money to cultivate a particular national narrative about the Philippines—one that acknowledged that the revolution had produced a nation, but argued that the nation still needed to undergo a period of tutelage under US rule before independence.[128] The designs the colonial government placed on US-Philippine currency were an attempt to shape Filipino national identity and cement that new nation's colonial relationship to the United States.

Figueroa's designs were, according to the BIA, "at the same time typical of the Philippines, while showing the sovereignty of the United States" (figure 2.8).[129] The obverse bore symbols of Philippine identity: a Filipino or Filipina (depending on the denomination) wielding a hammer, with Mount Mayon in the background. The reverse, however, featured a heraldic US eagle atop a shield with thirteen stars. The BIA called the coin's design "unmistakably American," and wrote that it "conveys the thought that it is by earnest labor that the Filipinos must work out their destiny, under the guidance of the United States."[130] Even for those who could not read the words "United States of America" on the coins, the iconic symbols of the United States would have been familiar to most Filipinos, who were by that time accustomed to seeing the US flag in schools, post offices, and other government buildings, and on national holidays like Flag Day and the Fourth of July.[131]

FIGURE 2.8. US-Philippine one-peso coin, 1906. National Numismatic Collection, National Museum of American History, Smithsonian Institution.

By July of 1902, the Philippine Commission and the Bureau of Insular Affairs had decided the design of Philippine coinage even though no legislation had been passed. Conant had proposed the creation of the US-Philippine peso, using a "gold-exchange standard"—a silver coin pegged to the US gold dollar at a rate of two to one.[132] While the actual bill stalled in Congress, embroiled in the same gold and silver debates that delayed the Hawaiian Coinage Act, the Philippine Commission officially adopted Figueroa's designs and the War Department asked the US Mint to begin preparing dies.[133]

On March 2, 1903, Congress passed the Philippine Coinage Act, creating the US-Philippine peso and making it the law of the land that Philippine colonial coinage "shall express the sovereignty of the United States."[134] Because of their behind-the-scenes preparation, the treasury secretary had a sample specimen of the new Philippine peso coin ready for inspection and approval just five days later.[135] Conant had gotten what he wanted: a gold-backed currency. As he moved on to currency reform in Mexico and China, others were left to actually implement currency reform in the Philippines.[136]

The Philippine Commission authorized the redemption of Spanish-Filipino coins, which were shipped to San Francisco and, like the Kalākaua coins, reminted into US money. Not trusting that this would supply enough metal, the BIA spent $6.3 million on raw silver bullion, and an additional $86,000 on metals for minor coins. In those first eight months, the US Mints in San Francisco and Philadelphia coined and shipped to Manila 14.5 million pesos in one-peso, half-peso, and twenty-, ten-, five-, and one-centavo coins. The Philippine Commission decided that they would not redeem Mexican currency, hoping that "the ordinary laws of supply and demand" would "produce a constantly accelerated flow of Mexican dollars out of the islands" once they were demonetized.[137]

Initially, there were no laws prohibiting the use of other currencies. But the colonial government began requiring that all civil employees be paid in US-Philippine pesos starting on August 1, 1903. Mary Fee, a US teacher in the Philippines, wrote about receiving her first paycheck in US-Philippine pesos: "The beautifully made, bright new silver coins had an engaging appearance after the tarnished mongrel coins to which we were accustomed." The local treasurer gave Fee most of her pay in peso coins, then "produced two bags of small pennies, and announced that I should have to take that sum in small coins in order to get the pennies into circulation." Fee reported that the minor coinage was "of beautiful workmanship, yellow as gold and heavy as lead"—so heavy that she had to hire a small boy to help her "lug home" her bags of coins.[138]

What happened next is an ideal account of how new currency begins to circulate. Fee made her first purchase in the new coins from the man from whom she bought eggs and chickens three times a week, giving him three new silver coins and a "handful of gleaming copper." She reported that her Filipina maid, observing the transaction, exclaimed "Jesus!" under her breath, and the man, "Dios mio!" But the man did not accept the government's valuation of the coins. Fee tried to explain that the silver pesos were worth more than the copper centavos he thought were gold, but, she wrote, "his Filipino habit of relying on his own eyes was in full command of him."[139] At his request, Fee exchanged one of his silver pesos for an equal amount in copper coins.

Word spread quickly. A woman soon arrived selling chickens at an incredibly low price. Suspecting the woman only wanted the new coins, Fee offered to pay her in Mexican money. The woman vehemently refused, claiming that "she wanted the bright new money."[140] Fee wrote that at home she was bombarded with sellers that day, people who normally never made house calls but came because they had heard about the curious "Señora" giving away "gold."[141]

In addition to enlisting civil employees like Mary Fee, the government printed proclamations and notices in several languages and dialects and posted them "in every municipality and barrio, advising them of the necessity of exchanging the old coins for the new Philippine currency and of the rate of exchange." Just one year after the US-Philippine peso's introduction, the Philippine Commission proclaimed that the "efforts thus made to establish a sound currency in the islands have, we are pleased to say, been crowned with success." They thanked the banks, which "were especially helpful in aiding in retiring the old currency and emitting the new," as well as the secretary of the treasury, the secretary of war, the chief of the BIA, and of course their trusted advisor Charles Conant, whose influence in the exchange was so great that people had begun calling U.S-Philippine coins "Conants."[142]

However, in the same 1904 annual report in which the Philippine Commission declared currency reform a success, R. F. Santos, the provincial governor of Albay, reported that, "humiliating as it is to confess it, the fact is that Mexican and the other fluctuating moneys have been the masters over gold in the markets and stores here."[143] Even when people did receive new US-Philippine pesos, Santos reported, "they ship it at once to Manila and exchange it there for Spanish-Filipino and Mexican at the ratio prevailing."[144] Governor Demetrio Larena of Negros Oriental explained that everyday transactions were still "made in Mexican or Spanish-Filipino currency, while the provincial and municipal taxes have to be paid in Conant, the taxpayers in exchanging the circulating currency with the official having consequently to suffer a discount."[145] Making matters worse, Edwin Kemmerer, the chief of the Division of the Currency in the Philippines, noted that "the new peso" the government claimed was worth twice as much as the Mexican peso "was no larger than the Mexican peso, upon the basis of which prices had been adjusted for generations, and the Chinese and the natives could not see why it should be worth any more." Just like in Puerto Rico, "the great majority of merchants and shopkeepers . . . accepted the new peso simply as the equivalent of the old."[146] The refusal to adopt US-Philippine pesos was less an act of resistance to US sovereignty and more a matter of practicality. The buyers who came to Albay and Negros Oriental to purchase hemp and other agricultural products traded in Mexican and Spanish-Filipino currency. When local merchants opted to use this currency, they were not resisting US rule; they were just going about their business.[147]

To government officials, however, allowing Filipinos to go about their business was a direct impediment to their efforts to transform the Philippines and "civilize" its inhabitants through monetary practices.[148] Conant and other financial experts wholeheartedly believed that introducing a gold-exchange standard would help uplift Filipinos since, as Emily Rosenberg has argued, they believed silver-based currencies "were characteristic only of 'backward' lands."[149] In order to prove that they, too, were civilized and thus fit for self-rule, some elite Filipinos became champions of currency reform.[150] So Governor Larena, even while lamenting that currency reform was failing in Negros Oriental, echoed Conant's logic when he acknowledged that the US-Philippine peso could place "the islands on a sound financial basis, in view of the fact that the Conant currency has a fixed value with relation to the gold standard prevailing in the principal markets of the world."[151] In

Albay, Governor Santos was so invested in currency reform that he would
"take up-country with him several hundred pesos' worth of coppers at a
time, to be introduced into the local markets there." He lamented that the
US-Philippine pesos would "somehow miraculously disappear shortly after-
wards."[152] Despite their best efforts to get people to begin using US money
in their economic transactions, ordinary Filipinos largely refused to change
their monetary behavior.

The Philippine Commission, feeling that elite Filipinos had failed to implement currency reform, sought once again to enlist the aid of US financial
experts. Conant and his fellow economist Jeremiah Jenks had moved on from
the colonies to spreading the gold-exchange standard to foreign countries
like China and Mexico.[153] Meanwhile, its failed implementation in the Philippines presented a problem. Grudgingly admitting that currency reform in
the Philippines was "apparently in certain respects not working satisfactorily,"
Jenks (at the request of the secretary of war) penciled in a visit to the Philippine Islands on his way to China to try to help the Philippine Commission
figure out how to make the gold-exchange standard work in practice.[154]

In 1904 Jenks and his former graduate student Edwin Kemmerer concluded that success would require greater coercion from the colonial government. They proposed two measures to the Philippine Commission. The first
law made the importation of Mexican currency, Spanish-Filipino currency,
or any currency not backed by a gold standard punishable by the forfeiture
of said currency, and by an additional fine of up to ten thousand pesos or a
prison sentence of up to one year.[155] This allowed the government to prevent
new foreign currency from undermining its efforts, but it did nothing to stop
the circulation of foreign money already in the Philippine Islands. Jenks and
Kemmerer's second measure would finally allow colonial officials to police
how Filipinos used money among themselves. The Local Currency and Taxa-
tion Act placed a tax "upon all checks, draft notes, etc. drawn in the old currency, and upon bank deposits and transactions therein."[156] As the tax gradu-
ally increased from 1 percent in October of 1904 to 5 percent by December,
the business community, realizing that the tax was prohibitive, quickly began
conducting affairs on the basis of the US-Philippine peso.[157] In Albay, Governor Santos gave up his routine of carrying currency to the countryside, and
celebrated the "triumph of Philippine currency over Mexican," which he at-
tributed to "the well-placed efforts of the central government, [and] its many
stringent laws against the use of Mexican and Spanish-Filipino coins which
served to enliven the dullness of apprehension of those who ordinarily fail to
lend their aid to the implanting of new processes in economic conditions."[158]
Santos allied himself firmly with the colonial government's civilizing mission,

celebrating that its coercive tactics had finally forced those who were, in his words, too "dull" to comprehend its benefits to use the U.S-Philippine peso.

Other provincial governors continued to struggle. In 1905 Larena reported that despite local authorities' efforts to publicize the policy changes even "in the most remote barrios of the pueblos" in Negros Oriental, the "ignorant classes" still held two to three hundred thousand pesos in Mexican currency.[159] In La Union, the governor reported that Igorots—a group US officials and elite Filipinos regarded as particularly "uncivilized"—were still holding onto old currency.[160] Other governors like Juan Clímaco in Cebu were more sympathetic, and reported, as Governor Davis had done in Puerto Rico, that most people still using old currency were rural farmers unable to exchange their currency within the time frame provided by the law. In Clímaco's estimation, the coercive laws had not "civilized" the inhabitants of Cebu, but instead forced many small business owners to close their shops in fear of the penalties for doing business in old currency.[161] Indeed, multiple provincial governors reported that the switch to the US-Philippine peso had caused serious financial crises that, just as in Puerto Rico, had negatively affected trade and overall economic prosperity in their provinces.[162]

By 1914, a decade after Conant and Jenks had initially proclaimed the Philippine currency question "settled," the Philippine Commission estimated that just 330,000 Spanish-Filipino pesos remained—mostly in Moroland, where US officials continued to face resistance and struggled to establish civil government.[163] Over the course of a decade, the US Mint sent more than fifty million US-Philippine pesos to the Philippine Islands, and the Philippine colonial government had harnessed the power of the state to make it the dominant currency in the colony.

While the monetary debate about US-Philippine currency focused on the metallic content of coins, many of the design decisions were about paper money. US-Philippine silver certificates designed and produced by the Bureau of Engraving and Printing in Washington began circulating in the Philippines with the passage of the 1903 Coinage Act.[164] Initially, US colonial officials believed that Filipinos would prefer coins over paper money, since in a climate so "hot and moist, every purse and pocket which carries silver certificate will be sweatty [sic]."[165] But paper money proved immensely popular. The Philippine secretary of finance and justice reported that the certificates "form an exceedingly convenient means of exchange and relieve the burdensomeness of making payments in the heavy silver coin, either old or new, and come as a great relief for business men and all others who have occasion to receive or pay out money."[166] Data compiled from 1904 to 1918 prove the silver certificates' popularity: they made up about half of the total circulation

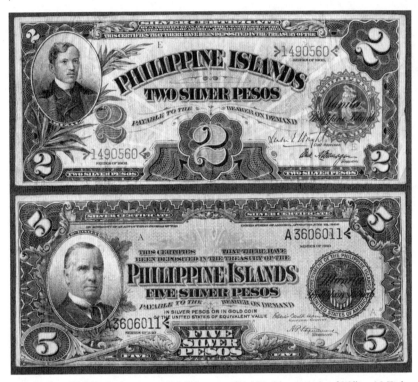

FIGURE 2.9. US-Philippine paper money with portraits of José Rizal (two pesos) and William McKinley (five pesos), designs adopted 1903. National Numismatic Collection, National Museum of American History, Smithsonian Institution.

of US-Philippine pesos in any given year.[167] Like coins, these notes were legally required to show the sovereignty of the United States.[168] And while they would feature some of the same portraits that that graced US money, officials decided to make these notes smaller than US money—about 2.5 × 6 inches, rather than the 3 × 7 inch US notes then in circulation (figure 2.9).[169]

With the advent of distinct US-Philippine paper money, the BIA began to consider whether it might produce unique postage stamps for the Philippines, to replace the overprinted US stamps that were still in use. It noted that "each of the colonies of Great Britain has its postage, characteristic and individual to such colony; this step has now been taken by us so far as the Philippine money is concerned and therefore why should we not take one step more and have our own Philippine stamps." The BIA also wanted stamps that showed "the Philippine government as different from the states and territories and at the same time showing the United States' sovereignty for its foreign communication."[170] In early 1904 the Philippine Commission authorized the creation of US-Philippine stamps, and directed the Philippine director of posts to confer with the Bureau of Engraving and Printing on the designs.[171] The director of posts and Bureau of Engraving and Printing officials decided to adopt the portraits from US-Philippine silver certificates for use on the new US-Philippine stamps.

It was not inevitable that these objects would contain portraits of US national heroes. Initially Philippine stamps were not going to feature people at all, since the BIA worried that "any series of portraits would promote discussion of the real right of the individual to be so honored."[172] But officials soon agreed that the Filipino patriot José Rizal should be placed on the two-centavo stamp and the two-peso bill. Rizal, considered a martyr after his execution by Spanish officials for anticolonial activity in 1896, at first seems an unwise choice to present to Filipinos, still resisting US rule. However, since Rizal had died at the hands of the Spanish and had not lived long enough to comment on US rule, US colonial officials determined that he could be made into the perfect Philippine national hero—allowing them to emphasize their role in helping throw off Spanish imperial rule, while drawing attention away from their own subsequent brutal subjugation of the Philippine independence movement.[173] US Governor-General William Cameron Forbes wrote that the US colonial government helped make Rizal "the acknowledged national hero of the Philippine people" mainly by declaring the anniversary of his death a national holiday, teaching "the young Filipinos to revere his memory" in schools, erecting monuments to him throughout the Philippines, and placing "his picture on the postage stamp . . . and on the currency."[174]

However, the Philippine director of posts argued, "If we put Rizal on one stamp and don't even put one American on either of the others we may look for criticism from our American contingent in the Islands."[175] The BIA decided that it could begin to erase the history of US violence in the Philippines and turn the figures associated with the US conquest and subsequent war into Philippine national heroes by putting them on money and stamps. The four-centavo stamp and five-peso silver certificate honored William McKinley; like the US ten-dollar bill in the Hawaiian Islands, this reminded Filipinos of the president who had denied their country its independence. The fifty-peso note and ten-centavo stamp venerated an even more uncomfortable figure: Major General Henry Lawton, the highest-ranked US officer killed in the Philippine-American War. A US captain in the Philippines wrote to the BIA that "the war is too recent to make it advisable to put pictures of the men who fought in it upon postage stamps."[176] But US officials wanted Filipinos to see Lawton as a national hero, alongside Rizal and McKinley.

The decision to move from overprinted US stamps to a distinct US-Philippine stamp series paid off—literally. Stamp sales nearly doubled after the new series was introduced in 1906 (figure 2.10), and continued to climb steadily.[177] Three historical figures from the Spanish period also appeared on US-Philippine stamps: Ferdinand Magellan, who landed in the Philippines in 1521, and Manuel Legaspi and Francisco Carriedo, both governors-general of the Philippine Islands under Spanish rule. However fraught, McKinley and Lawton did have a connection to the Philippines. But many US national figures with no Philippine connection also appeared on stamps and currency, including Admiral William T. Sampson (who had fought in the 1898 war, but in Cuba, not the Philippines), Abraham Lincoln, Benjamin Franklin, and of course George Washington. As early as 1905, BIA Chief Edwards warned that using the same people on US and US-Philippine stamps and currency might cause confusion.[178] As we know, this would come to a head in 1928. The ten-peso bill with Washington's portrait was, like US-Philippine coins, "unmistakably American" (see figure 2.1). Treasury officials balked when it seemed the bill might actually be *mistaken* for US currency. But when the treasury secretary insisted that Washington's portrait be removed to avoid confusion, the US governor-general of the Philippines, Henry Stimson, refused.

George Washington was an important symbolic figure in the Philippines. Children learned about him in schools, and the colonial government had made his birthday a national holiday.[179] In 1901 the newly formed Federal Party, which advocated US statehood for the Philippines, held a grand celebration in Manila for Washington's Birthday. Pardo de Tavera, the party's president, called Washington a "glorious figure" who represented "justice, honesty, and all the other virtues."[180] He proclaimed that in the future, "George Washington will not simply be the glory of the American continent, but also our glory, because he will be the father of the American world, in which we shall feel ourselves completely united and assimilated."[181] Pardo de Tavera argued that Washington was not just a US hero but a Philippine hero as well. Placing his portrait on stamps and money was an attempt to circulate this idea among the Filipino population.

Of course, not everyone in the Philippines agreed that George Washington symbolized the glory of US colonial rule. Many saw him as a symbol of *anti*colonialism, even calling Emilio Aguinaldo the "Washington of the Orient."[182] Aguinaldo himself compared Washington's fight for independence from Britain to his own fight for independence from the United States.[183] For many in the Philippines, Washington's portrait on the ten-peso note would not have produced the intended feeling of gratitude for US rule. Rather, it would have symbolized the hypocrisy of the United States, a nation born from Washington's anticolonialism, now colonizing a country that wanted its independence.

FIGURE 2.10. US-Philippine stamps with portraits of José Rizal (two centavos), William McKinley (four centavos), Ferdinand Magellan (six centavos), Manuel Legaspi (eight centavos), Henry Lawton (ten centavos), Abraham Lincoln (twelve centavos), William Sampson (sixteen centavos), George Washington (twenty centavos), Francisco Carriedo (twenty-six centavos), and Benjamin Franklin (thirty centavos), designs adopted 1906. National Postal Museum, Smithsonian Institution.

FIGURE 2.11. US-Philippine ten-peso bill with new Washington portrait and design, 1936. National Numismatic Collection, National Museum of American History, Smithsonian Institution. Compare to figure 2.1.

Because these stamps and pieces of currency were laden with national iconography, they always carried more meaning than just their denominational value. Governor-General Stimson held firm in his belief that Washington's portrait was doing important work in the Philippines. Stimson and the US Treasury officials reached a compromise, moving Washington's portrait to the left of the US-Philippine ten-peso bill and replacing the familiar Stuart portrait of Washington with one based on Jean-Antoine Houdon's *George Washington* (figure 2.11). And to avoid confusion between the McKinley five-peso and ten-dollar bills, they added a portrait of George Dewey on the right obverse of the US-Philippine five-peso bill.

Signs of the Times

As the above episode indicates, the design of these objects did not remain static. As conditions in the colonies changed, those changes were reflected in new designs for money and stamps. The 1930s, for example, were a period of transition for the US colonial empire. The Philippines became a US Commonwealth, with the promise of independence by 1946. The ceremonies themselves were intended to show the United States as a benevolent colonial ruler, slowly granting Filipinos more autonomy. A new stamp series released in 1934 reflected this shift.

The director of posts in the Philippines—by then a Filipino—wrote to the chief of the BIA to propose a change in stamps. Instead of portraits, he suggested stamps "for the purpose of advertising the Philippine Islands and attracting tourists."[184] The proposed series contained almost exclusively Philippine iconography. Rizal, "the foremost Filipino patriot and martyr," would remain on the two-centavo stamp. The four-centavo McKinley stamp would now feature a "woman carrying palay cuttings standing by carabao," an allegorical design that the BIA felt symbolized agriculture in the Philippines.[185] Fort Santiago replaced General Lawton, "pearl fishing" in Mindanao replaced Benjamin Franklin, "salt springs" in Nueva Vizcaya replaced Abraham Lincoln, and the twenty-centavo stamp bearing George Washington's portrait would now have Juan de la Cruz, a figure who "symbolizes the Philippine Islands much in the same way Uncle Sam personifies the United States."[186]

George Washington remained on Philippine stamps, however, finding a new home on the five-peso stamp, "mounted on his white charger."[187] The chief of the BIA explained the decision to the Bureau of Engraving and Printing: "George Washington is recognized as one of the greatest men of all times and that his memory is held in significant reverence, not only by the people of all outlying territories where the American flag flies, but in every corner of the world."[188] A Filipino stamp collector agreed, writing that "the Father of the American people is quite familiar to Filipino boys and girls. First President of a great nation, George Washington is one of the outstanding objects of their hero-worshiping." To this stamp collector, Washington's portrait on Philippine stamps had "served as an inspiration to Filipino boys and girls."[189]

When the Philippines became a commonwealth in 1935, the government overprinted the 1934 series with the word "COMMONWEALTH" to reflect the change in status (figure 2.12).[190] It also issued a set of five commemorative stamps for the occasion. One stamp in particular was an attempt to convey this shift in status in great detail. Titled "The Philippines Admitted to the Temple of Universal Progress," the Bureau of Engraving and Printing's draft drawing shows the layers of symbolism included in the stamp's design, originally prepared by Filipino artist Dominador Castañeda (figure 2.13).[191]

The official explanation of the design stated: "The Philippine Islands, having attained such progress in almost any endeavor of human intelligence,

FIGURE 2.12. US-Philippine four-centavo stamp (1934) overprinted for the Commonwealth (1935). Author's collection.

FIGURE 2.13. Draft drawing, "The Philippines Admitted to the Temple of Universal Progress," stamp design 1935. Bureau of Engraving and Printing Historical Resource Center.

which compare favorably with the most progressive and cultured countries in the world, is admitted to the temple of human progress, represented by several figures which symbolize the Arts [1 and 2], Science [3], Agriculture [4], Industry [5] and Commerce [6]. Leading the Philippines is a matron representing the United States of America [7], as her (the Philippines [8]) guide and guardian."[192] But even as the Philippines were being "admitted to the Temple of Universal Progress," and stamps with Philippine scenes and symbols devoid of US iconography were beginning to circulate throughout the Philippine Islands, Philippine stamps still had to express US sovereignty. In 1938 the US high commissioner of the Philippines (the new name for the US governor under the Commonwealth) wrote to the secretary of war asking if they could substitute "U.S.A." for "United States of America" to save space on stamps. The secretary of war sent the request to the US postmaster general, who, after conferring with the Bureau of Engraving and Printing, declined.[193] No matter how much autonomy the Philippines had as a commonwealth, US officials still wanted their stamps to send the clear message, just as the overprints had done in 1899, that the Philippines remained under the sovereignty of the "United States of America."

While the designs on 1930s US-Philippine stamps foreshadowed eventual Philippine independence, a new series of stamps affirmed the continued attachment of other territories to the United States. The idea came when

San Juan's postmaster asked the Post Office Department to produce a commemorative stamp for Puerto Rico. Worried that giving Puerto Rico special treatment "might arouse criticism," the department decided to create a series honoring Puerto Rico alongside the US Virgin Islands, Hawai'i, and Alaska— which, since it had been acquired decades before the war of 1898, was often not included in continental conceptions of the United States' overseas empire.[194] The series excluded the Philippines (now a commonwealth), but also Guam and American Samoa—despite people sending protests to the director of territories and insular possessions.[195]

Officials saw the series as a unique opportunity to promote tourism and, more broadly, as one official put it, to "diffuse knowledge of the Territory's existence throughout the United States."[196] Colonial governors selected the designs, giving them the power to decide what knowledge about the territory would circulate in the continental United States and among collectors around the world. The governor of the Virgin Islands chose a scene showing the harbor of the territory's capital city, Charlotte Amalie.[197] The governor of Alaska, after considering showcasing iconography from Native Alaskan culture, chose instead a scene depicting Denali—then called Mount McKinley—with a presumably white settler tilling the land and homes resembling New England's colonial architecture in the foreground.[198] A popular stamp-collecting periodical noted that "no such scene as shown on the stamp may be found in Alaska," suspecting that the design was more aspirational than reflective of current realities, as the Post Office Department had written in its official announcement of the stamp "symbolizing present-day developments in the Territory."[199]

For the Hawaiian Islands stamp, the governor chose the statue of the first Hawaiian monarch, King Kamehameha I, in Honolulu. The statue itself had been controversial since its inception, with many insisting it favored European features over Kamehameha's likeness.[200] After this stamp's release in 1937, the collectors' magazine *Linn's Weekly Stamp News* also noticed that the figure depicted on it, "supposedly a native chief," looked "every inch a Roman emperor"—writing that, if not for the legend "Hawaii," people might think the Post Office Department was "helping Mussolini celebrate the 2,000th anniversary of the magnificent autocracy of Augustus Caesar."[201] The *Honolulu Star Bulletin*'s stamp editor noted that if the Post Office Department "had exerted the least bit of effort they could have obtained reproductions of an original portrait of Hawaii's greatest king."[202] Nevertheless, the Post Office Department's decision to circulate the image of a Hawaiian monarch on stamps reveals how much its thinking had changed since the 1890s, when the Republic of Hawaii had destroyed all stamp dies with images of Native

FIGURE 2.14. US flag flying over La Fortaleza on commemorative stamp for Puerto Rico, part of US Territorial Stamp Series, 1937. Author's collection.

Hawaiian monarchs. The Post Office Department's actions sought to make King Kamehameha a part of official US national iconography, even while it reminded viewers of Hawaiʻi's independent past. Indeed, the *Honolulu Star Bulletin's* stamp editor lamented, "Although the new stamp is designed to honor Hawaii as a territory of the United States, nowhere in the postoffice department's publicity releases is any mention made of Hawaii as a territory, an incorporated part of the nation."[203]

For Puerto Rico, Governor Blanton Winship controversially decided to show the US flag flying over La Fortaleza—the governor's palace (figure 2.14).[204] As we will see in the next chapter, Winship was engaged in brutal repression of the Puerto Rican independence movement in the 1930s, focusing especially on challenges to the supremacy of the US flag in Puerto Rico. This stamp, showing the US flag and the palace—the seat of US colonial power in Puerto Rico— symbolically reaffirmed US sovereignty in this moment of crisis.[205]

These pocket-sized objects sent a distinct message to people in the continental United States ("These are our territories"), and a different message to people in the colonies ("You are linked to the United States"). For people in Guam and American Samoa, the stamps would send the message that while they lived under US rule, they did not deserve representation on these symbolic national objects—a debate that would reappear at the turn of the twenty-first century, with the advent of state quarters. Importantly, the combining of the names of these places with the legend "US Postage" implied that they were domestic space. And like the initial overprints of US stamps used in the early twentieth century, this territorial series showed that symbolic colonization was a two-way street. US iconography was imprinted on the colonies, and colonial imagery was imprinted on the United States.

Conclusion

The images on stamps and money tell a story about national sovereignty and national character. Forcing people in Puerto Rico, Hawai'i, Guam, the US Virgin Islands, and American Samoa to exclusively use US money and stamps meant that they only encountered US national iconography on these objects. And in the Philippines, the combination of US and Philippine iconography was meant to convey that the national histories and cultures of those two nations were inextricably linked. US officials hoped that, once it became a given that colonial subjects should use money and stamps with images that honored US history and cultural traditions, those objects would become a banal, unconscious reminder that they were tied to the United States.

These objects, in both their functional and their symbolic valences, were significant to colonial officials. In his book on US colonial policy, Theodore Roosevelt Jr., son of President Theodore Roosevelt and governor of Puerto Rico from 1929 to 1932, listed many accomplishments of US colonial rule that would likely be familiar to scholars of US imperialism: establishment of a board of health and a department of education, organization of an insular police force, and abolition of lotteries and cockfighting. Alongside those accomplishments, however, he included that "our currency replaced that of Spain, our stamps the Spanish stamps."[206]

These objects mattered to colonial subjects, too. In the early twentieth century, many were legally denied citizenship; but the images that the US government had chosen to be part of their everyday lives implied that colonial subjects were part of the US national community. As the twentieth century wore on, many began to realize that the actions of the United States did not live up to the images presented on these pocket-sized objects. And because US officials had already established the importance of the objects to colonial rule, the colonial subjects began to use them, along with the flag, to challenge US colonial rule in creative ways.

3

Symbolic Supremacy

Imagine, for a moment, an average day in a US colony. Whether they lived in a major metropolis like Manila in the Philippines or a small town like Yauco, Puerto Rico, a person could walk outside their home and see the flag flying over every schoolhouse. The Stars and Stripes hung at the post office in Hagåtña, Guam, and at the courthouse in Honolulu, Hawai'i. Thousands of miles away from the continental United States, children in US colonies routinely pledged their allegiance to the flag of the United States of America and to the republic for which it stood—despite their exclusion from that republic's representative government.

Consider, for a moment, the level of intimacy involved with these symbolic objects. Children placed their hands over their hearts while pledging their allegiance, women spent hours with needle and thread sewing US flags, people held and carried US money and used their mouths to lick US postage stamps and attach them to their private letters. It is not surprising that, given this intimacy, these nationally symbolic objects often became sites of resistance to US rule. Because of the mass effort to establish and spread them, people in the colonies were well aware of how seriously US colonial officials and other continental US Americans in the colonies took these symbolic performances of allegiance. It was not just about a desire to create patriotic subjects; it was also about gauging the subjects' loyalty to the United States, and thus their potential for organized resistance to US rule—something many continental US Americans living in the colonies always feared. If colonial subjects had been influenced by colonial education, US Americans worried that they could be influenced by anticolonial education as well.

US imperialists had created a situation in which nationally symbolic objects would be central to defining one's place within a polity and national community. But in teaching colonial subjects how to perform their allegiance to the flag, they also gave them a clear way to perform resistance: by subverting those same rules. In this chapter we will see the different ways in which colonial subjects have subverted the rules laid out by colonial officials for flag veneration. We will also see how colonial officials have reacted and over-reacted to these actions. The same people who expended incredible effort to spread the US flag throughout the colonial empire reacted harshly to perceived challenges to the flag's supremacy.

This chapter examines how, even after the initial establishment of symbolic objects in the colonial empire, those objects continued to be an arena in which contests over national identity played out. While thus far we have broadly discussed the entire colonial empire, this chapter focuses on the Hawaiian Islands, the Philippines, and Puerto Rico. These were the only US colonies that had their own national flags before the United States claimed sovereignty, and US officials saw that preexisting iconography, and people's attachment to it, as a potential threat to the supremacy of US national symbols.[1]

The perceived threat to the US flag's supremacy in the Philippines led the colonial government there to officially ban the Philippine flag from 1907 to 1919. In the 1920s and 1930s, the pro-independence Puerto Rican Nationalist Party explicitly sought to challenge the supremacy of the US flag in Puerto Rico and to reassert the Puerto Rican flag as the national banner. US colonial officials reacted harshly, and would eventually criminalize the display of the Puerto Rican flag, but not until after World War II.

US officials could monitor public performances of allegiance and address public displays of resistance. The women's world of sewing, however, was largely outside their purview. And in Hawai'i, quilting became a space in which women could create objects that expressed their views on sovereignty in the Hawaiian Islands, privately challenging the symbolic supremacy of US national iconography that they encountered outside their homes. But the range of messages that quiltmakers conveyed in response to US rule often defied the binary discourses of opposition and allegiance seen in the public sphere.

These seemingly distinct episodes—Hawaiian flag quilting, the Philippine flag ban, and Puerto Rican flag protests—are well known in their individual contexts.[2] When placed side by side, they can help us think about the importance of flag supremacy across the US colonial empire. Conflicts over flag supremacy were not a sideshow, nor were they merely a symbolic representation of other problems. To US imperialists, resistance (real or perceived) to US flag supremacy *was* the problem. But saying someone was engaged in "resistance" often implies that they were hoping their actions would provoke change, usually in the political system, whether that be civil rights or outright independence. This chapter will help us think more broadly about resistance, because not all actors sought political change. Hawaiian women who quilted the deposed kingdom's national flag, or people who flew their national flags in the Philippines or Puerto Rico, did not always do so to challenge US colonial rule. Some were simply affirming their own personal attachment to those symbols. But because many US imperialists were fixated on the supremacy of US national symbols, they saw attachment to any other symbols as a threat to the United States. Their crackdowns on use and display of alternate symbols, and the way nationalists, particularly in Puerto Rico, were able to use those objects to directly challenge US colonial rule, again shows a mutual recognition by all sides that the symbols and the way they were used mattered.

Stitching Sovereignty

After the official raising of the US flag in Hawai'i in 1898, Queen Lili'uokalani's companion Bernice Piilani Irwin recalled that "a great wave of patriotism had filled the hearts of the Hawaiians. The streets were filled with men wearing hatbands inscribed Aloha 'Aina (Love of Country). Hawaiian women busied themselves making flag-patterned bed quilts . . . in order to keep their beloved emblem constantly before their eyes."[3] While men tended to be at the forefront of public displays of allegiance and resistance, the private world of women's sewing was often overlooked. Even in the world of art, sewing has typically been classed as a "craft," an expression of femininity that has little to do with politics or high art.[4] But taking these objects seriously presents an opportunity to examine what kind of objects women chose to create and what kinds of national iconography they chose to include when colonial officials weren't watching. And many of them chose to create Hawaiian flag quilts (figure 3.1). The typical features of such a quilt were these: four Hawaiian flags around each of the four edges, and in the center some rendition of the Hawaiian kingdom's coat of arms—a crown over the high chiefs Kamanawa and Kame'eiamoku standing on opposite sides of a quartered shield—sometimes accompanied by other symbols of the monarchy.

The Hawaiian flag's design was adopted by King Kamehameha I in 1816. Like many countries, there are competing versions of the flag's origin story. The primary narrative asserts that Kamehameha, monarch of the independent Hawaiian Kingdom, was gifted a British flag toward the end of the eighteenth century.[5] Since the Hawaiian Kingdom had no flag of its own, Kamehameha raised this British flag—much to the irritation of the US citizens in Hawai'i, especially during the War of 1812. Shortly thereafter, Kamehameha ordered that a new flag be designed that would appeal to (and appease) both

FIGURE 3.1. "Ku'u Hae Aloha" (My Beloved Flag) Hawaiian flag quilt, maker unknown, late nineteenth to early twentieth century. Honolulu Museum of Art.

British and US citizens in Hawai'i. A British naval captain designed the flag, which combined elements of both British and US flags—and used the eight stripes to represent the eight major Hawaiian Islands.[6] While the Kingdom of Hawai'i remained independent until 1893, its design, with the British flag in the upper left hand corner, resembled those of many flags used throughout the British Empire, including the flag of the East India Company.

Quilting became prevalent in the Hawaiian Islands despite quilts not being necessary for warmth in most places. Native Hawaiians had their own practice of making clothing and bedding out of a fabric called *kapa*, which was produced through the time-consuming, labor-intensive process of pounding *wauke*, or paper mulberry plant.[7] In the late eighteenth century, the introduction of foreign-manufactured fabrics began to replace *kapa*, and possessing foreign fabric soon became a way for elite Hawaiian women to signal their status.[8] US missionaries introduced their kind of sewing to Hawaiian women in the 1820s, and the methods blended together to form a new practice: Hawaiian quilting.[9] Though initiated by missionaries, sewing was something that, once taught, could be practiced by Hawaiian women in intimate spaces that US missionaries and, later, US colonial officials could not monitor or control.[10]

In the continental United States, quilts were utility objects, usually made with leftover scraps of fabric to provide warmth. In Hawai'i, however, quilts were luxury items made with large pieces of imported fabric and an appliqué technique of layering pieces of fabric on top of one another.[11] The most common designs had natural elements like plants, or royal motifs like crowns or other insignia. Hawaiian quilting differed from continental quilting in one other crucial way: the patterns were not shared or circulated widely, and it was actually considered a serious offense to copy another quilter's design.[12] Hawaiian quilts served more of an artistic and symbolic rather than utilitarian purpose.

Because Hawaiian quilts were not made out of necessity to survive a coming winter, the quilters had the luxury of time. Hawaiian quilting was often a lengthy, intimate process in which a woman or group of women would spend months painstakingly stitching one quilt.[13] Thus, many believed that the spirit of the person who created the quilt became part of the quilt itself; it was common practice to burn quilts after their creators had died, so that their spirits could pass with them.[14] So choosing a design and creating a Hawaiian quilt was a slow, deliberate process of creating a work of art. The Hawaiian flag quilts were objects women created to express their loyalty to the Hawaiian flag.

Hawaiian women often made quilts that offered commentary on current events. The introduction of regular mail service, the building of a new harbor, the appearance of Halley's comet, and the introduction of gas lighting at 'Iolani Palace were all significant events that appeared on quilts.[15] It is difficult to say with certainty when the first Hawaiian flag quilt was sewn, because many such quilts were destroyed upon the death of their creators. But it likely came out of a moment of uncertain sovereignty in 1843, when a British naval captain occupied the Hawaiian Islands for six months.[16] Creating flag quilts was a way to express loyalty to the Hawaiian Kingdom in that time of crisis. Unsurprisingly, then, the quilts became extremely popular in the 1890s, when the independent monarchy's sovereignty was once again threatened—this time by the United States.

People in Hawai'i did not readily accept the coup that had unseated Queen Lili'uokalani, or the raising of the United States flag over their islands. Royalists continued to resist the new US-led government, and some even mounted a counterrevolution, attempting to restore Lili'uokalani to the throne. More than four hundred Hawaiians were eventually arrested and jailed for

involvement in the plot.[17] Though Liliʻuokalani had publicly asked her supporters to be patient and not rise up, the so-called Provisional Government
(comprised of people who had organized the coup against her) arrested her
for supposed knowledge of the plot. Liliʻuokalani was arraigned and tried in
the throne room of her own former ʻIolani Palace, fined five thousand dollars, and sentenced to five years hard labor. The hard labor was commuted
to imprisonment in an upstairs bedroom of her former palace. She was held
there for eight months.

While imprisoned, Liliʻuokalani and her attendants began to sew a quilt
that would eventually measure 95½ × 97½ inches with nine 28-inch square
blocks.[18] On the quilt they embroidered the words, "Her Majesty Queen Liliuokalani. Imprisoned at Iolani Palace January 17th 1895. . . . We began this
quilt there."[19] The quilt was a political piece, displaying crossed Hawaiian
flags between each quadrant. The center block contained the coat of arms of
King Kalākaua (monarch from 1874 to 1891) framed by a pair of crossed Hawaiian flags. To the right of center, the women included a small commemorative ribbon from the July 1865 celebration of the restoration of the Hawaiian
flag; the ribbon included the Hawaiian flag, motto, and coat of arms. And in
the bottom right block the women stitched one of the patriotic hatbands Hawaiian men were wearing in the streets after the 1893 coup, which contained a
Hawaiian flag and the words "Kuu Hae Aloha" (My Beloved Flag).[20]

After her release, Liliʻuokalani wrote in her diary that as she drove past
the palace, she could not bring herself to look at the flags flying there: "Time
may wear off the feeling of injury by and by. But my dear flag—the Hawaiian flag—that a strange flag should wave over it!"[21] The former monarch was
dismayed not just by the presence of the US flag, but by the subordinate position of the Hawaiian flag underneath it. US colonial officials had not simply replaced the Hawaiian flag; they had co-opted it and made it the official
ensign of their new Territory of Hawaii, where by law it flew below the US
flag. Because the colonial government had co-opted the symbol, displaying it
could signify any number of sentiments. A missionary from the continental
United States in 1901 noted "ardent annexationists as well as loving royalists
keep the Hawaiian colors flying from the tall poles in their yards."[22] The flag's
association with the monarchy was muddled, such that an outside observer
could not know if its display was a message of support or protest, allegiance
or resistance.

Edith B. Williams, herself a Native Hawaiian, later wrote that "if by taking this flag, which had flown over the Hawaiian kingdom for seventy-eight
years, they thought to appease the Hawaiians, they were gravely mistaken."
Hawaiians "resented the Republic and . . . its use of the monarchical flag."[23]

Hawaiian women found that they could eschew this new designation of the Hawaiian flag as a symbol of the US territorial government by continuing to include crowns, royal coats of arms, and other insignia related to the monarchy on their quilts, thus signaling that *these* Hawaiian flags represented the independent Kingdom of Hawaiʻi, not the US Territory of Hawaii. Some even included the Hawaiian monarchy's motto, "Ua Mau ke Ea o ka ʻĀina i ka Pono" (The life of the land is perpetuated in righteousness), or "Kuʻu hae aloha" (My beloved flag).[24] One 1899 quilt placed small, crossed Hawaiian flags above and below a crown. The quiltmaker positioned the flags upside down—a nautical practice meant to signal a vessel in distress, here used to signal a nation in distress. The identity of the maker is unknown, but the quilt was believed to have been a gift to its owners from Liliʻuokalani.[25]

While the US colonial government in Hawaiʻi attempted to imbue the Hawaiian flag with new meaning in *public*, the flags on quilts were used in decidedly more intimate ways.[26] US and Hawaiian flags on flagpoles were meant to be raised, lowered, saluted, and revered from below. In these quilts, the symbols of the deposed kingdom were stitched onto an object explicitly designed to provide comfort to the user. Hawaiian flag quilts invited users to literally wrap themselves in the symbols of the Hawaiian Kingdom. Victoria Ward, a close friend of Queen Liliʻuokalani, decided to hang a Hawaiian flag quilt inscribed with the phrase "Kuʻu hae aloha" in the canopy of her four-poster bed. Ward reportedly remarked that it would ensure that, even though the United States had taken over, her children would all be born under the Hawaiian flag just as she was, and she could die under that flag, as she had always intended.[27] By combining the Hawaiian flag with royal symbols on quilts, Hawaiian women were able to use sewing to express their continued loyalty to the kingdom. Creating Hawaiian flag quilts and keeping them in the privacy of one's home did not directly challenge the supremacy of US national symbols in public spaces. But women like Ward could use these quilts to create their own iconographic worlds in their own homes.

But women did not just create traditional Hawaiian flag quilts, and the imagery found on other quilts suggests a variety of responses to the annexation of the Hawaiian Islands. Some quilts combined US and Hawaiian iconography with designs that contained US and Hawaiian flags crossed over one another. The pattern of Kelliʻiahonui Richard's hand-embroidered quilt from 1910, for instance, repeated a rendition of the Hawaiian coat of arms. It had the usual crown at the top, but instead of the high chiefs Kamanawa and Kameʻeiamoku standing on opposite sides of a quartered shield, Richard instead embroidered simplified versions of the US and Hawaiian flag *together* under the crown. This much embroidery would have been painstaking, and Richard repeated the design nine times on the six-by-six-foot quilt. The effort says something about how important this sentiment was to Richard, as does the fact that the quilt was passed down four generations to today.[28] Another "annexation quilt" from the early twentieth century contained four sets of large, crossed US and Hawaiian flags around the royal coat of arms at the center. The Hawaiian quilter and quilt historian Elizabeth Akana argued unequivocally that "the quilt was made to celebrate annexation."[29]

Some flag quilts from the early twentieth century went even further, following the traditional pattern of a Hawaiian flag quilt but replacing all Hawaiian iconography with that of the United States. These quiltmakers placed four US flags around the border of the quilt, and the US coat of arms at the center.[30] Where Hawaiian flag quilts usually had the Hawaiian Kingdom's motto or "Ku'u hae aloha," these quilters stitched the United States unofficial motto, "E pluribus unum."[31] The anthropologist Joyce D. Hammond has suggested that, rather than being evidence of the imposition of US national iconography onto Hawaiians, these quilts "may be interpreted as a visual statement of the accommodation of an American identity into the foundational Hawaiian identity."[32] The US flag quilts were not performative; they were never displayed in public as evidence of Native Hawaiian patriotism, or loyalty to the United States. They remained private, and were passed down as family heirlooms for generations just as traditional Hawaiian flag quilts were.[33] People spent months of their lives in the early twentieth century creating these quilts to express their loyalty to the United States, even as their fellow quilters continued to honor the deposed Hawaiian Kingdom.

These quilts and the messages they carried were political. But they were not used as part of an effort to enact political change. US officials were concerned with public displays of loyalty in their colonies: whether Hawaiian children were reciting the Pledge of Allegiance, whether people were flying the Stars and Stripes on the Fourth of July, and whether they knew the words to "The Star-Spangled Banner." While the officials did often concern themselves with the intimate realms of people's lives, there is no record of them trying to dictate what symbols women stitched on their quilts. As Vernadette Vicuña Gonzalez has argued, "Transgressive quilting often escaped the colonial gaze because women's work was seen as nonthreatening."[34] In public, it seemed there was only room for allegiance or resistance. In the private world of quilt making, however, women were able to express a variety of viewpoints on the overthrow of the Hawaiian Kingdom and the advent of US colonial rule—ranging from allegiance to resistance, and including a variety of sentiments in between.

Prohibiting Patriotism

When Philippine revolutionaries designed their new nation's flag in 1897, they chose red, white, and blue to "commemorat[e] the flag of the United States"—then an ally in the fight for independence from Spain.[35] After the United States purchased the Philippines from Spain, the Philippine flag remained the symbol of the independent Philippine Republic, now fighting for its independence from the United States. The United States declared the Philippine-American War over in 1902, but the fight for independence in the Philippines continued. And in those tense years, continental US Americans in the Philippines remained acutely aware of the revolutionary potential of the Philippine flag and its ability to challenge the supremacy of the US flag in the islands.

While the Philippine flag was not officially banned in the early years of US colonial rule, continental US Americans in the Philippines closely monitored its use and reacted strongly to any perceived challenges to the supremacy of the US flag. In 1903, continental US Americans attacked Filipino performers during what the *Washington Post* called a "seditious play."[36] According to the *Post*—which relayed the story alongside reports of Filipinos killing US soldiers—during the play the leading lady, playing the role of an allegorical Independencia, "tore the American flag from its standard, revealing the flag of the Katipunan." The Katipunan—a secret pro-independence society formed under Spanish rule—was typically represented by a red flag with three *K*'s. But many US Americans in the Philippines often mistakenly called the red, white, and blue flag of the Philippine Republic with the sun and stars a "Katipunan flag."[37] The *Post* reported that after the actress lowered the US flag and raised the Katipunan (or Philippine) banner in its place, a "little brown brother"—an infantilizing term US Americans often used for Filipinos—began "jumping up and down and spitting on Old Glory."[38] Chaos ensued. The continental US Americans in the audience rushed the stage, attacking the cast. One "brawny-armed invader," as described by the *Post*, "grabbed the leading man by his ankles and swung him crashing through several acres of bamboo brake and jungle brush." A "second invader" hurled the Filipina playing Independencia down a steep flight of stairs. After attacking the actors, "the crowd proceeded to demolish everything that remained."[39] The actors had not threatened physical violence in their performance; they had critiqued US rule by subverting the established rules for flag veneration. Instead of raising the US flag and pledging their allegiance to it, they had lowered that object and trampled upon it. But to the continental US Americans in the audience, symbolic violence against the US flag was enough to warrant physical violence toward the perpetrators. The flag itself was an inanimate object; but any perceived attack on it was, to their minds, an attack on the United States.

The Philippine flag was not illegal, but the Philippine revolutionary Carlos Ronquillo recalled that "any individual who used any trinket, watch chain, button or pin with the colors or design of the Philippine flag was prosecuted and incarcerated by the Constabulary"—the colonial police force.[40] Ronquillo was even arrested in 1903 because "the number of his house was written on a tablet upon which was painted the Philippine Flag." Ronquillo understood that flying of the flag "was tolerated not as a political right but only as an exceptional privilege."[41] And it was a privilege that many continental US Americans, especially those who had fought against that flag during the war, were eager to take away. They found their opportunity to do so during the 1907 elections.

Up to that point, the only governing body in the Philippines had been the Philippine Commission, appointed by the president of the United States. The year 1907 marked the beginning of a bicameral legislature in the Philippines, with the appointed Philippine Commission forming the upper house and the elected Philippine Assembly the lower. It was the first time Filipinos would have representation in the US colonial government, and the first time Filipinos would participate in elections. Much to the US colonial officials' dismay, the newly formed pro-independence Nacionalista Party won a majority of seats. And in the aftermath of the July 30, 1907, elections, Filipinos took to the streets—not to protest, but to celebrate. Newspapers at the time reported that during these parades, Filipinos carried both Philippine *and* US flags. This display enraged continental US Americans in the Philippines.

Various US observers reported that "yes, the American flag was in evidence, but it was not given such prominence as the other flag."[42] Others complained that the US flags were "smaller than the Filipino flag," and that "too often it was either conspicuous by its total absence or by its insignificant size as compared with the Katipunan standard."[43] In Malabon it was reported that celebrants paraded with a Philippine flag about eight feet long and a US flag about two feet long. From a continental US perspective, "the comparison was odious," such that man "stepped into the crowd and took from the bearer of the American flag his burden." He told the *Manila Times*—a paper run by continental US Americans—that he "wouldn't have the good old flag subjected to the ignominy of such a display."[44]

Compared to the "seditious play" in 1903 and to the challenges to the US flag Puerto Ricans would mount later, this seems relatively innocuous. Filipinos were not tearing down or trampling US flags, nor had they disregarded the Stars and Stripes—they were carrying it alongside the Philippine flag. The problem, it became clear, was that US Americans did not appreciate Filipinos carrying Philippine flags at all. According to the *Manila Times*, this was a holdover from the war: "It cannot be expected that the old soldier who saw his commanders give their lives and who risked his own in raising the Stars and Stripes triumphant over the Sun and the Tricolored Triangle should not feel something burn within him on seeing those two flags now placed side by side and more reverence shown the latter than the former."[45] The memories of "those red days," wrote the *Times*, were "still too fresh."[46]

One story in particular incensed the continental US American community in the Philippines. On August 11, supporters of Fernando Guerrero—a recently elected Nacionalista and head of the newspaper *El Renacimiento*—had a parade. A US flag was at the head of the procession—a "disgrace" according to the continental US-run *Manila Opinion*, which noted that the US flag was small in comparison to the "immense and numerous Katipunan banners" behind it. The parade marched to the Luneta—the same park in Manila where patriotic holidays like the Fourth of July were celebrated every year. The police directed the crowd to the nearby Wallace Field, where, the *Opinion* wrote, "was committed the worst crime against constituted authority. One of the rioters tore the American flag out of the hands of the Filipino who carried it, and throwing Old Glory in the dirt, trampled upon it. This was the signal that others had been looking for. In less time than it takes to tell it every Filipino who could get at it jumped on the flag and ground its stars and stripes into the dirt, tearing it into shreds."[47] As this story spread throughout the continental US American community, tensions rose. The *Manila Times* warned Filipinos that for their own good, they ought not display their flag: "There are Americans, who are not their friends, who would welcome nothing more than an outbreak which would call for the stern repression of the iron hand."[48] In a particularly harsh statement, one continental US American remarked, "Those bearers of the Katipunan banner have forgotten the lesson taught them when ballots were bullets."[49] Again, a symbolic challenge to the US flag's supremacy in the Philippines prompted physical threats of violence from continental US Americans.

Remarkably, this flag-trampling incident may or may not have even happened. The anti-imperialist Helen C. Wilson reported that "these stories were of purely malicious fabrication." Writing from Manila to the *Springfield Republican* back in Massachusetts, Wilson said that Filipinos carried the flag of the Philippine Republic in this parade—"the use of which has been tolerated by the Government for some years"—not to challenge US sovereignty, but because the Philippine flag "represents to the Filipino people their hopes for the future." Wilson also clarified for her continental audience that while "Americans have apparently supposed that the flag of the Philippine Republic carried in the parades was identical with the Katipunan flag with its three K's," the latter "never appeared," and the two flags "are quite distinct." Wilson also emphasized the presence of US flags in the demonstrations, and blamed "the excitable and truckling American papers of Manila" for spreading such "false reports." [50]

The Filipino press also attempted to assuage continental US concerns after the August 11 parade for the newly elected Guerrero. Guerrero's own *El Renacimiento* reported, "We sincerely believe that in all those public demonstrations the people have not the slightest intention of insulting the people or the flag of the United States." Yes, Filipinos were displaying the Philippine flag—"but we can swear that there was never in the minds of the Filipinos the idea or intention of inflicting an insult against American sovereignty." *El Renacimiento* provided an "economical reason" for the smallness of the US flags: the larger US flags available for purchase were "too costly," and "the making of them by adjusting one piece of cloth to another is very complicated and difficult on account of the bars and stars." The Philippine flag, however, with just two large stripes and a triangle, was easier to make, and so "came within reach of the means of the poor class which formed the large majority of the paraders in Manila. It was but natural then that the people had to exhibit American flags of smaller size and of ordinary cloth." [51]

But continental US Americans in the Philippines remained incensed. The real or perceived disrespect to the US flag led one man, Theobald Diehl, to call for a mass meeting to be held at Manila's Grand Opera House on August 23, 1907. Diehl himself was German-born and had been naturalized as a US citizen before coming to the Philippines as part of the hospital corps in 1898 and joining the colonial customs service after the war. [52] The entire events surrounding the mass meeting were recorded by the newspaperman and participant Robert Westcott, in what Helen Wilson called an "ill-made little book entitled 'The Exaltation of the Flag.'" [53]

In the days leading up to the August 23 mass meeting, Westcott wrote, a committee of a "number of the representative Americans of Manila" began hanging up posters all over Manila, which read:

> PATRIOTIC MEETING. AMERICANS ATTENTION. Deeply moved by the occurrences of the last few weeks in Manila out of which has arisen the question: *'Is the sovereignty of these Islands to be represented by other than the American flag?'* a meeting of all Americans of these Islands is called to settle this question and to take steps to secure the peaceful adjustment of this problem. [54]

The poster listed the members of the planning committee: prominent US businessmen, military men, religious leaders, journalists, teachers, and more.

Even the chairman of the meeting, the veteran and businessman William H. Anderson from Ohio, noted that it was rare for the entire continental US American community in the Philippines to come together, as different groups often disagreed about how the colony should be run and for whose benefit.[55] But the local US press explained why they united around the flag: "We who live far away from the land where Old Glory was born and waves in undisputed triumph, who are exiles in this distant outpost of our nation, feel more keenly our kinship with her sons than did we when in our own land there was no need of defense." Indeed, they admitted that the US flag had "none but enforced respect" in the Philippines, but that it only made the symbol "doubly dear to us in these islands." Almost a decade after US troops had first planted the flag in the Philippines, these US Americans felt a special duty to uphold the US flag there because—as the presence of Philippine flags in the recent parades had reminded them—its supremacy in the islands was not a given. "Here," the *Cablenews* wrote, "America has planted her pennon on the utmost ramparts of the world, and we are sent to keep it."[56] No matter their profession or purpose in the Philippines, these continental US Americans shared this obligation.

But this mass meeting was not meant just to uplift Old Glory; the planners sought legal change: "to ask the Philippine Commission to take the necessary steps to prevent and to punish further indignities to the national emblem, and to punish the authors of seditious utterances against the United States Government."[57] They wanted to ban the Philippine flag and punish anyone who challenged the supremacy of the US flag. The posters promoting the mass meeting concluded: "Every American Man. Every American Woman. Every American Child Ought to Attend and Hear the Patriotic Address."[58]

As the August 23 mass meeting approached, the pressure on government officials mounted. But officials did not appear to share the mass meeting planning committee's anger or urgency. W. Cameron Forbes, commissioner of commerce and police and future governor-general of the Philippines, wrote in his journal on August 20 that the whole matter was "an unfortunate, and rather silly incident, or series of incidents." He himself had never supported a ban on the Philippine flag. In fact, he had "authorized a factory to make and sell buttons with these emblems on them"—with the approval, he noted, of William Howard Taft, secretary of war and former governor-general of the Philippines.[59] While the mass meeting committee continued to pressure the US colonial officials, *El Renacimiento* pleaded with them not to ban the Philippine flag. It argued that "Filipinos are well aware that they are a subject people," and that they "accept this condition resignedly, respecting here American sovereignty." But the Philippine flag, the paper argued, was "the national symbol of a thought"—that thought being Philippine independence, which was something the US government had promised to grant once it deemed Filipinos capable of self-government. "To prohibit a flag . . . which is a real representation of the ideal of independence recognized by America, is it not to violate that fundamental principle and give the lie to solemn promises of freedom made to us by the federal government?" The editorial ended with a warning: "If the government begins by prohibiting emblems or symbols it will end by suppressing every expression of that free thought which is the basis of peoples, governments, and human greatness."[60] *El Renacimiento* hoped that calling on US traditions of free speech and promises of Philippine independence would prevent a flag ban. Its reasoning fell on deaf ears. As Forbes wrote in his journal, the incidents following the 1907 elections had created "a great deal of feeling among the Americans here," he wrote; and so, to appease them, "we shall probably prohibit the use of the Katipunan flag and emblem."[61]

Early on the day of the mass meeting on August 23, 1907, the Philippine Commission passed Act no. 1696, banning the Philippine flag in the Philippines.[62] Punishment for possessing or displaying the Philippine flag in public *or* in the privacy of one's own home was a fine of five hundred to five thousand pesos, imprisonment from three months to five years, or both. Having their demands encoded in law, however, did not stop enraged continental US Americans from holding their mass meeting.

On August 23, 1907, at 7:30 p.m., the crowd met at the Veteran Army of the Philippines Hall. The entire evening was an ostentatious display of US flags and patriotic paraphernalia, thanks to the efforts of John H. Dow, another veteran-turned-businessman from St. Paul, Minnesota, named "chairman of the Committee on Hall and Decorations" for the mass meeting.[63] At the hall, the three thousand participants—men, women, and children—received red, white, and blue walking canes and marched to Manila's Grand Opera House. As the marchers entered, they found a military band playing patriotic songs and the theater fully decorated in red, white, and blue. Behind the stage, "there was displayed in colored incandescent lights the national emblem."[64] Most attendees found standing room only, and hundreds more stood outside—a testament to the crowd's commitment to the mass meeting's purpose: asserting the supremacy of the US flag in the Philippines.[65]

Having already convinced the Philippine Commission to ban the Philippine flag, the speakers spent the evening railing against the colonial government's policy of "benevolent assimilation," and insisting on harsher treatment of Filipinos. One speaker from Mississippi proclaimed, "The time has come, my countrymen, when we should talk plainly and honestly to the Filipino people. . . . The United States Government *owns* these Islands. . . . It is time for us to tell the Filipinos that they cannot insult with impunity the nation or the flag of the United States Government."[66] Captain Thomas E. Leonard, who had fought in the Philippine-American War, took a more violent approach: "I believe in peace and harmony. I always did. And when I had a battalion of volunteers behind me I felt *awful* peaceful." With his sarcastic comments punctuated by laughter from the audience, he continued: "I believe that if we could put about one hundred thousand American troops over here it would be *very peaceful* (Laughter.)—exceedingly so (More laughter); and you would not see any more Katipunan banners, eight or ten feet long . . . like that which passed my house the other night, *with a little six-cent American flag carried underneath it!* (Laughter.) It would be *too peaceful* for that (More laughter). . . ."[67]

These speeches from Philippine-American war veterans were a far cry from the sentiments Civil War veterans representing the Grand Army of the Republic had expressed when introducing the US flag to Philippine schools just seven years earlier. The GAR had told US colonial subjects that the US flag was "the ensign of freedom," a symbolic representation of power but also mercy.[68] And the GAR's mission to plant a US flag on every schoolhouse had emphasized patriotic education—teaching Filipinos to respect and venerate the US flag as their own—rather than violent coercion. By contrast, Captain Leonard, misquoting "Andy Jackson," announced: "If any man trample upon the American flag, shoot him on the spot."[69]

Not all speakers agreed on the need for violence, however, and the proceedings of the mass meeting revealed some of the fissures within the US American community. Reverend Stealy B. Rossiter, pastor of the First Presbyterian Church, directly followed Leonard and began by noting that he would be giving a different kind of speech than the military men—a comment that Westcott noted "was taken by some in the audience as a little 'dig' at the previous speakers." While Rossiter fully supported banning the Philippine flag, he argued, unlike the soldiers, that "this meeting is called in the interests of peace" and "in the interest of good fellowship and friendship which we hope to secure between the Filipino people and the American people."[70] Rossiter believed that Filipinos were not being malicious, they just did not yet grasp the meaning of the US flag. That flag, he argued, represented "home, fellowship, ideals, institutions, a hundred battles, red life blood poured out like water, a willingness to die for our country . . . a welded nation, an advanced civilization, a poor man's paradise. Justice between man and Heaven."[71] It was understandable, Rossiter argued, that continental US Americans were "easily hurt" by any insult to that flag. "Do the Filipinos understand this? I fear they do not. The Filipino who does not take off his hat, when the band plays the Star-Spangled Banner on the Luneta, as a salute to our flag and to his flag for the time being, has not entered a little bit into the merits of the question."[72]

However, the leader of the evening's proceedings, John W. Hausserman, yet another veteran-turned-businessman from Ohio, believed it was "of no great importance what the Filipino may at this time think of the Stars and Stripes." Because of the violence of US conquest, he admitted that for many Filipinos the Stars and Stripes represented murder, violence, and "other depredations."[73] This was irrelevant to Hausserman. He did not care if Filipinos believed in the US flag's "benevolence," as Rossiter wished; he cared just that they followed the rules.

The mass meeting concluded with Rossiter reading the committee's resolutions, which plainly proclaimed the supremacy of the US flag in the Philippines: "Resolved, That it is the opinion of patriots here assembled, that but one flag be recognized on these Islands . . . the Stars and Stripes, and that so long as we are on these Islands as the governing nation we can permit no other flag. . . ." Westcott reported that Rossiter was frequently interrupted by "deafening" applause, while the audience was "thrown into a delirium of enthusiasm." After the resolutions, attendees gave three more "rousing cheers" for the US flag as the band played the "Star-Spangled Banner" before leaving the opera house.[74]

The following day, the *Manila Times* reported that "the most striking feature of the demonstration was the unanimous opinion" among speakers that "our Government has gone too fast and too far in its benevolent efforts to prove to the Filipinos that we are disposed to give them a Government of their own."[75] But not everyone's opinions were represented at the mass meeting. Indeed, there were no women on the program at all. Interestingly, at the very end of his compendium of the events, Westcott included—without comment or context—a poem written by Minerva Agnes Davis the day after the mass meeting, outlining the role of women in upholding the supremacy of the US flag: "You and I are weak 'women-folks,' Girlie, / And 'tis true we can't fight for our flag / As our husbands and fathers and brothers / Fought the foemen who called it a rag." But, even if "weak 'women-folks'" could not fight, Davis argued, "Our duty / Is just to keep on teaching school." While the speakers at the mass meeting scoffed at the efficacy of education, Davis's poem made the case for its long-term benefits: "Fifty years from to-day all these children / Will be telling their children's small sons / Reminiscent and spell-binding stories,— / And *those* children will stand by the guns / On the ramparts where Old Glory flutters! / So that when we make offer to go / And to rid them of flag and protection, / Those children will all ballot, 'No!'" The fight for the US flag's supremacy in the Philippines, Davis's poem suggested, would be waged on multiple fronts. And if women fulfilled their roles in the classroom, Davis predicted, in "three generations" Filipinos themselves would be the ones to "cling to the *Red, White and Blue!*"[76]

After the drama of the August 23, 1907, mass meeting, US colonial officials in the Philippines quickly set about enforcing the new flag ban. The first proscription happened when the collector of customs held up a shipment of cotton goods that bore the Philippine flag on its label. The matter was taken to the governor-general, who confirmed that the collector had done the right thing and told the consignees that they would have to remove all Philippine labels before customs officials would let the shipment through. Shortly after that, the chief of police of Manila began informing merchants that they had to pull the Philippine and Katipunan flags they had for sale from their shelves.[77]

The first public enforcement of the ban took place during another political parade between Santa Ana and Paco, celebrating the election of the Nacionalista politician Cayetano Lukban to the Philippine Assembly.[78] Three girls dressed in red, white, and blue rode on a float at the center of the parade decorated with US and Philippine flags. Police Captain Jose de Crame, a former member of the Spanish secret service and commander of the Paco precinct in Manila, had that very day received the order from the Manila chief of police banning the Philippine flag. Upon hearing about the float, he went to the parade to enforce the new law.[79] *El Renacimiento* reported that Crame seized the Philippine flags, but "repeated that he was only complying with a superior order, in view of the silent protest of the persons present." But the limits of the new law were unclear. A detective from the continental United States called Crame's attention to a button that a man nearby was wearing on his lapel, bearing the colors red, white, and blue. The man protested that the colors represented the US flag. Crame seized the badge anyway (but it was later returned).[80] The colors of the Philippine flag had been inspired by the US flag. So, while designed to reinforce the supremacy of the US flag in the Philippines, the flag ban also cast suspicion on its colors.

When the US flag had first come to the Philippines, US imperialists had presented it as a symbol of freedom and liberty. *El Renacimiento* reflected somberly on "the restriction of freedom imposed by those imperial edicts." It wrote, "Bitter is the disillusion, deep the sorrow that fills the Filipino hearts, [but] . . . we shall pick up our sacred emblem, fold it with loving care, kiss it with affection and respect, and deposit it in the sanctuary of our national soul to cover with it our holy ideal."[81]

On October 16, 1907, almost two months after the mass meeting, Manila's Grand Opera House was once again filled with US flags for the inauguration

FIGURE 3.2. Inauguration of the Philippine Assembly at the Grand Opera House with William Howard Taft at the center in front, October 16, 1907. American Historical Collection / Filipinas Heritage Library.

of the Philippine Assembly. When the independent Republic of the Philippines had inaugurated its congress in 1898, the hall had been filled with Philippine flags. But now, at the inauguration of the Philippine Assembly, there was not a Philippine flag in sight (figure 3.2).

Flying Side by Side

Over the next decade, many people in the Philippines were fined and arrested for violating the flag ban. Some, like the nationalist Juan Panganiban, did fly the Philippine flag in support of Philippine independence.[82] Others—like Go Chico, a Chinese merchant in Manila whose shop window display included a medallion with a small picture of Emilio Aguinaldo and the Philippine flag— were punished despite claiming no knowledge of the law.[83] Between 1908 and 1914, the Philippine Assembly drafted thirteen bills and one resolution to repeal the flag ban. The five that passed were ignored by the Philippine Commission—that upper house appointed by the US president.

But by the mid-1910s, official moods were changing in the Philippines. The appointment of Governor-General Francis Burton Harrison in 1913 ushered in a new era of "Filipinization." An appointee of US President Woodrow Wilson, Harrison committed himself to implementing Wilson's widely espoused ideals of self-determination in the Philippines.[84] He immediately began replacing continental US Americans in the colonial government with Filipinos. The 1916 Jones Act abolished the presidentially appointed Philippine Commission and created the Philippine Senate, giving Filipinos control of both houses of the legislature, though the presidentially appointed governor-general maintained veto power. And the act, for the first time, codified a US commitment to eventual Philippine independence.[85]

By 1919, much had changed in the twelve years since three thousand angry continental US Americans filled Manila's Grand Opera House. Filipinos had continued to demonstrate their loyalty to the US flag through the routine rituals the government required, and by enlisting to fight for the United States. Manuel Quezon, president of the Philippine Senate and a future president of the Philippine Commonwealth, remarked that during World War I, Filipinos "showed their fealty to the democratic ideals of America," and "must have made all suspicion or doubt to disappear forever."[86] One Philippine Assembly representative noted, "The war gave occasion for the strengthening of relations. Our loyalty to the United States swept away all barriers, all suspicion. . . ."[87] Governor-General Harrison agreed.

In a message to the Fifth Legislature of the Philippines on October 16, 1919, Harrison proclaimed: "The time has now long passed for suspicion and distrust between the two peoples, and Act No. 1696 known as the Flag Law was passed during a period of temporary feeling which has long since been alloyed; I recommend, therefore, the repeal of the Flag Law, so that it may no longer be a crime for a Filipino to exhibit in public that flag under which his people had set up a generation ago their own form of government."[88]

Following Harrison's recommendation, Philippine Senator Rafael Palma immediately introduced Senate Bill no. 1 to repeal Act no. 1696.[89] Palma and other legislators spoke about what this would mean for Filipinos, who had waited patiently to see their flag "wave majestically" in the open air "where it may be kissed by the sun, caressed by the storms, and where it may not be reached by the mud splatter of our journey or the noise of our petty grudges, that immortal banner, blessed among all."[90] Act no. 2871 to repeal the ban on the Philippine flag passed on October 22, 1919.[91]

Not all continental US Americans in Manila agreed with Governor-General Harrison. Manila's *Cablenews-American* wrote that lifting the flag ban "smacks of disloyalty and will be resented, both here and in the United States."[92] They argued that "the emblem of the American nation, wherever it flies over American territory, must be accorded first place."[93] A schoolteacher from Kansas in Naga Camarines took it upon himself to write to his US senator back home protesting the decision. He believed that Filipinos would "seize the opportunity to slight and show disrespect to the American flag," and included a not-so-subtle threat that harked back to 1907: "You may be very sure that the Americans here will not stand for anything like that and will make it pretty interesting for the first little 'Brown Brother' who tries [*sic*] to show off in that manner." He hoped the senator would "feel justified in using [his] influence in Congress to put a stop to this *nonsense* over here." The senator forwarded the letter to the Bureau of Insular Affairs—the War Department agency in charge of the government of the Philippines—who did respond, but only to let the schoolteacher know there were regulations in place for how to properly display the US and Philippine flags together.[94]

With the events of 1907 still fresh in their minds, Filipino leaders preached caution. "We are to remember to exercise due respect to the American people, to American sovereignty and the American flag," Quezon argued, "which is to be all the more respected and beloved because beneath its shadow our flag is about to be unfolded, and it is not to supplant it yet a while." The Philippine flag ban was lifted, yes, but Quezon advised that "the use of our up to now proscribed flag be guided by moderation, self-control and courtesy."[95] Even Emilio Aguinaldo warned that Filipinos would still have to "respect and honor the American flag just as they want theirs to be respected and honored." He remarked, "The restoration of the Filipino Flag is a source of rejoicing for the people; and for me, of immense satisfaction, a solace."[96] Aguinaldo asked to participate in the Philippine flag's official debut, but the planning committee declined, their stated reasoning being that they believed he was too ill.[97] But he *would* take part in an official Philippine flag raising ceremony years later—when an independent Philippine Republic was declared under Japanese occupation during World War II.

On October 30, 1919, the Bureau of Insular Affairs reported that "over 100,000 people from Manila and the provinces participated in the official restoration of the Philippine flag." Aurora Quezon, the spouse of Manuel Quezon, had the honor of raising the Philippine flag to "tremendous applause."[98] A local newspaper wrote: "One must be blind in order not to perceive and admire the magnificent spectacle and the enthusiastic outburst of national feeling upon the recovery today of that beloved ensign. It is as if, without it, the Filipino people was a dead body, and that its return has restored the soul to that body."[99]

In his speech, Speaker of the House Sergio Osmeña argued that the meaning of the Philippine flag had changed: "Gaze on it, its colors are the same as those which in time past gave exultation to our arms and which also with our arms fell. Its folds and lines are the same. But if the flag of yesterday was bathed in blood it was because it was stained with blood, the blood of so many patriots sacrificed in the altar of war. . . . The present flag boasts with propriety the pure whiteness of the time of peace." Unlike the continental US Americans who insisted the US flag should fly alone, Osmeña argued that "these flags are not incompatible with each other. . . . The two flags should fly side by side in these Islands to work for the same end—the happiness and liberty of the Filipino people."[100]

The pro-US *Philippine Review* devoted the cover of its next issue to the momentous event (figure 3.3). The cover art depicted Governor-General Harrison handing a Philippine flag to an allegorical Filipina. The return of the Philippine flag was not shown here as a return to a flagpole, where it might wave over the Philippines from a place of honor. Instead, the flag was draped delicately between Harrison and the Filipina as they shared an intimate gaze. The Filipina appeared completely submissive, reinforcing familiar fantasies of US domination of consenting subjects.[101] The cover sent a clear message: the return of the Philippine flag was not a hard-fought victory achieved by Filipinos; it was a gift benevolently bestowed by the US colonial government.

Soon after the repeal of the ban, the US colonial government made the Philippine flag its own official flag in the Philippines, to "be used publicly, in

FIGURE 3.3. Cover of *Philippine Review* showing Governor-General Harrison giving the Philippine flag back to an allegorical Filipina, October 1919. Filipinas Heritage Library.

FIGURE 3.4. US and Philippine flags flying side by side outside a hospital in the Philippines after the lifting of the flag ban, 1934. Bureau of Insular Affairs photo. US National Archives.

the place next to that belonging to the flag of the United States." By law, that place—like that of the Hawaiian flag in the Territory of Hawaii—was a subordinate position, either underneath or to the right of the US flag (figure 3.4).[102] Rather than undermining the US flag's supremacy in the Philippines, allowing the display of the Philippine flag became tangible evidence of the benevolence of US rule. And the US colonial government was able to enact this symbolic change without granting Filipinos any more autonomy. Secretary of War John W. Weeks candidly expressed the benefits of this symbolic change in a letter to the secretary of state in September 1921: "Experience has shown the advisability of recognizing regional flags and giving them an established place subordinate to the National flag rather than to attempt to suppress the use of regional flags to enable ill disposed persons to use them as separatist or independence flags." In other words, it was wise imperial policy to co-opt a colony's national symbol rather than suppress it. This is what the Republic and then the Territory of Hawaii had done by making the Hawaiian Kingdom's flag its official emblem. And while Weeks did not mention the Hawaiian case, he did note that the British Empire regularly "recognize[d] in its colonial regulations arms or badges of its colonies and protectorates."[103]

The article inside the *Philippine Review* with Harrison and the allegorical Filipina on the cover proclaimed that the Philippine flag now flew "side by side with the Stars and Stripes, its best friend, its unselfish ally, its most determined protector." The writer hoped "that the two may forever be the symbol of our union—'The union of hearts—the union of our hands'—that the two may clearly proclaim the world over that THEY WILL EVER REMAIN TOGETHER."[104] If on the surface, repealing the Philippine flag ban appeared to undo an unfair act of colonial domination, its outcome was anything but anticolonial. In classrooms and on schoolhouses and other government buildings, where the US flag had once flown alone, it now flew alongside the Philippine flag, symbolically strengthening the bond between the Philippines and United States.

Nationalist unrest continued, but as Osmeña argued at the flag raising, the meaning of the Philippine flag had changed. Those who sought to challenge US rule would have to use other symbols. In the 1930s, a new independence movement called the Sakdalista movement arose in the Philippines. When an estimated sixty thousand Sakdalistas all over the Philippines rose up on the night of May 2, 1935, seizing nearly twenty towns across the provinces of Bulacan, Cavite, Rizal, and Laguna, they lowered all US *and* Philippine flags and raised a plain red banner in their places. The *Philippine Free Press* published a photo of a communist rally in Pampanga and asked readers to "try to find an American or Philippine flag in this picture. There aren't any."[105] This new generation of independence advocates did not rally around the Philippine flag. In their minds, that flag was the emblem of the US colonial government and the Filipinos who collaborated with it.[106]

The Puerto Rican independence movement, however, still had its flag.

Nascent Nationalism

In 1917, Pedro Albizu Campos, then a student at Harvard University, wrote that Puerto Ricans "welcomed the American flag in 1898 because we believed it . . . to be a symbol of democracy and justice."[107] Since the Grand Army of the Republic's initial gift of a flag for every schoolhouse in 1898, an entire generation of Puerto Ricans had grown up pledging its allegiance to the US flag. But after some time under that flag without any change in Puerto Rico's colonial status, many began to question whether the symbol of liberty, freedom, and democracy had lived up to its promises.[108] Even President Wilson told Congress that the United States had "created expectations of extended privilege which we have not satisfied" in Puerto Rico, leading to an "uneasiness among the people of the Island, and even a suspicious doubt with regard to our intentions concerning them."[109]

In the mid-1910s, US policymakers began to coalesce around the idea of extending US citizenship to Puerto Ricans.[110] Wilson suggested that it could help "satisfy the obligations of generous justice towards the people of Porto Rico" and save the United States "embarrassment" on the international stage—something that would become even more important to the United States as the century wore on.[111] Others saw strengthening ties between the continental United States and Puerto Rico as a wise strategic move on the eve of war. Along with the newly purchased US Virgin Islands, the United States wanted Puerto Rico to prevent Axis powers from reaching the prized Panama Canal.[112] And William Jones, one of the Democratic congressmen responsible for writing the law that granted Puerto Ricans citizenship, plainly stated another benefit: "I believe it will result in putting an end to all agitation in favor of independence."[113] In short, granting Puerto Ricans US citizenship was meant to pacify the colony and prepare it for World War I.[114] On March 2, 1917, Wilson signed the Jones-Shafroth Act into law.[115] Despite Jones's hopes, the conferral of citizenship did little to tamp down unrest in Puerto Rico.[116] Instead, it ushered in an era of discontent in the colony, as new Republican colonial officials took office after the war.

Across the empire, Republican officials appointed by Republican President Warren G. Harding took a harsher approach to colonial governance than did Wilson's Democratic appointees. In 1920, Harding sent the Wood-Forbes Commission, headed by Leonard Wood and W. Cameron Forbes, to determine the Philippines' readiness for independence. They unsurprisingly concluded that Filipinos were not ready for independence, and that the United States would be shirking its responsibility if it continued to give Filipinos more autonomy.[117] Harding appointed Leonard Wood governor-general in 1921, and began to reverse Filipinization, bringing continental US Americans back into government positions. On Guam, Naval Governor William W. Gilmer controversially banned intermarriage between whites and nonwhites.[118] And the following year, Gilmer even banned *whistling* within the city limits of the capital of Hagåtña.[119] The action was criticized in Guam and even in the continental US press. The *Philadelphia Public Ledger* mocked Gilmer's order, saying, "Ain't democracy a wonder?"[120] One person, while criticizing Guam's colonial government as a "naval czardom," asked, "Was it worth the natives' while to give up the fun of whistling for the privilege of saluting the Stars and Stripes and eating salmon out of a can instead of fresh fish from the ocean?"[121] One US official reported that during an inspection trip, "one of the natives pointed to the US flag and asked what that represented. When he was told that it represented liberty and freedom he said, 'Take it down and send it back to Agana; we have no freedom any more but we are going back to the days of slavery, so we don't need that flag.'"[122] Unlike Filipinos and Puerto Ricans, people on Guam did not have a national flag they might rally around. Yet, they still voiced their displeasure with these new policies in terms of the unfulfilled promises of the US flag.

While people on Guam dealt with Gilmer's ridiculous restrictions and Filipinos dealt with Wood rolling back Filipinization and delaying independence, Puerto Ricans also welcomed a new governor, E. Montgomery Reily, in July 1921. Reily's first order of business, in his inauguration speech, was to proclaim the supremacy of the US flag in Puerto Rico, saying there was not "any room on this island for any flag other than . . . the Stars and Stripes, and there never will be."[123] The Puerto Rican flag had not been an anti-US symbol. In fact, its design had been originally conceived of *in* the United States in 1895 during a meeting of the Puerto Rican branch of the Cuban Revolutionary Party in New York City, where those present decided that in a show of solidarity, the new Puerto Rican flag would invert the colors of the Cuban flag.[124] And until Reily's arrival, people had not viewed it as a threat to the US flag.

After Reily's inaugural proclamation that the US flag should be the only flag in Puerto Rico, things continued to escalate. Early in his term, while on a tour of the island, Reily referred to the Puerto Rican flag as a "rag."[125] Shortly thereafter, his chief of secret service removed a Puerto Rican flag from someone's car, tore it to shreds, and stomped on it.[126]

Puerto Ricans responded quickly to this disrespect to their flag. Thirty-nine of the fifty-eight elected officials in the Legislative Assembly signed a petition asking President Harding to remove Governor Reily. Félix Córdova Dávila, the nonvoting resident commissioner from Puerto Rico in the US Congress, testified about Reily's behavior on March 2, 1922. Córdova Dávila explained that Reily "had come to the island with 'deep-rooted prejudices,'" and that his disrespect of the Puerto Rican flag was emblematic of a larger problem.[127] As in Governor-General Wood's rollback of Filipinization in the Philippines, Reily had begun to replace experienced Puerto Rican civil servants with inexperienced people from the continental United States.[128] His commissioner of education, Juan B. Huyke, was the first Puerto Rican to have been appointed to that position, but was no less committed to Americanization. Indeed, after Reily's inauguration speech, Huyke proclaimed: "I am in perfect harmony with the ideas of Governor Reily, expressed in his brilliant inaugural address, in connection with the school problems of Porto Rico. Our schools are agencies of Americanism. They must implant the spirit

of America within the hearts of our children."[129] Huyke pushed for increased
patriotic education in schools, emphasizing flag veneration.[130] In June of 1922,
when Puerto Rican students graduating from Central High School in San
Juan wanted to have the Puerto Rican flag at the venue, Huyke ordered the
superintendent to call the police on the students and halt distribution of di-
plomas until the flag came down.[131] The presence of the Puerto Rican flag also
led to the suspension of graduation exercises at Caguas and Vega Alta, and
ceremonies at Fajardo only continued after students and officials agreed that
neither the US nor the Puerto Rican flag would be present.[132]

Córdova Dávila testified to Congress that the behavior of Reily and his
compatriots ultimately had "made this man intolerable to the people of the
island."[133] He presented a resolution of the Puerto Rican Senate, adopted by a
15–3 majority, to the US House of Representatives, declaring Reily "a vulgar
agitator and an irresponsible despot."[134] The chairman of the Rules Committee, however, said that though the House had the power to impeach Reily, it
would be "wholly impracticable" and "would take too long."[135] The following
year, Reily stepped aside amid political conflict, and was replaced by Huyke
as acting governor. But before Reily left La Fortaleza, he made one last proclamation of symbolic supremacy: standing on the balcony, addressing the
crowd below, he avowed: "These flags (American) here show that Puerto Rico
is American and will remain so to the end of time."[136]

The same year that Reily publicly insulted the Puerto Rican flag, Pedro
Albizu Campos graduated from Harvard Law School. In 1922 he returned to
Puerto Rico, and two years later he officially joined the Nationalist Party. At
that time, Albizu later recalled, Puerto Rican nationalism was not yet "ma-
ture," and Nationalists often felt it was necessary to have US flags at their
events "to protect themselves against aggression." At a Nationalist celebration of José de Diego's birthday on April 16, 1924, the grandstand had a large
Puerto Rican flag along with small three-inch US flags. Albizu was not one
of the recognized speakers on the program that day, but he walked up to
the grandstand and removed the US flags, declaring that "the shadow of a
three-inch flag, if it is of tyranny, can mean death."[137] After conducting what
he called a "patriotic pilgrimage" through Latin America in the late 1920s,
Albizu became even more committed to Puerto Rican independence.[138] He
was elected president of the Nationalist Party on May 11, 1930.

One of his first tasks, in late 1930, was that of mounting a challenge to US
national iconography on currency, through a series of Puerto Rican Nationalist bonds. The bonds, of course, had a practical purpose. The Nationalist
Party needed money, and people buying bonds would fund the independence
movement.[139] However, just as the US federal government viewed money as

FIGURE 3.5. One-peso Puerto Rican Nationalist bond featuring portrait of Francisco Ramírez, issued 1930. Photo by El Alternativo.

an opportunity to spread national iconography, the Nationalist Party, too, went beyond printing simple bond certificates bearing only their denominations. It decided to place Puerto Rican national figures—heroes of the independence movement—on these bonds, creating a kind of counter currency that challenged the primacy of US national iconography on money.

The Nationalist Party printed five denominations: the one-peso bond note had a portrait of Francisco Ramírez, the first president of the Republic of Lares in 1868 (figure 3.5). Mariana Bracetti, the woman who had sewn the flag used in the Lares Revolution of 1868, appeared on the five-peso note. The revolutionaries José de Diego and Ramón Emeterio Betances, regarded as fathers of Puerto Rican independence, appeared on the ten-peso and fifty-peso, respectively. And the independence advocate Eugenio María de Hostos graced the one-hundred-peso note. The text on the bonds referred to an already-existing independent "República de Puerto Rico" in its sixty-third year—dating from the 1868 Grito de Lares. Each note also contained the signature of Pedro Albizu Campos as "presidente."[140]

Monetarily speaking, the bonds were a failure. Sales lagged, and very few bonds were sold, especially of the higher denominations.[141] But, like US money, the Puerto Rican Nationalist bonds operated on two levels: monetary and symbolic. The Nationalist Party may not have raised much money, but it was able to distribute a fair number of the different denominations of bonds among people it trusted throughout the island. Symbolically, the bonds were a significant challenge to the primacy of US national iconography on currency established in the early twentieth century. The legal currency, including bonds, produced by the US Treasury for circulation in Puerto Rico featured portraits of people like Thomas Jefferson, Andrew Jackson, and Abraham Lincoln. The Puerto Rican Nationalist bonds envisioned an alternate set of nationally symbolic objects, in which currency in Puerto Rico was produced by an independent Republic of Puerto Rico and contained Puerto Rican national iconography.

No symbolic object was more important to the Nationalist Party than the Puerto Rican flag. In 1932, pro-statehood Puerto Ricans in the Senate challenged the Nationalist Party by attempting, as US colonial governments in Hawaiʻi and the Philippines had done, to co-opt the Puerto Rican flag and make it the official flag of the US colonial government.[142] On April 16, 1932, the Legislative Assembly was considering that law on the same day as the Nationalist Party was celebrating the anniversary of José de Diego's birth in San Juan. When Albizu learned of the legislation, he claimed that he and the other Nationalists "immediately saw that what they were trying to do was snatch from Puerto Rico the symbol of its independence, to snatch the flag from the mind and the heart."[143]

Albizu ended his speech with an exhortation against the law, and proceeded to lead the crowd of hundreds of protesters to the Capitol, shouting "Long live the Republic! Down with the bandits!" The crowd rushed past the police stationed at the Capitol. The police pushed back. Amid the chaos, the handrail on a staircase broke and a high school student named Manuel Rafael Suárez Díaz died.[144] The bill did not pass. And at a small tobacco shop in Mayagüez, a woman named Dominga de la Cruz Becerril read about Albizu's efforts to save the Puerto Rican flag from colonial co-optation, and was inspired to join the Puerto Rican Nationalist Party.[145]

A Flag off Every Schoolhouse

In 1934 President Franklin D. Roosevelt appointed Blanton Winship governor of Puerto Rico. Former adjutant general of the War Department, Winship was the first governor from a military background appointed to Puerto Rico since the transition to civil government in 1900. Most Puerto Ricans, suffering in the Great Depression, had been hoping for a New Deal reformer who would bring economic recovery to the island. Winship's goal, however, was to destroy the Nationalist Party.[146]

Conflict began in 1935. First, symbolically on the Fourth of July, Puerto Rican Nationalists bombed US government buildings where the US flag flew:

the Puerto Rican Reconstruction Administration office in Old San Juan, the US Court Building at Puerta de Tierra, a telephone building in San Juan, and an island police station in Barrio Obrero.[147] No one was harmed in the bombings. Conflict continued on October 24, 1935, at the Río Piedras campus of the University of Puerto Rico, where tensions were rising between students on campus who supported the US-appointed chancellor and those who supported the Nationalist Party. During this conflict, police shot and killed four Nationalists as they approached the campus in their car. The police were never held responsible for their actions.[148] To hold police accountable for what became known as the Río Piedras Massacre, two Nationalists, Elías Beauchamp and Hiram Rosado, assassinated Police Chief Colonel E. Francis Riggs on February 23, 1936. Beauchamp and Rosado were killed while in police custody, never taken to trial for the assassination.[149] On April 3, Albizu and several other Nationalist Party leaders were arrested and charged with conspiracy to overthrow the US colonial government in Puerto Rico.[150] Albizu was imprisoned in Atlanta until 1943.

The assassination of Riggs prompted the introduction of Puerto Rican independence legislation for the first time. On April 23, 1936, US Senator Millard Tydings of Maryland, a personal friend of the deceased Riggs, introduced the independence legislation in Congress, but on harsh terms, including almost no transition aid and an immediate 25 percent tariff on all goods exported from Puerto Rico to the continental United States.[151] He made it clear that the harsh terms for independence were revenge for Riggs's assassination.[152]

Pro-statehood Puerto Ricans vehemently opposed the bill. The resident commissioner from Puerto Rico in US Congress, Santiago Iglesias, claimed that "independence, as it has been offered," meant that "the great American Government would ask our people to commit suicide." Iglesias downplayed the actions of Nationalists, claiming they were a minority jeopardizing the rights of the majority who wanted a permanent union with the United States.[153] The Tydings Bill led many Nationalists to believe that the independence they had sought for so long was a foregone conclusion.[154] So, while their leader, Albizu, was imprisoned, they took further action. On the day the Tydings independence bill was introduced in Congress, students at San Juan's Central High School—the same school that had insisted on having the Puerto Rican flag at its graduation in 1922—lowered the US flag and raised the Puerto Rican flag in its place.[155] It was the first time the Puerto Rican flag had flown alone on a schoolhouse since the GAR's arrival with US flags in 1898. From Central High, these actions spread throughout the island. On May 1, Nationalists raised the Puerto Rican flag over schools in Ponce, as well as City Hall and other public buildings in the city. The demonstrators also removed prominent pictures of President Roosevelt and former US President Herbert Hoover.[156]

On May 2, 1936, José Padín, acting as governor in Winship's absence, declared that "over the island's public buildings no one has the right to hoist any other flag but that of the United States of America," and that "any substitution made for that flag, no matter how respectable the substitute, must necessarily be interpreted as a challenge to the sovereignty of the United States." Padín gave the Nationalists the benefit of the doubt, saying that their flag raisings were simply a "product of the prevailing excitement" over the prospect of independence. However, he was clear: "It is my duty to warn all that the government will employ all the means at its disposal to offer the flag of the United States and its institutions the full guarantee and consideration they deserve."[157] Padín's stern declaration did not halt the demonstrations. In fact, things escalated from there.

On the night of May 12, 1936, after letting the Puerto Rican flag fly for almost three weeks, the principal of Central High School, George Audas, decided that it should come down. Night students emerged from the school building to find "a single-starred Puerto Rican flag in the dust at the foot of the flagpole." The students reacted strongly; the press reported that they wrecked classrooms, broke ink bottles, and smashed windows and furniture. Joined by other protesters, they then marched to La Fortaleza, the governor's residence, and booed Winship, taunting him by raising a Puerto Rican flag on a stick just outside his window.[158]

The next morning, May 13, instead of going to school, Central High students marched through the streets, spreading their protest to other schools. At Pedro Goyco, a large grade school in San Juan, older students entered the classrooms, tore down the US flags, and, according to some eyewitnesses, trampled them. The Puerto Rican flag was even raised over City Hall and schools near Guánica, where the first US troops had planted their flag during the war against Spain in 1898.[159]

Meanwhile, back at Central High, students had once again raised the Puerto Rican flag. Winship, who had been watching all this unfold, was enraged. He turned to the interim police chief and barked, "Go out and pull that down!" In fact, the police had made no efforts to tear down the Puerto Rican flags; they were still without a chief after Riggs's assassination. And the students were a force to be reckoned with; they had vowed they would defend the Puerto Rican flag with their lives.[160]

Winship called in the Puerto Rico National Guard to put down the student protests.[161] On May 14, with the National Guard policing the schools—two decades before the Arkansas National Guard would be deployed to schools in Little Rock, Arkansas, to enforce integration—San Juan's schools reopened without incident. What one continental journalist had called "Puerto Rico's 'one-day revolution'" was over.[162]

As the dust settled, people began to try to make sense of the events. Winship, for his part, refused to acknowledge that this had been a genuine uprising of students who wanted independence. Instead, he told the press that "an irresponsible group composed mostly of all full grown men not connected with the public schools and some undisciplined students have perpetrated a series of acts of sabotage that have brought alarm to the community and aroused the indignation of many persons who love order and prize our reputation as a civilized people."[163] An editorial in the Puerto Rican newspaper *El País* warned that the demonstrations perhaps had hurt the independence movement: "Such violence as yesterday's will be used here and elsewhere as an argument against Puerto Rico's capacity for self-government."[164] Puerto Rico Supreme Court Justice Félix Córdova Dávila, who a decade before had fought in US Congress for the removal of Governor Reily for his comments against the Puerto Rican flag, agreed: "Demagogy and anarchy never achieved the happiness of any people."[165] Luis Muñoz Marín, at the time a Puerto Rican senator, took a different view, blaming the Tydings Bill and the United States more generally for the disorder: "The offering of an independence measure filled with injustices puts the responsibility for any collective tragedy that may occur in Puerto Rico squarely on the shoulders of the United States."[166]

A *New York Times* writer got at the heart of the problem: that the promises of what would follow the US flag to Puerto Rico remained unfulfilled. "In a few weeks it will be thirty-eight years since US troops landed in Puerto Rico," he wrote, saying that early on "it was found, much to island disappointment, that the flag didn't bring American citizenship." After gaining citizenship in 1917, he wrote, Puerto Ricans had "found that citizenship did not bring the Constitution." Thus, he added, "Puerto Rico finds that its future remains uncertain. Resurgent nationalism is the outstanding political consequence of this continued uncertainty."[167] In other words, the failure of the US flag to live up to its promises had led Puerto Rican students to directly challenge the US flag's place in Puerto Rico.

The *Listin Diario*, a Dominican newspaper, agreed, writing that it did not find the resistance surprising because "to live without a flag results in an authentic anachronism in the full 20th century."[168] The Dominican Republic's former secretary of state for education and fine arts wrote that Dominicans were "amazed to not hear Spanish songs in many rural schools" in Puerto Rico. They "noted the silence of national episodes from the humble lecture-halls of the very young to the university chair." Americanization had removed those things from Puerto Rican education, but there were consequences: "For this reason the students who did not receive civic nourishment in the planned lesson, missed in the lecture-halls, now seize the nationalist flag of Puerto Rico and nail it to the flag-staff in a flight of retribution. It was because they received, outside of the official atmosphere of studies, the teaching that makes men, the lesson that boring into the minds, makes resurrections of citizenry."[169] Once the contradictions of colonial education were laid bare, anticolonial education easily took hold.

In Puerto Rico, students were at the forefront of challenges to the US flag because they had been at the forefront of the early Americanization efforts to spread that flag. They had been the ones forced to raise the US flag every morning, hold their hands over their hearts as they recited the Pledge of Allegiance, and learn about the sacred meaning of the Stars and Stripes. This type of education left no room for the Puerto Rican flag, which, because of its history before US colonial rule, was hugely important to many people. The spread of US flag veneration had been remarkably successful in Puerto Rico, and so the reaction against it was equally intense.

Instead of acknowledging these grievances, Winship opted for a crackdown. On May 15 he issued a stern declaration to all mayors, judges, prosecuting attorneys, and police chiefs in Puerto Rico, demanding prosecution of those who desecrated the US flag. He wrote that they, "as agents of the law, [were] expected to take immediate action against such violators," and that as governor he would "employ the forces at my command to the limit necessary to protect children, women and all other citizens abiding by the law." Winship also signed a new bill into law that would require all government employees and officials to take an oath of allegiance to the United States, its Constitution, and the laws of Puerto Rico.[170]

In this tense environment, Winship insisted, perhaps more vehemently than ever, that patriotic rituals continue. He wrote to Ernest Gruening, the director of the Division of Territories and Island Possessions (the United States' colonial office, in effect), that "in view of recent events and corresponding press comments about conditions in the Island, the coming Fourth of July celebration should have unprecedented prominence." He wanted the festivities to leave "a very good impression on the Continent" and "show conclusively that the majority of Puerto Ricans are eager to demonstrate their allegiance to the flag and to the institutions of our country." Winship hoped that the so-called "exaggerated newspaper versions" in the continental United States about the student flag protests would "be upset by the evidence of loyalty to the United States expected on July 4th."[171]

The resulting parade was pure Americana: Puerto Rican veterans, Insular Police, the American Legion, and others marched through San Juan carrying US flags. Floats covered in Stars and Stripes carried people dressed as US national heroes—one George Washington on a white steed, another George Washington crossing the Delaware with his Revolutionary troops, Betsy Ross sewing the US flag.[172] Winship stood atop the reviewing stand, surrounded by US flags, and gave a speech proclaiming that Puerto Ricans and continental US citizens had "been united for many years, under one flag, by the bonds of a common citizenship. We are Americans."[173] Winship's new chief of police, Colonel Enrique Oberta, had declared that he would "shoot down anyone who dared demonstrate for independence."[174] There was not a Puerto Rican flag in sight.

According to Winship, "the parade was a tremendous success, attended by many thousands of people, who as the ceremonies progressed gained confidence in the situation and became more and more enthusiastic."[175] His message reached the continental press; the New York Times reported that this Fourth of July gave an "opportunity to those who opposed island independence a chance to demonstrate their feelings." And that "despite the opposition propaganda against the day's celebration," it had "turned out to be the biggest since the American occupation in 1898."[176]

Whatever good feelings were created by the 1936 Fourth of July celebrations were lost the next year. Winship's crackdown continued, reaching its violent culmination on Palm Sunday, March 21, 1937. On that day, Nationalists planned a parade both to commemorate the anniversary of the abolition of slavery in Puerto Rico in 1873 and to demonstrate against Albizu's continued imprisonment. Dominga de la Cruz Becerril, the woman who had joined the Nationalist Party after reading about Albizu's 1932 protest against the colonial co-optation of the flag, had by this point risen to become head of the women's chapter of the Nationalist Party in Mayagüez. She traveled to Ponce to take part in the demonstrations. Police had initially authorized the parade that day in Ponce, and then had revoked the permit at the last minute. Organizers resolved to continue the march as planned. Male organizers tried to exclude women from the march, given the increased risk of violence in marching without a permit, but de la Cruz and the other Nationalist women refused to sit on the sidelines.[177]

De la Cruz remembered that on that day, the Ponce Cadets led the march, with the Mayagüez Cadets close behind, "all of them, waving their [Puerto Rican] flags." The band struck up Puerto Rico's national anthem, "La Borinqueña," and as they began to march, police opened fire on the crowd, killing eighteen. While trying to flee the chaos, de la Cruz noticed that one of the women carrying a Puerto Rican flag had been wounded, and that the flag she carried was headed for the ground. "This could not be," de la Cruz recalled thinking in that moment. "Don Pedro [Albizu] had said, 'The flag must never touch the ground.'" De la Cruz ran toward the flag, rescuing it from falling to the ground, and then carrying it to a nearby house where she and others sought shelter from the violence. Police arrested de la Cruz there, and she became widely regarded as a heroine of the Nationalist Party for rescuing the Puerto Rican flag that day.[178]

Winship, who had ordered the police to respond to Nationalists harshly, was largely blamed for what became known as the Ponce Massacre.[179] Letters from Puerto Rico flooded into the federal government asking officials to condemn the massacre, remove Winship, punish the Ponce police, and even release Albizu from prison. People in the continental United States, too, began to take notice of Winship's harsh policies, and asked whether they fit with US values. In an article titled "Have We Forgotten 1776?" the *New York Post* reminded US Americans of their own anticolonial fight: "If Puerto Rico wants freedom, our answer should be to grant it. Reply by machine gun is unworthy of a people that cherishes memories of its own 'seditious' nationalists in 1776."[180]

After the Ponce Massacre, Winship was largely discredited and seen as a tyrant, even by those in the US federal government.[181] Undeterred, Winship doubled down on flag supremacy again for Occupation Day in 1938—the fortieth anniversary of US troops landing in Puerto Rico on July 25, 1898. While Occupation Day festivities usually took place in San Juan, Winship brazenly decided to hold them in Ponce. As on the Fourth of July in 1936, he hoped the celebration would demonstrate the success of his campaign to suppress nationalism and restore law and order in Puerto Rico. Winship reenacted the raising of the first US flag in Ponce forty years earlier in 1898—a stern message to those who questioned its place in Puerto Rico, and a clear indication that he felt no remorse about the massacre.

Everything seemed to be going according to plan. Forty thousand people showed up for the celebration, and the press reported that ten thousand US flags filled the city.[182] But as Winship prepared to give his speech, bullets flew at the reviewing stand. The assassination attempt was unsuccessful, and Winship was unscathed, but thirty-six people were wounded, including several government officials. Two people, both Puerto Rican, died: Luis Irizarry, a National Guard colonel who had been standing next to Winship, and Ángel Esteban Antongiorgi, a Nationalist shooter.[183] Winship exclaimed, "What damn poor shots they are!" and continued with his speech as though nothing had happened. He did not change his remarks, which opened with a declaration: "President Roosevelt and millions of your other fellow-American citizens in the United States are most happy to be reminded that the Puerto Rican people have seen fit to celebrate so enthusiastically the fortieth anniversary of the arrival of the American flag on these shores." But his planned remarks included a warning to those who challenged the supremacy of the US flag in Puerto Rico: "It is highly important to the future of Puerto Rico . . . that the people of Puerto Rico do nothing to cast doubt on the unquestionable fact that the island as a whole is decidedly loyal to the United States Government and the American flag."[184]

The two surviving shooters later charged with Winship's attempted assassination, Tomas Lopez de Victoria and Elifaz Escobar, had both participated in the Ponce parade that had turned into a massacre the previous year.[185] Their bullets had left five holes in the US flag that the First Battalion of the Sixty-Fifth US Infantry was carrying in Winship's Occupation Day parade.[186]

The Winship administration's efforts to instill US flag supremacy in Puerto Rico continued. In May 1939 he declared a "National Flag Week," and encouraged "the people of Puerto Rico to show our love of our country, our pride in its glorious history, our elation in its magnificent achievements, and our belief in the fulfillment of its destiny, by flying the Stars and Stripes at their homes and other suitable places, as well as on their cars, and holding in every community special exercises at which they shall renew their allegiance to the ideals symbolized by our Flag." He asked people generally to "give grateful expression to their good fortune to be living under the protecting folds of 'Old Glory' in these troublous times of racial and religious intolerance, aggression and greed, strife and violence."[187]

Throughout the year, Winship's commissioner of education led a campaign "to create flag consciousness in the minds of school children," which would include a prize for the best essays on the subjects "What Americanism Means to Me" and "What Americanism Means to Puerto Rico." And in response to reports that "the custom of saluting the American flag and the singing of hymns is no longer followed in our schools, the Commissioner announced that he planned to redouble efforts to ensure that the Pledge of Allegiance was recited every day during opening exercises."[188] Pro-US Senator Celestino Iriarte, who back in 1932 had proposed the law that would make the Puerto Rican flag the official flag of the colonial government, told the press he believed that doubling down on the practice of saluting the US flag regularly would be "the best way of familiarizing the people with the supreme symbol of the country."[189] At the Fourth of July parade in 1939, its official US flag, which normally contained forty-eight stars, bore an additional forty-ninth star in gold, symbolizing hope for Puerto Rican statehood.[190] But the colonial government skipped the official Occupation Day celebration that year, fearing that the violence of 1938 might be repeated.[191]

Toward the end of the decade, things were shifting in Puerto Rico. As the threat of war grew, so did the United States' urgency for Caribbean bases. Puerto Rico became a strategic location in the Caribbean, just as before World War I.[192] And just as Wilson had warned during World War I, nationalist resistance there could make the United States look bad on the international stage. In February 1939, *Das Schwarze Korps*—the official propaganda organ of the Nazi Schutzstaffel (SS)—accused the Winship regime of using Soviet-style repression on Puerto Ricans—citing the 1937 Ponce Massacre as evidence.[193] President Roosevelt wanted above all to build bases on Puerto Rico. And that's what finally led to the ousting of Winship in June 1939. By the time Winship left office, war already covered the front pages of Puerto Rican newspapers, and warships and military planes were becoming commonplace sights.[194] Under the new governorship of Admiral William Leahy, Puerto Rico experienced a huge military buildup: the expansion of Fort Buchanan, the fortification of El Morro and Borinquen Field, and base construction at Isla Grande.[195] Leahy did not face the same challenges Winship had—partly because of his character, and partly because, as he wrote in his diary, "the world has changed in the last three months," and people now understood that the "liberty of Puerto Rico is now bound up in the liberty of the whole of America."[196] In November 1938 the journalist Ruby Black had written to Muna Lee, Luis Muñoz Marín's wife, that in this new environment, and given "the present international situation," Puerto Rico was more important than ever to protecting the Panama Canal, and Congress would not consider granting independence.[197]

Luis Muñoz Marín, until now a prominent independence supporter, was also changing his tune, just as he and his Popular Democratic Party were coming to power in Puerto Rico, filling a power vacuum left behind by the collapse of the *Coalición* of pro-statehood politicians. Muñoz claimed that his change of heart had come after he realized independence would not bring about social justice for working-class Puerto Ricans. And because he believed in the US war effort, he saw no reason for the cause of independence to bring international embarrassment to the United States during the war. Muñoz Marín publicized his new support for the president at "Roosevelt Day," standing beside a little Puerto Rican boy dressed as Uncle Sam.[198] With Nationalist leaders like Albizu imprisoned, and former independence supporters like Muñoz Marín supporting the United States, resistance to Americanization in Puerto Rico would be put on pause during World War II.

Preparing for War

As the threat of war loomed, unwavering loyalty to the US flag became paramount across the US colonial empire. In the US Virgin Islands, where the promises of Americanization had already shown themselves to be empty, many people had become disillusioned with US rule in the 1930s. But in 1941 a St. Thomas newspaper reminded people, "It is very important for us, as loyal American citizens, to show in a visual manner the deep feeling, and abiding faith we have in the American Government." The "visual manner," it said, was flag veneration, as "the Flag of the United States is the outward, visible symbol of a type of government which is based on spiritual values, equality, justice, truth, and faith."[199] On February 1, 1939, when people on Guam celebrated the fortieth anniversary of the first raising of the US flag over their island, B. J. Bordallo, chairman of the House Council of the Guam Congress, argued that with war on the horizon, "we owe that flag our full allegiance and all that it implies. I mean, our loyalty, our faith in the invincibility of the nation which that flag represents."[200]

But while the 1920s and 1930s had been marked by nationalist challenges to the US flag in Puerto Rico, a new threat to the supremacy of that flag in US Pacific colonies was emerging in this period: the Japanese empire. For decades, US officials had worried about Japan's imperial ambitions and its willingness to support independence movements in the region.[201] On January 31, 1921, the Japanese steamer *Shinyo Maru* had entered Manila Harbor flying Japanese and Philippine flags—but no US flag. Although displaying the Philippine flag without the US flag was illegal on land, authorities in the Philippines were not able to act on this, as it was only "regarded as a discourtesy."[202] In January 1935, Japanese fishing boats in Occidental Negros, Philippines, actually started flying the Philippine flag underneath the *Japanese* flag.

Local businessmen in Davao reportedly "resent[ed] the discarding of the American flag" and considered the positioning of the Philippine flag below the Japanese "insulting." The act, in their estimation, constituted "a presumptuous anticipation of what the Japanese expect to happen to the Philippines if the United States or the Filipinos allow the state of affairs in Davao to develop to their logical consequences." The smallness of the Philippine flag compared to the Japanese, they believed, was meant to indicate "the smallness and helplessness of the Philippines in comparison to the powerful Japanese empire."[203]

At the time, the Japanese empire was rapidly expanding its holdings in the Pacific, surrounding US possessions like Guam and the Philippines. The *Philippine Herald* reported the next day that Atsushi Kimura, the Japanese consul general, said the violation by Japanese fishing boats was unintentional, and that he would prepare a circular explaining the proper use of flags.[204]

Things returned to normal for the time being, but the incident led the *Philippine Herald* to ask an ominous question: "Has the Japanese flag replaced the American flag in the Philippines?"[205]

The Object(s) of Occupation

In 1939, people on Guam commemorated the fortieth anniversary of the first official raising of the US flag. That same year, W. B. Courtney, a correspondent for *Collier's* magazine, traveled to the small island to report back to the continental United States on its Pacific colony. The article included a few basic facts, since most of his continental audience would have been unfamiliar with Guam. As Courtney put it, if you "have a fairish idea of where it is you are one up on at least 99¾ out of every 100 of your fellow Americans." Even with the advent of air travel it took four days to reach Guam, which, Courtney told readers, lay thirteen degrees north of the equator, 3,337 miles west of Honolulu, and 1,500 miles east of Manila.[1] But despite the distance, "you come to earth again in a territory under the same flag."[2] Not only was Guam a US territory under the US flag, but it was the site of a most impressive patriotic display. Like continental journalists who had traveled to the island before him, Courtney was stunned to witness the impressive routine of flag veneration on Guam. Every single school day, all the children of the capital city of Hagåtña—more than one thousand of them—gathered in front of the Governor's Palace, raised the US flag, recited the Pledge of Allegiance, and sang the "Star Spangled Banner."[3] Courtney noted, however, that as Hagåtña's children conducted their routine flag veneration, "there is a little catch in their voices these days, for they know the talk that goes on around oil lamps in the evenings."[4] And the image on the first page of the article showed why. The caption read: "Tiny Guam . . . lies in the midst of Japan's far-flung string of mandated islands."[5]

Spain had ceded Guam, the southernmost island in the Mariana Islands archipelago, to the United States after the 1898 war, but sold the rest of the Marianas to Germany, which the League of Nations transferred to Japan as

part of the South Seas Mandate following World War I. This series of unre-
lated interimperial arrangements resulted in the Marianas archipelago and
their indigenous CHamoru inhabitants being divided between Japanese and
US territory.⁶ Since World War I, the flag of the Rising Sun had flown less
than fifty miles from the Stars and Stripes, and with the rapid expansion of
the Japanese empire, US sovereignty over its Pacific colonies was no longer
a given. As Courtney's airplane took off from Guam in early 1939, he wrote:
"You leave Guam at sunrise color and when you look back regretfully upon
its morning peacefulness you find another phrase belling in your mind: 'The
Rising Sun.'"⁷

While people on Guam dutifully pledged their allegiance to the US flag,
they also had a keen understanding of how people in the continental United
States viewed their island—an unincorporated territory neither foreign nor
domestic.⁸ As one CHamoru man told Courtney, "It is not probable that you
would give Ohio to Japan in order to avoid war, but we are a remote little
chick far away from the shelter of its mother's wing and can see the hawk's
shadow. Washington politics might very well lead you sometime to let us slip
in order to avoid general bloodspilling."⁹ While both Guam and Ohio were
under the US flag, the difference, this CHamoru man knew, was perception.
People from the continental United States knew that Ohio was part of the
United States. They thought of the people there as fellow "Americans." The
same could not be said for Guam. No matter how fervently they performed
patriotic rituals—and by all accounts people on Guam performed them
more fervently than anyone else—Guam would never seem as "American" as
Ohio to most US citizens. This man knew that when push came to shove, the
United States would privilege the continent over the colonies.

Those in charge of "Washington politics" did hear this CHamoru man's
words; the entire *Collier's* article was entered into the congressional record by
an Ohio representative who wanted his fellow Congress members to have "a
picture of a paradise caught in the path of a juggernaut."¹⁰ Yet just as the CHamoru man predicted, the United States would indeed let Guam—along with the
Philippines, Wake Island, and even parts of Alaska's Aleutian Islands—"slip"
to Japanese occupation during World War II. There, the flag of the Rising Sun
replaced the Stars and Stripes, "Kimigayo" ("His Imperial Majesty's Reign")
replaced the "Star-Spangled Banner," and "Japanese Military Government" replaced "United States of America" on people's money and stamps.

This chapter uses this nationally symbolic material culture to think
through the experience of people in US colonies who lived under Japanese
occupation during World War II. Both the US and Japanese empires deployed symbolic objects in their efforts to colonize the Pacific; indeed, this

chapter reveals surprising similarities in their approaches. And while each imperial power had the brute force strength to dictate how people interacted with said objects in public spaces, neither could dictate what meanings people would attach to those objects or how their meanings might change over time. Drawing on firsthand accounts from CHamorus and Filipinos, official sources—both military and civilian—from Japan and the United States, and close readings of the symbolic objects themselves, we see that examining the brief period of Japanese imperialism in these colonies actually deepens our understanding of US imperialism. Under Japanese occupation—or the threat thereof—US symbols that had faded into the background of daily life over the previous four decades suddenly occupied center stage, and activities that had been completely mundane suddenly became charged with meaning. Before the war, pledging allegiance to the US flag had been a matter of routine. During the war, it could get one killed. As the CHamoru scholar Keith Camacho has argued, "The war now required Chamorros to contemplate, if not openly accept or resist, their loyalty to their colonizers," both US and Japanese.[11]

As we have seen, in the decades since the United States claimed Pacific colonies, US imperialists—officials and nonstate actors alike—had invested an incredible amount of time, energy, and resources into the process they called "Americanization." Rather than mere stepping-stones to Asia, US officials wanted these spaces to resemble the continental United States, and the people there to resemble their idea of "Americans." We have seen how the proliferation of US national symbols on flags, stamps, and currency was central to these Americanization efforts. Colonial officials believed that a US flag in the public square or George Washington's visage on a piece of money could be a visible, tangible, and consistent reminder that, regardless of legal and political status, these places were part of the United States. Not all colonial inhabitants accepted these symbolic objects and the messages US imperialists claimed they carried. And we have seen that, when faced with challenges, US imperialists were willing to use coercion and violence to uphold the symbolic supremacy of US national iconography in the colonies.

But not all colonial inhabitants rejected US national symbols. After decades of living with them, some (not unlike people in the continental United States who lived with the same symbols) had begun to feel that the US flag was their flag, that the "Star-Spangled Banner" was their national anthem, and that, despite their legal status, they too were "Americans."[12] On February 1, 1939, two months before the publication of the *Collier's* piece, people on Guam celebrated the fortieth anniversary of the first raising of the US flag there. On that occasion, the CHamoru politician B. J. Bordallo delivered a passionate address about the meaning of the flag on Guam. He talked about how it had brought material comforts, security, and national tranquility to the island. And while he acknowledged that the United States had not yet granted Guam "full adoption under the 'Stars and Stripes' thus assuring us the privilege to enjoy equal opportunities, equal rights, and equal protection," he still believed that the people of Guam, "owe that flag our full allegiance . . . our loyalty, our faith in the invincibility of the nation which that flag represents." Well aware of the threat US sovereignty on Guam faced from the expanding Japanese empire, Bordallo ominously proclaimed, "Our welfare and future security depends entirely upon the time that that flag shall remain with us."[13]

The US naval governor praised the speech, but said, "I regret very much that only a few Americans are here to witness this and other patriotic exercises."[14] Perhaps the governor hoped that if more people from the continental United States knew of the US patriotism on Guam, they would think of the people there as part of the national community, and thus worthy of protection from Japan. But even his statement that "only a few Americans" were in attendance shows that he, too, did not truly think of people from Guam as "Americans." In their accounts of World War II, many scholars have followed suit.

Though not often named as such, US territories have consistently featured prominently in mainstream US narratives about World War II, from the attack on Pearl Harbor to the Battles of Manila, Midway, and Wake. While these narratives have traditionally portrayed the Pacific theater as conflict between a nation-state and an empire, more recent work insists we recognize this as an interimperial conflict in which both the Japanese and the US empires sought to maintain and expand their colonial holdings in the region.[15] While there is much to be said about the battles that took place on these islands, following material objects rather than military strategy reveals something different: namely, what everyday life was like in US colonies under Japanese occupation. And as the Philippine scholar Genevieve Clutario has argued, examining people's everyday lives under occupation "can help us think anew life under overlapping empires."[16] It helps us better understand the experiences of the Filipinos, CHamorus, and Hawaiians who had been told for decades that they were Americans, but who during the war suddenly faced the fear or reality of the United States abandoning them to Japanese occupation.

Much of this chapter focuses on the experiences of people in the Philippines and Guam. World War II was and remains a defining moment in the history and historiography of both places, but they are rarely discussed in tandem despite being the only inhabited US colonies to come under foreign occupation. Telling their stories together helps us better understand the extent of Americanization in each place, specifically how deeply US symbols had or had not penetrated the people's sense of themselves and their place in the world. In the Philippines, responses to Japanese occupation ranged from those of people who decided to work with the new Japanese regime, and those of people who hid their US flags from sight but outwardly performed loyalty to Japan, to those of people who took up arms against the Japanese occupation. On Guam, a smaller island where armed resistance was less feasible for most of the war, CHamorus largely went along with Japanese occupation in public, while some people's private actions revealed an abiding loyalty to the United States and its symbols.[17]

As the Rising Sun replaced the Stars and Stripes in Pacific US colonies, people who had been told for decades that they should imagine themselves as part of the "Greater United States" were now told they should imagine themselves as part of the "Greater East Asia Co-Prosperity Sphere"—Japan's vision for a new regional order.[18] The United States had called its own idea Americanization. This was Japanization—another diffuse set of policies and practices, including language education, holidays, national symbols, and patriotic routines that, as the Japanese historian Wakako Higuchi has argued, were intended to make people within Japan and its expanding empire "something like Japanese."[19]

There was lack of clarity among Japanese officials about whether the Greater East Asia Co-Prosperity Sphere was an economic bloc, a slogan for Japanese imperialism, an expression of Pan-Asianism, or all or none of the above. But as the war advanced, the historian Jeremy Yellen argues, "visions of order followed the Rising Sun battle flag."[20] Japan's exact aims for its new regional order remained in flux, but one goal was crystal clear: that of eliminating all US influence in the Pacific and Southeast Asia.[21] The new Japanese symbols colonial subjects encountered became consistent reminders that their status as "Americans" had been conditional. They were forced to face the limits of US power and the limits of their inclusion in an imagined US national community. This shattered the view US colonial officials had promoted since the turn of the twentieth century that the Philippines and Guam were inextricably linked to the United States. And although Japanese troops never invaded the Hawaiian Islands, the symbolic changes made to currency there under martial law showed that the Hawaiians' inclusion in the US national community was conditional, too.

For both the United States and Japan, producing and spreading symbolic objects while prohibiting and policing the use of the other imperial power's emblems required a lot of work. Yet even in the midst of total war, governments and officials were willing to invest money and manpower into these objects. Compared to other events that took place between 1941 and 1945, symbolic objects might seem inconsequential. But we will see that both Japanese and US colonial officials and ordinary people caught between these empires decided they were willing to kill and die for these seemingly inconsequential objects. Under extreme conditions, people's willingness to risk their lives for these objects repeatedly affirmed the importance of these symbols both to establishing colonial order and to colonial inhabitants' own understanding of themselves and their place in the world.

The Rising Sun

On the morning of December 8, 1941 schoolchildren in the Philippines and Guam were in the middle of their US flag routines—reciting the Pledge of Allegiance and singing the "Star-Spangled Banner"—when they heard the news that, as one Filipina recalled in her memoir, "something happened in Hawaii."[22] That something (across the international date line, where it was still December 7) was the attack at Pearl Harbor, which, it soon became clear, was just the first attack in a strategic assault on the United States' Pacific empire. Within a few hours, Japan had launched attacks on the Philippines, Guam, Midway, and Wake. Two days later, on the morning of December 10, Japanese troops landed simultaneously in the Philippines and on Guam.

The Japanese forces' first action was the same as the one US troops had taken when they invaded the Spanish Filipinas and Guam in 1898: that of tearing down the flag of the former colonizer and raising their own flag in its place (figure 4.1). Indeed, flags were so important to signaling the change in sovereignty that immediately after communicating the news of the US surrender of Bataan, the Japanese consul's first command was "to rush ordering the Japanese flags."[23] Manila's *Tribune* ran photos of troops bringing in the Japanese flag and lowering the US flag with the caption: "Star-Spangled banner makes way for the Rising Sun."[24]

The US military had all but abandoned Guam and the Philippines before the invasion. And as Manuel Quezon, president of the US Commonwealth government of the Philippines, sat exiled on Corregidor in early 1942 while the Japanese flag flew over Manila, he was forced to reckon with the limits of the Philippines' inclusion in the US national community. After hearing President Roosevelt announce more military aid to fight Germany rather than Japan, Quezon erupted to General Douglas MacArthur's intelligence chief: "For thirty years, I have worked and hoped for my people. Now they burn and die for a flag that could not protect them. *Por Dios y todos los Santos*," he exclaimed, his Spanish expressions a reminder that Japan was the third colonial power to occupy the Philippines in his lifetime. "I cannot stand this constant reference to England, to Europe. . . . I am here and my people are here under

FIGURE 4.1. Raising the Japanese flag in the Philippines, 1942. Japanese Navy File / Filipinas Heritage Library. Compare to figure 1.1.

the heels of a conqueror. . . . *Que demonio*—how typically American to writhe in anguish at the fate of a distant cousin while a daughter is being raped in the back room."[25]

Given the many ills and injustices of US colonialism, and the United States' unwillingness to stay and defend the Philippines and Guam, Japanese officials were surprised to find that not only did people there not greet them as liberators, but some were even willing to lay down their lives to protect the US flag. In the Philippines, Japanese troops shot a high school principal, Buenaventura Bello, and left him for dead after he tried to stop Japanese soldiers from lowering the US flag at his school.[26] And on Guam, an Insular Guardsman, Angel Flores, lost his life trying to prevent Japanese troops from lowering the US flag in front of the Governor's Palace—at the same spot where more than a thousand schoolchildren gathered to raise the US flag every morning.[27] In that moment there was a powerful recognition from all sides—the Japanese troops who tore down the US flag and the CHamorus and Filipinos who died trying to prevent it from being torn down—that the flag was far more than just a piece of cloth.

After tearing down US flags and banning the Philippine flag as well, Japanese officials sought to cultivate negative associations with the Stars and Stripes.[28] Just five days after the invasion of Guam, Japanese officials held a "demonstration of the might of Japan" in the capital city of Hagåtña, which all

residents were required to attend. One teenager recalled that the festivities included target practice using the US flag.[29] Another early parade on Guam featured a float "showing a young nisei boy wearing a Japanese military uniform
and pointing a rifle at another boy dressed in American navy attire, with the
nisei youngster stepping on an American flag."[30] And in the Philippines, one
man recalled that when Japanese troops cleaned out the American Bazaar (an
early department store), they made a point of tearing a US flag to pieces and
using it to wipe the floor while Filipinos looked on, "angry and indignant, but
unable to do anything."[31]

The Japanese empire's stated policy was "to facilitate the organic integration of the entire region into the Japanese Empire."[32] And, like US colonial
officials who had taken over from Spain four decades before, Japanese officials believed that to achieve their goal, new colonial subjects would have
to be taught not just to loathe US national symbols but to revere Japanese
ones. So just as US imperialists had sought to make the Stars and Stripes and
routines of US flag veneration part of everyday life in their colonies in the
early twentieth century, Japanese officials wanted the Japanese flag and their
flag routines to become a part of everyday life in these new additions to their
Co-Prosperity Sphere.

Like Americanization before it, Japanization began in earnest in schools.
Unlike the US educators who only reached schoolchildren, however, Japanese
administrators required that all people from ten to sixty years of age attend
their weekly night schools.[33] Japanese officials scoured the textbooks in use in
the Philippines and Guam, and line by line they ordered the elimination of all
mentions of the US flag, lyrics of songs like "The Star-Spangled Banner" and
"America," and the seal of the US Commonwealth of the Philippines.[34] Even
arithmetic textbooks, the Filipino historian Teodoro Agoncillo recalled, were
not spared, since math problems denoted money in US currency.[35] The portraits of US national heroes like George Washington and Abraham Lincoln
that had once hung in Philippine classrooms were removed and destroyed.[36]
Where people in the Philippines and Guam had once raised the Stars and
Stripes, they now raised the flag of the Rising Sun. And instead of reciting the
Pledge of Allegiance, they now bowed in the direction of the Imperial Palace
in Tokyo and recited slogans like "We are children of the emperor, we'll do
our best to be loyal, and we will become splendid Japanese."[37] Many who were
children during the war remember being kicked, slapped, and beaten by their
Japanese teachers for not showing enough patriotism during these rituals.[38]

Japanese officials had another (literally) captive audience in the prisoner-
of-war camps. At Camp O'Donnell—the final destination of the infamous
Bataan Death March—Filipino prisoners of war participated in a daily flag

FIGURE 4.2. "Welcome Premier—Among the crowd of 100,000 that turned out yesterday to welcome Premier Gen. Hideki Tozyo of Japan were school children, right, and government employees, nurses, each carrying a small Rising Sun flag." *Manila Tribune*, May 6, 1943. National Library of Australia. Compare to figure 1.7.

ceremony at 8 a.m..[39] A Japanese journalist described the routine: "The flag ceremony begins with the boys going out to the grounds and bowing towards the direction of the Imperial Palace in Tokyo. They salute as the flag is being hoisted, and sing the . . . Nippon National Anthem." In the journalist's words, "This was made part of the daily program with the idea of inculcating in the prisoners of war the spirit of respect and amity for the leader nation of the Orient. They bow towards the Imperial Palace and sing the Kimigayo [national anthem], not as slaves and serfs, but as privileged members of the Greater East Asia Co Prosperity Sphere."[40] Just like US flag routines before them, these flag routines invited people in the Philippines and Guam to imagine themselves as part of a larger national-imperial community.

In addition to daily routines, on national holidays Japanese officials would require large public flag displays. For the 1943 anniversary of the fall of Bataan and Corregidor to Japan, Filipinos were given the day off work to join in a flag parade and celebration that became all the more important once officials learned that Japanese Prime Minister Hideki Tōjō would be in attendance. The Japanese consul gave specific instructions, requiring that "all residents along the streets he is expected to pass, greet him with the Japanese flags and shout 'Banzai,'" and that at Luneta Park in Manila—the same place US officials had hosted Fourth of July celebrations for decades—the "public assembled shall wave flags when the visitors arrive."[41] The Japanese government provided free flags in order to ensure that Tōjō would find Manila filled with the Rising Sun (figure 4.2). The official announcement of the holiday included the following orders: "I call upon all residents of Manila to display the Flag of the Rising Sun on May 5, 6, and 7, 1943 in their homes and offices in connection with these celebrations."[42] After the war, Jose B. Vargas, the Filipino official who had promulgated these orders, would be charged with treason by the US-Philippine Commonwealth Government for ordering Filipinos to "display the flag of the Rising Sun" on this and other occasions.[43]

Many people went along with the Japanese flag orders. Jose P. Laurel, soon to be president of the Second Philippine Republic under Japanese occupation, explained his reasons for praising the Japanese flag, stating in a speech during a celebration of the end of US rule that the Japanese flag was "a flag that should be venerated by all Filipinos since it symbolizes the unselfish attempt of a great Oriental people to liberate not only Filipinos but all other peoples of East Asia."[44] But not all compliant performance signified loyalty. As Keith Camacho has argued in the case of Guam, "Whenever possible, they resisted the policies by simply refusing to obey them. When there was no choice, many Chamorros honored the policies, such as bowing to Japanese officials, just so they could move on with their daily lives and familial obligations."[45] CHamorus also used sarcasm as a form of resistance.[46] For example, some CHamorus twisted the lyrics of a Japanese flag song. The original said, "The Japanese flag is pretty, its center red, its border white." Changing the word for "white," a'paka', to applacha' meant they sang that the flag was not red and white, but red and dirty. Japanese officials never caught on.[47]

These acts of resistance reveal some people's private feelings about the Japanese flag, but did not keep Japanese officials from accomplishing their goals. With a mixture of encouragement and coercion, like that of Americanization before it, symbolic Japanization was largely a success. In the Philippines and Guam, place names were a mixture of local, Spanish, and US American names. Under Japanese rule, the schools on Guam named after US naval governors all had their names changed. All fourteen villages on the island were given Japanese names, and even the name of the island itself was changed from Guam to Omiya Jima—Great Shrine Island.[48] In the Philippines, Dewey Boulevard became Heiwa Boulevard, Jones Bridge became Banzai Bridge, and by December 1942—one year after Japan invaded the Philippines—the Japanese had changed the names of 131 streets and roads, thirteen plazas and public parks, four bridges, eleven towns, and thirteen schools.[49]

Whether or not Japanese imperial officials had won the hearts and minds of their new colonial subjects, they had won the landscape. In their memoirs of the war years, many Filipinos recorded the shock they felt upon returning to familiar places and finding the Japanese flag flying where the US flag had once been (figure 4.3). One man traveling through Luzon in May 1942 remarked that from the bus he could see that "houses in the barrio were flying the Japanese flag. . . . The flag was flying on bridges and walls and even on the buses. . . . It seemed that my country was topsy-turvy." Everywhere he looked, he "saw the same picture—the same changes brought on by the War."[50]

FIGURE 4.3. The Japanese flag flying on Escolta Street, Manila, March 1942. American Historical Collection, Ateneo de Manila University. Compare to figure 1.8.

Pocket-Sized Imperialism

Pocket-sized objects were not spared in this transformation. In the first decade of US rule, colonial officials had created a system in which currency, stamps, and the iconography they carried became a tangible connection between the United States and its far-flung territories. On the eve of World War II, however, US government officials began to fear the economic consequences of Japan acquiring the large amounts of US currency held in the Philippines. US colonial officials decided that to prevent US currency "from falling into the hands of the enemy," they would destroy all US and US-Philippine money in the islands.[51]

US High Commissioner (the new title for the governor-general under the Commonwealth) Francis B. Sayre put the financial expert Woodbury Willoughby in charge of this task.[52] The Commonwealth government asked all people in the Philippines to turn in their currency, and planned to make "a careful record" of deposits; but Japan invaded sooner than expected. Treasury officials abandoned Manila, boxed up the remainder of the currency, and took refuge on the island of Corregidor with the rest of the government now in exile.[53] There, Willoughby and his associates "labored under great difficulties," counting and recording millions in paper currency all by hand— and, after shelling from Japanese troops took out the electricity, by lamplight as well.[54] Once it became clear they would have to abandon Corregidor before finishing their task, the team decided the best course of action would be to destroy the money immediately—despite knowing that "the owners in many cases would in all probability have difficulty after the war in establishing proof of their claims."[55] They radioed what information they were able to hastily gather to Washington, where officials in the US Division of Territories and Island Possessions were left to decipher the typo-ridden list. Officials tried to cross-reference misspelled names with the Manila directory, wondering if the name written as "Jessie Liceauco" was "maybe Jessie Lichauco, or possibly José M. Lichauco." They failed to cross-reference others, like "Edward Zfkng," which they thought was "probably garbled but correct name unknown."[56] Then, the Treasury officials began to prepare for a mass burning.[57]

On January 14, 1942, officials on Corregidor "opened all the trunks and boxes" of currency "and shoveled the bundles of bills into the furnace."[58] High Commissioner Sayre recalled that "five and ten and twenty and hundred dollar bills—were burned by the armful to the intense interest and wonderment of the soldiers standing by."[59] This would have been an extraordinary event to witness. There was nothing inherently valuable about these pieces of paper; money only holds value because governments say it does and enough people agree. But the subversion of the rules made the mass burning all the more thrilling. A reporter on site recalled that they "made a good lively fire, and with a big cast-iron hoe we stirred until the last well-thumbed dollar was gray ash."[60] One naval aide "got the thrill of his life by nonchalantly lighting his cigaret with a tightly rolled $100 bill."[61]

The mass burning took care of the paper currency on Corregidor, but the committee would have to find another way to dispose of the 350 tons of silver pesos stashed in wooden boxes weighing three hundred pounds apiece.[62] Officials decided to dump the sizeable fortune into Caballo Bay, an ideal location for two reasons: mountains would shield the activity from Japanese troops on Bataan, and the water was deep enough so that even if the Japanese did later learn of the plan, it would be difficult for them to retrieve the coins.[63] Over a span of ten nights, US ships carried the 350 tons of silver and, by moonlight, dumped them into the bay. Later in the war, three Filipino divers would die while following Japanese orders to retrieve the sunken treasure.[64]

Under US rule, money in the Philippines had provided a tangible symbolic connection between people in the Philippines and US sovereignty. Economic experts and local officials toiled tirelessly to make US-Philippine pesos the only legal circulating currency in the Philippines. The Philippine Commission had painstakingly pored over designs for US-Philippine coins that they felt would accurately reflect the sentiment that the future of the Philippines was inextricably linked to that of the United States.[65] In the 1920s, a US colonial governor had even taken on a Cabinet member in a fight to keep George Washington on Philippine money, because it was that important to US colonial rule in the Philippines.[66] Now, those coins with the US seal lay at the bottom of Caballo Bay, and Washington's portrait on the ten-peso bill had been reduced to ashes on Corregidor.

Whatever US currency did remain in circulation, Japanese officials banned in February 1942. They replaced US-Philippine pesos with a new currency backed by the Imperial Japanese government (figure 4.4), and noted: "All the people in the occupied areas should not only have full trust in their value but also cooperate in their smooth circulation." The message invited people to put their faith in Japanese currency, but a violent warning followed two weeks later: "Any person or individual refusing to receive . . . the aforesaid note or notes will be severely punished."[67]

With this new money, every transaction became a reminder that people in the Philippines were ruled by "THE JAPANESE GOVERNMENT." People were made to hold, carry, and feel this new money, now a tangible representation of Japanese imperial rule. That feeling prompted a response. The money, one Filipino recalled, "was printed on ordinary bond paper and had no value."[68] While no kind of paper is inherently more valuable than another, Filipinos had come to expect a certain quality from the US Bureau of Engraving and Printing that Japanese officials could not match. As they handled this money in their everyday lives, the poorer quality of the paper affected people's perceptions about its value. Filipinos often called Japanese currency "Mickey Mouse Money."[69] The nickname reveals much about Filipino perceptions of the worthlessness of Japanese money, and the prevalence of a US cultural phenomenon like Disney in the Philippines.

Japanese officials did not immediately introduce new postage stamps. Like US officials in 1898, they opted to overprint existing stamps. But while US officials imported and overprinted US stamps in 1898 for use in their new colonies, Japanese officials decided to overprint the existing stock of US-Philippine stamps in the Philippines.[70] Postal service in Manila reopened

FIGURE 4.4. Japanese occupation currency, 1942. National Numismatic Collection, National Museum of American History, Smithsonian Institution. Compare to figures 2.1, 2.9, and 2.11.

on March 4, 1942, with two stamps: the two-cent Rizal and the sixteen-cent "Magellan's Landing."[71] One stamp collector commented after the war on "how well the Japanese technical advisers to the Filipino postal authorities" did to choose these stamps in particular. He supposed their goal was to "strike a concordant note in the hearts of the people to honor once again their foremost national hero, Dr. Jose Rizal."[72] But the US-Philippine stamps now had black bars censoring the words "United States of America" and "Commonwealth." They no longer bore any trace of US sovereignty. Only when the overprint was incomplete or slightly off-center, like on the sixteen-centavo "Magellan's Landing" or the fifty-centavo "Barasoain Church" stamps pictured in figure 4.5, could people catch a glimpse of the words "United States of America."

Japanese officials even transformed old US stamps into commemorative stamps celebrating US losses. A stamp issued in May 1942, whose legend had previously affirmed the sovereignty of the "United States of America" over the Philippines, now celebrated the US defeat at Bataan and Corregidor.

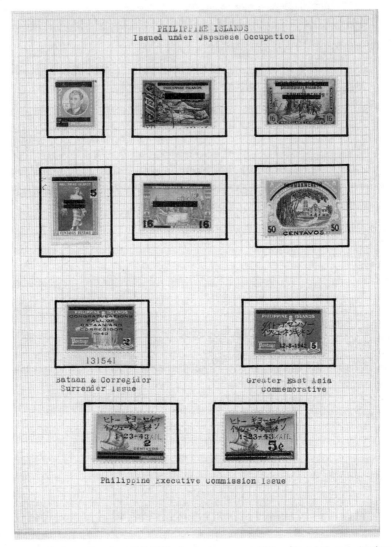

FIGURE 4.5. Japanese overprints of US-Philippine stamps, 1942–43. National Postal Museum, Smithsonian Institution. Compare to figures 2.10 and 2.12.

By December of 1942, the same stamp was overprinted again, this time in Japanese—a testament to official perceptions of how well the language was spreading—to commemorate the anniversary of the "outbreak of the "Greater East Asia War."[73]

Former US colonial subjects living under Japanese occupation soon found that Japanese officials took these pocket-sized objects as seriously as they did flags, even executing people for using US money.[74] Some decided to hide their

US money. Gilbert Perez "hid away a few paper dollars in a jar near a certain post of my shanty" in the Philippines. "Unfortunately, after the liberation," he wrote, "I forgot the *certain post* and had to dig around three different posts before finding out which one was really the certain post where my surviving treasure was hidden away."[75] On Guam, a soldier recalled a "story about a elderly gentleman who took his money out of the Bank of Guam . . . and buried his money in the jungles." After the war, "the first day the bank was open, he deposited his money . . . tattered, in shreds."[76] These people hid their money for practical purposes, to have something of value should the United States return. But if Japanese officials had discovered them in possession of US currency, it could have cost them their lives.[77]

US currency was not the only currency that could get someone killed under Japanese occupation. In the Philippines, some local governments that could no longer use US-Philippine pesos but lacked a sufficient supply of Japanese military currency printed their own "emergency currency" out of necessity (figure 4.6). People used whatever they could find. In a town in Mountain Province, a committee co-opted a local church's printing press and paper from local offices and businesses to start printing currency.[78] And hidden deep in the Philippine interior, guerrillas fighting against Japanese rule used handmade woodblocks and dyes and whatever they could find—scraps of newspaper, office forms, ledger books, even cloth—to create their own guerrilla currency. Possessing these small, crude pieces of paper was incredibly risky. In the words of the Filipino statesman Carlos P. Romulo, "the man who said that a guerrilla note was not currency but a death warrant was hardly indulging in exaggeration."[79]

Japanese military notes were the only legal standard but were not always available, and by the end of the war they were essentially worthless. The US high commissioner to the Philippines wrote in 1946 that toward the end of the occupation, the value of Japanese military currency had plummeted so much

FIGURE 4.6. Emergency currency from Negros, Philippines, 1944. National Numismatic Collection, National Museum of American History, Smithsonian Institution.

that "even Japanese officials conducted black-market operations in prewar money."[80] But for ordinary people, using US-Philippine money was too risky, and they were stuck with Japanese money. As one Filipino put it, "We needed this worthless money to buy valuable rice."[81]

Independence Day

While many Filipinos joined the guerrillas fighting to oust the Japanese, others decided to accept Japanese rule and begin building a Philippine future without the United States. The United States had promised Filipinos independence during the transition to commonwealth, but had yet to make good on that promise. On June 16, 1942, Prime Minister Tōjō announced that the Philippines would become an independent republic within the Greater East Asia Co-Prosperity Sphere.[82]

President-Elect Jose P. Laurel appointed a special committee of Filipinas headed by the suffragist and writer Pura Villanueva Kalaw to prepare a Philippine flag for the inauguration ceremony. Kalaw reported that more than a hundred women contributed to the creation of the flag—a task that certainly didn't require that many hands. It was not the most efficient way to sew a flag, but the joint effort symbolically showed women from all over the country coming together. Kalaw wrote, "Women from different regions and of different faiths united together like sisters" and "busied themselves night and day, heedless of recompense, in order to help give success and happiness to the land."[83] She presented the flag to President Laurel with the following message: "We pray God that our Republic may succeed and that this Holy Flag given by this group of women may float forever, alone, over this land, as long as the world shall stand."[84] This flag raising would be different than those organized under US rule in 1919 and 1935 because, for the first time since Emilio Aguinaldo had raised the flag in 1898 to declare the independence of the First Philippine Republic, the Philippine flag would fly *alone*.

On October 14, 1943, the inauguration of the Second Philippine Republic took place. After having been excluded from attending the Philippine flag raising under US rule in 1919, Aguinaldo was given place of honor at the inauguration of the new republic as one of the notable people to raise the flag. *La Vanguardia* reported that many "cried openly at the sight" of the Philippine flag flying alone at last.[85] Kalaw recalled that even though "50,000 small Filipino flags had been distributed for the occasion . . . not a single torn flag was found on any roadside thrown by careless hand. In the two years that they had not seen their flag, the Filipinos had learned to love it deeply and well."[86]

FIGURE 4.7. Stamps of the Second Philippine Republic. Philippine Independence stamp, October 14, 1943; Apolinario Mabini National Heroes stamp, February 17, 1944; Jose P. Laurel one-year anniversary stamp, October 14, 1944. Author's collection.

Laurel argued that the Second Philippine Republic was an "opportunity to govern ourselves, run our affairs, have our own flag, and enjoy real complete and absolute independence."[87] But others questioned whether the flag denoted real independence. Commonwealth President Quezon, by then exiled in Washington, argued that the Philippines would become another Manchukuo—Japan's puppet state in China.[88] The Philippine statesman Claro Recto protested to the Japanese government that, considering reports of thousands of Filipinos still suffering "physical torture" at the hands of Japanese troops, it seemed that "the only sign of independence" in the Second Philippine Republic was "the display of the Philippine flag."[89]

Stamps became another sign of independence. The Filipino artist Guillermo Tolentino prepared the design for a commemorative stamp celebrating Philippine independence, which was released on the day of the inauguration (figure 4.7). The legend at the top read "Independence of the Philippines" in both Tagalog and Baybayin—an indigenous script predating Spanish colonization. The stamp showed an allegorical Filipina standing in front of the Rizal monument, and the Philippine flag with broken chains on either side, representing liberation from US rule.[90]

Whereas Philippine stamps under the United States had depicted US revolutionary heroes like Washington and Franklin, in February 1944 the Second Philippine Republic issued its own "National Heroes" series with images of the Philippine revolutionary heroes Jose Burgos, Apolinario Mabini, and Jose Rizal. While images of Rizal had been on US-Philippine stamps, this was the first time he had appeared on one without the accompanying legend "United States of America." The Second Philippine Republic may not have granted the Philippines complete independence in political terms, but it did give Filipinos the kind of symbolic independence the United States had never allowed:

the ability to fly their national flag alone, and to have their national culture represented without references to the colonizing country.

On October 14, 1944, the Second Philippine Republic issued another stamp to commemorate the one-year anniversary of the inauguration. It featured President Laurel's portrait and the legend "Pilipinas"—no reference to any colonial power. The stamp came late, however: just a few weeks before US troops invaded the Philippines.[91]

"Just a Precaution"

Japan never invaded the Hawaiian Islands, but the looming threat of occupation and the imposition of US martial law in the islands still changed the national symbols people routinely encountered.[92] As they had done in the Philippines, US Treasury officials feared that if Japan invaded Hawai'i, large amounts of US legal tender would fall into Japanese hands. In 1942 they decided to have people living in Hawai'i turn in all their US money in exchange for currency overprinted "HAWAII" (figure 4.8). US officials called it a "'scorched earth' program to prevent our usual securities, currency, etc. from falling into the hands of the invading army." They referenced the Philippine currency destruction program but recognized a difference in geography: "We understand that the 'scorching of the earth' really consisted in taking all movable and valuable personal property to Corregidor, where any destruction could be carried out with plenty of time. There is no Corregidor available here." Thus, in February 1942 Honolulu bankers recommended to the territorial governor of the Hawaiian Islands that US money be removed to the continental United States as soon as possible.[93]

A special committee of Treasury officials worked with local banks to "prepare, check, and classify all currency on hand in the Banks and all currency returned to the Banks from general circulation."[94] Treasury officials soon realized that "millions would have to be destroyed and that millions of the New Hawaii Series would be required to complete the Herculean task." Martial law helped. The US military governor declared that no person in Hawai'i was allowed to possess more than $200 of currency in any given month, which, unsurprisingly, led to "congestion of money in the Banks." The committee soon gave up on safely transporting the dollars people turned in to the continental United States, and decided instead to follow the Philippine example. Armored trucks under heavy guard transported money from the banks to the crematory at Nu'uanu Cemetery and to the furnaces of the sugar mill at the Honolulu Plantation Company, where the mass burnings took place. Burnings of US dollars continued in the Hawaiian Islands until 1945.[95] Meanwhile,

FIGURE 4.8. Hawaiian series one-dollar bill, 1942. National Numismatic Collection, National Museum of American History, Smithsonian Institution.

more than $25 million in new paper money—silver certificates and Federal Reserve notes—made their way from San Francisco to the Hawaiian Islands.[96]

The exchange was quick—quicker than any currency exchanges that had introduced the US dollar to the colonies in the early twentieth century. People in Hawaiʻi were given less than three weeks—from June 26 to July 15, 1942—to turn in all of their regular US bills and exchange them for the new Hawaiian series. After July 15, regular US currency would no longer be accepted in the Hawaiian Islands.[97] Those who violated currency regulations faced fines of up to five thousand dollars, or up to five years in prison.[98] As in previous currency reforms, US colonial officials had to affirm the value of the new currency: "This is a precautionary measure and I don't want anyone to get the idea that there is a change in value," one official said. "The Hawaiian series for use in the territory is worth the same as regular currency used in other sections of the United States." He added that the Hawaiian series was "all new and clean which should be a welcome treat to the people of the territory, who have been handling dirty, old bills since the war."[99]

During the war, traveling between the continental United States and the Hawaiian Islands suddenly resembled traveling to a foreign country. Only Hawaiian currency could be used within Hawaiian borders.[100] A *San Francisco Chronicle* correspondent described his arrival at the airport: "You are greeted casually, informally—naval officers with automatics instead of hula girls with leis. You turn in all your American currency and get bills marked 'Hawaii' on the backs, which are good for use only in the territory. 'Why,' you want to know. The cashier shrugs. Just a precaution, he explains, initiated by the military governor in case the Japanese should land on the island." The cashier was nonchalant enough—"but it's a grim thought," the reporter noted, "'if the Japanese should land.'"[101]

Indeed, it was no secret to people in the Hawaiian Islands that the United States was making contingency plans in case of a Japanese invasion. The official press release announcing the Hawaiian Series currency stated that the purpose of the measure was "to concentrate all securities in a relatively few places, where they will be readily available for removal or destruction by the authorities should an invasion attempt impend." It also reminded people that it was their "patriotic duty" to comply with these regulations.[102] People living in Hawai'i had seen other US territories fall under Japanese occupation, and now the money they used in their everyday lives—money that used to assure them they were no different from any other part of the United States—created a boundary between the Hawaiian Islands and the United States. US military tanks rolled down the streets, people lived with frequent blackouts and strict curfews, and now every transaction was a reminder that they could be next.[103]

People in Hawai'i were forced to use this special currency until October 21, 1944. On that date the military governor proclaimed that "with the danger of invasion definitely removed, the precautionary measures prescribed by the regulations are no longer necessary."[104] It was one day after General Douglas MacArthur landed in the Philippines.

"VICTORY"

General Douglas MacArthur returned to the Philippines on October 20, 1944. In a radio address, he told Filipinos he had brought with him "the indomitable spirit of Bataan and Corregidor," a commitment to restore "the liberties of your people," and a new Commonwealth president, Sergio Osmeña.[105] But MacArthur brought something else with him he did not mention: thousands of new US stamps and currency overprinted with the word "VICTORY."[106]

In the middle of a world war, when one might assume that the federal government had more pressing matters to attend to, US federal and Philippine

Commonwealth government officials in Washington began debating what kind of iconography they should put on the stamps and currency to be circulated upon the reinvasion of the Philippines—a conversation they began as early as 1942, when it was not a given that the United States would ever return. It was also not a given that Filipinos should continue using US currency if the United States *did* return. Andres Soriano, the commonwealth's secretary of finance, expressed concern that the reintroduction of US currency "might be used by propagandists to support a thesis that the United States would not relinquish the Philippines once they had been reoccupied." But Soriano was outnumbered. US government officials favored continuing to issue money with the legend "United States of America."[107] Secretary of Interior Harold Ickes even added that that any "changes in the character of the legitimate currency" would have to be approved by the US Congress.[108] Despite the promise of autonomy under the commonwealth, the federal government still had final say over such matters.

In July 1943, while preparations were being made in the Philippines for the inauguration of the independent Second Philippine Republic, Secretary of Interior Harold Ickes and Secretary of War Henry Stimson—the former governor-general of the Philippines who had fought the secretary of the treasury to keep Washington on Philippine money—came up with a plan. They proposed reintroducing prewar US-Philippine money and stamps with the same designs as before, but overprinted with the word "VICTORY" (figures 4.9 and 4.10).[109] A year and a half later, US troops began circulating these new symbolic objects as their reinvasion of the Philippines advanced. In these so-called liberated areas, US troops declared that US-Philippine pesos were once again legal tender and that Japanese military notes had no recognized value.[110] This created a "financial dilemma" for many Filipinos, as one man found after returning from a "liberated" city to Manila, which was still under Japanese control: "My Victory Notes from Iloilo were useless because the Japanese declared that spending them was illegal and people caught using them were executed." He had to hide them in the back of a drawer.[111]

To spread the message that the Japanese Military Government's money no longer held value in the Philippines, the US military began airdropping Japanese occupation currency overprinted with the phrase "The Co-Prosperity Sphere: What Is It Worth?" in territory still occupied by Japan. The US military said the purpose of the notes was "to impress on the Filipino people the worthlessness of Japanese occupation currency, with consequent embarrassment and loss of face to the Japanese."[112] Even if the Japanese notes were not worth much by the end of the war, most people would still stop to pick up free money falling from the sky and see the US military's message.

FIGURE 4.9. US-Philippine ten-peso "Victory" bill, 1944. National Numismatic Collection, National Museum of American History, Smithsonian Institution.

FIGURE 4.10. US-Philippine four-centavo "Victory" stamp, 1944. Author's collection. Compare to figures 2.12 and 4.5.

FIGURE 4.11. Filipina throwing Japanese-Philippine pesos into a crowd of US soldiers and sailors in Leyte, November 15, 1944. Photo courtesy of the Allison Collection of the MacArthur Museum of Arkansas Military History.

The US high commissioner announced, "The Japanese military peso was declared null, void, and unredeemable," and that "no attempt was made to gather up the Japanese notes."[113] Indeed, US authorities actively encouraged the destruction of Japanese military currency. A month after MacArthur's return, in Tacloban—the temporary seat of the Commonwealth government while US troops waited to retake Manila—the Red Cross hosted a party. In a scene that mirrored the thrill soldiers in Corregidor had felt while destroying US-Philippine currency at the beginning of the war, a Filipina threw four million pesos in Japanese-Philippine paper money into a crowd of US soldiers and sailors (figure 4.11).

After being forced under pain of death to use only Japanese money under occupation, Filipinos now found that money worthless with the return of US sovereignty. Even the emergency and guerrilla notes printed by Philippine forces who had fought Japan throughout the occupation were not all redeemed.[114] The Philippine Legislature did pass a law that would at least recognize debts Filipinos had paid down with Japanese currency during the war, and the large amounts of Japanese military notes that Philippine banks held as a result. Commonwealth President Osmeña signed the law, but US President Harry Truman vetoed it.[115] The independent Second Philippine Republic had ended, and currency matters in the Philippines were once again the purview of the United States.

The "Victory" series was the latest iteration in a long propaganda war that played out on these symbolic objects. The same stamps that had been overprinted by Japan to eliminate mention of US sovereignty and commemoration of US losses were now overprinted to preemptively declare the United States' "victory" in the Philippines. Indeed, as one Philippine stamp collector put it, "Successive political changes have so left their indelible marks in the form of overprints and surcharges on stamps that today a complete collection of them is a miniature pictorial history of the Philippines."[116] The US government saw the "Victory" series as a visible way to signal the reestablishment of its sovereignty in the Philippines. But these objects also became important to many Filipinos. Another stamp collector wrote that to the Filipinos, "who had undergone untold sufferings and privations, cruelties, tortures, [and] insults," the "Victory" series meant "life itself, resurrection, liberation, the end of the Kempetai—of enemy occupation. It is a symbol of freedom, liberty and the return of the democratic ways of life."[117] These pocket-sized pieces of paper carried substantial meaning.

It is incredible that, in the middle of a world war, government officials would make the creation of this "Victory" series such a priority. But their actions were not entirely surprising. Since the early twentieth century, officials had used material objects with US national symbols to assert US sovereignty over the colonies. More surprising, perhaps, was what former US colonial subjects had kept hidden during the occupation.

Hidden Flags

The United States began its reinvasion of Guam on July 21, 1944. Ten days later, US troops came to a concentration camp into which Japanese troops had forced CHamorus.[118] The two thousand people interned in Camp Asinan were not expecting the arrival of US troops. Indeed, many believed more Japanese troops were arriving, and only began to emerge from the camp after they realized this was indeed the long-awaited return of the United States to Guam.[119]

Ben Blaz, a CHamoru teenager who had escaped the camps early and was traveling with the US Army, said it was "the most unforgettable sight that I think I have ever seen . . . this long line of people coming out" of the camp. And the most surprising thing: "Each one of them was carrying an American flag." Blaz and the US soldiers accompanying him found that in

FIGURE 4.12. "Tiny natives of Guam hold home-made American flags made by their mothers from parts of dresses while in custody of the Japanese, Aug. 10, 1944. The children waved the flags when the Yanks moved in." Associated Press photo by Joseph Rosenthal.

the internment camp, women had been gathering scraps of fabric and were "clandestinely . . . in utter defiance of the enemy occupation . . . making little bitty American flags out of the shreds" (figure 4.12).[120]

People had hidden their US flags in the Philippines, too.[121] In her memoirs, one Filipina recounted a harrowing story of Japanese troops coming into her family home to conduct a surprise search—they suspected the family of assisting guerrillas who were resisting Japanese rule. She remembered a cold sweat engulfing her body, her mother's lips moving in silent prayer beside her as Japanese troops opened the trunk where they had hidden their US flag. The Japanese soldier, she recalled, was only one pillowcase away from discovering the flag—a pillowcase, she recalled, through which he might have seen the red stripes if he had looked more closely—when he suddenly closed the trunk and left the room.[122] Even Buenaventura Bello, the high school principal whom Japanese troops had shot for refusing to take down the US flag at his school, kept that bullet-riddled flag hidden for the duration of the war.[123]

Before the war, US imperialists had put a great deal of effort into trying to get people who lived in these places to form an attachment to the US flag. On Guam, the daily performance of flag veneration in Hagåtña was impressive, to be sure, but there was no way of knowing whether it *was* just a performance. Women from the continental United States had taught Filipinas and CHamorus to sew US flags by hand in the early twentieth century, but never knew if they completed the task with patriotic feeling.[124] Sewing a US flag or pledging allegiance to the US flag while living under US rule was simply following the script laid out by those in power. But here, under Japanese occupation, women risked their lives to stitch US flags and keep them hidden from Japanese officials.

As we have seen in other US colonies, those who wanted to challenge colonial rule could do so by challenging the supremacy of the current colonial ruler's flag. But unlike Puerto Rican Nationalists who tore down US flags around San Juan and raised Puerto Rican flags in their place, CHamoru women and Filipinos were not using their US flags to mount a public challenge to the Japanese flag's supremacy in Guam or the Philippines. In this way, these secret flags were more like the Hawaiian flag quilts Hawaiian women had stitched and displayed in the privacy of their homes after the United States annexed the islands. And, like Hawaiian flag quilts, these secret flags were not designed to send a political message to anyone. Indeed, these women went to great lengths to ensure the flags were never seen by Japanese officials, and they hoped but did not know that US officials would one day return. Like the Hawaiian women who carefully stitched their flag quilts, these CHamoru women and Filipinos created and kept their flags for themselves.

What do we make of these colonial subjects who risked their lives to secretly make and keep US flags? Perhaps the attachment to the flag simply signals that many found US imperialism preferable to Japanese. But US troops had brutally repressed the independence movement in the Philippines for more than a decade, leaving more than three quarters of a million Filipinos—men, women, and children—dead, burning entire villages, torturing suspected independence supporters, and putting people in concentration camps.[125] On Guam, US colonization had been less violent (not hard to achieve, given the scale of violence in the Philippines), but hardly more benevolent. The island was ruled by the US Navy, with no civilian government—Courtney's 1939 *Collier's* article had called it "the trimmest little dictatorship on earth, a perfected military despotism."[126] Naval governors held such arbitrary authority that one even passed an executive order prohibiting whistling within the capital city of Hagåtña, just because he found it an "irritating noise."[127] People in the Philippines and Guam had for forty years been forced to pledge their allegiance to the flag of a nation that had violently subjugated them and legally and politically excluded them—forced to pledge allegiance to a flag that had a star for each state, but nothing to represent them. And now the nation that flag represented had abandoned them to Japanese occupation. Whatever their feelings about Japan, it is remarkable that anyone risked their life to secretly have a US flag.

The CHamoru scholar Michael Lujan Bevacqua has argued that during the war, people on Guam were stuck between "the American red, white, and blue and the red rising sun of the Japanese: what Chamorro symbol could match those, could represent a distinctive Chamorro agency amid these massive empires of steel clashing around them?"[128] It is important to note, however, that the women in internment camps were not being forced to choose a national symbol in that moment.[129] The easiest course of action for them would have been to stitch no flags at all. And, unlike the performative flag-waving after the war, there was no intended audience for these secret patriotic actions, since, by all accounts, people in the camps did not know when or even whether the United States was coming back.[130] Their decision thus presents a paradox of, as Bevacqua has put it, "the perceived patriotism of those who by admission are not supposed to be patriotic."[131] But if US colonial subjects "are not supposed to be patriotic," it raises a question: Who is?

Some have argued that those US colonial subjects who claimed "American identity" did so as a result of "false consciousness perpetuated by Americanization and colonialism."[132] But at the same time as Filipinos and Guam CHamorus were secretly hiding and making US flags, Black and Japanese Americans were fighting and dying for the United States despite the lack of basic civil and human rights the country afforded them. Indeed, the political scientist Rogers M. Smith has estimated that "for at least two-thirds of American history, the majority of the domestic adult population was"—because of race, national origin, or gender—"ineligible for full citizenship."[133] If all nations are imagined communities, then why should people in US colonies have any less right than people in the continental United States to, if they choose, imagine themselves as "American"? Is their consciousness any more "false" than that of those in the continental United States who pledge their allegiance to the US flag?

This moment pushes us to consider that people from the continental United States do not have exclusive ownership over "American" identity. During the decades in which colonial subjects had incorporated US national symbols into their everyday lives, the borders of US national identity had expanded beyond the continental United States. As the CHamoru teacher and civic leader Agueda Iglesias Johnston proudly proclaimed, she was "Guamanian-Chamorro by birth but American patriotic by choice."[134] As scholars, we should take such claims as seriously as if they were made by someone from the continental United States. Whether US patriotism of this degree existed on Guam before the war has been debated, but its existence in 1944 is certain. As Bevacqua ironically notes, "The Japanese had accomplished in thirty-two

intense months what the U.S. had failed to do" in forty years of colonial rule—
"the ascension of excessive Chamorro patriotism for the United States."[135]

Recalling the women and children coming out of the camps with their
handmade flags, Blaz—who would himself go on to join the US Marines and
serve as Guam's territorial delegate in the US Congress—said "that if anyone
at that point had any doubt as to what this war was all about their questions
were answered then . . . because it is demonstrative to the intense loyalty that
people have out there for the United States."[136] The significance of this moment was not lost on US troops. The first US flag they ran up the flagpole in
front of the Governor's Palace in Hagåtña—the same spot where a thousand
schoolchildren would gather for flag routines before the war, and the same
spot where Angel Flores had died for the US flag three years earlier—was one
of the small handmade flags from the camps.[137]

Island Hopping

US troops had returned the US flag to the Philippines and Guam. But as they
advanced throughout the Pacific, invading other islands under Japanese rule,
they planted the Stars and Stripes in places where it had never flown before. On
January 31, 1944, they raised it on Gehh, in the Marshall Islands.[138] They raised
the flag on Majuro on February 9, on Arno Atoll on February 12, on Engebi
on February 19, on Enewetak Atoll on February 25, on Wotho on March 9, on
Lib on March 11, on Bikini Atoll on March 30, on Utirik on April 5, on Ujelang
on April 22, in Palau on December 3, and, the following year, on Mili, Pagan,
Kosrae, Pohnpei, Chuuk, Wotje, and Yap.[139] As one military report put it, "The
[flag raising] ceremony appealed to the natives, and was an aid in inculcating
the idea that they now were under American protection and no longer subject
to Japanese rule."[140] Indeed, military officials were clear that the US flag was
not meant to be a symbol of temporary occupation in these islands previously
under Japanese rule; when Admiral Raymond Spruance raised the US flag in
Majuro, he told the inhabitants (via an interpreter): "This is your flag now."[141]

Where they raised the flag, US troops also read out two proclamations:
Proclamation no. 1 established that Admiral Chester W. Nimitz, commander-
in-chief of the US Pacific Fleet, assumed all power in areas occupied by US
forces. And as local chiefs and officials throughout the Pacific surrendered
their Japanese insignia of authority, "to evidence that the authority they now
exercised came from the United States," US commanders presented them
with new badges: large brass discs with the American eagle and an inscription
of their title, for example: "King, Majuro Atoll, U.S.A." Proclamation no. 2,
titled "War Crimes," laid out a number of rules for those now living under

FIGURE 4.13. "Fais Islanders try out a new custom: saluting the American flag," January 1945. US Navy photo. UHM Library Digital Image Collections.

US occupation—including making anyone who "displays the flag or colors of the Japanese Empire or sings or plays its national anthem" subject to fine or imprisonment.[142] During the war, people in Guam and the Philippines who had lived under the US flag for decades suddenly found that flag illegal under Japanese occupation. The people who had spent decades under the Japanese flag before the war now experienced the same thing, with the symbols swapped, as they came under US occupation.

The Navy admitted that "no definite plans for the future control of the islands existed at the end of the war."[143] As it had done during the war in 1898, the US military planted its flag on new island territories without knowing whether they would remain under US sovereignty. They were better prepared this time, however, having set up schools as early as 1942 to train Navy personnel for military government in "liberated areas."[144] Japan's former Pacific Island empire would remain under US naval occupation for the time being. And naval officials did not hesitate to rule these new islands the same way they had ruled over American Samoa, Guam, and the US Virgin Islands. People across the Pacific who had saluted the Japanese flag since World War I now pledged their allegiance to the flag of the United States. As naval officials wrote on the back of a photo of a flag raising (figure 4.13): "A flagpole erected in front of the island's men's house provides the appropriate prop for symbolizing new loyalties."[145]

At an official flag raising in November 1945, Iroij Tomeing—likely wearing a badge designating him "King, Wotje Atoll, U.S.A."—spoke on the meaning of the US flag on Wotje: "The bars are telling us to be true and brave and to be loyal to our country; the stars are bright that people can see by their light and understand their message of freedom." People in Wotje had heard about "the message of the stars" while under Japanese rule, he said, "but the skies were overclouded and we did not get to see them. Now the sky is clear, and the stars are shining brightly over our island and over the whole world."[146] To Tomeing, the coming of the US flag signaled a new era of "freedom" for people in the Marshall Islands.

What Followed the Flag

By the end of 1945, the US flag once again flew over the Philippines and Guam, and now also flew over Wotje and hundreds of other islands formerly under Japanese rule. But it is worth asking—as we did after the war in 1898—what followed the flag?

As US troops raised the Stars and Stripes over the "skeleton remains" of the Marine barracks on Guam, a US general proclaimed that "under our flag," Guam "again stands ready to fulfill its destiny as an American fortress in the Pacific."[147] His words were an ominous warning. In the reestablishment of US sovereignty on Guam, 2,500 out of 3,286 homes were destroyed.[148] The capital city of Hagåtña "was a heap of rubble," and the next largest communities— Agat, Sumi, Piti, and Asan—"were leveled."[149] Two years later, things had not improved. The *New York Times* reported on "forgotten Guam" and "the callous way in which our government is treating 23,000 loyal natives whose homes and cities were destroyed in the process of driving the Japanese from that island." Congress had only appropriated six million of the requested twenty-five million dollars to rebuild Hagåtña and Agat—cities which, the *Times* reminded its readers, had been "leveled by our own shells and bombs." And lack of recovery funds was not the only problem: "Land now is being taken by the Navy for military purposes without any provision for the people who once lived on it."[150] Having just "liberated" Guam CHamorus from Japanese internment camps, US troops now put them back in camps while they built a naval basing complex on CHamoru land.[151] The US "record on Guam was bad enough before the war," reported the *Times*. "Now we repay their loyalty during the war with unconscionable action. What must they think as they see millions of dollars being poured into military installations while nothing is being done to restore the homes that we pounded into rubble?"[152]

In the newly occupied Marshall Islands, too, the US flag quickly came to symbolize displacement and destruction. Some people, like those on Delap and Uliga, were displaced immediately so that US troops could build airfields to continue fighting Japan.[153] For others, though, displacement would last long after the war's end. In February 1946, Commodore Ben H. Wyatt—military governor of the Marshall Islands—arrived in Bikini Atoll and asked the inhabitants to leave, "for the good of mankind." King Juda, their leader, agreed to go, responding, "Men otemjej rej ilo bein Anij" ("Everything is in God's hands").[154] The US military sent Bikini's inhabitants to Rongerik—an atoll 125 miles east that had been uninhabited due to its small size and lack of adequate food and water. There, Bikinians living under the US flag on Rongerik began to starve while the US military dropped nuclear bombs on their former home. After facing international criticism, in March of 1948 naval officials relocated Bikinians briefly to Kwajalein—where they were forced to live, in Iroij Kilon Bauno's words, "a strange life" in tents by an airstrip—and eventually to Kili, where lack of food continued to be a problem.[155]

The US flag had been raised in the Marshall Islands, but had not brought the "freedom" Iroij Tomeing had hoped it would. The flag also failed to bring back to Guam the material comfort, security, or tranquility that B. J. Bordallo had praised before the war. Even the proud patriot Agueda Johnston, linking postwar CHamoru dispossession to a longer history of US imperialism, confronted US Marines who were trying to bulldoze someone's home and asked, "How far west are you pushing us Indians, Captain 'John' Smith?"[156]

Like "Indians" in the continental United States, Guam CHamorus would be dispossessed of their land but eventually granted US citizenship—something people there had been fighting for since the 1920s.[157] In the end, their demonstrated loyalty to the US flag during the war had made their patriotism indisputable. In 1947 Secretary of Interior Ickes wrote, "Those of us who have heard of the record of the people of Guam during World War II marvel at the loyalty of these long suffering people." They had endured "forced labor, tortures, beatings, and privation beyond description . . . many were executed. And yet I am told that not one single Guamanian was convicted of disloyalty to the United States."[158] He added, using language that again implied Guam was not part of the United States, "That record cannot be matched even in the United States itself." Attempting to assuage racist anxieties, Ickes proclaimed, "They are not little black men on a tropical island. . . . They speak our language; they have our social and religious institutions; they live in an American economy. . . . They are Americans!"[159] The secretary's comments emphasized that Guam CHamorus were not just a foreign group loyal to the United States; they themselves *were* Americans. Japanese occupation had put

Americanization on Guam to the test and, in Ickes's estimation, proved it a success. Although it took the Guam Congress staging a walkout to draw attention to the issue, in 1950 the US Congress did grant Guamanians US citizenship and transfer Guam from the Navy to the Department of the Interior, thus ending the era of "military despotism."[160]

These changes in Guam's status were part of a larger postwar shift in the US colonial empire largely motivated, as we will see, by the changing international climate. As Ickes wrote in a scathing editorial condemning the Navy's treatment of Marshall Islanders, "Apparently it has not yet penetrated the navy mind that every case of arrogant injustice to a native people has become an international question. . . . America can be so outraged by the oppression of a minority group by any other nation . . . , but the navy can not see the mote in its own eye." Ickes's solution, however, was not the end of US colonial rule, but the transfer of the Marshall Islands, along with Guam, American Samoa, and the rest of the formerly Japanese islands under Navy rule, to civilian rule under his Department of Interior—all of which happened between 1950 and 1951.[161] Around the same time, Congress granted Puerto Ricans the right to elect their own governor and then write their own constitution. Later that decade, the Hawaiian Islands would become a US state. But the only US colony to gain full independence in this period was the Philippines. On July 4, 1946, less than a year after the end of the war and against the backdrop of wartime destruction, the Philippine flag rose alone once again, this time finally declaring the islands' independence from the United States.

Symbolic Decolonization

On July 4, 1946, people throughout the United States and its colonial empire celebrated Independence Day. It was a double celebration of decolonization: the 170th anniversary of the United States' independence from Great Britain, and the day the Philippine Islands became independent from the United States. The inauguration of the independent Philippine Republic was an extravagant ceremony meant to signal to the world that the United States was leading the charge for postwar decolonization. As former US High Commissioner to the Philippines Francis B. Sayre proclaimed, "July 4, 1946 will stand out in history as an important milestone date when the ways of nineteenth century imperialism were discarded and supplanted by twentieth-century ways of international brotherhood."[1]

In a way, Sayre was right. The world looked different after World War II. There was no reason it should; empires had weathered world wars before, and US and European colonizers had emerged victorious from World War II. But after the war, anticolonial nationalists around the world began taking on their colonizers and winning. A combination of factors led to this shift, including the new power of anticolonial nationalists themselves; domestic concerns in imperial metropoles about the costs of continuing empire; the Japanese Empire's slogan "Asia for the Asiatics," which continued to resonate even after its defeat; and a new international organization: the United Nations, which devised a list of "non-self-governing territories" that would be monitored by members of the international organization.[2] In this new environment, anticolonial nationalists could rally international support for their cause and do serious damage to a colonizing country's reputation. When, for example, Marshall Islanders called for an end to nuclear testing, or Puerto

Rican Nationalists accused the United States of continued colonialism, US officials found that the world was now watching.

This new context, the historian Gretchen Heefner has argued, put US colonial policy "in the global spotlight."[3] And while they had that spotlight, US officials decided to put on a show. This chapter shows how, with the inaugurations of Philippine independence in 1946, the Puerto Rican Commonwealth in 1952, and Hawaiian statehood in 1959, the United States sought to perform decolonization for the world. Each story deals with events occurring on local, national, imperial, and international scales, as the intended audience for these performances included dissatisfied colonial inhabitants in the territories, embarrassed citizens in the continental United States, stubborn European imperial powers, critical communist countries, and skeptical yet hopeful decolonizing nations around the world. As we will see, State Department officials were especially concerned with convincing the last group of the United States' commitment to ending imperialism, and were eager to draw these newly independent countries to their side in the Cold War against the Soviet Union. And just as national symbols had been central to colonization in the early twentieth century, so they would be central to these mid-century performances of decolonization—a term used here to refer to the process of colonies gaining formal independence.[4]

The United States was not the only imperial power in this period using symbolic objects in performances of decolonization. In the decades after World War II, dozens of countries gained independence from their former colonizers. These status changes were often accompanied by lavish ceremonies that centered around the lowering of the colonial flag and the raising of the new national flag.[5] After independence, new countries began circulating postage stamps and currency that bore their own national symbols. While historians have tended to dismiss these symbolic objects and ceremonies as "insubstantial pageants and tinsel ephemera," they were not a sideshow to decolonization.[6] As Kwame Nkrumah, Ghana's first head of state, argued in a piece called "Why the Queen's Head Is Coming Off Our Coins," the people have "got to be shown that they are now really independent. And they can only be shown by signs."[7] Newly independent countries used these symbols and ceremonies to forge their new national identities.[8] And former colonial powers used them as proof positive that imperialism had ended.

The decline of European colonial empires is a familiar episode in the history of US imperialism. The post–World War II moment saw the rise of US power on a global scale; even more than the events of 1898, people cite it as a birth of US empire.[9] But they refer to it as a different kind of empire, usually called "informal" to distinguish it from "formal" imperialism, in which one country claims sovereignty over another. After the war, the United States perfected informal imperialism—how to get what it wanted from another country without having to deal with the responsibility of formal colonization or its effect on the colonizer's reputation. And as it pursued this new kind of imperialism, the United States led the global charge for the end of colonial empire—showing the world that, in Sayre's words, they were discarding nineteenth-century imperialism.

But the United States did not "discard" its colonial empire in this period. Its largest colony, the Philippines, did gain formal independence. Its other overseas territories, however, remained under US jurisdiction. The official status of Hawai'i and Puerto Rico under US jurisdiction did change enough to convince the UN to remove them from their list of non-self-governing territories. But Native Hawaiian scholars have challenged whether statehood constituted decolonization; and, as we will see, even under commonwealth status, Puerto Rico's legal relationship to the United States remained the same: that of an unincorporated territory.[10] American Samoa, Guam, and the US Virgin Islands remained unincorporated territories, too, though all were transferred from the Navy to the Department of Interior by the early 1950s. And while the United States claimed to be divesting itself of colonial possessions after the war, it acquired *more* territory in this period: Japan's former Pacific empire, which in 1947 became the Trust Territory of the Pacific Islands. While formally administered through the United Nations, US officials—initially naval, and then civilian—did not hesitate to treat these spaces the same as they did the other US colonies.

This is the puzzle this chapter seeks to understand: how after World War II the United States claimed it was decolonizing its colonial empire while only ever granting one colony—the Philippines—independence, and even acquiring new territory in that period. This chapter shows how, just as US officials had understood the importance of symbolism and national iconography in early-twentieth-century colonization, they understood the importance of symbolism and symbolic gestures in this postwar period of global decolonization. It offers a bird's eye view of these postwar imperial transitions, highlighting the contingency and unevenness of US colonial policy. Different colonies had different outcomes, and some acts even seem contradictory: the US flag came down in the Philippines while the Hawaiian Islands gained a seemingly permanent place on the nation's most sacred symbol as the fiftieth star on the flag. But US officials argued that both symbolic moves were acts of decolonization. Indeed, the United States used these symbolic objects to define what constituted decolonization as it staged these performances for itself, its colonies, and the rest of the world.

Independence Day, Again

July 4, 1946, had been the scheduled date for Philippine independence since the inauguration of the Commonwealth a decade earlier, according to the terms of the 1934 Philippine Independence Act. But independence was not a guarantee; the United States had broken its promises to the Philippines before.[11] And after Japan invaded in 1941, the matter was no longer up to the United States. Nevertheless, preparations for Philippine independence continued even while the archipelago remained under Japanese occupation. State Department officials knew it had become a matter of international importance. Throughout the war, they boasted that Philippine independence could offer "a perfect example of how a nation should treat a colony or a dependency in cooperating with it in all essential respects calculated to assist it in making all necessary preparation for freedom."[12] But pushing decolonization at this time had its risks; US officials had genuine concerns that the British, Dutch, and other colonial powers might refuse to recognize Philippine independence, for fear that it might threaten their own colonial holdings.[13]

Some in the US government, however, were starting to think of empire differently from their fellow colonizers. They imagined decolonization could be a performance for the rest of the world—particularly for other countries' colonies, with which they sought to have positive relationships after those colonies achieved independence. In September 1944, one month before MacArthur returned to the Philippines, the Secretary of State Cordell Hull wrote to President Roosevelt about the need to secure "the good will of the native peoples of southeast Asia" for the United Nations. Hull pushed for "early, dramatic, and concerted announcements" with specific dates on which independence or self-government would be granted. And while this was primarily a postwar strategy, he noted that "definite commitments" such as these also had "great value as psychological warfare," and could "save many American and Allied lives and facilitate military operations." The United States, for its part, would of course reaffirm its commitment to Philippine independence.[14] Its public show of good faith was to admit the Philippines, still officially a US commonwealth, as an original member state of the United Nations.

The situation in the Philippines itself was, of course, dire. As US High Commissioner Paul V. McNutt noted in January 1946, the United States had "failed miserably" in protecting Filipinos from external aggression: "The principal duty of a sovereign towards its wards." Everything the United States had "boasted" about in the Philippines—"public schools, health service, good roads, democracy"—lay in ruins after Japanese occupation and US reinvasion.[15] But the situation in the Philippines was no longer as important to most fed-

FIGURE 5.1. "At Malacañan Palace—Mrs. Manuel Roxas, Mrs. Sergio Osmeña, Mrs. Pura Villanueva Kalaw, and Mrs. Rosario Acuña Picazo embroidering the stars of the last American Flag on Philippine soil."
From Pura Villanueva Kalaw, *A Brief History Of The Filipino Flag* (Manila: Bureau of Printing, 1947), 23.

eral government officials as was the cultivation of a new reputation as a global
leader of decolonization. Philippine independence would be a shining example of decolonization for the world.

Flags would be central to signaling the change in sovereignty. The Joint
Executive Committee ("composed of prominent Filipinos and Americans,"
according to the *New York Times*) took the planning of the July 4, 1946, flag
raising ceremony very seriously.[16] It decided that the creation of the flags for
the ceremonies should be a joint effort in which each nation would be tasked
with sewing the other's national flag. The Philippine Commonwealth government decided that the creation of the last US flag to officially fly in the Philippines would be a highly publicized event.

While men occupied the most prominent political positions, women
would create the symbolic objects for the ceremony (figure 5.1). Pura Villanueva Kalaw—the same woman who had organized the creation of the Philippine flag used in the inauguration of the Second Philippine Republic under
Japanese occupation—received a special invitation to join in the making of
the US flag at the Presidential Palace on June 30, 1946. When she arrived

that Sunday afternoon, Kalaw found a veritable "who's who" of prominent Filipinas: current and former first ladies and spouses of important government officials, but also women who were accomplished in their own right: the president of the Philippine Women's University, the director of the Welfare Bureau, a district court judge, lawyers, writers, newspaperwomen, pharmacists, and doctors.[17]

The creation of the last US flag to fly in the Philippines was a transnational effort: continental US women had sewn the red and white stripes, and the prominent Filipinas were to stitch the stars into the blue field.[18] When Kalaw arrived at the palace, she found the unfinished US flag spread across a table at the center of the room, and "conveniently placed cut-out stars ready for sewing" laid out on small tables throughout the room.[19] The event began with the wives of the former president, current president, and future president of the Philippines—Trinidad de Leon Roxas, Aurora A. Quezon, and Esperanza Limjap Osmeña—embroidering stars with silver thread while the rest of the guests looked on. Kalaw and the others had to wait for their turn to sew; there were not enough needles for everyone present. As sewing circles go, this one was hardly practical. The women had, in Kalaw's words, come together to "perform this symbolic gesture of affection for America."[20] And, as with any performance, there was an audience.

Because the press was there to cover the event, in this moment, the usually private world of women's sewing was on display for public consumption. At one point the cameramen even made the women move outside to the veranda because it was too dark inside the palace to take pictures. The women played their part: "Mrs. Roxas seemed oblivious of the crowd. Although she was courteous and amiable to all, her attention was on her sewing."[21]

After the women had affixed all forty-eight stars to the US flag, the press captured Kalaw and the other women marveling at their creation. Much had changed since US troops had first planted the Stars and Stripes in the Philippines in the late summer of 1898. Kalaw, for her part, wrote that staring at the finished flag—the last US flag that would ever officially fly over the Philippines—prompted her to reflect on how much her "country has advanced and progressed under the shadows and shelter of this flag."[22]

As women prepared the flags, the Philippine Commonwealth government commissioned the US Bureau of Engraving and Printing to create new postage stamps for the independent Third Philippine Republic. The same artist who in 1943 had designed the independence stamps for the Second Philippine Republic under Japanese occupation, Guillermo Tolentino, had now designed this independence stamp (figure 5.2). According to the bureau's notes, it showed an allegorical "Filipina preparing to enter the National Flag of the

FIGURE 5.2. Philippine independence stamp, issued July 4, 1946. Author's collection.

Philippines among those of the nations of the world."[23] The US and British flags were the most visible in the background. The stamp may have been produced by the US Bureau of Engraving and Printing, but the legend signaled the change in sovereignty. Where Philippine stamps had once read "United States of America, Philippine Islands," they now read "Independence of the Philippines" and "Republic of the Philippines."

On July 4, 1946, a crowd of six hundred thousand people massed in the Luneta in Manila—on the other side of the park from where the inauguration of the Second Philippine Republic had taken place not three years before—to witness the inauguration of the Third Philippine Republic. National iconography from both the Philippines and the United States was everywhere. The cover of the official program showed Lady Liberty and the allegorical Filipina from the independence commemorative stamp.[24] The parade included floats with Lady Liberty and Las Filipinas, and people dressed in red, white, blue and gold in the formation of the Philippine flag. Even General Aguinaldo, president of the First Philippine Republic, who had led troops into war to repel US sovereignty in 1898, was in attendance. With a group of other Philippine Revolution veterans, he carried the first Philippine flag that had been unfurled at Kawit when they declared Philippine independence from Spain.[25]

Although the US government had already declared the Philippines independent, according to the *New York Times*, it was not treaties or documents that would signal that change in sovereignty, but flags: "With the exchange of flags, [High Commissioner] McNutt will automatically become the United States Ambassador. Then President Manuel A. Roxas will bow out the Philippine Commonwealth and usher in the Philippine Republic in an address to the nation."[26]

The moment would be recounted dramatically a year later, in a volume the Public Relations Office of the new republic produced to commemorate the first anniversary of independence: McNutt, with his "silver hair," arose "and slowly, gracefully, patiently pull[ed] the great American Flag from the top of the pole" while the US Army Band played "The Star-Spangled Banner," "solemn, sweet, and sad." Then Roxas "slowly, gracefully, patiently raised the Flag of the Filipinos to the top of the silver pole" while the Philippine Army Band played the Philippine national anthem (figure 5.3). "At this point the two flags met on the way—one going up, the other coming down. There was a brief, split-second pause. They touched each other for a fleeting instant as if in a last caress, a last kiss." The moment the Philippine flag was raised, a siren blew in Manila, church bells rang all over the Philippines, and a twenty-one-gun salute signaled the end of colonial rule in the Philippines.[27] As the US flag was "folded carefully, solemnly, tenderly," and the Philippine flag blew alone in the breeze, "the spell was broken."[28]

Roxas, now officially president of the independent Philippine Republic, proclaimed: "I have raised the Philippine flag to wave henceforth alone and unshadowed over the entire Philippines. American sovereignty has been withdrawn. It has been transferred and is now possessed in full measure by the Filipino people."[29]

The meaning of the Philippine flag changed in that moment, from the symbolic representation of a commonwealth of the United States to the emblem of an independent nation. But in his inaugural speech, Roxas argued that the meaning of the US flag was changing in that moment as well. He proclaimed that the "flag which was first raised in conquest here has been hauled down with even greater glory," and that the "American flag flies more triumphantly today than ever before in its history."[30] Senator Millard Tydings, one of the original architects of Philippine independence legislation, agreed: "While in the physical sense we shall lower that flag for the last time over the Philippines, in truth and in fact—by that very act—it will unfurl itself at a height it has never reached before. . . . That flag, because of Philippine independence, will take on a new lustre and become, I am sure, a symbol of hope for the Peace, Progress and Humanities between nations."[31] At the turn

FIGURE 5.3. Lowering of the US flag and raising of the Philippine flag at Philippine independence ceremonies, July 4, 1946. From *Blue Book: First Anniversary of the Republic of the Philippines* (Manila: Bureau of Printing, 1947), 3.

of the century, anti-imperialists had argued that acquiring colonies sullied the US flag, an emblem meant to represent liberty and freedom. July 4, 1946, gave them reason to celebrate, too. James Morgan, for example, stated plainly that he believed the entire period of colonialism in the Philippines to be an "unhappy adventure," but that by being removed from the Philippines, "Old Glory will take on new glory."[32]

The glory of the flag ceremonies was tainted, however, by lingering devastation from the war. The preparations, a *New York Herald Tribune* reporter noted, had been "accentuated by the frantic efforts of Filipino carpenters and painters to dress up their war-smashed city for the independence celebration." But, she wrote, "no last-minute slicking" could "conceal the ruined buildings, which slump like decayed dinosaurs throughout the center of the capital."[33]

On the actual day, Filipinos who could not fit on the Luneta watched from blown-out buildings nearby. Even the official program of the inauguration, which contained sketches by Ferdinand Amorsolo of significant events in Philippine history, included a sketch of the Legislative Building in ruins.[34] Carlos P. Romulo, former resident commissioner of the Philippines in the US Congress, didn't shy away from the topic in his speech: "The Philippines was more devastated by the war than any of the United Nations. Our cities and homes destroyed, our industries still at a stand-still, our agriculture ravaged. It is difficult for any nation to embark on independence. . . . It is thousand-fold more difficult to do so, when a nation starts from a foundation of universal destruction."[35] The Philippines had their independence and their flag, but still had a long road to recovery. The departure of the US flag also signaled the end of the United States' formal responsibility for postwar reconstruction.[36]

Most US officials were less concerned about actual conditions in the Philippines than about the independence ceremonies. Much effort had been put into this performance of decolonization, and US officials wanted the world to see it. Representatives from fifty different nations were present at the inauguration.[37] For those who could not attend, a special shortwave radio program was broadcast to twenty-five countries, from Europe to South America to Asia, opening with the Philippine national anthem, including a message from President Truman to the Philippines, and closing with "The Star-Spangled Banner."[38] And it was the symbolism in particular that drew peoples' attention. As Roxas noted, "It can be said that the eyes of the world are upon us. But the world is not listening especially to the brittle words we say, words which pass quickly from hearing and fade soon from even the printed page. The peoples of the earth see in this occasion a magnificent flowering of the human spirit, an interval of grandeur in an epoch in which the grandeur of unselfishness is rare indeed."[39] People would forget what was said on July 4, 1946, but they would not forget the feeling the ceremonies had invoked.

On that day, Philippine flag ceremonies took place throughout the continental United States as well. In Washington, the chief of the Philippine Division of the State Department stood in front of the Philippine Commonwealth Building, lowered the US flag, and raised the Philippine flag, marking the moment the Commonwealth Building became the Philippine embassy.[40] In New York City, five hundred Filipino-Americans celebrated at Essex House while others gathered in Central Park to perform a double-flag raising ceremony—after all, this was Independence Day for the United States, too.[41] The Filipino community in Chicago held a similar flag raising celebration at the Merchandise Mart.[42] And in Los Angeles, Philippine independence was

commemorated with a full parade with more than seven thousand participants, and a grand ball attended by more than twelve hundred people.[43]

The ceremonies in the Philippines and throughout the United States had
the intended effect. While some questioned the terms of independence and
whether the Philippines would simply become "another Cuba," the over-
whelming response was positive.[44] Chiang Kai-Shek, the leader of the Republic of China, proclaimed that Philippine independence "illustrates that the
United States always is willing to help friendly neighbors realize their ideals
of democracy."[45] In the *Hindustan Times*, Indians, as the British feared, found
solidarity with Filipinos: "To peoples of Asia the event is of more than symbolic importance. It marks the beginning of the end of the colonial era and
stands as a beacon of hope and fulfillment for those other peoples whose battle for freedom is not yet won."[46] But in this new climate, even the British had
to chime in, if begrudgingly. A member of the House of Lords sent regards to
the US government, saying that the date "will always be remembered as one
of the great historic dates in the long history—slow and often painful—of the
liberation of the human race."[47]

A "Dissatisfied Colony"

On December 15, 1947, about a year and a half after the world witnessed the
United States grant the Philippines independence, Pedro Albizu Campos
returned to Puerto Rico. In the decade since his arrest and imprisonment,
things in Puerto Rico had changed. On a personal level, some sixty thousand Puerto Ricans had served in World War II, each one, pro-US Senator
Celestino Iriarte argued, "giv[ing] his blood for his flag, the flag of the stars
and stripes."[48] Politically, Luis Muñoz Marín's Partido Popular Democrático,
or Popular Party, had moved away from its prewar independence platform.
And while many expected that Muñoz Marín would resume the fight for independence after the war, that did not happen.[49] Internationally, the US federal government's thinking about Puerto Rico had shifted. The island had
always been strategically important, but in the postwar period it became a
point from which the United States felt it could contain communism in Latin
America.[50] While State Department officials prepared for the independence
of the Philippines, they had no intention of granting independence to Puerto
Rico. In one congressman's words, "Puerto Rico cannot become independent
because the United States has to maintain an army, and a navy in the island to
defend the territory against the Russian menace, which after this war will try
to dismember this continent to take possession of South America."[51]

At the same time, in this new era of decolonization, keeping a colony, especially for military and strategic purposes that only served the colonizer, was becoming less acceptable on the global stage. A Texas newspaper in 1947 asked its readers to imagine "that a certain powerful nation had held another weak nation in military subjection for about 50 years and continued to deny to the people of this little country the rights enjoyed by the people of the United States." Readers might guess they were referring to "the ruthless colonialism of some European nation—France, perhaps; Great Britain or Holland. But the nation that has done this is that champion of democracy, the United States, and the complaining witness is Puerto Rico."[52] The United States' task, then, would be to convince the world that Puerto Rico was decolonizing without being granted actual independence.[53]

During the war, the United States made many lofty statements about self-determination. Secretary of the Interior Harold Ickes had asked the US delegation at San Francisco "to vote for the incorporation of independence for all colonial peoples into the Charter of the World Security League."[54] As the title of an *El Imparcial* editorial, "Ickes Amazes Us," suggests, these proclamations surprised Puerto Ricans. In the wake of the Atlantic Charter, local government officials in Puerto Rico, the Puerto Rico Farmers Association, and the Parent Teacher Association of Puerto Rico used the charter's language of self-determination to call on the federal government to end colonial rule.[55] In the continental United States, too, colonial rule in Puerto Rico was coming under fire. The New York College Teachers Union Board, in demanding the release of Albizu and other Puerto Rican political prisoners, argued that Puerto Rican independence would "improv[e] our moral standing in the eyes of the world."[56] A *Washington Post* editorial remarked that in this new era, "Puerto Rico presents a live, urgent and real test of trusteeship right in our own backyard. We shall have to meet it a great deal more satisfactorily than we have met it in the past if we are to lecture the British and the French on colonial policy with any ease of conscience."[57]

However, Puerto Rico still suffered from a lack of continental awareness. Governor Jesus T. Piñero—the first Puerto Rican appointed to the role—wrote in a letter to the editor of the *New York Times* that "the question of what we Americans shall do with our colonial empire 'must seem remote to the average citizen.' Puerto Ricans understand that." But Piñero could not help feeling "puzzled by the continued protestations of our government in Washington against the failure of other governments elsewhere situated in the world to give dependent peoples a voice."[58] The hypocrisy was undeniable; but to the military, so was the strategic importance of Puerto Rico. The special assistant to the US secretary of state, in his "Balance Sheet of Interests," stated things plainly: "The main objective is to keep the peace. Peace means the elimination of 'friction points.' Dissatisfied colonies are friction points. Puerto Rico is dissatisfied and is a colony."[59] President Truman, for his part, professed neutrality, repeatedly stating that he believed Puerto Ricans should decide their own destiny.[60]

This was the Puerto Rico to which Albizu returned in December 1947. Although much had changed in the previous decade, he still drew an impressive crowd. An estimated forty thousand people welcomed him at the dock,[61] and students at the University of Puerto Rico (UPR) decided to raise the Puerto Rican flag in his honor. The ensuing conflict over the flag sparked a period of chaos in the university that eventually led to Public Law 53, which criminalized supporting Puerto Rican independence.

Albizu's return was not the first time UPR students had raised the Puerto Rican flag. The flag had traditionally flown at the university on patriotic occasions, and the chancellor, Jaime Benítez, had enthusiastically participated in such events.[62] But on March 21, 1947, to commemorate the tenth anniversary of the Ponce Massacre, students had raised the Puerto Rican flag and placed a portrait of Albizu at the foot of the flagstaff.[63] In response, Benítez had decided to raise the US flag on a pole improvised on the University Tower, where it would fly *above* the Puerto Rican flag the students had raised.[64] Seeing this as a challenge, the students had asked the chancellor to lower the US flag. Benítez had refused, arguing that flying both flags maintained "respect for the symbols and laws of Puerto Rico," because "the North American flag represented great figures of liberty such as Oswald Garrison Villard and Arthur Garfield Hays," who both had worked with the American Civil Liberties Union (ACLU) to investigate abuses in Puerto Rico.[65] A student had replied, "Today this flag does not represent here those great men, but rather the assassins of the Ponce Massacre." In an statement about Benítez's new attitude, titled "How Men Change!" students and professors had written, "The American flag is not a symbol of Puerto Rico, but rather a symbol of the nation that has subjugated our people."[66]

It was in this already tense environment that UPR students now decided to raise the Puerto Rican flag in honor of Albizu's return, with an accompanying message: "University Students Welcome Maestro Albizu Campos." From there, a tug-of-war ensued. The UPR chief of police lowered the Puerto Rican banner and raised the US flag in its place; then students lowered that US flag and—against Benítez's direct order—raised the Puerto Rican flag again. With their symbol in place, the students called an assembly under the flag and decided to invite Albizu to speak at the university. In response, Benítez suspended three students—José Gil de Lamadrid, Jorge Luis Landing, and

Juan Mari Bras—"indefinitely," and recommended their expulsion from the university.[67]

Benítez immediately faced backlash. Faculty members released a statement on behalf of the suspended students, attempting to clarify that the Puerto Rican flag itself, as an object, posed no threat. "To raise our flag constitutes no insult to anyone," they argued, because it did not have the force of the state behind it. Lowering it, on the other hand, "does constitute an insult to everyone who feels Puerto Rican, and a provocation when such a deed is committed under such circumstances as those of that day and moment."[68] Dr. Nestor Vicenty, a UPR psychology professor who lost his job over the flag incident, pointed out that in this new era of global decolonization, Puerto Rico was unique in not being able to display its flag: "Everywhere in the world the flag is a symbol of nationality that merits the respect and the reverence of all its sons and of all other men." He claimed that "the raising of the Puerto Rican flag in the University of Puerto Rico is an act of patriotism, and not an act of student indiscipline."[69] The UPR police chief even described "the pain it caused me to find myself obliged to lower the [Puerto Rican] flag," and said he had done so "with tears in my eyes."[70]

Ruth Reynolds, an activist who had traveled to Puerto Rico from the continental United States to investigate the situation for the American League for Puerto Rico's Independence, reported that "a very substantial portion of the people to whom I talked believed that the expulsion of the students on December 15, 1947, resulted from their having raised the Puerto Rican flag in *homage to don Pedro Albizu Campos*."[71] The flag itself was not necessarily a revolutionary object; but when combined with the president of the Nationalist Party, it became an incendiary symbol.

On April 14, 1948, UPR students staged a one-day strike with the goal of getting the suspended students, Dr. Vicenty, and other dismissed faculty reinstated.[72] In response, Chancellor Benítez closed the university for two weeks. In preparation for the university's reopening on Monday, May 3, Benítez had ordered the removal of the main flagpole from UPR's campus. If there was no place for a flag to fly, he reasoned, there could be no conflict over which flag flew there. But after three days of workers digging up the concrete base of the flagpole, Benítez received a message from Celestino Iriarte—the pro-US former Puerto Rican senator who had proposed the law to make the Puerto Rican flag the official flag of the colonial government back in 1932. Iriarte informed Benítez that according to university rules and regulations, it was mandatory that the United States flag be raised on UPR's campus every morning and lowered every evening. The workers began to refill the holes they had dug.[73]

The reopening of the university was dubbed by Reynolds "the Week of Terror." Benítez ordered more than two hundred policemen, uniformed and in plainclothes, onto and around campus.[74] UPR students reported "threats, intimidation, use of police force, use of revolvers, blackjacks and tear gas bombs."[75] Observers told Reynolds that police targeted newspaper reporters in the violence, and that government officials even cut off the electricity to students' loudspeakers through the Puerto Rico Water Resources Authority.[76] On May 8, 1948, for the second time in the colony's history—and still a decade before they would be called in to enforce school integration in Little Rock, Arkansas—the National Guard was brought in to put down flag protests in Puerto Rico's schools.

The conflict at the university led directly to the June 10, 1948, passage of Public Law 53 in the Puerto Rican Legislature, popularly known as the Ley de Mordaza, or Gag Law. Public Law 53 made it a felony, punishable by a maximum of ten years in jail or a maximum fine of ten thousand dollars, "to encourage, plead, advise, or preach the necessity, desirability, or suitability of overthrowing, paralyzing, or destroying the insular government, or any political subdivision of this by means of violence," or to "print, publish, edit, circulate, sell, distribute, or publicly exhibit any writing or publication which encourages, pleads, advises, or preaches the necessity, desirability, or suitability of overthrowing the insular government."[77] Unlike the Philippine flag ban in 1907, the language of the Gag Law did not explicitly target the Puerto Rican flag. But because the flag was so connected to the Nationalist Party and the independence movement, it was understood, by police and by citizens, to be prohibited.[78]

From then on, any show of support for independence—including the Puerto Rican flag—could be construed as a crime; and without trial by jury in Puerto Rico, it was up to judges appointed by the presidentially appointed governor to decide who would be charged with a felony under the act. But the Gag Law, which was meant to stifle nationalist expression, only lent power to its symbols. For years the Puerto Rican flag had been displayed innocuously by ordinary people and political parties not pushing for independence. Through this law, the colonial government definitively marked the flag as a subversive symbol. This was a subversive power the Nationalist Party could use. The very next day after the law was passed, on June 11, 1948 (and three days before US Flag Day), Puerto Rican Nationalists held their own "El Día de la Bandera" celebration in Manatí—a Puerto Rican Flag Day. They visited the grave of Antonio Vélez Alvarado, the creator of the Puerto Rican flag, and Albizu praised him "for designing the flag that united all Puerto Ricans" and gave birth to the Puerto Rican nation.[79]

Nationalists flew the Puerto Rican flag defiantly on Occupation Day—the celebration the colonial government held every year on the anniversary of US occupation—and in their annual commemorations of El Grito de Lares, the Ponce Massacre, and the birthdays of Puerto Rican independence fighters like José de Diego.[80] The US colonial government in Puerto Rico and the FBI surveilled the Nationalist Party closely, always noting when Puerto Rican flags were displayed at their events.[81] Albizu knew why the Puerto Rican flag was such a threat to the US and Puerto Rican colonial governments. "As long as a nation has symbols," he proclaimed in a 1950 speech, "it cannot be defiled and they cannot defeat it."[82]

On the anniversary of the Ponce Massacre that year, Albizu condemned Governor Muñoz Marín for claiming that Puerto Ricans were happy with the US flag. Albizu reminded crowds that the governor's father, Luis Muñoz Rivera, had revered the Puerto Rican flag. "I wish his son had a bit of shame," he said.[83] Muñoz Marín responded to Albizu's charges with measured moderation: "It is a duty of conscience to fight to see to it that that [Puerto Rican] flag shall never wave over the destruction of the people whose symbol it is . . . [and] to see that that flag waves over real freedom . . . of the people of Puerto Rico in all its forms, kinds, and essentials." He argued that Albizu's proclamations that the Puerto Rican flag should be the "only one flag" in Puerto Rico "show[ed] irresponsibility to want to gamble the whole life of the people on the capricious impatience to have the name of independence."[84]

Puerto Rico was slowly gaining more autonomy, and Muñoz Marín was living proof. In 1947, the US Congress had granted Puerto Rico the right to elect its own governor for the first time, and the people had elected Muñoz Marín. Again, this action was intended to improve the United States' global reputation. A press release from the Department of the Interior said the new law would "catch the eye of the people and nations all over the world who will see in it evidence that the people of Puerto Rico have taken another step on the road to full self-government, and," more importantly, "that the United States puts into practice its principles of democracy and self-determination."[85]

The Bureau of Engraving and Printing set about designing a new stamp to further publicize the change. The first proposed design commemorated the fiftieth anniversary of the annexation of Puerto Rico in 1898.[86] The governor warned that "such a move at this time is not advisable from the Island's point of view." Occupation Day had become a flashpoint, and "some kind of resentment is apt to burst open by at least a voiceful and boisterous minority."[87] Muñoz Marín asked the artist Irene Delano to provide a new design. Delano had first come to Puerto Rico in the early 1940s with her spouse, the photographer Jack Delano, then on assignment with the Farm Security Administration. And

FIGURE 5.4. Stamp commemorating the first gubernatorial elections in Puerto Rico, issued April 27, 1949. National Postal Museum, Smithsonian Institution.

despite her experience in the Puerto Rican government's Division of Cinema and Graphics producing posters to disseminate information about public health, housing, and voting to the Puerto Rican people, she was stumped by this smaller assignment: "For heaven's sake, I've used stamps all my life, but, like everybody else, I guess, I couldn't tell you what is on a single one of them. What the devil am I to do?"[88] After receiving a crash course in stamp design from local collectors, and advice from fellow artists, Delano delivered the requested design to Muñoz Marín.[89]

Delano's design depicted an archetypal rural Puerto Rican jíbaro—a potent national symbol in and of itself—with the wheel of industry in one hand and the ballot box in the other, commemorating both the growth of industry and the advent of gubernatorial elections in Puerto Rico (figure 5.4).[90] Luis Muñoz Marín wrote that the design was "symbolic of this country's gallant fight for the achievement of a better life through democratic processes."[91] The emphasis on advancement through hard work and voting stood in direct opposition to Albizu's refusal to participate in the US colonial electoral system. The stamp, which would circulate throughout Puerto Rico, the United States, and among collectors around the world, was part of the federal government's effort to show the world that it was beginning to decolonize Puerto Rico. The secretary of the interior wrote that in addition to its "educational value and assistance in developing tourism in Puerto Rico," the stamp emphasized

Puerto Rico's elections "especially at a time when the attention of the world is fixed on dependent areas as never before in history."[92]

This positive view of increasing autonomy was espoused not just by US federal officials, but by Puerto Ricans themselves. At Fourth of July celebrations in 1949, the floor leader of the Puerto Rican Senate, Victor Gutierrez Franqui, proclaimed: "As for myself I can say that I do not consider myself the citizen of a colony—that I do not consider Puerto Rico a colony." While Nationalists expressed their pro-independence views through flying the Puerto Rican flag, those who, like Gutierrez, wanted a closer relationship with the United States expressed their sentiments through attachment to the US flag. "My generation is an American generation," Gutierrez continued; "1,900,000 of us Puerto Ricans were born under the flag of the United States and of these 1,500,000 were born American citizens. I, as a Puerto Rican, feel a part of a community of free citizens of the United States of America, for whom the life of liberty and of democracy is a reality."[93] This sentiment also came through in letters written by ordinary people, especially veterans and their loved ones. One Puerto Rican veteran wrote to President Truman saying that, as someone who had served under "our glorious flag," he hoped that Puerto Rico would become a state.[94] And a mother of a veteran wrote to Truman that if Puerto Ricans should ever lose their glorious standard, "our American flag," they would surely die of hunger and cold, and return to the days of slavery.[95] While the Nationalist Party condemned the Stars and Stripes, these people thought of it as "their" flag.

Granting Puerto Ricans the right to elect their own governor, federal officials knew, would not be enough to convince the world that Puerto Rico had ceased to be a colony. A more concrete status change was in order. The idea of transforming Puerto Rico into a commonwealth had first been proposed in 1943 by an advisory committee set up by President Roosevelt, comprising the secretary of the interior, the governor of Puerto Rico (Rexford Tugwell at the time), Muñoz Marín (then president of the Puerto Rican Senate), and other prominent government officials, to study the possibilities of redefining the relationship between Puerto Rico and the United States.[96] A key feature of this commonwealth, according to Pedro Capo-Rodríguez, who testified in front of the House Committee on Insular Affairs in 1944, would be Puerto Rico's own flag. Capo-Rodríguez argued that "a Puerto Rican flag, waving side by side with the American flag in the Island would be both a symbol of a more perfect union between Puerto Rico and the United States and a categorical and unquestionable affirmation of our faith in the principles of democracy." Capo-Rodríguez reminded representatives that the symbolic gesture would matter in this new international environment: "Such formal action on the part of Congress could only enhance the prestige and promote the interests of the United States not merely in Puerto Rico, but even more so throughout Latin America and the rest of the world."[97]

On July 3, 1950, Truman signed Public Law 600, the Puerto Rico Federal Relations Act of 1950, which allowed Puerto Ricans, if they approved the law, to elect a constitutional assembly that would create a new constitution for Puerto Rico—subject to approval by the US Congress. The law stated that Congress "has progressively recognized the right of self-government of the people of Puerto Rico," and that this latest step gave Puerto Ricans "government by consent."[98] Colonialism by consent, however, was still colonialism, and officials suspected that Nationalists would not be satisfied with the change. The secretary of the interior and Muñoz Marín—by then governor of the island—met several times to discuss the possibility of a nationalist uprising, based on information received from the FBI, but they concluded that there was no real threat of insurrection, and that federal intervention would not be necessary.[99] They were wrong.

On October 30, 1950, before there could be a vote on the new constitution, Nationalists organized an island-wide uprising.[100] Blanca Canales was one of three leaders, and the only woman, to lead a small group in the revolt. But while the uprising had been in the works for years, Canales believed the timing was "premature." After an October 28 jailbreak from the Río Piedras penitentiary, police blamed Nationalists and began raiding their homes.[101] Believing he would be arrested again soon, Albizu ordered that the island-wide uprising begin two days later, on Monday October 30, 1950.

Canales, for her part, was to cut the telephone wires from the calling center in Jayuya, and then proceed to the River Palace Hotel, where she would proclaim the independence of the Republic of Puerto Rico from the second-floor balcony. At 6 a.m. on Monday morning, men began to assemble at her home.[102] The revolt was to begin at noon, but police had conducted a predawn raid that morning on Nationalist supporters in Ponce.[103] By 10:30 a.m., Canales heard the news that there had been a shootout between Ponce Nationalists and police; and soon after her cousin informed her of that, Nationalists in Arecibo had risen up, attacked the police station, and killed four officers.[104] Fearing that the road might soon be blocked, Canales decided to begin the revolt in Jayuya early.

Searching for a way to inspire the men who had gathered for the uprising, Canales took down the Puerto Rican flag hanging in her foyer and carried it downstairs. "This flag has a long history," she said, "for it was flown at the San Juan gate . . . the day Don Pedro returned home (December 15, 1947) . . . and in Manatí (June 1948) and Lares (September 1949)." While waving the flag before the men, Canales proclaimed: "This is the moment to act. We will go and seize the town. . . . Kneel and swear to defend Don Pedro, this flag and the liberty of Puerto Rico." The men pledged their allegiance to the flag of Puerto Rico, then left to seize Jayuya and declare Puerto Rican independence.[105]

Soon afterward, Canales stood on the second-floor balcony of the River Palace Hotel. As she watched the police station and US post office burn, she unfurled the Puerto Rican flag, and cried out in Spanish, "Long live free Puerto Rico!"[106] By this time, the revolt had spread throughout the island, from Ponce to Arecibo to Utuado, and even to La Fortaleza—the Governor's Palace—in San Juan. Muñoz Marín called in the National Guard, which "in scores of sharp, bloody little battles," according to *Time* magazine, used "bazookas, tanks, and planes" against its own citizens to put down the rebellion.[107] More than two dozen people died—a death toll higher than in the United States' conquest of Puerto Rico in 1898.[108]

Concerned that this would make Puerto Rico look unstable to US policymakers who would have the power veto Puerto Rico's new constitution, Muñoz Marín downplayed the violence and its origins in a report to the secretary of the interior: "Total number of nationalists on island are estimated by FBI at about 400. Most of them are fanatical but situation seems to be well in hand. Such words as 'uprising' 'revolution' 'rebellion' make interesting headlines but are misleading."[109] In turn, federal officials, mindful of the international community, sought to localize the uprising. In an attempt to preempt Soviet criticism in the United Nations, the US secretary of state announced that it was "purely an internal matter which is being dealt with effectively by appropriate authorities."[110] When US officials did connect the uprising in Puerto Rico to the broader international context, it was only to invalidate the motivations of Nationalists by suggesting, as Muñoz Marín did in a public radio address, that communists might have persuaded them to rise up against the government.[111]

Two days later, the revolt that Muñoz Marín had tried to contain to the island spread to the continental United States. On November 1, 1950, Oscar Collazo and Griselio Torresola traveled to Blair House, the guest house where Truman had been living since 1948 while the White House underwent renovation. They approached the guest house, opened fire, and succeeded in shooting a police officer and two secret service agents, killing one of them, before agents shot and killed Torresola and captured Collazo.[112] Truman, who had been napping inside Blair House when the assassination attempt began, survived unscathed.[113] Later, Collazo was clear about his and Torresola's motivations, testifying that they had decided to assassinate Truman to draw attention to Puerto Rico's plight in the continental United States. He lamented that "ninety per cent of the American people, don't know where Puerto Rico is. . . . They don't know that Puerto Rico is a possession of the United States, even though it has been so for the last fifty-two years." He and Torresola had hoped that "by coming to Washington and making some kind of demonstration in the capital of this nation," they could "make the American people understand the real situation in Puerto Rico."[114]

The continental US press, however, did not relay that message to the "American people." They reported Truman's regret at the death of one of his secret service agents, and his confusion about Puerto Rican demands, since, he again claimed, he had always supported Puerto Ricans' right to choose their own destiny.[115] Some reports repeated Muñoz Marín's line that the uprising was inspired by communists, and even said that "it would be dignifying an abortive revolt to call it a rebellion" rather than "violence incited by fanatical nationalists."[116] Tugwell, the former governor, told the press that "practically all Puerto Ricans are loyal Americans," and that Truman, through Public Law 600, had "gone out of his way to further Puerto Ricans' aspirations for independence within the United States system."[117] The last part of Tugwell's sentence revealed the problem: to the Nationalist Party, "independence within the United States system" was not independence at all.

While Tugwell dismissed the significance of the uprising to US officials, back in Puerto Rico, Muñoz Marín reacted harshly, ordering police to arrest *all* Nationalists. Albizu, a primary target, was "flushed out of his home with tear gas," in the words of the *Washington Post*.[118] The authorities worked swiftly, estimating that within two days, members of the Insular Police and National Guard arrested approximately one thousand people.[119]

While police were ordered to target known Nationalists, possession of a Puerto Rican flag was enough to mark a person eligible for arrest. A Puerto Rican teacher, Modesto Gotay, was arrested for flying the flag outside his home. He was eventually released, but authorities did not return his confiscated flag for another two months.[120] Gotay had flown the same flag outside his home for more than thirty years without incident—even under the repressive regimes of the governors E. Mont Reily and Blanton Winship. And yet, as Puerto Rico was purportedly decolonizing under its first elected governor, Gotay was now arrested for flying his national emblem.

The Single-Star Flag

On June 4, 1951, Puerto Ricans voted on Public Law 600. While the Puerto Rican Independence Party (a postwar offshoot of Muñoz Marín's Popular Party that remained committed to independence) and the Nationalist Party boycotted the elections, over three-fourths of those who voted chose to approve the law. Later that year, elected delegates held a constitutional assembly to draft and ratify a new constitution, which Puerto Rican voters and eventually the US Congress approved, and which Truman signed into law on July 3, 1952.[121] The new constitution maintained the three-branch government Puerto Rico already enjoyed, with an elected governor, an elected bicameral legislature, and a judicial branch. It did, however, change the procedure for appointees: those who previously had been appointed by the US President and confirmed by the US Senate would now be appointed by Puerto Rico's governor and confirmed by its Senate.[122] With these changes, the Constitutional Convention of Puerto Rico announced: "We attain the goal of complete self-government, the last vestiges of colonialism having disappeared in the principle of Compact, and we enter into an era of new developments in democratic civilization."[123] The first law passed under the new constitution adopted the single-star Puerto Rican flag as the official flag of the Commonwealth—or, as it was called in Puerto Rico, el Estado Libre Asociado (ELA).[124]

While they had downplayed the 1950 uprising and assassination attempt on Truman to the continental US and international community, US and Puerto Rican officials wanted all eyes on the inauguration of the Commonwealth of Puerto Rico. Three days of celebration would culminate at noon on a Friday afternoon, with the raising of the Puerto Rican flag in every city and town.[125] But this was not just any Friday. It was July 25—the holiday known as Occupation Day, which marked the anniversary of US troops first landing and raising their flag in Puerto Rico in 1898. On July 25, 1952, Muñoz Marín would raise the Puerto Rican flag, and Occupation Day would become Constitution Day. As the scholars César Ayala and Rafael Bernabe have argued, this was no coincidence: "The image of Muñoz Marín raising the Puerto Rican flag was expected to complement that of the landing in Guánica" and send a clear message: "U.S. rule had led to Puerto Rican self-government."[126]

On July 25, 1952, a crowd of thirty-five thousand assembled in San Juan. A hundred prominent guests joined Muñoz Marín, including governors, senators, and representatives from the United States, and dignitaries from ten Central and South American countries.[127] After a ninety-minute parade, UPR Chancellor Jaime Benítez—who had expelled students for raising the Puerto Rican flag on campus just four years before—introduced Chief Justice Roberto H. Todd Jr., who read the Commonwealth proclamation, followed by Resident Commissioner Antonio Fernós's reading of the preamble of the new constitution. Then, before raising the flag, Muñoz Marín took to the podium to deliver his inaugural address.

Perhaps sensing the restlessness of the crowd, Muñoz Marín began by re-
assuring his audience that he would raise the flag of Puerto Rico as soon as
he finished his speech. His brief remarks that day did not focus on the meaning of the constitution, on self-government, or on decolonization. Instead,
Muñoz Marín focused entirely on the Puerto Rican flag. In Spanish, he proclaimed that "Puerto Rico is honored to see its flag float next to that of the
great American Union" and that it made those two countries "equal in dignity." He hoped that the Puerto Rican people would now see in their flag "the
symbol of their spirit before their own destiny and together with America."[128]

This was a dramatic shift from the previous meaning of the Puerto Rican
flag. When originally introduced in the 1890s, it was a symbol of revolution
against Spanish rule. In the early years of US rule, it was associated with the
desire for independence, but was also commonly encountered as an innocuous symbol of Puerto Rican national pride. The 1948 Gag Law unequivocally
transformed the Puerto Rican flag into a revolutionary emblem, possession
of which put one at risk of arrest. And now, in 1952, Muñoz Marín made the
case, both to the Puerto Rican people and to the world, that the flag's meaning had changed yet again. "The flag of Puerto Rico is not one of narrow
nationalism," he argued. "It is of all Puerto Ricans." It was, he said, the flag
of "those who used it for terrorism in the past," and "of those who raise it as
a badge of peace and courage in the present." Indeed, Muñoz Marín argued
that making the Puerto Rican flag the official flag of the Commonwealth was
"rescuing it for Puerto Rico," saving it from being "reduce[d] to a banner of
division." The ability to work hard for a good living, education, a fraternal
feeling towards all men on earth, and "a culture of freedom, work, serenity,
justice, generosity"—these were the things, Muñoz Marín argued, with which
the Puerto Rican people imbued their flag on that day. "In the folds of this
flag is a humanist attitude that keeps our people at a distance from obso-
lescent nationalism," he argued.[129] While Muñoz Marín's language suggested
that Puerto Rican nationalism was a thing of the past, newspapers noted that
Truman had commuted the death sentence of his attempted assassin, Oscar
Collazo, to life in prison that very day.[130]

At noon, Muñoz Marín raised the Puerto Rican flag beside the US flag,
and a US general ordered a seventeen-gun-salute to the US Commonwealth
of Puerto Rico—not the twenty-one-gun salute reserved for sovereign nations.[131] The only difference between the Puerto Rican flag previously used
by the Nationalist Party and the Puerto Rican flag officially raised from that
day forward was that the new flag used a darker shade of blue—to match the
blue on the US flag.[132]

FIGURE 5.5. US and Puerto Rican flags flying side by side outside a hospital in Puerto Rico after the inauguration of the Commonwealth, July 1952. Instituto de Cultura Puertorriqueña Archivo General de Puerto Rico, Departamento de Instrucción Pública, Ce71 A4051.

In an article titled "At Last, Puerto Rico Has Ceased to Be a People without a Flag!" the Puerto Rican newspaper *El Mundo* reflected on the significance of the moment: "From now on there will be no fear of raising the single-star flag."[133] Indeed, much like after the end of the Philippine flag ban in 1919, Puerto Rican and US flags now flew side by side throughout Puerto Rico, on schools, hospitals, post offices and other government buildings, and the two were displayed prominently together during patriotic holidays, with the Puerto Rican flag in the subordinate position (figure 5.5).

This was what Nationalists had feared since pro-US Puerto Rican legislators had first attempted to make the Puerto Rican flag the official flag of the colonial government in 1932: the colonial co-optation of their national symbol. Isabel Freire de Matos Paoli, whose spouse, the poet Francisco Matos Paoli, had been arrested under the Gag Law, protested the move in an *El Imparcial* article called "The Kidnapping of the Puerto Rican Flag."[134] The Puerto Rican Independence Party noted the hypocrisy of the recent arrests: "The men who yesterday ordered the search of dwellings and the arrest of heads of households and young men, for the horrendous crime, for the terrible crime of having the Puerto Rican flag in their homes, or high on a flagpole . . . today glorify what barely yesterday they repudiated."[135] From La Princesa prison, Albizu and the other imprisoned Nationalists could see the Puerto Rican flag now flying in its official capacity as the flag of the Commonwealth government, but, *El Imparcial* reported, they had offered no comment on the change.[136] Even in the government's eyes the single-starred flag had been stripped it of its revolutionary potential; surveillance of Nationalist activities after July 25, 1952, refer to it as "la bandera del Estado Libre Asociado," not the flag of the independence movement.[137]

On the other side of the political spectrum, the raising of the Puerto Rican flag irritated some pro-US Puerto Ricans. One man wrote to the chairman of the Committee on Insular Affairs in the US Congress in September 1952 to complain about the flag's prevalence after the Commonwealth inauguration. "The other night in a show of the Caribbean festival only this hymn [La Borinqueña] was played. Continental US citizens were puzzled as well as American citizens of Puerto Rico because they did not play our National Anthem The Star Spangled Banner." He argued that the prevalence of Puerto Rican national symbols sent a misleading message about sovereignty: "Some tourists had the idea they were in a foreign country or that the new status had brought about a change."[138] Another man wrote to the secretary of the interior about how Muñoz Marín was misleading the Puerto Rican people with "a public campaign proclaiming that Puerto Rico is now free from the sovereignty of the United States," including "legaliz[ing] the sovereign flag of the island and the national anthem." He nostalgically recalled the "good old days" when "everybody (the people) in Puerto Rico was pro American, felt American, English was taught in the schools, the children paid allegiance to the flag and the Star Spangled Banner."[139]

While some supported it and others condemned it, there was no consensus on what the Commonwealth or Estado Libre Asociado was. The United States had other commonwealths that were also states (Massachusetts, Pennsylvania, Kentucky, and Virginia) and the Philippines had been a commonwealth from 1935 to 1946. Muñoz Marín argued that the Puerto Rican Commonwealth was "a new kind of statehood," a "political mutation."[140] According to the Nationalists, however, Puerto Rico's status had not changed at all. In a statement to the US House of Representatives they argued that the "colonial reform" of 1952 was "a typical case of colonial semantics." Military conscription, commercial treaties, customs duties, courts, passports, currency, and the general subjection of the Puerto Rican government to the federal government of the United States all remained unchanged.[141] Adding further to the confusion, a Hong Kong newspaper announced that Puerto Rico had become a US state, and a Florida congressman argued on the House floor that the United States had granted Puerto Rico independence.[142]

The latter viewpoint was the one the US federal government wanted the world to believe as it sought to convince other countries to vote for removing Puerto Rico from the UN's list of non-self-governing territories. But behind closed doors, US government officials spoke the truth. The director of the Office of Territories (the US equivalent of a colonial office) wrote to the attorney general that the US Constitution "makes provision for only three kinds of political entities under our federal system: States, the district set aside for the seat of the government of the United States, and territory of the United States." Since Puerto Rico had not become a state and was certainly not independent, it followed that it must still be a territory. In the words of the Office of Territories, "the term 'Commonwealth' should not be regarded as descriptive of any change in Puerto Rico's political relationship to the United States or in the form of government in Puerto Rico."[143]

This was not what many Puerto Ricans—including Luis Muñoz Marín—wanted the Commonwealth to mean. When Muñoz Marín sent the federal government a draft of the official letter that would request Puerto Rico's removal from the UN list of non-self-governing territories, the Office of Territories took issue with certain phrases—particularly his assertion that Puerto Rico had "ceased to be a territory of the United States." The Office of Territories also eliminated the statement that "Puerto Rico's laws cannot be repealed or modified by external authority"—which, in their words, expressed "a conclusion of law which is probably not correct."[144] Congress still maintained ultimate authority. Muñoz Marín was deeply troubled by these edits, and particularly by the statement that Puerto Rico remained a territory of the United States. He wrote that the status of Puerto Rico as no longer a territory was "the clear understanding of the people of Puerto Rico." Furthermore, he retorted that, having "created a political entity which, in substance and in form, is free from any vestige of colonialism," the Puerto Rican people "would be profoundly disturbed if the terms 'territory,' 'dependency' or 'possession' were applied to the Commonwealth."[145] Muñoz Marín seemingly had received confirmation of the Nationalist Party's accusation that the Commonwealth was merely "colonial semantics." Nevertheless, he submitted the letter to the federal government on January 19, 1953. With the inauguration of the Commonwealth, US and Puerto Rican officials had put on their symbolic show of decolonization. Now they had to convince the rest of the world that Puerto Rico was no longer a US colony.

Proceedings in the United Nations did not go smoothly. Perhaps unsurprisingly, the sharpest resistance in the UN came from former colonies. The delegate from India reminded the General Assembly that Puerto Rico had no voting representation in the US Congress, which conducted Puerto Rico's foreign relations and national defense.[146] US officials, Secretary of State John Foster Dulles argued, had expected opposition from India, along with "anti-U.S. propaganda" from the Soviet bloc, Guatemala, Yugoslavia, and Indonesia. They were more surprised at the "invidious" opposition from Mexico, whose delegate reminded the UN that the US assistant secretary of state himself had told the US Senate that "it would help the prestige of the United States and its programme throughout Latin America if the added recognition of self-government were given Puerto Rico." In addition to pointing out the US officials' ulterior motives, Mexico's representative, proclaiming affinity with Puerto Ricans "as a Spanish-American people," expressed that "many Latin Americans were disappointed that Puerto Rico, which had broken away from Spain at the same time as Cuba and the Philippines, had not been as fortunate in its final status as they had."[147] The Commonwealth, in other words, fell short of real independence.

As opposition mounted, President Dwight Eisenhower decided to throw a Hail Mary pass, and asked UN Ambassador Henry Cabot Lodge, just before the General Assembly's vote, to make a dramatic announcement from Eisenhower himself: that if the Puerto Rican legislature ever adopted a resolution in favor of complete independence, he would order Congress to approve it.[148] Secretary of State Dulles worried that such a bold proclamation might upset various actors, from pro-statehood Puerto Ricans, to Puerto Ricans in New York City wanting to retain their freedom of movement between Puerto Rico and the continental United States, and to congressional leaders who would resent the president speaking on a matter of congressional authority. Dulles even wondered about the announcement's international implications, and whether it might "be seriously embarrassing to the French and be used by the extreme nationalists and perhaps communist-inspired elements in North Africa."[149] Despite these concerns the plan went ahead, and Lodge made the declaration to the UN on November 27, 1953.[150] He reported triumphantly back to Eisenhower that his idea had been "a ten-strike," met with "an unprecedented burst of applause." Lodge estimated "the effect will be tremendous in Latin America and all colonial areas."[151]

The stunt had the intended effect. By a vote of 26 to 16, the General Assembly approved the resolution to remove Puerto Rico from its list of non-self-governing territories. But not all voices had been heard in the proceedings. Outside the UN headquarters in New York City, eleven protestors—all women—had been arrested for disorderly conduct. Representing the Women's Committee for the Liberation of Puerto Rican Political Prisoners, they had been handing out leaflets and demanding a hearing before the Committee on Non-Self-Governing Territories. The *New York Times* reported that "the leader of the women gave her name as Mrs. Lolita Lebron."[152]

On March 1, 1954, six months after being rebuffed at the United Nations, Lolita Lebrón, along with Irving Flores Rodriguez, Andrés Figueroa Cordero, and Rafael Cancel Miranda boarded a train from New York City to Washington. After lunch in Union Station, they entered the visitor's gallery at the House of Representatives. While House members engaged in debate over a Mexican guest worker program, Lebrón rose, unfurled a Puerto Rican flag, shouted "¡Viva Puerto Rico Libre!" (Long Live Free Puerto Rico!), and then, along with her compatriots, opened fire. They wounded five congressmen before being apprehended.[153] Lebrón had hand sewn the Puerto Rican flag herself, leading the guard who disarmed her to call her "the Betsy Ross of Puerto Rico."[154]

The date had been carefully chosen, Lebrón told police, to coincide with the opening of the Inter-American Conference in Venezuela—another attempt to bring international attention to Puerto Rico's continued colonial status.[155] Cancel Miranda later testified at his trial that the House shooting was meant "to demonstrate to the world that the Puerto Ricans not only want their independence but also that [a Puerto Rican] fights, he defends, and that he would offer his life for the independence of his country."[156] In the aftermath of the Commonwealth's co-optation of the Puerto Rican flag, Lebrón's decision to display the Puerto Rican flag during the shooting was also its reclamation as the emblem of Puerto Rican independence. The continental US press eagerly amplified this message, reprinting photos of Lebron's Puerto Rican flag alongside sensationalist headlines about the shooting.[157] Some photographers even posed the pistols used in the shooting alongside Lebrón's flag, associating the Puerto Rican flag—the emblem Muñoz Marín had tried so hard to transform into a symbol of the shared future between Puerto Rico and the United States—not only with Puerto Rican independence, but with a violent independence movement (figure 5.6).

Legally, the Commonwealth of Puerto Rico remained a US territory. But symbolically, it had most of the things that characterize an independent nation: a national flag, patriotic commemorations, and foundational myths.[158] In stark contrast to the Americanization policies of the early twentieth century, the Institute of Puerto Rican Culture, founded in 1955, was tasked with defining, promoting, and defending a distinct Puerto Rican national identity and portraying that identity to the rest of the world.[159] Politicians had argued that with the 1952 constitution, "the last vestiges of colonialism" had disappeared, but even while they forged a distinct national identity after the

FIGURE 5.6. Cameramen photographing Lolita Lebrón's homemade flag with guns used in the House of Representatives shooting, March 1, 1954. Associated Press photo.

advent of the Commonwealth, the US flag continued to fly, and people continued use US money and stamps bearing US—not Puerto Rican—national iconography.

The Fifty-Star Flag

When US imperialists began planting the flag in new colonies in 1898, it had forty-five stars—one star, they informed colonial inhabitants, for each state in the Union. People in these overseas colonies began pledging their allegiance to this forty-five star flag as part of their daily routines, and engaging in public flag veneration on US national holidays. After 1898, that flag changed, adding new stars for Oklahoma, New Mexico, and Arizona. By 1912 the US flag had forty-eight stars, each one representing a distinct space within the United States. But the design of the flag did not represent all the spaces under US jurisdiction, and people in overseas colonies knew they were not represented by the stars on the flag to which they pledged their allegiance. More than sixty years after imperialists officially raised the US flag in the Hawaiian Islands, this would change for people there.

FIGURE 5.7. Young women of Honolulu pose with forty-nine star flag, July 1959. Hawaii Statehood Commission photo. Hawai'i State Archives.

The idea of Hawaiian statehood was not new. Territorial delegate Robert William Wilcox had proposed bringing statehood legislation to Congress as early as 1901, the Hawaiian legislature had passed numerous resolutions in favor of statehood, and there had been more than thirty congressional hearings and reports on the matter by the beginning of World War II.[160] As other scholars have shown, Hawaiian statehood had been stymied thus far because of racist opposition, primarily from Southern Democrats, to admitting a state with Hawai'i's racial diversity. After the war, however, Hawai'i's racial diversity shifted from the "con" to "pro" column, as more people began to consider the myriad ways in which Hawai'i as a state could benefit the United States: as a multicultural paradise for tourists and consumers, a strategic hub for East and West to meet and fight communism in Asia and the Pacific, and a way to make the United States appear both anticolonial and racially tolerant to the rest of the world.[161] A large part of this imagining of Hawai'i as a future state was the imagining of its inclusion on the ultimate national symbol: the US flag.[162] In one pro-statehood publicity photo (figure 5.7), the caption read, "Honolulu girls pose with a 49-star flag, showing how Old Glory will look when Hawaii's state star has been added to the other 48" (at the time, many believed Hawai'i would become a state before Alaska). The photo sold the idea of racial harmony in Hawai'i, the caption arguing, "The girls typify the racial medley of Hawaii."[163]

Back in the continental United States, too, people made sense of the potential incorporation of a new, distant state into the Union through the flag.[164] But people's ideas were varied about how a star for Hawai'i should be incorporated, revealing different visions of the islands' relationship to the rest of the United States. Some thought the new star should be central to the design. For example, Arthur Walter of Peckskill, New York, suggested a design with forty-eight stars surrounding one star in the center, arguing that Hawaiians' wartime sacrifice had earned them a place of honor on the US flag.[165] Others believed that a new star for Hawai'i should be separate from the rest (figure 5.8). Roman Smith of Youngstown, Ohio, wrote that placing the new star among the others would "spoil our flag," and thought it better to have it in its own field.[166] Louis R. Kelley of Philadelphia was more explicit about why he opposed placing a new star for Hawai'i alongside those representing the other states: "All the 48 states are within the blue horizon, when you come to the edge of one state you look across the border and see the next state. They are all within the horizon, all within the blue field of the flag." He believed "that blue field should not be changed unless at some future time adjacent territory should join the union." He suggested that, should Hawai'i become a state, its star should be placed in the middle red stripe of the flag.[167]

Others, like Marjorie S. Lewis and her daughter, proposed a more conservative seven-by-seven arrangement of forty-nine stars, "To keep our Flag, its Beauty / Tho' Hawaii makes Forty-nine," as she wrote in a poem accompanying the design.[168] Many other designs, however, were far more creative. One man suggested arranging the stars to spell out "U.S.A.," and a schoolboy from Wisconsin arranged the stars in the shape of a screaming American eagle.[169] Tomas Chavez Jr., of San Antonio, Texas, suggested swapping the design elements to give the flag forty-nine stripes and thirteen stars, since more stripes could always be added to the bottom.[170] One woman sent in a total of six designs for forty-nine-, fifty-, and even fifty-one-star flags.[171] Students at Beaver Creek School in Montana also recommended leaving space "for other possessions which may be annexed as states later."[172] In this moment, the future shape of the nation, and thus the future shape of the national emblem, was not set in stone. To these citizens the US flag was not a static object, but one designed to accommodate change.

Even though there were no set plans for Hawaiian statehood in the 1940s, the director of the Division of Territories and Island Possessions (the precursor to the Office of Territories) sent the citizens' letters to President Truman

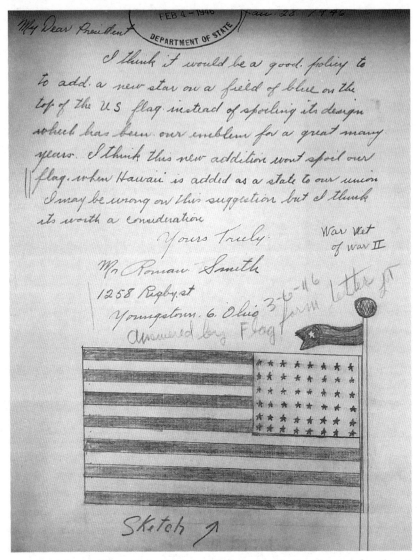

FIGURE 5.8. Proposed forty-nine star flag design with the new star for Hawai'i separate from the rest, January 28, 1946. US National Archives.

anyway because, as the director wrote, "Although many of the letters are elementary, they do reflect an interest in the flag by segments of the population."[173] People expressed their feelings about the incorporation of Hawai'i as a state through their ideas about how its star would be incorporated on the nation's most prominent symbol.

More than a decade later, President Eisenhower finally formed a commission to propose designs for a new flag.[174] The design for the eventual fifty-star flag that would welcome the Hawaiian Islands into the Union came from Ohio high school student Robert Heft, who spent $2.87 making the flag for a history class project.[175] Per an 1818 law, the new flag with an additional star would first be raised at Fort McHenry—the place where Francis Scott Key wrote "The Star-Spangled Banner" during the War of 1812—on the first Fourth of July following the passage of statehood. Since Hawai'i was admitted as a state after July 4, 1959, the first official raising of the fifty-star flag was scheduled for July 4, 1960.

Stamps could be put out earlier, so a run of ninety million commemoratives celebrating Hawaiian statehood was released in August 1959. Joseph Feher, the Hungarian-born head of the design department at the Honolulu Academy of Arts, designed the stamp (figure 5.9), which he argued expressed "the final integration of Hawaii in the United States, symbolized by the Alii [sic] warrior accepting with pride and dignity the membership offered into the United States from across the sea," in the form of "the star of statehood."[176] The stamp suggested that statehood, symbolized by the star coming across the Pacific, was a gift given by the United States and accepted by Native Hawaiians—obscuring the fact that the voting populace that had approved Hawaiian statehood was by that time majority *non*-Native. The stamps broke

FIGURE 5.9. Hawaiian statehood commemorative stamp, issued August 21, 1959. National Postal Museum, Smithsonian Institution.

local records for first-day sales in Hawai'i—and sales in the continental United States, the Honolulu postmaster reported, were "tremendous."[177] While awaiting official ceremonies the following year, Honolulu Postmaster George T. Hara suspected that the stamp's "widespread use in the months ahead should do much to interest every American in Hawaii and the significance of her admittance to the Union today."[178]

Hawaiian statehood, like Philippine independence and the Puerto Rican Commonwealth, would be marked by impressive ceremonies. Jan Jabulka, executive director of the Hawaiian Statehood Celebration Commission, wrote, "We are going to build this up to a great event, with the tourist bureau exploiting it on the mainland. I figure we will draw 25,000 people to the palace grounds to witness this historic event." The highlight, Jabulka wrote, "will be the July 4th ceremony when we raise for the first time the 50 starred flag over Iolani palace."[179] Jabulka was determined to make it a momentous occasion. He even tried unsuccessfully to have the first fifty-star flag raised at Fort McHenry, as required by law, then flown by military jet to Honolulu, estimating that with the time difference it could arrive in time to be raised again in the official ceremonies there.[180]

The commission chose to host the statehood celebration at 'Iolani Palace—the former seat of government of the overthrown Hawaiian Kingdom. And, despite the first official US flag-raising on August 12, 1898, being a date of mourning for Native Hawaiians, it actually decided that "insofar as possible the ceremony will duplicate the program which was held on August 12, 1898 at Iolani Palace where the first American flag was raised over the Territorial capitol."[181] The commission even placed the original carpet from the Hawaiian throne room—"once trod by Kamehameha III," the press noted—on the platform where they would raise the US flag.[182] Among the 3,500 invited guests, the commission arranged to include people who had been present at the first flag raising in 1898.[183]

On July 4, 1960, people throughout the United States raised the fifty-star flag for the first time. Because they lay across the international date line, the fifty-star flag was actually raised on US soil for the first time in two overseas colonies: Wake Island and Guam.[184] In the continental United States, the fifty-star flag was first raised at Fort McHenry at 12:01 a.m.; then towns in Maine battled to be the first to raise the flag at dawn.[185] Flag raisings continued across the continental United States throughout the day. A special crew raised and lowered thousands of fifty-star flags outside the Capitol building in Washington, so that members of Congress could give them to their constituents as mementoes.[186] At the flag's official debut at Independence Hall in Philadelphia, Hiram Fong—US Senator from the new state of Hawai'i—marveled at how much the US flag had changed since its inception. Who among the Founders, he wondered, could have predicted that "their flag of thirteen Atlantic seacoast states, would have, one day, fifty stars, representing a nation reaching to the Arctic and into the midst of the Pacific Ocean?"[187] Each raising of the fifty-star flag was an opportunity for those present to reflect on the inclusion of the new star on the flag as the physical manifestation of Hawai'i's political inclusion in the United States.

Situated just east of the international date line, Hawai'i itself was the last state to raise the fifty-star flag. On the morning of July 4, 1960, ten thousand people gathered at 'Iolani Palace to see a US flag with a star representing Hawai'i raised over the islands for the first time. At 11:35 a.m., the official party emerged from the palace onto the platform while the Hawaiian National Guard Band played the "Hilo March." Two groups of four men, each representing one of the four military branches, were tasked with lowering the forty-nine-star flag and raising the new one. The *Honolulu Advertiser* reported that "the 50-state flag slid unhaltingly up the 141-foot halyard, hung limply for a moment, then flared majestically in a puff of trade breeze. Onlookers packing the palace grounds watched in hushed awe, then broke into applause for the new national emblem."[188] Then Gary Doi, the winner of a school essay contest put on by the Statehood Celebration Commission, led the ten-thousand-strong audience in reciting the Pledge of Allegiance.[189] It was the first time people in the Hawaiian Islands pledged their allegiance to a US flag that included them in its design. They then raised the Hawaiian flag again, still in a position subordinate to that of the US flag.[190] Once the flag of an independent kingdom, it had also been the flag of a provisional republic run by US citizens, and the flag of a US territory. Now it was the official flag of the state of Hawaii.[191]

In his address, Governor William Quinn proclaimed that "America's symbol of freedom—its flag—is changed today. It is different because of us in Hawaii." While the government had rejected designs that proposed making the Hawai'i star central or separate from the others on the flag, Quinn still argued, "There is something special about our star. It stands for a state where peoples of every nationality and culture have learned to live in harmony with each other. . . . We believe that Hawaii's star can be made to shine like the Star of Bethlehem, leading all men in the cause of peace."[192]

In his speech, Quinn claimed that "since July the 4th, 1776, the United States of America has been the symbol of the kind of independence that was available to all nations," though "much of the impact of our own revolution is just making itself felt in some parts of the earth." Indeed, Quinn argued that "the nations which have thrown off the yoke of colonialism in the past fifteen years" were following the path the United States had laid out in 1776. Among these he included the Democratic Republic of the Congo, which had gained its independence from Belgium just a few days earlier, and the Philippines—which, he admitted, had "earned, and achieved their independence from us" fourteen years before that.[193] In Quinn's mind, the United States had remained an anticolonial nation at heart even though it had been a colonial power in practice. And Hawaiian statehood, he argued, proved that the United States had done away with its colonial power: "By making Hawaii a state, we have struck a great blow for freedom in the world of the Pacific," and "no more will we be challenged as a colonial nation."[194]

Conclusion

Indeed, Hawaiian statehood was the final piece of a narrative of decolonization that US government officials wanted to present to a world divided by the Cold War. The secretary of the interior boldly proclaimed that "the United States has neither sought nor acquired new territory, except for the peaceful acquisition of the Virgin Islands in 1917. To the contrary, it has willingly given independence to the Philippines and self-government to the Commonwealth of Puerto Rico and now has granted a full share of one of history's greatest privileges—statehood—to its former organized territories." The secretary contrasted these "peaceful processes" with concurrent events in "the Communist world": namely, "the blood baths and ruthless trampling out of liberty in Hungary and Tibet." This was the story the United States wanted its own citizens and people around the world to believe: that acquisition of territory had been an aberration, and that these recent status changes had corrected it. Philippine independence, the Puerto Rican Commonwealth, and Hawaiian statehood, he argued, were "there for all the world to see, to ponder, and to weigh, today, tomorrow, and for all time as men everywhere consider the ideological path which they and their fellows, given a choice, will choose to tread."[195]

Of course, the secretary of the interior knew that the United States had not relinquished all its territorial possessions; by that time, his own department oversaw the governments of American Samoa, Guam, the US Virgin Islands, and Japan's former Pacific islands. The latter—which covered a sea area roughly the same size as the continental United States—were first occupied by the US military in 1944 and 1945. In 1947 these islands taken from Japan officially became a United Nations "Trust Territory" administered by the United States. Like the Puerto Rican "Commonwealth," UN "trusteeship" was a new category that evaded clear definition. Chinese and Soviet delegates wanted "independence" to be the stated objective of the trusteeship system. The US delegate, along with the French and British, however, preferred the noncommittal phrase "progressive development toward self-government," which could entail independence but did not require it. "If one goes beyond that phrase," the US delegate said, it might present the "danger that we would be interpreted as butting in on colonial affairs."[196] "Trusteeships," then, became the UN's version of League of Nations mandates—colonies that had a measure of oversight from fellow UN members on the Trusteeship Council.

For people living in these US-administered territories, however, UN oversight left much to be desired. In 1954, Marshall Islanders officially petitioned the UN to halt nuclear testing and hold the United States accountable for its ill effects.[197] Again, US officials found actions in their territories under international scrutiny, with the Soviet Union calling on the United States to desist from all testing, and India pushing for the matter to be reviewed by the International Court of Justice.[198] US officials' primary concern was not the well-being of Marshall Islanders, but "that international consideration and publicity of this matter be terminated at the earliest possible moment, since it serves only to embarrass the United States and to provide material for the communist propaganda grist mills."[199] The United States convinced the majority of Trusteeship Council members to vote in its interests, and nuclear testing in the Marshall Islands continued for another four years.[200]

The islands may have officially been a UN Trust Territory administered by the United States, but as one researcher in the 1970s noted, "It is obvious to even the casual observer that the United States exercises considerable power over Micronesia. All islands have postal ZIP codes, rely on the American dollar as legal tender, and fly the American flag."[201] The same conditions prevailed in the Commonwealth of Puerto Rico, the state of Hawaii, and the unincorporated territories of American Samoa, Guam, and the US Virgin Islands. After the status changes of the 1940s and 1950s, US officials may have proclaimed that the United States was no longer "a colonial nation," but the imperial material remained.

CONCLUSION

When the Hawaiian Islands became a US state in 1959, the US government added a fiftieth star to the national flag to symbolize the change. The governor at the time proclaimed: "Today Hawaii's star is set in the firmament for the first time, and for all time."[1] In 2009, during what the state hoped would be a celebration of the fiftieth anniversary of statehood, hundreds of protesters took to the streets of Honolulu. The march mounted a direct challenge to the supremacy of US national symbols. At the head of the march, protesters pushed a twelve-foot effigy of Uncle Sam, with dollar signs for eyes, holding two cardboard guns, one labeled "GENOCIDE" and the other "IMPERIALIST."[2] As they marched, the protestors chanted, "We are not Americans," repeating a powerful proclamation made back in 1993 by the Native Hawaiian activist and scholar Haunani-Kay Trask on the one-hundredth anniversary of the 1893 illegal overthrow of the Hawaiian monarchy.[3]

Once the march reached the Convention Center—the venue of the official 2009 statehood commemoration—protesters pulled a US flag out of Uncle Sam's hat, cut out the fiftieth star, and set it on fire (figure 6.1).[4] "We were never the 50th state," one protester told an Associated Press reporter. "It was an illusion, a fabrication." The choice of words evoked how for fifty years Hawai'i's supposed inclusion in the United States had literally been woven into the fabric of the US flag.[5]

Hawai'i's star, it seemed, was not "set in the firmament." And, according to these protesters, the rest of the US colonial empire should not be set in the firmament either. The symbolic protest extended beyond the Hawaiian Islands. As the participant and scholar Dean Saranillio explained: "Uncle Sam's hat was decorated with feathers inscribed with the names of different nations whose sovereignties have been violated by the United States: First

FIGURE 6.1. "Native Hawaiian activist Jean Stavure cuts a star out of the U.S. flag to represent the State of Hawaii during a Hawaiian independence march in Honolulu on Friday, Aug. 21, 2009." Associated Press photo by Marco Garcia.

Nations, the Philippines, Guam, Puerto Rico, Cuba, and Iraq." And Uncle Sam had rolled in on a cardboard tank, with cutouts of bombs inscribed with the names of places devastated by US bombings in Hawaiʻi—Kahoʻolawe and Mākua—and elsewhere: Hiroshima and Nagasaki in Japan, Bikini Atoll in the Marshall Islands, and Vieques in Puerto Rico.[6]

In 2009, the same year in which protesters in Hawaiʻi removed themselves from the US national flag, delegates from other parts of the colonial empire celebrated the culmination of a decade-long fight for *inclusion* on a different symbolic object. Congress had initially created the 50 States Commemorative Coin Program in 1997.[7] The program promoted a certain image of the United States as a "great Nation made up of individual States," or a "voluntary association of once independent States."[8] Of course, this vision of the United States as a "republic of 50 states" excluded people living under US rule in Puerto Rico,

FIGURE 6.2. US territorial quarters, issued 2009. Coin images from the US Mint.

American Samoa, the US Virgin Islands, Guam, the Northern Mariana Islands, and even the District of Columbia from this symbolic representation of the nation.[9] Starting in 1998, nonvoting delegates from the excluded territories began introducing legislation to amend what they felt was an oversight.[10]

Kenneth McClintock-Hernandez of Puerto Rico told the House Subcommittee on Domestic and International Monetary Policy that including the territories in the commemorative quarters program would "help implement a policy of inclusion capable of symbolizing an accurate picture of the political reality of our Nation," and would recognize the contributions of the territorial inhabitants, "who quite often, for cultural or political reasons, feel left out of the national mainstream."[11] Robert Underwood of Guam agreed that many people in the territories saw "noninclusion in the commemorative quarter program as the latest manifestation of the lack of acknowledgment of our membership and contributions to the full breadth of American society."[12] Underwood believed that a shift in cultural nationalism might even lead to a change in political status: "Who knows, a full examination of representative democracy for all these areas under the American flag could follow this effort to include the Territories and the District."[13] He and his fellow territorial delegates in the House of Representatives did not have the right to vote on this bill.

In December 2007, after a decade of effort, the District of Columbia and United States Territories Circulating Quarter Dollar Program Act finally became law after its addition to the yearly omnibus spending bill.[14] In 2009 the US Mint began issuing quarters commemorating the overseas colonies (figure 6.2). The obverse of these coins featured the same bust of George Washington that all US quarters did, but the reverse was meant to depict something of each territory's unique heritage and history: an ava bowl and coconut tree for American Samoa, the fortresses of San Juan for Puerto Rico, the Bananaquit bird and a palm tree for the Virgin Islands, and CHamoru latte stones and sailing vessels for both Guam and the Northern Mariana Islands.

A few years later in Minnesota, the travel writer Doug Mack and his wife Maren added Montana's state quarter to what they thought was a completed collection, in which the quarters were ordered by the date each state was admitted to the Union, from Delaware in 1787 to Hawai'i in 1959. Then they noticed spaces in the coin portfolio for more quarters after Hawai'i. "Oh, right—we have territories," Mack remarked. He "plucked the coins from the portfolio" and noticed that "the designs bore mottoes in wholly unfamiliar languages and objects that [he] couldn't identify." Maren asked, "What's the deal with the territories, anyway?" Mack embarked on a tour of the US colonial empire to find out—traveling to the US Virgin Islands, American Samoa, Guam, the Northern Mariana Islands, and Puerto Rico.[15]

Underwood was right. These small symbolic objects did have the power to disrupt people's notions about the shape of their country, and invited them to grapple with the existence of twenty-first century US colonies—or, in Mack's words, the "Not-Quite States of America." But the design of these coins, one side carrying US iconography and the other bearing symbols unique to a colony, recalled an earlier colonial currency: the US-Philippine peso (figure 2.8). The Bureau of Insular Affairs wrote in 1903 that those coins would express that the future of the Philippines was tied to the United States. The territorial commemorative quarters suggested a similar bond between the United States and its twenty-first-century colonies. Viewed alongside the fifty state quarters, the territorial additions implied that US jurisdiction over American Samoa is as banal as its jurisdiction over Alabama, despite the vast difference in political status.[16] Indeed, the inclusion of the colonies in the state quarters series both challenged and upheld the status quo. On the one hand, these pocket-sized objects shattered the myth that the United States was a nation of fifty states, and forced ordinary citizens to reckon with the reality of US imperialism. But these coins—with the design on one side representing the United States and the design on the other representing an individual territory—also innocuously affirmed that these overseas territories should remain connected to the United States, as two sides of the same coin.

In the introduction to this book, I argued that following certain symbolic objects allows us to see the longevity and durability of US colonial rule. In the twenty-first century, flags remain a tool for people to use in challenging US colonial rule; and the designs on currency reflect people's fight for inclusion in the national community. These symbolic objects remain at the center of debates about national identity, inclusion, and exclusion. As this book has shown, these

symbols have never been a mere sideshow to seemingly more important political transformations; they have been absolutely central to them, from the initial
planting of the US flag to the promotion of patriotic education and the upholding of the US flag's supremacy against challenges both internal and external.

In setting aside the question of how the history of the colonies changes
our understanding of US history, I hope this book has started to develop a
history of the US colonial empire itself. While the places under study have
distinct histories and cultures and have had distinct experiences under US
rule, with this new approach we can begin to sketch a historical narrative of
the colonial empire as a whole—a history that at times intersects and overlaps
with that of the continental United States, and at times diverges from it. We
might see the first decade of the twentieth century as a period of Americanization, with steps toward self-rule in the 1910s, a doubling down on empire
in the 1920s, economic depression and resistance in the 1930s, world war in
the 1940s, and the creation of a new postwar order in the 1950s. These periods have been marked by flag raisings and the introduction of currency and
stamps in the first decade of the twentieth century, imperial doubling down
on the supremacy of US national symbols in the 1920s, nationalist challenges
to those same symbols in the 1930s, an interimperial battle with Japan over
national symbols in the Pacific in the 1940s, and displays of symbolic decolonization in the 1950s. As people continue to write histories of the US colonial
empire—a field that is rapidly growing but still less established than other
imperial historiographies—they will undoubtedly come up with new chro-
nologies and turning points. I hope this book reassures those interested in
writing such histories that it can and should be done.

For people who study, live in, or hail from one or more of the US colonies, I hope this history has provided an opportunity to learn more about the
rest of the colonial empire. Perhaps it has revealed some moments, like official
flag raisings, in which an important historical episode in one particular place
has happened in other places as well. I'm sure other moments have hammered
home the absolute specificity of each particular place, and the pitfalls of zoom-
ing out too far. For those whose primary focus is the continental United States,
I hope that this work, along with other recent work on the US colonial empire,
will encourage all of us who live in the United States to recognize the country
as a nation and empire that includes both states and territories, citizens and
colonial subjects. Finally, I hope that for experts on US empire, the focus on
national symbols and material culture has shed new light on already familiar
episodes, and perhaps has introduced some new moments as well.

In this book I have used national symbols and material culture to approach
difficult questions of identity and allegiance in the colonial empire: What does

conquest look like during a flag raising ceremony in the US Virgin Islands? What does World War II look like in overprinted stamps in the Philippines? What does the era of decolonization look like as the former flag of Puerto Rico's independence movement commemorates the inauguration of the US Commonwealth of Puerto Rico? We have seen how colonial subjects grappled with and actively shaped "what followed the flag," whether that flag was planted by imperialists in 1898, 1917, or 1945. In following these symbolic objects, I have told stories about people who have resisted colonial rule as well as those who have fought for recognition and inclusion in the national community. We have seen the US flag and various other flags—of Hawaiʻi, the Philippines, Puerto Rico, Japan—rise, fall, and rise again. We have seen people take to the streets in protest and quietly stitch quilts in defiance of US symbolic supremacy. We have seen others, like Ines Caparros Soler, proclaim that in receiving these symbolic objects they "became American," offering their own understanding of what assuming that identity entailed. We have also seen individual people move between acceptance and resistance: Pedro Albizu Campos welcomed the US flag in 1898, then led the largest nationalist movement against US colonial rule in the 1930s and 1940s. Alternatively, Luis Muñoz Marín began his political career advocating for the Puerto Rican flag to fly alone, then raised it alongside the US flag at the inauguration of the Commonwealth. Hawaiian independence advocates who cut the fiftieth star off the US flag and territorial delegates who fought for inclusion in the state quarters program reveal that both sides of this debate are alive and well in the twenty-first century.

The history presented in this book is important for people who either oppose or accept US national symbols, and for those in the colonies or anywhere else who have never considered the innocuous yet insidious role these symbolic objects play in their everyday lives. For sovereignty movements that seek to dismantle this symbolic system, or for those that seek to operationalize it to gain further inclusion in the United States, this book offers a history of how and why this symbolic system was constructed, how it has been challenged, how it has been maintained, and to what end. As independence movements grapple with the prevalence of US national symbols in their countries, this history provides examples of how the supremacy of these symbols has been challenged in the past. This book has also taken seriously the stories of those who have sought greater inclusion in the national community. They have had as much right to claim US national identity as anyone in the continental United States. After all, they, too, grew up pledging their allegiance to the flag of the United States of America.

Acknowledgments

This project began with a Philippine postage stamp bearing George Washington's portrait. Having always thought the United States preferred to downplay its colonies, I was surprised to find the likes of Washington, Benjamin Franklin, and Abraham Lincoln on stamps bearing the legend "Philippine Islands, United States of America"—making empire plainly obvious.

These objects might have remained a curiosity if not for the scholarly community I found at Northwestern University, from Susan Pearson encouraging me to dig deeper into those stamps, to Ken Alder introducing me to the world of material culture, and to Daniel Immerwahr, who set the gold standard for advising. While he wrote *How to Hide an Empire* and I worked on this project, we shared exciting revelations and productive disagreements about how to approach this history. I am most grateful that Daniel treated me as a colleague from day one, and am proud to have now become one. I also want to thank Kevin Boyle, Gerry Cadava, Deborah Cohen, Jonathan Holloway, Melissa Macauley, Kate Masur, Amy Stanley, and Helen Tilley, as well as Annerys Cano, Susan Delrahim, Elzbieta Foeller-Pituch, and Lesley Lundeen for their support. And to my peers—those who read my work and offered advice and (perhaps just as important) those who never did but provided the best community I could have asked for—I thank you from the bottom of my heart. I also want to thank Nick Cullather for his early encouragement, while I was still at Indiana University, that I would "be really good at this historian thing."

The research for this book brought me to sixteen archives in the continental United States and seven overseas territories, and was generously funded by the American Historical Association, the Bentley Historical Library, the Buffett Institute for International Studies, the Smithsonian Institution, the

Society for Historians of American Foreign Relations, and the Tobin Project. Thank you to the staff at the Bentley Historical Library, the US National Archives (especially Tab Lewis), Ellen Feingold and the team at the National Numismatic Collection at the National Museum of American History, Susan Smith and Baasil Wilder at the National Postal Museum, Hallie Brooker at the US Bureau of Engraving and Printing's Historical Resource Center, and everyone in Washington who opened their homes to me over the years. Thank you to María Isabel Rodríguez Matos at the Archivo General de Puerto Rico, and to the staff at the University of the Virgin Islands Library at St. Thomas and the St. Croix Landmarks Society. Thank you to La Vaughn Belle for sharing her incredible art and insights about the history of colonialism in the Virgin Islands, and for introducing me to Gerard Emanuel, Frandell Gerard, Stephanie Hanlon, Akeem McIntosh, and Aminah Saleem, who all graciously took the time to speak with me. Thank you to Joy Sales for taking time away from research to acquaint me with Manila. Thank you to the staff at the American Historical Collection at the Ateneo de Manila University, the Filipinas Heritage Library at the Ayala Museum in Makati, and the National Library of the Philippines. Thank you to Dora Herrero and the staff at the Micronesian Area Research Center at the University of Guam. Thank you to the Hawai'i State Archives staff, and to Sherman Seki at the University of Hawai'i at Mānoa. Thank you to Siata Siaosi and Justin Maga at the Feleti Barstow Library, David Herdrich at the Territorial Archive of American Samoa, and Jim Himphill at the American Samoa Historic Preservation Society.

I was lucky to begin revising this project in the Society of Fellows and the History Department at the University of Michigan. I am grateful to Anna Bonnell Freidin, John Carson, Jay Cook, Henry Cowles, Deirdre de la Cruz, Ian Shin, Tim Lorek, Matthew Spooner, and SaraEllen Strongman, and to all the senior and postdoctoral fellows, especially Scotti Parrish, Laura Finch, and Marlous van Waijenburg, for their support. I was equally lucky to finish this project at Yale, where so many colleagues have offered advice and support, including Jennifer Allen, Rohit De, Anne Eller, David Engerman, Crystal Feimster, Beverly Gage, Elizabeth Hinton, Denise Ho, Jennifer Klein, Regina Kunzel, Naomi Lamoreaux, Dan Magaziner, Joanne Meyerowitz, Alan Mikhail, Isaac Nakhimovsky, Steve Pitti, Nana Quarshie, Paul Sabin, Hannah Shepherd, and Arne Westad. Special thanks to Dana Lee for all her help and hard work.

Many have graciously commented on this work over the years on panels, at workshops, on coffee or Zoom dates, and in casual conversation. Special thanks to Michelle Bezark, Mary Bridges, Andi Christmas, Ruby Daily, Yuri Doolan, Michael Falcone, Dexter Fergie, Katie Hladky, Niko Letsos, Caity Monroe, and Angela Tate. Thank you to the organizers of the German

Historical Institute's conference on Transoceanic American Studies, the participants in the Americanist Workshop at Northwestern, and everyone who asked probing questions in question-and-answer sessions over the years. Thank you to Ashanti Shih and everyone at the Northeast Pacific Island Studies Symposium for their comments on the introduction to this book; to Christopher Dietrich, Nicole Sackley, Naoko Shibusawa, and the History Department at the University of North Carolina Wilmington for their insights on chapter 4; and to Kristin Oberiano, Erez Manela, and everyone at the Harvard International and Global History Seminar for their comments on chapter 5. Portions of chapter 2 and the conclusion first appeared in an article: "Pocket-Sized Imperialism: U.S. Designs on Colonial Currency," *Diplomatic History* 41, no. 5, (November 2017): 874–902. That content is reproduced here by permission of Oxford University Press. Thank you to the editors and anonymous reviewers for their feedback.

I am so grateful for Tim Mennel, who saw this project's potential in its earliest stages, and who enthusiastically and patiently shepherded it through the publication process. The anonymous reviewers provided invaluable feedback that greatly improved the manuscript. I'd also like to thank Susannah Engstrom, Renaldo Migaldi, Anne Strother, Brian Chartier, and everyone else at the University of Chicago Press who helped bring this book into the world. Thank you to Derek Gottlieb for putting together the index. Thank you to the Whitney Humanities Center Frederick W. Hilles Publication Fund for offsetting the publication costs.

To my loved ones in Indianapolis, Chicago, Washington, New York, my "tour family," and beyond: Your enthusiasm and encouragement have helped bring this project to fruition more than you know. I especially want to thank my grandfather, a retired social studies teacher who never answered even my simplest questions when I was growing up, but instead took me on my first "research trips" to a bookshelf of encyclopedias, teaching me early on that I could find answers (and sometimes more questions) for myself. Finally, to Sir Paul—thank you for the music, for the shows, for everything.

Notes

Introduction

1. The interview was conducted between July 2000 and August 2001. Manuel Madriaga, "The Star-Spangled Banner and 'Whiteness' in American National Identity," in *Flag, Nation, and Symbolism in Europe and America*, ed. Thomas Hylland Eriksen and Richard Jenkins (London: Routledge, 2007), 62.

2. Peter C. Stuart, *Isles of Empire: The United States and Its Overseas Possessions* (Lanham, MD: University Press of America, 1999), 438.

3. *Downes v. Bidwell* 182, U.S. 222, at 341 (1901). James Edward Kerr, *The Insular Cases: The Role of the Judiciary in American Expansionism* (Port Washington, NY: Kennikat Press, 1982); Christina Duffy Burnett and Burke Marshall, eds., *Foreign in a Domestic Sense: Puerto Rico, American Expansion, and the Constitution* (Durham, NC: Duke University Press, 2001); Bartholomew Sparrow, *The Insular Cases and the Emergence of American Empire* (Lawrence: University Press of Kansas, 2006); Kal Raustalia, *Does the Constitution Follow the Flag? The Evolution of Territoriality in American Law* (Oxford, UK: Oxford University Press, 2009); Gerald L. Neuman and Tomiko Brown-Nagin eds., *Reconsidering the Insular Cases: The Past and Future of the American Empire* (Cambridge, UK: Cambridge University Press, 2015).

4. Madriaga, "The Star-Spangled Banner," 62.

5. Delano himself experienced the process of "becoming American" after immigrating from Ukraine in the 1920s. Hilda Lloréns, *Imaging the Great Puerto Rican Family: Framing Nation, Race, and Gender during the American Century* (Lanham, MD: Lexington Books, 2014), 78.

6. Paul A. Kramer, "Power and Connection: Imperial Histories of the United States in the World," *American Historical Review* 116 (December 2011): 1366; Alyosha Goldstein, "Toward a Genealogy of the U.S. Colonial Present," in *Formations of United States Colonialism*, ed. Alyosha Goldstein (Durham, NC: Duke University Press, 2014), 1–21; Daniel Immerwahr, *How to Hide an Empire: A History of the Greater United States* (New York: Farrar, Straus and Giroux, 2019), 10; Moon-Ho Jung, *Menace to Empire: Anticolonial Solidarities and the Transpacific Origins of the US Security State* (Berkeley: University of California Press, 2022), 9–11.

7. Arnaldo Testi, *Capture the Flag: The Stars and Stripes in American History* (New York: New York University Press, 2010), 79.

8. As Amy Kaplan asked, "If Puerto Rico was deemed foreign in a domestic sense, then where did that place the American nation?" Amy Kaplan, *The Anarchy of Empire and the Making of U.S. Culture* (Cambridge, MA: Harvard University Press, 2002), 4.

9. For a definition of colonial empire and its variations, including settler and administrative colonialism, see Julian Go, *Patterns of Empire: The British and American Empires, 1688 to the Present* (Cambridge, UK: Cambridge University Press, 2011), 9–10; Goldstein, "Toward a Genealogy of the U.S. Colonial Present," 7–11.

10. Sparrow, *The Insular Cases*, 212–16.

11. Christine Taitano DeLisle, " 'Guamanian-Chamorro by Birth but American Patriotic by Choice': Subjectivity and Performance in the Life of Agueda Iglesias Johnston," *Amerasia Journal* 37, no. 3 (2011): 71; Sarah Steinbock-Pratt, *Educating the Empire: American Teachers and Contested Colonization in the Philippines* (Cambridge, UK: Cambridge University Press, 2019), 7.

12. Benedict Anderson, *Imagined Communities: Reflections on the Origin and Spread of Nationalism* (London: Verso, 2006).

13. For an overview of the scholarship on Indian boarding schools, see John R. Gram, *Education at the Edge of Empire: Negotiating Pueblo Identity in New Mexico's Indian Boarding Schools* (Seattle: University of Washington Press, 2015), 4–7.

14. Matthew Frye Jacobson, *Barbarian Virtues: The United States Encounters Foreign Peoples at Home and Abroad, 1876–1917* (New York: Hill and Wang, 2001).

15. David W. Blight, *Race and Reunion: The Civil War in American Memory* (Cambridge, MA: Harvard University Press, 2002).

16. For an overview of Americanization literature, see Victoria de Grazia, *Irresistible Empire: America's Advance Through Twentieth-Century Europe* (Cambridge, MA: Harvard University Press, 2005), 552–56.

17. Alfred McCoy, Francisco Scarano, and Courtney Johnson, "On the Tropic of Cancer," in *Colonial Crucible: Empire in the Making of the Modern American State*, ed. Alfred W. McCoy and Francisco Scarano (Madison: University of Wisconsin Press, 2009), 22–23. Aída Negrón de Montilla compiled a list of fifteen different criteria that might constitute Americanization in Puerto Rico's schools: Aída Negrón de Montilla, *Americanization in Puerto Rico and the Public School System 1900–1930* (Río Piedras, PR: Editorial Edil, 1970), xi–xii. See also Lillian Guerra, *Popular Expression and National Identity in Puerto Rico* (Gainesville: University Press of Florida, 1998), 21–23, 48–52.

18. Alice L. Conklin, *A Mission to Civilize: The Republican Idea of Empire in France and West Africa, 1895–1930* (Stanford, CA: Stanford University Press, 1997).

19. Steinbock-Pratt, *Educating the Empire*, 24. Additional works that deal with Americanization in the US colonies include Aída Negrón de Montilla, *Americanization in Puerto Rico and the Public School System 1900–1930* (Río Piedras, PR: Editorial Edil, 1970); Glenn Anthony May, *Social Engineering in the Philippines: The Aims, Execution, and Impact of American Colonial Policy, 1900–1913* (Westport, CT: Greenwood Press, 1980); Stanley Karnow, *In Our Image: America's Empire in the Philippines* (New York: Random House, 1989); Ken De Bevoise, *Agents of the Apocalypse: Epidemic Disease in the Colonial Philippines* (Princeton, NJ: Princeton University Press, 1995); Pedro A. Cabán, *Constructing a Colonial People: Puerto Rico and the United States, 1898–1932* (Boulder, CO: Westview Press, 1999); José-Manuel Navarro, *Creating Tropical Yankees: Social Science Textbooks and U.S. Ideological Control in Puerto Rico, 1898–1908* (New York: Routledge, 2002); Jorge Duany, *The Puerto Rican Nation on the Move: Identities on the Island and in the United States* (Chapel Hill: University of North Carolina Press, 2002); Alfred W. McCoy and

Francisco Scarano, eds., *Colonial Crucible: Empire in the Making of the Modern American State* (Madison: University of Wisconsin Press, 2009); Alfred W. McCoy, *Policing America's Empire: The United States, the Philippines, and the Rise of the Surveillance State* (Madison: University of Wisconsin Press, 2009); Luis H. Francia, *A History of the Philippines from Indios Bravos to Filipinos* (New York: Overlook Press, 2010); Solsiree del Moral, *Negotiating Empire: The Cultural Politics of Schools in Puerto Rico, 1898–1952* (Madison: University of Wisconsin Press, 2013).

20. Anderson, *Imagined Communities*, 133; Robert Bellah, "Civil Religion in America," *Daedalus* 96, no. 1 (Winter 1967): 1–21; Michael Kammen, *Mystic Chords of Memory: The Transformation of Tradition in American Culture* (New York: Vintage Books, 1991); John Bodnar, *Remaking America: Public Memory, Commemoration, and Patriotism in the Twentieth Century* (Princeton, NJ: Princeton University Press, 1992), 13–20; Anne McClintock, "Family Feuds: Gender, Nationalism and the Family," *Feminist Review* 44 (Summer 1993): 61–80; Michael Billig, *Banal Nationalism* (London: Sage Publications, 1995); Harcourt Fuller, *Building the Ghanaian Nation-State: Kwame Nkrumah's Symbolic Nationalism* (New York: Palgrave Macmillan, 2014); Lloréns, *Imaging the Great Puerto Rican Family*, xxii–xxiv; Jeffrey Herlihy-Mera, *After American Studies: Rethinking the Legacies of Transnational Exceptionalism* (London: Routledge, 2018), 3, 13, 20–28.

21. Thomas Hylland Eriksen, "Some Questions about Flags," in *Flag, Nation, and Symbolism in Europe and America*, ed. Thomas Hylland Eriksen and Richard Jenkins (London: Routledge, 2007), 4; Mona Ozouf, *Festivals and the French Revolution* (Cambridge, MA: Harvard University Press, 1988), 2.

22. Herlihy-Mera, *After American Studies*, 2, 6.

23. Sarah M. S. Pearsall, "Madame Sacho: How One Iroquois Woman Survived the American Revolution," *Humanities* 36, no. 3 (May/June 2015).

24. E. Berkeley Tompkins, *Anti-Imperialism in the United States; The Great Debate, 1890–1920* (Philadelphia: University of Pennsylvania Press, 1970); Michael Patrick Cullinane, *Liberty and American Anti-Imperialism: 1898–1909* (New York: Palgrave Macmillan, 2012); Stephen Kinzer, *The True Flag: Theodore Roosevelt, Mark Twain, and the Birth of American Empire* (New York: Henry Holt and Company, 2017).

25. Herlihy-Mera, *After American Studies*, 13, 23–26.

26. René Alexander Disini Orquiza Jr., *Taste of Control: Food and the Filipino Colonial Mentality under American Rule* (New Brunswick, NJ: Rutgers University Press, 2020); Rebecca Tinio McKenna, *American Imperial Pastoral: The Architecture of US Colonialism in the Philippines* (Chicago: University of Chicago Press, 2017).

27. Jean Gottmann, "The Political Partitioning of Our World: An Attempt at Analysis," *World Politics* 4, no. 4 (July 1952): 516–17; Benedict Anderson, "Census, Map, and Museum," in *Imagined Communities*, 163–86; Billig, *Banal Nationalism*.

28. Stanley D. Brunn, "Stamps as Iconography: Celebrating the Independence of New European and Central Asian States," *GeoJournal* 52, no. 4 (2000): 316–17.

29. Karen A. Cerulo, "Symbols and the World System: National Anthems and Flags," *Sociological Forum* 8, no. 2 (June 1993): 266.

30. Gottmann, "Political Partitioning," 516.

31. Louis A. Pérez Jr., *Cuba between Empires, 1878–1902* (Pittsburgh: University of Pittsburgh Press, 1983), 275.

32. On the inclusionary nature of politics of recognition, see Paul A. Kramer, *The Blood of Government: Race, Empire, the United States, and the Philippines* (Chapel Hill: University of North Carolina Press, 2006), 18.

33. Michael Adas, *Dominance by Design: Technological Imperatives and America's Civilizing Mission* (Cambridge, MA: Harvard University Press, 2009), 167.

34. Wilder opts for the term "imperial nation-state" to describe France in this period. Gary Wilder, *The French Imperial Nation-State: Negritude and Colonial Humanism between the Two World Wars* (Chicago: University of Chicago Press, 2005).

35. Wilder, *French Imperial Nation-State*, 10.

36. Italics mine. Wilder, *French Imperial Nation-State*, 7.

37. Frederick Cooper similarly discusses West African claims to Frenchness during and after decolonization. Anne Rush, Sukanya Banerjee, and Mrinalini Sinha write about how British colonial subjects rejected the hierarchies imposed on them by colonial officials and instead fashioned themselves as "imperial citizens" of the British Empire. Frederick Cooper, *Citizenship between Empire and Nation: Remaking France and French Africa, 1945–1960* (Princeton, NJ: Princeton University Press, 2014); Anne Rush, *Bonds of Empire: West Indians and Britishness from Victoria to Decolonization* (Oxford, UK: Oxford University Press, 2011); Sukanya Banerjee, *Becoming Imperial Citizens: Indians in the Late-Victorian Empire* (Durham, NC: Duke University Press, 2010); Mrinalini Sinha, *Specters of Mother India: The Global Restructuring of an Empire* (Durham, NC: Duke University Press, 2006).

38. Mary Renda, *Taking Haiti: Military Occupation and the Culture of U.S. Imperialism, 1915–1940* (Chapel Hill: University of North Carolina Press, 2004), 12.

39. Immerwahr, *How to Hide an Empire*, 3–19.

40. A. M. Dockery, "Domestic Rates and Conditions Applicable to Alaska, Hawaii, Porto Rico, and the Possessions of the United States," *The Post Office Clerk* 15, no. 10 (1917).

41. Alfred W. McCoy and Francisco Scarano, eds., *Colonial Crucible: Empire in the Making of the Modern American State* (Madison: University of Wisconsin Press, 2009); Immerwahr, *How to Hide an Empire*.

42. Ann Laura Stoler, *Along the Archival Grain: Epistemic Anxieties and Colonial Common Sense* (Princeton, NJ: Princeton University Press, 2009), 7.

43. Epeli Hau'ofa, "Our Sea of Islands," *The Contemporary Pacific* 6, no. 1 (Spring 1994): 155.

44. Jung, *Menace to Empire*, 12.

45. On hyphenated-American identity, see Herlihy-Mera, *After American Studies*, 9–10, 44–45.

46. Nancy Morris conducted a study on Puerto Rican self-identification from 1990 to 1991. See the responses here: Nancy Morris, *Puerto Rico: Culture, Politics, and Identity* (Westport, CT: Praeger, 1995), 103–26. Solsiree del Moral discusses how Puerto Rican teachers saw no contradiction in their efforts to create a Puerto Rican national identity without challenging US colonial rule. Del Moral, *Negotiating Empire*, 5. See also Duany, *The Puerto Rican Nation on the Move*, 5–7, 15–18; Lloréns, *Imaging the Puerto Rican Family*.

47. Julian Go, *American Empire and the Politics of Meaning: Elite Political Cultures in the Philippines and Puerto Rico During U.S. Colonialism* (Durham, NC: Duke University Press, 2008); Lanny Thompson, *Imperial Archipelago: Representation and Rule in the Insular Territories under U.S. Dominion after 1898* (Honolulu: University of Hawai'i Press, 2010); Go, *Patterns of Empire*; Vernadette Vicuña-Gonzalez, *Securing Paradise: Tourism and Militarism in Hawai'i and the Philippines* (Durham, NC: Duke University Press, 2013); JoAnna Poblete, *Islanders in the Empire: Filipino and Puerto Rican Laborers in the Empire* (Urbana: University of Illinois Press, 2014); Colin D. Moore, *American Imperialism and the State, 1893–1921* (Cambridge, UK: Cambridge University Press, 2017); Funie Hsu, "The Coloniality of Neoliberal English: The Enduring

Structures of American Colonial English Instruction in the Philippines and Puerto Rico," *L2 Journal* 7 (2015): 123–45; Daniel Immerwahr, *How to Hide an Empire*; Jung, *Menace to Empire*.

48. Daniel Immerwahr, "Puerto Rico in the U.S. Empire: A Reply to Anne Macpherson," *S-USIH Blog* (March 2020).

49. Poblete, *Islanders in the Empire*, 3.

50. Christina Duffy Ponsa-Kraus has argued that scholars have exaggerated these distinctions. Christina Duffy Burnett, "*Untied* States: American Expansion and Territorial Deannexation," *University of Chicago Law Review* 72 (2005): 801.

51. Romeo V. Cruz has argued that the Bureau of Insular Affairs in the War Department functioned as a de facto colonial office until the creation of the Division of Territories and Island Possessions centralized colonial administration in 1934. Romeo V. Cruz, *America's Colonial Desk and the Philippines, 1898–1934* (Quezon City, Philippines, 1974). On the creation of the DTIP, see Daniel Immerwahr, *How to Hide an Empire*, 156–57.

52. Neil Smith, *American Empire: Roosevelt's Geographer and the Prelude to Globalization* (Berkeley: University of California Press, 2003), 16.

53. Immerwahr, *How to Hide an Empire*, 11.

54. Arjun Appadurai, ed., *The Social Life of Things: Commodities in Cultural Perspective* (Cambridge, UK: Cambridge University Press, 1986); Mihaly Csikszentmihalyi and Eugene Rochberg-Halton, eds., *The Meaning of Things: Domestic Symbols and the Self* (Chicago: University of Chicago Press, 1981); Patricia Spyer, ed., *Border Fetishisms: Material Objects in Unstable Spaces* (New York: Routledge, 1998); Trevor Pinch and Weibe Bijker, "Social Construction of Facts and Artifacts," in *Social Construction of Technological Systems: New Directions in the Sociology and History of Technology*, ed. Weibe Bijker, Thomas Hughes, and Trevor Pinch (Cambridge, MA: MIT Press, 1987), 17–50; Langdon Winner, "Do Artifacts Have Politics?" in *The Whale and the Reactor: A Search for Limits in an Age of High Technology* (Chicago: University of Chicago Press, 1986), 19–39; Sandra H. Dudley, ed. *Museum Materialities: Objects, Engagements, Interpretations* (London: Routledge, 2010).

55. Paul Kramer has argued that this language of being "under the flag" was often used to avoid terms like "territory" or "colony." Kramer, *Blood of Government*, 329–30.

56. Just one example: Stuart, *Isles of Empire*, 257, 270–71.

57. Robert Underwood, "Red, Whitewash, and Blue: Painting Over the Chamorro Experience," *Pacific Daily News*, July 17, 1977, p. 6.

58. Marial Iglesias Utset, *A Cultural History of Cuba During the U.S. Occupation, 1898–1902*, trans. Russ Davidson (Chapel Hill: University of North Carolina Press, 2011), 3–5.

59. Billig, *Banal Nationalism*, 8.

60. Stoler, *Along the Archival Grain*, 7.

61. Nancy Morris has argued in the case of Puerto Rico that "symbols provide a powerful shorthand for feelings attached to complicated and abstract phenomena." Morris, *Puerto Rico*, 158.

62. Robin Bernstein, *Racial Innocence: Performing American Childhood from Slavery to Civil Rights* (New York: New York University Press, 2011), 11.

63. Mona Ozouf has noted that French festival organizers after the revolution also "inherited a fervent belief in the ability to train minds." Ozouf, *Festivals and the French Revolution*, 197. Mona Domosh has made a similar argument about commodities doing the work of colonization: Mona Domosh, *American Commodities in an Age of Empire* (New York: Routledge, 2007), 9.

64. Mary Renda makes the same argument about "paternalism" in Haiti. Renda, *Taking Haiti*, 15.

65. Immerwahr, *How to Hide an Empire*, 1–7.

66. Michael Lujan Bevacqua, "Guam: Protests at the Tip of America's Spear," *South Atlantic Quarterly* 116, no. 1 (2017): 174–83.

67. Yarimar Bonilla and Marisol Lebrón, eds, *Aftershocks of Disaster: Puerto Rico before and after the Storm* (Chicago: Haymarket Books, 2019).

Chapter 1

1. *History of the Gift of Six Hundred National Flags to the Schools of Porto Rico by Lafayette Post, No. 140 Department of New York Grand Army of the Republic 1898* (New York: J. J. Little & Co., 1899), 44.

2. On the Constitution following the flag, see James Edward Kerr, *The Insular Cases: The Role of the Judiciary in American Expansionism* (Port Washington, NY: Kennikat Press, 1982); Christina Duffy Burnett and Burke Marshall, eds., *Foreign in a Domestic Sense: Puerto Rico, American Expansion, and the Constitution* (Durham, NC: Duke University Press, 2001); Bartholomew Sparrow, *The Insular Cases and the Emergence of American Empire* (Lawrence: University Press of Kansas, 2006); Kal Raustalia, *Does the Constitution Follow the Flag? The Evolution of Territoriality in American Law* (Oxford, UK: Oxford University Press, 2009); Gerald L. Neuman and Tomiko Brown-Nagin, eds., *Reconsidering the Insular Cases: The Past and Future of the American Empire* (Cambridge, UK: Cambridge University Press, 2015).

3. *Journal of the Thirty-Third National Encampment of the Grand Army of the Republic, Philadelphia, PA, September 6–7, 1899* (Philadelphia: Town Printing Company, 1899), 75.

4. *Journal of the Thirty-Fourth National Encampment of the Grand Army of the Republic, August 29–30, 1900, Chicago IL* (Philadelphia: Town Printing Company, 1901), 166.

5. Arnaldo Testi, *Capture the Flag: The Stars and Stripes in American History* (New York: New York University Press, 2010), 16.

6. Testi, *Capture the Flag*, 18–25.

7. Testi, *Capture the Flag*, 27.

8. Testi, *Capture the Flag*, 31.

9. Testi, *Capture the Flag*, 38–39, 41.

10. Testi, *Capture the Flag*, 32–34.

11. Michael Billig, *Banal Nationalism* (London: Sage Publications, 1995), 8.

12. Jean Gottmann, "The Political Partitioning of Our World: An Attempt at Analysis," *World Politics* 4, no. 4 (July 1952): 516.

13. Mihaly Csikszentmihalyi, "Why We Need Things," in *History from Things: Essays on Material Culture*, ed. Steven Lubar and W. David Kingery (Washington: Smithsonian Institution Press, 1993), 22–23.

14. "They Know the Flag: From Feb 1 to April 13, 1893, the Stars and Stripes Floated over the Hawaiian Islands," *Boston Daily Globe*, July 8, 1898, p. 7; Geo. Henry Preble, *Origin and History of the American Flag, Vol. II* (Philadelphia: Nicholas L. Brown, 1917), 785.

15. George Dewey quoted in Preble, *Origin and History of the American Flag*, 776.

16. Flag Lieutenant Thomas Mason Brumby to his sister Mrs. Walter Izard Heyward, quoted in Thomas Mason Brumby, "The Fall of Manila, August 13, 1898," *Proceedings of the United States Naval Institute* 86, no. 8 (August 1960): 88–93.

17. Oscar King Davis, *Our Conquests in the Pacific* (New York: Frederick A. Stokes, 1899), 69–76.

18. "American Flag Association: Their Motto 'One Flag, One Country, God Over All.' " *New-York Tribune*, June 10, 1898, p. 7.

19. An Address from Allan C. Bakewell, Commander of Lafayette Post, no. 140 Department of New York GAR on Presentation of United States Flags to the Schools of Hawaii, *Journal of the Thirty-Fourth National Encampment of the GAR, 1900*, 167; James A. Moss, *The Spirit of the American Flag* (Washington: United States Flag Association, 1933), 38.

20. "Flag of the Future: Union Jack and Stars and Stripes Worn as a Blended Banner in London," *Baltimore Sun*, June 4, 1898, p. 2; "Friends over the Sea: Significant Anglo-American Banquet in London," *Washington Post*, June 4, 1898, p. 1; "Anglo-American Banquet," *New-York Tribune*, June 4, 1898, p. 6.

21. William Jennings Bryan, "The National Emblem," speech delivered at Lincoln, Nebraska, December 23, 1898, in *Life and Speeches of Hon. Wm. Jennings Bryan* (Baltimore: R. H. Woodward, 1900), 66.

22. Testi, *Capture the Flag*, 83–86.

23. Bryan, "The National Emblem," 66.

24. Testi, *Capture the Flag*, 79.

25. Jane Burbank and Frederick Cooper, *Empires in World History: Power and the Politics of Difference* (Princeton, NJ: Princeton University Press, 2010); Paul A. Kramer, "Power and Connection: Imperial Histories of the United States in the World," *American Historical Review* 116 (December 2011): 1349.

26. "Our Flag Raised in Puerto Rico," *New York Times*, July 27, 1898, p. 1; "Puerto Rico Expedition: American Flag Hoisted at Ponce," *Irish Times* (Dublin), August 1, 1898, p. 6; "Another Town in Puerto Rico Ours: Flag Raised over Juan Diaz amid Cheers of the Inhabitants," *New York Times*, August 2, 1898, p. 1.

27. "The raising of the American Flag at the Governor's Palace on the 18th of Oct. 1898," no. 83, Álbum de Puerto Rico de Feliciano Alonso, Archivo Fotográfico, Archivo General de Puerto Rico, San Juan, Puerto Rico.

28. "Puerto Rico Is Now American Soil: The Stars and Stripes Raised over San Juan, the Capital," *New York Times*, October 19, 1898, p. 1.

29. *Reports of Henry K. Carroll Dec 30, 1898, and Oct 1899 and of U.S. Insular Commission May 1899* (Washington: Government Printing Office, 1899), 139.

30. Pedro Albizu Campos, "Porto Rico and the War," *Harvard Crimson*, April 14, 1917.

31. "Old Glory in Hawaii: Flag of the United States Replaces the Emblem of the Pacific Island at Honolulu," *Chicago Daily Tribune*, August 23, 1898, p. 1.

32. Bernice Piilani Irwin, *I Knew Queen Liliuokalani* (Honolulu: South Sea Sales, 1960), 64.

33. Ruth M. Tabrah, *Hawaii: A History* (New York: W. W. Norton, 1984), 9.

34. Irwin, *I Knew Queen Liliuokalani*, 102.

35. Trouble over Flag-Raising: Hawaii's Ex-Queen and Princess Kaiulani Spent a Sad Day," *New York Tribune*, August 24, 1898, p. 2.

36. Irwin, *I Knew Queen Liliuokalani*, 67.

37. Tabrah, *Hawaii*, 110.

38. B. F. Tilley to the assistant secretary of the Navy, April 19, 1900, in *Annual Reports of the Navy Department for the Year 1900: Report of the Secretary of the Navy: Miscellaneous Reports* (Washington: Government Printing Office, 1900), 99.

39. B. F. Tilley, "To the Tui Manua, the Chiefs of Manua, and the People of Manua," April 12, 1900, in *Annual Reports of the Navy Department for the Year 1900*, 105–6.

40. B. F. Tilley to the assistant secretary of the Navy, April 19, 1900, in *Annual Reports of the Navy Department for the Year 1900*, 100.

41. Declaration by Commandant B. F. Tilley upon the Hoisting of the United States Flag at Tutuila, Pago Pago, April 17, 1900, in *Annual Reports of the Navy Department for the Year 1900: Report of the Secretary of the Navy: Miscellaneous Reports*, 101.

42. B. F. Tilley to assistant secretary of the Navy, April 18, 1900, in *Annual Reports of the Navy Department for the Year 1900*, 102.

43. Program: *Ceremonies Attending the Hoisting of the American Flag*, April 17, 1900, Flag Day Programs: Fa'atonu, American Samoa Historic Preservation Office (hereafter ASHPO), Pago Pago, American Samoa; "Under the American Flag: Commander Tilley Hoists Old Glory in Samoa," *Los Angeles Times*, May 13, 1900, section 3, p. 5.

44. Edward Maurice Blackwell, *Book Two: Memoirs of Edward Maurice Blackwell* (Richmond, VA: Old Dominion Press, 1948), 38.

45. "'Tis Finished," *Lightbourn's Mail Notes*, April 2, 1917, reprinted in George E. Audain, "The 40th Anniversary of the Transfer," *St. Thomas Mail Notes*, March 31, 1957, vertical file: History of Transfer 1917, St. Croix Landmarks Society, St. Croix, US Virgin Islands.

46. Cheyenne Harty, "Transfer Day 1917: We Know What We Got, but We Don't Know What We Going to Get," *St. Croix Avis*, March 30–31, 2003, p. 5, vertical file: History of Transfer 1917, St. Croix Landmarks Society, St. Croix, US Virgin Islands.

47. Shelley Morehead, "We Have Much to Resolve," *St. Croix Avis*, March 31, 2007, vertical file: History of Transfer 1917, St. Croix Landmarks Society, St. Croix, US Virgin Islands.

48. Edward A. O'Neill, *Rape of the American Virgins* (New York: Praeger Publishers, 1972), 38.

49. Clarence Heyliger, "The Day the Dannebrog Came Down and Old Glory Flew," *St. Croix Avis*, May 1969, p. 15, vertical file: History of Transfer 1917, St. Croix Landmarks Society, St. Croix, US Virgin Islands.

50. "Tis Finished," *Lightbourn's Mail Notes*, April 2, 1917.

51. On the Philippine Revolution, see Gregorio F. Zaide, *The Philippine Revolution* (Manila: Modern Book Company, 1954); Teodoro A. Agoncillo, *The Revolt of the Masses: The Story of Bonifacio and the Katipunan* (Quezon City: University of the Philippines, 1956); Cesar Adib Majul, *The Political and Constitutional Ideas of the Philippine Revolution* (New York: Oriole Editions, 1967); David R. Sturtevant, *Popular Uprisings in the Philippines 1840–1940* (Ithaca, NY: Cornell University Press, 1976); Reynaldo C. Ileto, *Pasyon and Revolution: Popular Movements in the Philippines, 1840–1910* (Quezon City, Philippines: Ateneo de Manila University Press, 1979); Jonathan Fast and Jim Richardson, *Roots of Dependency: Political and Economic Revolution in the Nineteenth-Century Philippines* (Quezon City, Philippines: Foundation for Nationalist Studies, 1979); John N. Schumacher, *Revolutionary Clergy: The Filipino Clergy and the Nationalist Movement, 1850–1903* (Manila: Ateneo de Manila University Press, 1981); Nicole CuUnjieng Aboitiz, *Asian Place, Filipino Nation: A Global Intellectual History of the Philippine Revolution, 1887–1912* (New York: Columbia University Press, 2020).

52. Marcela de Agoncillo to Emanuel A. Baja, October 21, 1926, quoted in Emanuel A. Baja, *Our Country's Flag and Anthem* (Manila: Juan Fajardo Press, 1928), 48.

53. Speech of President Sergio Osmeña on the occasion of the exchange of flags between the United States and the Philippines at Philadelphia, May 14, 1945, box 748, folder 9-7-33, Publicity–Publications–Press Clippings, Central Files–Philippines, record group 126, Office of Territories

(hereafter RG 126), US National Archives and Records Administration (hereafter NARA), College Park, MD.

54. Appendix A-1, "Declaration of Philippine Independence, June 12, 1898," in Sulpicio Guevara, ed., *The Laws of the First Philippine Republic (The Laws of Malolos), 1898–1899* (Manila: National Historical Commission, 1972), 206.

55. Baja, *Our Country's Flag and Anthem*, 36, 61.

56. Colonel Bakewell to Major General Daniel Butterfield, December 30, 1898, in *History of the Gift of Six Hundred National Flags to the Schools of Porto Rico*, 23; "Lafayette Post's Gift: Six Hundred American Flags Presented to Puerto Rican Schools," *New York Times*, December 12, 1898, p. 3.

57. Bakewell to Butterfield, 24.

58. "Address of Comrade Bakewell on Presenting the Flags," in *History of the Gift of Six Hundred National Flags*, 32.

59. "Address of Comrade Bakewell on Presenting the Flags," 32–34.

60. "Address of Comrade Bakewell on Presenting the Flags," 35.

61. "Address of Comrade Bakewell on Presenting the Flags," 36.

62. Bakewell to Butterfield, 23.

63. Bakewell to Butterfield, 23.

64. "Big Flag for Morro: Largest Piece of Bunting Ever Unfurled Is Ready," *Chicago Daily Tribune*, June 3, 1898, p. 5.

65. "The *Dixie*'s Flag: Colors Raised over Ponce Were Sent by Lord Baltimore Chapter, Children of the Revolution," *Baltimore Sun*, August 8, 1898, p. 7.

66. "Address of Comrade Bakewell on Presenting the Flags," 31.

67. Major-General Daniel Butterfield, "Circular," August 22, 1898, in *History of the Gift of Six Hundred National Flags*, 13.

68. Butterfield, "Circular," 14.

69. *Journal of the Thirty-Third National Encampment of the Grand Army of the Republic 1899*, 74.

70. Adjutant-General H. C. Corbin to commanding general, Department of Puerto Rico, and other officers of military posts in that department, October 22, 1898, in *History of the Gift of Six Hundred National Flags*, 16.

71. Major-General Nelson A. Miles to Major Allan C. Bakewell, August 21, 1898, in *History of the Gift of Six Hundred National Flags*, 17.

72. "First Election in Guayama: Resulted in Many Indictments for Illegal Practices; Too Many Spanish Flags Being Flown in Puerto Rico–Progress of Census Enumerators," *Cincinnati Enquirer*, December 24, 1899, p. 7.

73. General Orders no. 208, December 13, 1899, in *Laws, Ordinances, Decrees, and Military Orders Having the Force of Law, Effective in Porto Rico May 1, 1900, Part 4* (Washington: Government Printing Office, 1909), 2346–47.

74. *History of the Gift of Six Hundred National Flags*, 39–40.

75. *History of the Gift of Six Hundred National Flags*, 40.

76. "Circular of Instructions, Printed in English and Spanish, Distributed to All the Schools," in *History of the Gift of Six Hundred National Flags*, 41–42.

77. *Journal of the Thirty-Eighth National Encampment of the Grand Army of the Republic, Boston, Massachusetts, August 17th and 18th, 1904* (Chicago: M. Umbdenstock, 1904), 260.

78. "Address of Comrade Bakewell on Presenting the Flags," 36.

79. Solsiree del Moral, *Negotiating Empire: The Cultural Politics of Schools in Puerto Rico, 1898–1952* (Madison: University of Wisconsin Press, 2013), 3–10.

80. *History of the Gift of Six Hundred National Flags,* 44.

81. Paul G. Miller, supervisor, "School District no. 10 San German, Puerto Rico," in *Report of the Commissioner of Education for Porto Rico* (Washington: Government Printing Office, 1902), 90.

82. Letter from S. M. Lindsay, commissioner of education at Puerto Rico July 1, 1903, in *Journal of the Thirty-Seventh National Encampment of the Grand Army of the Republic, San Francisco, August 20–21, 1903* (Philadelphia: Town Printing Company, 1903), 253.

83. O. M. Wood, supervisor, "School District no. 16, Bayamon," July 1, 1902, in *Report of the Commissioner of Education for Porto Rico* (Washington: Government Printing Office, 1902), 103.

84. *Journal of the Thirty-Third National Encampment of the Grand Army of the Republic 1899,* 357.

85. Letter from S. M. Lindsay, commissioner of education at Puerto Rico, July 1, 1903, in *Journal of the Thirty-Seventh National Encampment of the Grand Army of the Republic, 1903,* 253.

86. Henry L. Morehouse, D.D., "Our Spanish Speaking Neighbors: Porto Rico: Rapid Survey of Our Field Work as Seen by the Corresponding Secretary; Narrative Sketch of a Twenty-Five Days' Tour in the Islands," *Baptist Home Mission Monthly* 26, no. 5 (May 1904): 180.

87. The sentiment came from an 1895 poem by the same name, written by T. J. Crowe. "A Flag on Every Schoolhouse," *Werner's Magazine* 17, no. 1 (Jan. 1895): 134. The GAR misattributed the poem to Colonel J. A. Joel, "late editor *Grand Army Gazette.*" *Journal of the Thirty-Eighth National Encampment of the Grand Army of the Republic Department of Kansas; Dodge City, Kansas, May 16, 17, 18, 1916* (Topeka: Kansas State Printing Plant, 1916), 84.

88. *Journal of the Thirty-Fourth National Encampment of the Grand Army of the Republic, 1900,* 165.

89. *Journal of the Thirty-Fourth National Encampment of the Grand Army of the Republic, 1900,* 167.

90. *Journal of the Thirty-Fourth National Encampment of the Grand Army of the Republic, 1900,* 168.

91. *Journal of the Thirty-Fourth National Encampment of the Grand Army of the Republic, 1900,* 168.

92. *Journal of the Thirty-Fourth National Encampment of the Grand Army of the Republic, 1900,* 159.

93. *Journal of the Thirty-Fourth National Encampment of the Grand Army of the Republic, 1900,* 161. The eleven Manila schools French did not get to had flag raising ceremonies led by US American and Filipino schoolteachers under French's general directions.

94. *Journal of the Thirty-Fourth National Encampment of the Grand Army of the Republic, 1900,* 162.

95. *Journal of the Thirty-Fourth National Encampment of the Grand Army of the Republic, 1900,* 161, 162.

96. Paul A. Kramer, *The Blood of Government: Race, Empire, the United States, and the Philippines* (Chapel Hill: University of North Carolina Press, 2006), 262–69.

97. Kramer, *Blood of Government,* 39, 208–17.

98. *Fifth Annual Report of the Philippine Commission to the Secretary of War, 1904, Part 3* (Washington: Bureau of Insular Affairs, 1905), 110.

99. *Journal of the Thirty-Fourth National Encampment of the Grand Army of the Republic, 1900*, 159.

100. *Journal of the Thirty-Fourth National Encampment of the Grand Army of the Republic, 1900*, 165.

101. "Liberty on Fourth: General Amnesty May Be Declared in Philippines," *Washington Post*, June 16, 1902, p. 1; Photo of Central School, Gigquit, Surigao, Mindanao, P. I., box 9, folder Ca-8-7 Education-Provinces-Pupil Types-Classrooms, School Buildings-Moro Province, Mindanao, record group 350, Bureau of Insular Affairs (hereafter RG 350), Still Pictures, NARA, College Park, MD.

102. *Fifth Annual Report of the Philippine Commission to the Secretary of War, 1904, Part 1* (Washington: Bureau of Insular Affairs, 1905), 541.

103. Department of Public Instruction Bureau of Education, Manila, P. I., to office of General Superintendent Allan C. Bakewell, March 22, 1905, in *Journal of the Thirty-Ninth National Encampment of the Grand Army of the Republic, Denver, Colorado, September 7th and 8th, 1905* (Boston: Griffith-Stillings Press, 1905), 193.

104. *Annual Report of the Governor of Guam for Fiscal Year Ending June 30, 1930*, 17; *Annual Report of the Governor of Guam for Fiscal Year Ending June 30, 1931*, 16; *Annual Report of the Governor of Guam for Fiscal Year Ending June 30, 1935*, 12; *Annual Report of the Governor of Guam for Fiscal Year Ending June 30, 1936*, 10, box 531, folder 9-3-18 Reports-Governor-Annual, Central Files-Guam, RG 126, NARA, College Park, MD; "Flag Day Celebrated by Guam Schools," *GTA Advocate* no. 3 (February 1939): 15, box 517, folder Guam Bulletin, RG 126, NARA, College Park, MD.

105. Chaplain and Mrs. Hall, "When Santa Claus Visits Guam," *Red Cross Courier* (December 1938), box 517, folder: Guam Bulletin, RG 126, NARA, College Park, MD.

106. *Annual Report of the Governor of Guam for Fiscal Year Ending June 30, 1931*, 16, box 531, folder 9-3-18 Reports-Governor-Annual, Central Files–Guam, RG 126, NARA, College Park, MD.

107. *Journal of the Thirty-Third National Encampment of the Grand Army of the Republic, 1899*, 357.

108. Letter from Department of Education of Porto Rico, Office of the Commissioner, San Juan, March 7, 1905, in *Journal of the Thirty-Ninth National Encampment of the Grand Army of the Republic, 1905*, 193.

109. Steinbock-Pratt, *Educating the Empire*, 3–4.

110. Letter from S. M. Lindsay, Commissioner of Education at Puerto Rico, July 1, 1903, *Journal of the Thirty-Seventh National Encampment of the Grand Army of the Republic, 1903*, 253.

111. Letter from Department of Education of Porto Rico, Office of the Commissioner, San Juan, March 7, 1905, in *Journal of the Thirty-Ninth National Encampment of the Grand Army of the Republic, 1905*, 193.

112. *Journal of the Thirty-Fourth National Encampment of the Grand Army of the Republic, 1900*, 162.

113. Daily attendance rates in Puerto Rico, for example, were only 10.5 percent in 1901 and hovered between 30 and 40 percent from the 1910s to the 1930s. Lillian Guerra, *Popular Expression and National Identity in Puerto Rico* (Gainesville: University Press of Florida, 1998), 36–37.

114. Anne Perez Hattori, "Navy Blues: US Naval Rule on Guam and the Rough Road to Assimilation," *Pacific Asia Inquiry* 5, no. 1 (Fall 2014): 22; César J. Ayala and Rafael Bernabe, *Puerto Rico in the American Century: A History since 1898* (Chapel Hill: University of North Carolina

Press, 2007), 78. This was not unique to the US colonial context. The new regime in France after the Revolution had also tried to change time by introducing a new calendar of festivals. Mona Ozouf, "The Festival and Time," in *Festivals and the French Revolution* (Cambridge, MA: Harvard University Press, 1988), 158–96.

115. "Their First Fourth: How the Filipinos Celebrated the Day a Year Ago," *Evening Star* (Washington), June 30, 1900, p. 17.

116. "Their First Fourth," p. 17.

117. Alice Byram Condict, *Old Glory and the Gospel in the Philippines: Notes Gathered during Professional and Missionary Work* (Chicago: Fleming H. Revell, 1902), 87–88.

118. Condict, *Old Glory and the Gospel in the Philippines*, 87.

119. "Flag Day Observed in Puerto Rico: School Children Marched and Sang 'The Star Spangled Banner,'" *Washington Post*, June 16, 1901, p. 11; Roger L. Conant, Superintendent of School District no. 5, Caguas, Puerto Rico, to commissioner of education for Puerto Rico, June 13, 1903, in *Third Annual Report of the Governor of Porto Rico, Covering the Period from July 1, 1902 to June 30, 1903* (Washington: Government Printing Office, 1903), 200.

120. "Exhibit F. Report of the Commissioner of Education for Porto Rico," in *Annual Report of the Governor of Porto Rico for the Fiscal Year ended June 30, 1908* (Washington: Government Printing Office, 1909), 207.

121. Governor Milne, "Tutuila Flag Day Address, April 17, 1936," Governor's Office, reel 52-1, Holidays, Office of Archives and Records Management, Pago Pago, American Samoa.

122. Hattori, "Navy Blues," 23.

123. Joaquin Sablan, "Significance of the American Flag," *Guam Teacher* 6, no. 8 (February 1, 1936).

124. Michael Billig, *Banal Nationalism* (London: Sage Publications, 1995), 45.

125. Robert B. Westcott, *The Exaltation of the Flag: Proceedings at the Patriotic Mass Meeting Held by the Americans of the Philippine Islands, Which Took Place in the City of Manila, P.I., on the Evening of Friday, August 23, 1907* (Manila: John R. Edgar, 1907), 106.

126. *Journal of the Thirty-Ninth National Encampment of the Grand Army of the Republic, 1905*, 192.

127. *Journal of the Thirty-Fourth National Encampment of the Grand Army of the Republic, 1900*, 168–83.

128. *Journal of the Thirty-Fourth National Encampment of the Grand Army of the Republic, 1900*, 182.

129. John E. Gilman, adjutant general, "Report of the Flag Committee," New Haven, Connecticut, August 2, 1905, in *Journal of the Thirty-Ninth National Encampment of the Grand Army of the Republic, 1905*, 167.

130. José Trías Monge, *Puerto Rico: The Trials of the Oldest Colony in the World* (New Haven, CT: Yale University Press, 1997), 55.

131. *Revised Laws of Hawaii: Comprising the Statues of the Territory, Consolidated, Revised and Annotated* (Honolulu: Honolulu Star-Bulletin, 1915), 332.

132. Gilman, "Report of the Flag Committee," 167.

133. *Journal of the Thirty-Fourth National Encampment of the Grand Army of the Republic, 1900*, 168.

134. "The Glorious Fourth," *La Democracia* (Manila), July 3, 1912, box 148, entry 5 I-3 General Files 1898–1913, RG 350, NARA, College Park, MD.

135. Pedro Albizu Campos, "Porto Rico and the War," *Harvard Crimson*, April 14, 1917.

136. Albizu told this story in a speech he gave on April 16, 1950. Memorándum para el jefe de la policía insular, 17 de abril de 1950, 4, box 21, folder 22 (a,b), Archivo General de Puerto Rico, San Juan.

Chapter 2

1. A. W. Mellon, secretary of the treasury, to Dwight F. Davis, secretary of war, February 21, 1928, box 18, folder: Philippine–General, Circulation of Historical Value of U.S. and Foreign Securities (Series "K") Currency, 1890–1942, record group 53, Bureau of Public Debt, US National Archives and Records Administration (hereafter NARA), College Park, MD.

2. Romeo V. Cruz, *America's Colonial Desk and the Philippines, 1898–1934* (Quezon City: University of the Philippines Press, 1974).

3. Henry L. Stimson, governor-general of the Philippines, to Frank McIntyre, chief of Bureau of Insular Affairs, October 26, 1928, box 18, folder: Philippine–General, Circulation of Historical Value of U.S. and Foreign Securities (Series "K") Currency, 1890–1942, record group 53, Bureau of Public Debt, NARA, College Park, MD.

4. Emily S. Rosenberg, *Financial Missionaries to the World: The Politics and Culture of Dollar Diplomacy, 1900–1930* (Cambridge, MA: Harvard University Press, 1999); Yoshiko Nagano, *State and Finance in the Philippines, 1898–1941: The Mismanagement of an American Colony* (Singapore: National University of Singapore Press, 2015); Peter James Hudson, *Bankers and Empire: How Wall Street Colonized the Caribbean* (Chicago: University of Chicago Press, 2017); Allan E. S. Lumba, *Monetary Authorities: Capitalism and Decolonization in the American Colonial Philippines* (Durham, NC: Duke University Press, 2022).

5. Rosenberg, *Financial Missionaries to the World*, 104–5.

6. Michael Kevane, "Official Representations of the Nation: Comparing the Postage Stamps of Sudan and Burkina Faso," *African Studies Quarterly: The Online Journal for African Studies* 10, no. 1 (Spring 2008): 13.

7. Jean Gottmann, "The Political Partitioning of Our World: An Attempt at Analysis," *World Politics* 4, no. 4 (July 1952): 516.

8. *Downes v. Bidwell* 182, U.S. 222, at 341 (1901). For more on the *Insular Cases* see James Edward Kerr, *The Insular Cases: The Role of the Judiciary in American Expansionism* (Port Washington, NY: Kennikat Press, 1982); Christina Duffy Burnett and Burke Marshall, eds., *Foreign in a Domestic Sense: Puerto Rico, American Expansion, and the Constitution* (Durham, NC: Duke University Press, 2001); Bartholomew Sparrow, *The Insular Cases and the Emergence of American Empire* (Lawrence: University Press of Kansas, 2006); Kal Raustalia, *Does the Constitution Follow the Flag? The Evolution of Territoriality in American Law* (Oxford, UK: Oxford University Press, 2009); Gerald L. Neuman and Tomiko Brown-Nagin, eds., *Reconsidering the Insular Cases: The Past and Future of the American Empire* (Cambridge, UK: Cambridge University Press, 2015).

9. Sheila A. Brennan, *Stamping American Memory: Collectors, Citizens, and the Post* (Ann Arbor: University of Michigan Press, 2018), 1–2.

10. Todd Pierce, "Philatelic Propaganda: Stamps in Territorial Disputes," *IBRU Boundary and Security Bulletin* 4, no. 2 (1996): 62–64; Stanley D. Brunn, "Stamps as Iconography: Celebrating the Independence of New European and Central Asian States," *GeoJournal* 52, no. 4 (2000): 315–23; Jack Child, "The Politics and Semiotics of the Smallest Icons of Popular Culture: Latin American Postage Stamps," *Latin American Research Review* 40, no. 1 (2005): 108–37; Stanley D. Brunn, "Stamps as Messengers of Political Transition," *Geographical Review* 101, no. 1 (January 2011): 19–36.

11. Stanley D. Brunn, "Stamps as Iconography," 316–17.

12. Eric Helleiner, *The Making of National Money: Territorial Currencies in Historical Perspective* (Ithaca, NY: Cornell University Press, 2003), 2.

13. A. Piatt Andrew, "The End of the Mexican Dollar," *Quarterly Journal of Economics* 18, no. 3 (May 1904): 321.

14. J. L. Riddell, *A Monograph of the Silver Dollar: Good and Bad* (New Orleans: Norman, 1845).

15. Helleiner, *The Making of National Money*, 39; David A. Martin, "The Changing Role of Foreign Money in the United States, 1782–1857," *Journal of Economic History* 37, no. 4 (December 1977): 1027.

16. Stephen Mihm, *A Nation of Counterfeiters: Capitalists, Con Men, and the Making of the United States* (Cambridge, MA: Harvard University Press, 2007), 305, 321–30.

17. Letter from S. M. Clark to Treasury Secretary Chase, March 28, 1863, quoted in Helleiner, *The Making of National Money*, 106.

18. Mihm, *A Nation of Counterfeiters*, 359.

19. Theda Skocpol, "The Tocqueville Problem: Civic Engagement in American Democracy," *Social Science History*, 21 (Winter 1997): 461.

20. Brian Balogh, *A Government Out of Sight: The Mystery of National Authority in Nineteenth-Century America* (Cambridge, UK: Cambridge University Press, 2009), 13; Richard White, *"It's Your Misfortune and None of My Own": A New History of the American West* (Norman: University of Oklahoma Press, 1991), 57–59, 128, 174, 247.

21. Richard R. John, *Spreading the News: The American Postal System from Franklin to Morse* (Cambridge, MA: Harvard University Press, 1995), 112–68. Wayne E. Fuller, *RFD: The Changing Face of Rural America* (Bloomington: Indiana University Press, 1964), 110; On postal service and continental expansion, see Cameron Blevins, *Paper Trails: The US Post and State Power in the American West* (Oxford, UK: Oxford University Press, 2021).

22. George Minot, Esq. ed., *The Statutes at Large and Treaties of the United States of America, 1845 to 1851* (Boston: Little, Brown, and Company, 1862), 201.

23. David M. Henkin, *The Postal Age: The Emergence of Modern Communications in Nineteenth-Century America* (Chicago: University of Chicago Press, 2006), 37.

24. Brennan, *Stamping American Memory*, 68.

25. For instances of colonial subjects repurposing coins as jewelry, see G. L. Dyer, *Annual Report of the Naval Governor of Guam for Fiscal Year Ending June 30, 1905*, 26, box 536, folder: Annual Reports, 1905–1909, Central Classified Files–Guam, 1907–1951, record group 126, Office of Territories (hereafter RG 126), NARA, College Park, MD; Peter Gordon Gowing, *Mandate in Moroland: The American Government of Muslim Filipinos, 1899–1920* (Quezon City, Philippines, 1983), 139. For the theory of "scriptive things," see Robin Bernstein, *Racial Innocence: Performing American Childhood from Slavery to Civil Rights* (New York: New York University Press, 2011).

26. Bruce Cartright Jr. "Hawaii: Issue of 1893," *American Philatelist* 27, no. 10 (July 1914): 225.

27. Walter M. Giffard, "Descriptive Catalogue of the Postage Stamps of Hawaii (Sandwich Islands)," *Hawaiian Almanac and Annual for 1894* (Honolulu: Press Publishing, 1893), 116; *Report of the General Superintendent of the Census, 1890* (Honolulu: R. Grieve, 1891), 11.

28. Giffard, "Descriptive Catalogue of the Postage Stamps of Hawaii," 114.

29. Giffard, "Descriptive Catalogue of the Postage Stamps of Hawaii," 117.

30. Constitution of the Republic of Hawaii, article 16, p. 56, vol. 7: Constitutional Conventions, folder: Stenographic Record of Proceedings 1st, 2nd, 3rd, 4th days, Government Records Inventories, Hawai'i State Archives, Honolulu.

31. Brewster C. Kenyon, *History of the Postal Issues of Hawaii: A List of the Adhesive Postage Stamps, Stamped Envelopes and Postal Cards of the Hawaiian Government* (self-published, 1895), 23.

32. Charles Emory Smith, "The Mails Follow the Flag," *Collier's Weekly*, May 5, 1900, p. 3.

33. Frank W. Vaille had been in the Railway Mail Service before coming to the Philippines. "Report of the General Superintendent of Railway Mail Service," *Annual Reports of the Post-Office Department for the Fiscal Year Ended June 30, 1898* (Washington: Government Printing Office, 1898), 647.

34. Frank W. Vaille, "Report of the Postal Agent for the Philippine Island Military Service," *1898 Reports of the Post-Office Department*, 143.

35. Vaille, "Report of the Postal Agent," *1898 Reports of the Post-Office Department*, 143; John F. Willoughby, "The Manila Mail: How the Postal System of the Philippines Has Been Americanized," *Denison Review* (Iowa), August 29, 1899, p. 7.

36. Perry S. Heath quoted in Smith D. Fry, "Our Postal System: It Is Now Being Established All Over Puerto Rico," *Brookhaven Leader* (Mississippi), October 12, 1898, p. 3.

37. Vaille, *1898 Reports of the Post-Office Department*, 144.

38. "Postal Facilities in the Philippines: Agent Vaille at Manila Reports the Service Better Now Than under Spanish Rule," *San Francisco Call*, October 28, 1898, p. 2.

39. F. W. Vaille, "Report of F. W. Vaille, Director-General of Posts in the Philippine Islands," *Annual Reports of the Post-Office Department for the Fiscal Year Ended June 30, 1899* (Washington: Government Printing Office, 1899), 62.

40. "Report of the Committee Appointed by the Postmaster General to Investigate the Condition of the Postal Service on the Island of Porto Rico," *1898 Reports of the Post-Office Department*, 31; Heath quoted in Fry, "Our Postal System."

41. Fry, "Our Postal System."

42. "Puerto Rican Postal Service," *The Post Office: A Monthly Journal for Stamp Collectors* 8 (November 1898), 147; "Report of the Committee Appointed by the Postmaster General to Investigate the Condition of the Postal Service on the Island of Porto Rico," *1898 Reports of the Post-Office Department*, 63; "Postal Commission Returning," *Washington Post*, October 23, 1898, p. 2.

43. Henkin, *The Postal Age*, 3–5, 34–35, 121, 125, 136–37.

44. "Letters to the Philippines: How the Boys in Blue Can Be Reached," *St. Paul Globe*, May 18, 1898, pp. 1, 3.

45. "Philippine Postal Rates," *Hot Springs Weekly* (South Dakota), June 17, 1898, p. 2; "Mail for the Philippine Islands," *Dickinson Press* (North Dakota), June 18, 1898, p. 2; "Mail for the Front: How Soldiers with Shafter Got Letters from Home," *Jersey City News*, August 6, 1898, p. 7.

46. James E. Stuart, Chas. F. Trotter, John M. Masten, W. M. Mooney, D. H. Fenton, and Martin A. MacDonald, "Report of the Committee to Investigate Postal Service in Porto Rico," *1898 Reports of the Post-Office Department*, 32.

47. Smith, "Mails Follow the Flag," 3–4. On anti-imperialism debates, see E. Berkeley Tompkins, *Anti-Imperialism in the United States: The Great Debate, 1890–1920* (Philadelphia: University of Pennsylvania Press, 1970); Michael Patrick Cullinane, *Liberty and American Anti-Imperialism: 1898–1909* (New York: Palgrave Macmillan, 2012).

48. Section 90 of "Chap. 339.–An Act To Provide a Government of the Territory of Hawaii," April 30, 1900, *Statutes of the United States of America Passed at the First Session of the Fifty-Sixth Congress, 1899–1900* (Washington: Government Printing Office, 1900), 159; Carl H. Scheele and Constance Minkin, *Neither Snow, Nor Rain . . . : The Story of the United States Mails* (Washington: Smithsonian, 1970), 55; Henry F. Bryan, *American Samoa: A General Report by the Governor* (Washington: Government Printing Office, 1927), 48, 110.

49. Stuart et al., "Report of the Committee to Investigate Postal Service in Porto Rico," *1898 Reports of the Post-Office Department*, 31, 56, 67; Charles Emory Smith, "Report of the Postmaster-General," *Annual Reports of the Post-Office Department for the Fiscal Year Ended June 30, 1900* (Washington: Government Printing Office, 1900), 16.

50. Brennan, *Stamping American Memory*, 86.

51. Brennan, *Stamping American Memory*, 100; Jeffrey Herlihy-Mera, *After American Studies: Rethinking the Legacies of Transnational Exceptionalism* (London: Routledge, 2018), 100, 110–11.

52. Smith, "Report of the Postmaster-General," *1899 Reports of the Post-Office Department*, 13.

53. C. M. Cotterman, "Exhibit H. Bureau of Posts," *Annual Reports of the War Department for the Fiscal Year Ended June 30, 1902, Volume X: Report of the Philippine Commission, Part 1* (Washington: Government Printing Office, 1903), 226.

54. "Report of W. H. Elliott, Director-General of Posts of Porto Rico," *1899 Reports of the Post-Office Department*, 55.

55. "Report of F. W. Vaille, Director-General of Posts in the Philippine Islands," *1899 Reports of the Post-Office Department*, 64.

56. "Report of F. W. Vaille, Director-General of Posts in the Philippine Islands," *1900 Reports of the Post-Office Department*, 36.

57. "Report of F. W. Vaille, Director-General of Posts in the Philippine Islands," *1899 Reports of the Post-Office Department*, 63.

58. Table G. showing the gross receipts of post offices, by states and territories, in "Report of the Fourth Assistant Postmaster-General," *Annual Reports of the Post-Office Department for the Fiscal Year Ended June 30, 1903* (Washington: Government Printing Office, 1903), 593.

59. Table G. showing the gross receipts of post offices, by states and territories, in "Report of the Fourth Assistant Postmaster-General," *Annual Reports of the Post Office Department for the Fiscal Year ended June 30, 1901* (Washington: Government Printing Office, 1901), 904; Gross receipts of post offices, by states and territories, in "Report of the Fourth Assistant Postmaster-General," *Post-Office Department Annual Reports for the Fiscal Year Ended June 30, 1905* (Washington: Government Printing Office, 1905), 665.

60. "Report of the Fourth Assistant Postmaster-General," in *1903 Annual Reports of the Post-Office Department*, 593; "Report of the Fourth Assistant Postmaster-General," in *1905 Annual Reports of the United States Post Office Department*, 665.

61. "Postal Service," in *Report of the United States Philippine Commission to the Secretary of War for the Period from December 1, 1900 to October 15, 1901, Part 1* (Washington: Government Printing Office, 1901), 69–70.

62. Franklin Matthews, *The New-Born Cuba* (New York: Harper & Brothers, 1899), 162.

63. "Decree of August 29, 1899, Establishing a Postal System," in *The Laws of the First Philippine Republic (The Laws of Malolos), 1898–1899*, ed. Sulpicio Guevara (Manila: National Historical Commission, 1972), 182.

64. Percy A. Hill, "Philippine Stamps: The First Issue," *Philippine Magazine* 32, no. 1 (January 1935): 42.

65. Order given by military commander, Bacolod, Negros, March 16, 1900, quoted in Hill, "Philippine Stamps: The First Issue," 44.

66. Edwin C. Madden, "Report of the Third Assistant Postmaster-General," *1900 Reports of the Post-Office Department*, 707.

67. Virginia Benitez Licuanan, *Money in the Bank: The Story of Money and Banking in the Philippines and the PCIBank Story* (Manila: Philippine Commercial International Bank, 1985), 51.

68. Luther K. Zabriskie, *The Virgin Islands of the United States of America: Historical and Descriptive Commercial and Industrial Facts, Figures, and Resources* (New York: G. P. Putnam's Sons, 1918), 124.

69. Helleiner, *The Making of National Money*, 2–3.

70. John P. G. Arndt, "Coins of Hawaii: Subject of Talk by Numismatist," *Honolulu Star-Bulletin*, March 14, 1914, p. 3.

71. Arndt, "Coins of Hawaii."

72. S. M. Damon, minister of finance, to Sanford B. Dole, *The Report of the Hawaiian Commission to the Committee on Foreign Relations* (Washington: Government Printing Office, 1898), 92.

73. "Report of Committee on Finance," *Report of the Hawaiian Commission*, 91.

74. "Honolulu Bankers' Memorial," *Hawaiian Investigation Part 3: Exhibits, Memorials, Petitions, and Letters Presented to the Committee on Pacific Islands and Porto Rico, United States Senate* (Washington: Government Printing Office, 1903), 51.

75. *Manila Times*, quoted in Clarence R. Edwards, *Memorandum for the Secretary of War on Currency and Exchange in the Philippines* (Washington: Government Printing Office, 1900), 15.

76. Henry K. Carroll, "The Money Question: Preliminary Report of the Commissioner," *Reports of Henry K. Carroll Dec 30 1898 and Oct 1899 and of U.S. Insular Commission May 1899* (Washington: Government Printing Office, 1899), 449–97; "Testimony of Señor Balbas," *Report of the Philippine Commission to the Secretary of War, Vol. II: Testimony and Exhibits* (Washington: Government Printing Office, 1900), 152–60; *Virgin Islands: Report of the Joint Commission Appointed under the Authority of the Concurrent Resolution Passed by the Congress of the United States, January 1920* (Washington: Government Printing Office, 1920), 32.

77. Trumbull White, *Our New Possessions: A Graphic Account, Descriptive and Historical, of the Tropic-Islands of the Sea That Have Fallen under Our Sway* (Chicago: National Educational Union, 1898), 428.

78. Allan E. S. Lumba, "Imperial Standards: Colonial Currencies, Racial Capacities, and Economic Knowledge during the Philippine-American War," *Diplomatic History* 39, no. 44 (September 2015): 2.

79. Edwin Walter Kemmerer, *Modern Currency Reforms: A History and Discussion of Recent Currency Reforms in India, Porto Rico, Philippine Islands, Straits Settlements, and Mexico* (New York: The MacMillan Company, 1916), 159; Lumba, "Imperial Standards," 6.

80. *Manila Times* quoted in Edwards, *Currency and Exchange in the Philippines*, 15.

81. Mihm, *Nation of Counterfeiters*, 307.

82. Carlos M. Soler, "Change of the Money System: Opinion of the Spanish Bank of Porto Rico," in *Reports of Henry K. Carroll*, 472.

83. *Virgin Islands: Report of the Joint Commission Appointed under the Authority of the Concurrent Resolution Passed by the Congress of the United States, January 1920* (Washington: Government Printing Office, 1920), 34.

84. *Virgin Islands Joint Commission*, 32.

85. *Virgin Islands Joint Commission*, 35.

86. "Honolulu Bankers' Memorial," 51; Kemmerer, *Modern Currency Reforms*, 257–58.

87. Kemmerer, *Modern Currency Reforms*, 299.

88. Lumba, *Monetary Authorities*, 6.

89. Charles N. Fowler, *"The Fowler Financial and Currency Bill," Speech in the House of Representatives, June 26, 1902* (Washington: Government Printing Office, 1902), 4.

90. Paymaster-General A. E. Bates, quoted in Edwards, *Currency and Exchange in the Philippines*, 604.

91. George W. Davis, "The Currency," in *Report of Brigadier General George W. Davis on Civil Affairs of Puerto Rico, 1899* (Washington: Government Printing Office, 1900), 30; "The Currency of Puerto Rico: Interview with T. G. J. Waymouth," in *Reports of Henry K. Carroll*, 457; "Statement of Mr. Körber, of the Banking Firm of Müllenhof & Körber," in *Reports of Henry K. Carroll*, 477.

92. Kemmerer, *Modern Currency Reforms*, 203.

93. Dr. Cayetano Coll y Toste, "A Review of the Social, Economic, and Industrial Condition of the Island of Puerto Rico Immediately Preceding Occupation by the United States," in *Report of the Military Governor of Porto Rico on Civil Affairs, 1900, Part 13* (Washington: Government Printing Office, 1902), 232.

94. Kemmerer, *Modern Currency Reforms*, 208.

95. George W. Davis, "The Exchange of Currency," in *1899 Report on Civil Affairs of Puerto Rico*, 174.

96. Davis "The Exchange of Currency," 209.

97. Kemmerer, *Modern Currency Reforms*, 187.

98. Biago Di Venuti, *Money and Banking in Puerto Rico* (Río Piedras: University of Puerto Rico Press, 1950), 21.

99. Kemmerer, *Modern Currency Reforms*, 224.

100. Kemmerer, *Modern Currency Reforms*, 215.

101. Kemmerer, *Modern Currency Reforms*, 217.

102. Davis "The Exchange of Currency," 173; Kemmerer, *Modern Currency Reforms*, 219–20.

103. Pablo Martín-Aceña and Inés Roldán de Montaud, "A Colonial Bank under Spanish and American Sovereignty: The Banco Español de Puerto Rico, 1888–1913," *Caribbean Studies* 41, no. 1 (July-December 2013): 165.

104. Kemmerer, *Modern Currency Reforms*, 223.

105. Kemmerer, *Modern Currency Reforms*, 222.

106. Charles H. Allen, "Retirement of Porto Rican Coin," *First Annual Report of Charles H. Allen, Governor of Porto Rico Covering the Period from May 1, 1900 to May 1, 1901* (Washington: Government Printing Office, 1901), 66.

107. "Report of the Committee on Finance: The Hawaiian Currency," *Report of the Hawaiian Commission*, 91–92; L. J. Gage, secretary of the treasury, to Hon J. B. Foraker, US Senate, February 9, 1901, report no. 260: "Hawaiian Silver Coinage, etc.," 57th Congress, 1st Session, House of Representatives, *United States Congressional Serial Set, Volume 4400*, 3.

108. "Hawaii's Coins: The Trouble that Came of Wilcox's Blunders," *Pacific Commercial Advertiser*, March 14, 1901, p. 5.

109. Robert William Wilcox, speaking on HR 7091, 56th Cong., 2nd sess., *Congressional Record* (February 4, 1901): H 1915.

110. "Hawaii's Coins," 5.

111. Representative John Gaines, speaking on S 2210, 57th Cong., 2nd sess., *Congressional Record* (January 7, 1903): H 579.

112. Representative Ebenezer Hill, speaking on S 2210, 57th Cong., 2nd sess., *Congressional Record* (January 7, 1903): H 583.

113. Representative Oscar Underwood, speaking on S 2210, 57th Cong., 2nd sess., *Congressional Record* (January 7, 1903): H 583. The image of Queen Liliʻuokalani appeared on an unofficial coin minted in England in 1891, but only fifty-four such coins were ever struck. Bruce Cartwright, "The Money of Hawaii," *The Hawaiian Annual for 1929* (Honolulu: Thos. G. Thrum, 1928), 76.

114. Representative Hill, speaking on S 2210, 57th Cong., 2nd sess. *Congressional Record* (January 7, 1903): 578, 583–84.

115. "Chap. 186: An Act Relating to Hawaiian Silver Coinage and Silver Certificates," January 14, 1903, in *Statutes at Large of the United States of America from December 1901 to March 1903, vol. XXXII, Part 1* (Washington: Government Printing Office, 1903), 770–71.

116. "A Third of the Coin Redeemed," *Hawaiian Star*, March 19, 1903, p. 3; "Hawaiian Money Will Not Be Legal Tender," *Hawaiian Star*, December 3, 1903, p. 1.

117. Paul M. Pearson, *Annual Report of the Governor of the Virgin Islands for the Fiscal Year Ended June 30, 1934* (Washington: Government Printing Office, 1934), 4.

118. Robert S. Allen, "Hoover's Trip Step to Unify Insular Areas: President Said to Plan to Bring Possessions under One Department," *Boston Christian Science Monitor*, March 17, 1931; George Audain, "To Virgin Islanders," *Saint Thomas Mail Notes*, April 7, 1931; George E. Audain, "Virgin Islanders Hit U.S. Attitude: Editor Holds Unthinking Stand Here Has Blocked Port's Recovery," May 5, 1931, box 1271, folder 9-11-33, Press Clippings–General (part 1), Central Files Virgin Islands, RG 126, NARA, College Park, MD.

119. A bill to provide for the redemption of Danish West Indian coin now in circulation in the Virgin Islands of the United States, and for other purposes, act effective June 20, 1934, box 6, folder: Currency–Exchange, Replacement, and Redemption in the Virgin Islands K 314.3, Series K Currency 53-87-101, Entry UD Circulation of Historical Value of US and Foreign Securities (Series "K") Currency, 1890–1942, record group 53, Bureau of Public Debt, NARA, College Park, MD.

120. Box 1249, folder: Monetary Conditions–General (part 4), Central Files–Virgin Islands, RG 126, NARA, College Park, MD.

121. Kemmerer, *Modern Currency Reforms*, 214.

122. Richard Snow, *A Guide Book of Flying Eagle and Indian Head Cents: Complete Source for History, Grading, and Prices* (Atlanta: Whitman, 2009), 25.

123. Pablo Navarro-Rivera, "The Imperial Enterprise and Educational Policies in Colonial Puerto Rico," in Alfred W. McCoy and Francisco Scarano, eds., *Colonial Crucible: Empire in the Making of the Modern American State* (Madison: University of Wisconsin Press, 2009), 170.

124. Edwards, *Currency and Exchange in the Philippines*, 1.

125. Rosenberg, *Financial Missionaries to the World*, 15.

126. Clarence R. Edwards, "The Execution of the Philippine Coinage Act," in *Stability of International Exchange: Report on the Introduction of the Gold-Exchange Standard into China and other Silver-Using Countries* (Washington: Government Printing Office, 1903), 414.

127. Onofre D. Corpuz, *The Roots of the Filipino Nation, Volume 2* (Quezon City: Aklahi Foundation, 1989), 156.

128. For more on the formation of the Philippine national myth, see Reynaldo Ileto, *Knowing America's Colony: A Hundred Years from the Philippine War* (Honolulu: Center for Philippine Studies, 1999), 2.

129. Assistant chief of BIA to Mr. A. C. Van Rensselaer of Stockbridge, Massachusetts, September 19, 1902, box 268, folder 2325, entry #I-3 5-A: General Files 1898–1913, record group 350, Bureau of Insular Affairs (hereafter RG 350), NARA, College Park, MD.

130. Edwards, "Execution of the Philippine Coinage Act," 414.

131. "America in the Philippines: The Agitation for Independence and the Flag," *The Living Age* 267, no. 3468 (December 1910): 813–16; Florence Kimball Russell, *A Woman's Journey through the Philippines on a Cable Ship That Linked Together the Strange Lands Seen en Route* (Boston: L. Century Page, 1907), 152; "Cagayan, Misamis," *Philippine Education* 6, no. 7 (December 1909): 34.

132. "Proposed New Coinage," *1901 Report of the Philippine Commission*, 100–103; Rosenberg, *Financial Missionaries to the World*, 16; Lumba, "Imperial Standards," 13–14.

133. Edwards, "Execution of the Philippine Coinage Act," 415; Rosenberg, *Financial Missionaries*, 17.

134. "Chap. 980: An Act to Establish a Standard of Value and to Provide for a Coinage System in the Philippine Islands," March 2, 1903, in *Compilation of the Acts of Congress, Treaties, and Proclamations Relating to Insular and Military Affairs from March 4, 1897, to March 3, 1903* (Washington: Government Printing Office, 1904), 38.

135. Edwards, "Execution of the Philippine Coinage Act," 415.

136. Rosenberg, *Financial Missionaries*, 19.

137. Henry C. Ide, "Second Annual Report of the Secretary of Finance and Justice," *Fourth Annual Report of the Philippine Commission 1903, Part 3* (Washington: Government Printing Office, 1904), 282–84.

138. Mary H. Fee, *A Woman's Impression of the Philippines* (Chicago: A. C. McClurg, 1912), 163.

139. Fee, *Woman's Impression of the Philippines*, 164–65.

140. Fee, *Woman's Impression of the Philippines*, 165.

141. Fee, *Woman's Impression of the Philippines*, 166.

142. "Currency," *Fifth Annual Report of the Philippine Commission to the Secretary of War, 1904, Part 1* (Washington: Government Printing Office, 1905), 22–24.

143. R. F. Santos, "Report of the Governor of the Province of Albay," in *1904 Philippine Commission, Part 1*, 375.

144. Santos, "Report of the Governor of the Province of Albay," *1904 Philippine Commission, Part 1*, 374.

145. Demetrio Larena, "Report of the Governor of the Province of Negros Oriental," in *1904 Philippine Commission, Part 1*, 557.

146. Edwin Kemmerer, *First Annual Report of the Chief of the Division of the Currency for the Philippine Islands to the Treasurer of the Philippine Islands for the Period from October 10, 1903 to September 1, 1904* (Manila: Bureau of Public Printing, 1905), 13; Kemmerer, *Modern Currency Reforms*, 496.

147. Santos, "Report of the Governor of the Province of Albay," in *1904 Philippine Commission, Part 1*, 374; Larena, "Report of the Governor of the Province of Negros Oriental," in *1904 Philippine Commission, Part 1*, 557.

148. Lumba, *Monetary Authorities*, 5–6.

149. Rosenberg, *Financial Missionaries to the World*, 10.

150. For more on how elite Filipinos tried to prove their fitness for self-rule by participating in Americanization projects, see Ileto, *Knowing America's Colony*, 39; Paul A. Kramer, *The Blood of Government: Race, Empire, the United States, and the Philippines* (Chapel Hill: University of North Carolina Press, 2006), 220–25.

151. Larena, "Report of the Governor of the Province of Negros Oriental," *1904 Philippine Commission, Part 1*, 557.

152. R. F. Santos, "Report of the Governor of the Province of Albay," in *Sixth Annual Report of the Philippine Commission to the Secretary of War, 1905, Part I* (Washington: Government Printing Office, 1906), 138.

153. Rosenberg, *Financial Missionaries to the World*, 17.

154. "Report of Jeremiah W. Jenks, Commissioner Designated by the Commission on International Exchange, with the Approval of the President, to Carry on the Work of the Commission in the Far East," in Hugh H. Hanna, Charles A. Conant, and Jeremiah Jenks, *Report of the Commission on International Exchange on the Introduction of the Gold-Exchange Standard into China, the Philippine Islands, Panama, and Other Silver-Using Countries and on the Stability of Exchange*, (Washington: Government Printing Office, 1904), 34.

155. "Act No. 1042 Prohibiting the Importation into the Philippine Islands of Certain Kinds of Coins," in *Report of the Commission on International Exchange*, 307.

156. "Currency," *1904 Philippine Commission, Part 1*, 23; "Act No. 1045 to Maintain Parity of Philippine Coins by Imposing a Tax upon Written Contracts Payable to Certain Kinds of Currencies, a License Tax for Conducting Business in Certain Currencies, etc.," in *Report of the Commission on International Exchange* (1904), 308–12.

157. Kemmerer, *Report of the Chief of the Division of the Currency*, 15.

158. Santos, "Report of the Governor of Albay," *1905 Philippine Commission, Part 1*, 137–38.

159. Demetrio Larena, "Report of the Governor of the Province of Negros Oriental," *1905 Philippine Commission, Part 1*, 368.

160. J. Luna, "Report of the Governor of the Province of La Union," *1905 Philippine Commission, Part 1*, 430. For more on Igorots, see Kramer, *Blood of Government*, 68, 266, 339–40, 376.

161. Juan Clímaco, "Report of the Governor of the Province of Cebu," *1905 Philippine Commission, Part 1*, 226.

162. Salustiano Borja, "Report of the Governor of the Province of Bohol," *1905 Philippine Commission, Part 1*, 181; M. Arnedo, "Report of the Governor of the Province of Pampanga," *1905 Philippine Commission, Part 1*, 389.

163. Gregorio Araneta, "Circulation," *Report of the Philippine Commission to the Secretary of War, 1911* (Washington: Government Printing Office, 1912) 147. For more on US governance in Moroland, see Peter Gordon Gowing, *Mandate in Moroland: The American Government of Muslim Filipinos, 1899–1920* (Quezon City: New Day Publishers, 1983).

164. Neil Shafer, *A Guide Book of Philippine Paper Money* (Racine, WI: Whitman Publishing Company, 1964), 21.

165. M. E. Beall Memorandum for Colonel Edwards, August 22, 1903, box 522, entry #I-3 5-A: General Files 1898–1913, RG 350, NARA, College Park, MD.

166. Henry C. Ide, *Second Annual Report of the Secretary of Finance and Justice to the Philippine Commission for the Period from September 30, 1902, to September 1, 1903* (Manila: Bureau of Public Printing, 1904), 28.

167. George F. Luthringer, *The Gold-Exchange Standard in the Philippines* (Princeton, NJ: Princeton University Press, 1934), 36.

168. Shafer, *Guide Book of Philippine Paper Money*, 21.

169. Shafer, *Guide Book of Philippine Paper Money*, 21.

170. WLP Memorandum for Colonel Edwards, April 22, 1903, box 503, folder 7628, entry #I-3 5-A: General Files 1898–1913, RG 350, NARA, College Park, MD.

171. Assistant executive secretary of the Philippine Commission to chief of BIA, February 25, 1904, box 503, folder 7628, entry #I-3 5-A: General Files 1898–1913, RG 350, NARA, College Park, MD.

172. John R. M. Taylor, Capt. 14th Infantry memorandum for chief of BIA January 16, 1905, box 503, folder 7628, entry #I-3 5-A: General Files 1898–1913, RG 350, NARA, College Park, MD; C. M. Cotterman to W. Leon Pepperman, assistant to chief of BIA, February 17, 1905, box 503, folder 7628, entry #I-3 5-A: General Files 1898–1913, RG 350, NARA, College Park, MD.

173. Renato Constantino, *Insight and Foresight* (Quezon City: Foundation for Nationalist Studies, 1977), 29–30; Sharon Delmendo, *The Star-Entangled Banner: One Hundred Years of America in the Philippines* (Quezon City: University of Philippines Press, 2005), 25–26; Theodore Friend, *Between Two Empires: The Ordeal of the Philippines, 1929–1946* (New Haven, CT: Yale University Press, 1965), 15; Kramer, *Blood of Government*, 333–37.

174. W. Cameron Forbes, *The Philippine Islands, Revised Edition* (Cambridge, MA: Harvard University Press, 1945), 33.

175. C. M. Cotterman to W. Leon Pepperman, assistant to chief of BIA, February 17, 1905, box 503, folder 7628, entry #I-3 5-A: General Files 1898–1913, RG 350, NARA, College Park, MD.

176. John R. M. Taylor, Capt. 14th Infantry, memorandum for chief of BIA, January 16, 1905, box 503, folder 7628, entry #I-3 5-A: General Files 1898–1913, RG 350, NARA, College Park, MD.

177. Stamp sales were ₱222,701.36 in 1905, before the introduction of the new stamps; ₱425,261.50 in 1906; ₱607,203.44 in 1907; and ₱677,290.98 in 1908. For 1905 stamp sales, "Report of the Auditor," *Annual Reports of the War Department for the Fiscal Year Ended June 30, 1905, Volume XIII, Report of the Philippine Commission, Part 4* (Washington: Government Printing Office, 1905), 300. For 1906–8 stamp sales, see Wm. T. Nolting, "Exhibit H: Report of the Director of Posts," *Report of the Philippine Commission to the Secretary of War 1908, Part 2* (Washington: Government Printing Office, 1909), 500.

178. Edwards to Wright, March 8, 1905, box 503, folder 7628, BIA entry #I-3 5-A: General Files 1898–1913, RG 350, NARA, College Park, MD.

179. José-Manuel Navarro, *Creating Tropical Yankees: Social Science Textbooks and U.S. Ideological Control in Puerto Rico, 1898–1908* (New York: Routledge, 2002), 55, 62–63, 140–41.

180. Pardo de Tavera, quoted in Alice Byram Condict, *Old Glory and the Gospel in the Philippines: Notes Gathered during Professional and Missionary Work* (Chicago: Fleming H. Revell, 1902), 91.

181. Pardo de Tavera, quoted in Stanley Karnow, *In Our Image: America's Empire in the Philippines* (New York: Random House, 1989), 176.

182. David Starr Jordan, *Imperial Democracy: A Study of the Relation of Government by the People, Equality before the Law, and other Tenets of Democracy, to the Demands of a Vigorous Foreign Policy and other Demands of Imperial Dominion* (New York: D. Appleton, 1899), 65.

183. Karnow, *In Our Image*, 181.

184. Juan Ruiz, director of posts, Philippines, to chief of Bureau of Insular Affairs, April 24, 1931, box 715, folder 7628-293 with P. I. postage stamps and cards, orders, and correspondence, part 1, BIA 1914–45, RG 350, NARA, College Park, MD.

185. For more on the symbolism of the carabao, see Renato Constantino, "The Miseducation of the Filipino," in *Vestiges of War: The Philippine-American War and the Aftermath of an Imperial Dream*, ed. Angel Velasco Shaw and Luis H. Francia (New York: New York University Press, 2002), 182.

186. Creed F. Cox, chief of BIA, to director of Bureau of Engraving and Printing (hereafter BEP), January 24, 1934, PSPI 25 "Washington at Trenton" (on horse), 1934 series, 5 pesos, Bureau of Engraving and Printing Historical Resource Center, Washington (hereafter BEP-HRC).

187. Juan Ruiz, director of Philippine posts, to chief of BIA, July 17, 1933, box 715, folder 7628-293 with P. I. postage stamps and cards, orders, and correspondence, part 2, RG 350 BIA 1914–45, NARA, College Park, MD.

188. Cox to director of BEP, January 24, 1934, PSPI 25, BEP-HRC.

189. Enrico Palomar, "George Washington: Father of the American People on Philippine Stamps," *Philippine Journal of Philately* 3, no. 4 (March-April 1951): 13, National Postal Museum, Smithsonian Institution, Washington.

190. Edward A. Stockton Jr. acting chief of BIA, to director of BEP, September 11, 1935, box 715, folder 7628-293, with P. I. postage stamps and cards, orders, and correspondence, part 5, BIA 1914–45, RG 350, NARA, College Park, MD.

191. History Card (no. 597), PSPI 26 Temple of Human Progress, BEP-HRC; D. C. McDonald to director of Bureau of Engraving and Printing, September 25, 1935, box 715, folder 7628-293, with P. I. postage stamps and cards, orders, and correspondence, part 4, BIA 1914–45, RG 350, NARA, College Park, MD.

192. "The Philippines Admitted to the Temple of Universal Progress," PSPI 26, Temple of Human Progress, BEP-HRC.

193. McNutt to secretary of war, August 17, 1938; postmaster general to secretary of war, August 23, 1938, box 716, folder 7628, 334 postage stamps and cards for P. I., BIA 1914–45, RG 350, NARA, College Park, MD.

194. L. B. Sebring, "Stamp Notes: Puerto Rico Jubilant on Commemoration," *New York Herald Tribune*, January 17, 1937, p. I-18.

195. The Hawaiian Philatelic Society even suggested designs for Guam and American Samoa. Hawaiian Philatelic Society to Samuel Wilder King, delegate to Congress from Hawaii, February 15, 1937, enclosed in letter from Sam King, House of Representatives, to Ruth Hampton, assistant director, Division of Territories and Insular Possessions, March 6, 1937, box 87, folder 9-0-3, Publicity–Commemorative Stamps, Money & Stamps, RG 126, NARA, College Park, MD.

196. Joint resolution authorizing the issuance of a special stamp in behalf of the island of Puerto Rico, January 16, 1935, 74th Cong., 1st session. H.J. Res. 90, from the US House of Representatives, box 953, folder 9-8-84, Puerto Rico–Publicity–Commemorative Stamps–1935–50, Money & Stamps, RG 126, NARA, College Park, MD; Blanton Winship, governor of Puerto Rico, to secretary of the interior, April 6, 1935: Re: H.J. Res. 90, box 953, folder 9-8-84, Puerto Rico–Publicity–Commemorative Stamps–1935–50, Money & Stamps, RG 126, NARA, College Park, MD; R. A. Kleindienst Memorandum for Director Ernest Gruening, DTIP, April 25, 1935, box 953, folder 9-8-84, Puerto Rico–Publicity–Commemorative Stamps–1935–50, Money & Stamps, RG 126, NARA, College Park, MD.

197. Lawrence W. Cramer, governor of the Virgin Islands, to third assistant postmaster general, April 14, 1937, box 87, folder 9-0-3, Publicity–Commemorative Stamps, Money & Stamps, RG 126, NARA, College Park, MD; Kent B. Stiles, "Virgin Islands' Adhesives to Restore City's Name," *New York Times*, October 24, 1937, section 12, p. 10; R. A. Barry, "St. Thomas Is Charlotte Amalie Again and Stamp Seals the Name," *New York Herald Tribune*, November 27, 1937, p. 11.

198. Elizabeth Forman, "Alaska May Get Totem Stamp," *New York Times*, July 25, 1937, p. 150.

199. "The Alaska 'Picture,'" *Linn's Weekly Stamp News* 10, no. 6 (December 11, 1937): 93.

200. Jacob Adler, "The Kamehameha Statue," *Hawaiian Journal of History* 3 (1969): 87–100.

201. *Linn's Weekly Stamp News* 10, no. 8 (December 25, 1937): 131; "The Hawaiian Stamp," *Chicago Daily Tribune*, December 8, 1937, p. 12.

202. Donald Billam-Walker, "Post Office Publicity Boys Not Up on Hawaiiani," *Honolulu Star Bulletin*, quoted in *Linn's Weekly Stamp News* 9, no. 46 (September 18, 1937): 771.

203. Billam-Walker, "Post Office Publicity Boys Not Up on Hawaiiani," 771.

204. Ernest Gruening to Blanton Winship, governor of Puerto Rico, February 25, 1937, box 87, folder 9-0-3, Publicity–Commemorative Stamps, Money & Stamps, RG 126, NARA, College Park, MD.

205. Eliza B. K. Dooley, when sending in her drawing suggestions for the stamp, asked, "What is the political situation?"—a reference, one can safely assume, to the ongoing Nationalist conflict in Puerto Rico; see chapter 3. Eliza B. K. Dooley, Labor Department, to Ernest Gruening, Division of Territories and Island Possessions, July 29, 1937, box 87, folder 9-0-3, Publicity–Commemorative Stamps, Money & Stamps, RG 126, NARA, College Park MD.

206. Theodore Roosevelt Jr., *Colonial Policies of the United States* (Garden City, NY: Doubleday, Doran and Company, 1937), 93.

Chapter 3

1. The flags of Guam, the US Virgin Islands, and American Samoa date from 1917, 1921, and 1960, respectively.

2. On Hawaiian flag quilts: Joyce D. Hammond, "Hawaiian Flag Quilts: Multivalent Symbols of a Hawaiian Quilt Tradition," *Hawaiian Journal of History* 27 (1993): 1–26; Vernadette Vicuña Gonzalez, "Hawaiian Quilts, Global Domesticities, and Patterns of Counterhegemony," in *Transnational Crossroads: Remapping the Americas and the Pacific*, ed. Camilla Fojas and Rudy P. Guevarra Jr. (Lincoln: University of Nebraska Press, 2012), 87–115. On the Philippine flag ban: H. W. Brands, *Bound to Empire: The United States and the Philippines* (Oxford, UK: Oxford University Press, 1992), 93–94; Paul A. Kramer, *The Blood of Government: Race, Empire, the United States and the Philippines* (Chapel Hill: University of North Carolina Press, 2006), 329–33; Alfred W. McCoy, *Policing America's Empire: The United States, the Philippines, and the Rise of the Surveillance State* (Madison: University of Wisconsin Press, 2009), 175–76. On the protests in Puerto Rico: Ovidio Dávila Dávila, "Los bonos del Partido Nacionalista para la reconstitución de la República de Puerto Rico (1930)," *Revista del Instituto de Cultura Puertorriqueña* 6, no. 11 (2005): 32–43; Juan Manuel Carrión, "The War of the Flags: Conflicting National Loyalties in a Modern Colonial Situation," *Centro Journal* (September 2006): 101–23; Margaret Power, "Nationalism in a Colonized Nation: The Nationalist Party and Puerto Rico," *Memorias: Revista Digital de Historia y Arqueología Desde el Caribe Colombiano* 10, no. 20 (May-Aug. 2013): 120–37.

3. Bernice Piilani Irwin, *I Knew Queen Liliuokalani* (Honolulu: South Sea Sales, 1960), 46.

4. Roszika Parket, *The Subversive Stitch: Embroidery and the Making of the Feminine* (London: J. B. Tauris, 2010), 5.

5. Notes and Draft of Article on Hawaiian Flag, n.d., box M-68-1, folder 6. Research Material on Hawaiian History, personal papers, Victor S. K. Houston Collection, Hawai'i State Archives, Honolulu.

6. It's disputed whether George Beckley or Alexander Adams designed the flag. "The Maker of the Hawaiian Flag," *First Annual Report of the Hawaiian Historical Society* (Honolulu: Hawaiian Gazette Company, 1893), 9.

7. William T. Brigham, *Ka Hana Kapa: The Making of Bark-Cloth in Hawaii* (Honolulu: Bishop Museum Press, 1911).

8. Stacy L. Kamehiro, "Hawaiian Quilts: Chiefly Self-Representations in Nineteenth-Century Hawai'i," *Pacific Arts* 3/5 (2007): 24.

9. Lucy G. Thurston, *The Life and Times of Lucy G. Thurston* (Ann Arbor, MI: S. C. Andrews, 1882), 32; Poakalani Serrao, John Serrao, Raelene Correia, and Cissy Serrao, *The Hawaiian Quilt: The Tradition Continues* (Honolulu: Mutual Publishing, 2007), x; Gonzalez, "Hawaiian Quilts," 95–96.

10. Ann Laura Stoler, *Carnal Knowledge and Imperial Power: Race and the Intimate in Colonial Rule* (Berkeley: University of California Press, 2002); Ann Laura Stoler, ed. *Haunted by Empire: Geographies of Intimacy in North American History* (Durham, NC: Duke University Press, 2006).

11. Kamehiro, "Hawaiian Quilts," 29.

12. Loretta G. H. Woodard, "Communities of Quilters: Hawaiian Pattern Collecting, 1900–1959," *Uncoverings* 27 (2006): 4.

13. Elizabeth Root, *Menehune Quilts: The Hawaiian Way* (Kailua, HI: Erdhi Publishing, 2001), 8.

14. Root, *Menehune Quilts*, 11.

15. Reiko Mochinaga Brandon, *The Hawaiian Quilt* (Honolulu: Honolulu Academy of Arts), 13–14.

16. Hammond, "Hawaiian Flag Quilts," 6.

17. Irwin, *I Knew Queen Liliuokalani*, 51.

18. Rhoda E. A. Hackler and Loretta G. H. Woodard, *The Queen's Quilt* (Honolulu: Friends of Iolani Palace, 2004), 9.

19. Hackler and Woodard, *The Queen's Quilt*, 20.

20. Hackler and Woodard, *The Queen's Quilt*, 28.

21. Edith B. Williams, *Ka Hae Hawaii: The Story of the Hawaiian Flag* (Honolulu: South Sea Sales, 1963), 50; Gonzalez, "Hawaiian Quilts," 111–12.

22. W. D. Westervelt, "History of Hawaii's Flag," *Paradise of the Pacific* 14-7 (1901): 15, quoted in Hammond, "Hawaiian Flag Quilts," 24.

23. Williams, *Ka Hae Hawaii*, 54.

24. Hammond, "Hawaiian Flag Quilts," 7.

25. Jane Benson and Nancy Olsen, *The Power of Cloth: Political Quilts, 1845-1986* (Cupertino, CA: De Anza College, 1987), 23; Hammond, "Hawaiian Flag Quilts," 7–8.

26. Hammond, "Hawaiian Flag Quilts," 8.

27. Roger G. Rose, *Hawai'i, The Royal Isles, Bernice P. Bishop Museum Special Publication 67* (Honolulu: Bishop Museum Press, 1980), 214; Williams, *Ka Hae Hawaii*, 50.

28. Robert Shaw, *Hawaiian Quilt Masterpieces* (Fairfield, CT: Hugh Lauter Levin Associates, 1996), 58.

29. Elizabeth A. Akana, *Hawaiian Quilting as a Fine Art* (Honolulu: Hawaiian Mission Children's Society, 1986), 26

30. Brandon, *The Hawaiian Quilt*, 44–45.

31. Deborah Harding, *Stars and Stripes: Patriotic Motifs in American Folk Art* (New York: Rizzoli, 2002), 8.

32. Hammond, "Hawaiian Flag Quilts," 19.

33. Brandon, *The Hawaiian Quilt*, 24.

34. Gonzalez, "Hawaiian Quilts," 111.

35. "Appendix A-1: Declaration of Philippine Independence, June 12, 1898," in *The Laws of the First Philippine Republic (The Laws of Malolos), 1898–1899*, ed. Sulpicio Guevara (Manila: National Historical Commission, 1972), 206.

36. For more on nationalist plays in this period, see Vicente L. Rafael, *White Love and Other Events in Filipino History* (Durham, NC: Duke University Press, 2000), 39–51.

37. Alice Thacher Post, "A Shameful Record," *Public* 10, no. 505 (December 7, 1907): 862; "The Two Flags: The Philippine Flag Prohibited in Houses and Commercial Establishments," *El Renacimiento*, August 23, 1907, quoted in Emanuel A. Baja, *Our Country's Flag and Anthem* (Manila: Juan Fajardo Press, 1928), 108.

38. William Howard Taft coined the term "little brown brother." See Stuart Creighton Miller, *"Benevolent Assimilation": The American Conquest of the Philippines, 1899–1903* (New Haven, CT: Yale University Press, 1982), 134.

39. "Killed by Bolo Men: How Capt. Overton and Two Privates Met Death," *Washington Post*, June 23, 1903, p. SP11.

40. For more on the Philippine Constabulary, see Alfred W. McCoy, *Policing America's Empire: The United States, the Philippines, and the Rise of the Surveillance State* (Madison: University of Wisconsin Press, 2009); Moon-Ho Jung, *Menace to Empire: Anticolonial Solidarities and the Transpacific Origins of the US Security State* (Berkeley: University of California Press, 2022), 40–47, 80–104, 269–72; Christopher Capozzola, *Bound by War: How the United States and the Philippines Built America's First Pacific Century* (New York: Basic Books, 2020), 50–54.

41. Carlos Ronquillo to Emanuel Baja, September 8, 1926, quoted in Baja, *Our Country's Flag and Anthem*, 86.

42. "The Filipino Flag and Anthem," *Manila Times*, Aug. 12, 1907, quoted in Baja, *Our Country's Flag and Anthem*, 90.

43. "The Malabon Incident," *Manila Times*, August 19, 1907, quoted in Robert B. Westcott, *The Exaltation of the Flag: Proceedings at the Patriotic Mass Meeting Held by the Americans of the Philippine Islands, Which Took Place in the City of Manila, P.I., on the Evening of Friday, August 23, 1907* (Manila: John R. Edgar, 1907), 33; Westcott, *Exaltation of the Flag*, 4.

44. "The Malabon Incident," *Manila Times*, August 19, 1907, quoted in Westcott, *Exaltation of the Flag*, 33.

45. "The Filipino Flag and Anthem," *Manila Times*, August 12, 1907, quoted in Baja, *Our Country's Flag and Anthem*, 91.

46. The Resentment over the 'Flag' Incident," *Manila Times*, August 14, 1907, quoted in Baja, *Our Country's Flag and Anthem*, 92.

47. "Our Humiliation," *Manila Opinion*, August 17, 1907, quoted in Westcott, *Exaltation of the Flag*, 14–15.

48. "One Government: One Flag," *Manila Times*, August 15, 1907, quoted in Baja, *Our Country's Flag and Anthem*, 93.

49. "Why No Other Flag Shall Fly," *Cablenews American*, August 21, 1907, quoted in Westcott, *Exaltation of the Flag*, 43.

50. Letter from Helen C. Wilson, quoted in Alice Thacher Post, "A Shameful Record," *Public* 10, no. 505 (December 7, 1907): 861–63.

51. "An Account of the Interview with Governor-General James F. Smith on Aug. 21, 1907," *El Renacimiento*, August 22, 1907, quoted in Baja, *Our Country's Flag and Anthem*, 99.

52. "Death of Theo. Diehl," *Manila Bulletin*, August 21, 1928.

53. Wilson, quoted in Post, "A Shameful Record," 862.

54. Westcott, *Exaltation of the Flag*, 69.

55. William H. Anderson, *The Philippine Problem* (New York: G. P. Putnam, 1939), 116–18, 252–53.

56. "Why No Other Flag Shall Fly," quoted in Wescott, *Exaltation*, 41.

57. Westcott, *Exaltation of the Flag*, 8.

58. Westcott, *Exaltation of the Flag*, 9, 69.

59. Journal entry, August 27, 1907, 284, box 2, vol. 2, W. Cameron Forbes Papers, Library of Congress, Washington.

60. "An Account of the Interview with Governor-General James F. Smith on August 21, 1907," *El Renacimiento*, August 22, 1907, quoted in Baja, *Our Country's Flag and Anthem*, 99; "From Bad to Worse? The Prohibition of the Philippine Flag Is an Injury to the People and a Violation in the Philippine Islands of the Fundamental Principle of Free Expression of Thought: Sedition Act Amended," *El Renacimiento*, August 21, 1907, quoted in Baja, *Our Country's Flag and Anthem*, 97.

61. Journal entry, August 27, 1907, 283–4, box 2, vol. 2, W. Cameron Forbes Papers, Library of Congress, Washington.

62. "An Act to Prohibit the Display of Flags, Banners, Emblems, or Devices Used in the Philippine Islands for the Purpose of Rebellion or Insurrection against the Authority of the United States and the Display of Katipunan Flags, Banners, Emblems, or Devices, and for Other Purposes," *Philippine Gazette*, August 23, 1907.

63. Westcott, *Exaltation of the Flag*, 70; Henry A. Castle, *A History of St. Paul and Vicinity: A Chronicle of Progress and Narrative Account of the Industries, Institutions, and People of the City and Its Tributary Territory, Vol. III* (Chicago: Lewis Publishing, 1912), 862; Marrion Wilcox, ed., *Harper's History of the War in the Philippines* (New York: Harper & Brothers, 1900), 434.

64. Westcott, *Exaltation of the Flag*, 10.

65. Westcott, *Exaltation of the Flag*, 10; "Last night's call to patriotism—the eagle screamed," n.d., quoted in Baja, *Our Country's Flag and Anthem*, 127.

66. Address of Hon. Southworth of Mississippi, quoted in Westcott, *Exaltation of the Flag*, 83–84.

67. Address of Captain Thomas E. Leonard, quoted in Westcott, *Exaltation of the Flag*, 123–24.

68. "Address of Comrade Bakewell on Presenting the Flags," quoted in *History of the Gift of Six Hundred National Flags*, 32, 34.

69. Leonard, quoted in Westcott, *Exaltation of the Flag*, 116. On the origins of the quote, see "Gen. Dix's Order: 'If Any Man Attempts to Haul Down the American Flag, Shoot Him on the Spot," *New York Times*, September 14, 1872, p. 1; "Flag Day Recalls Famous Statement: Former Governor Wright Was Author of Historic 'Shoot Him on the Spot' Order," *Indianapolis Journal*, June 14, 1911, p. 5.

70. Address of Rev. Dr. S. B. Rossiter, quoted in Westcott, *Exaltation of the Flag*, 126–28.

71. "Account of August 23, 1907 meeting at the Grand Opera House," *Manila Times*, August 24, 1907, quoted in Baja, *Our Country's Flag and Anthem*, 123.

72. "Account of August 23, 1907," quoted in Baja, *Our Country's Flag and Anthem*, 123.

73. "Account of August 23, 1907," quoted in Baja, *Our Country's Flag and Anthem*, 118. Hausserman went on to be known as the "Gold King" of the Philippines because of his Benguet

Consolidated Mining company. "Their Gold Mines Are Their Ace in the Hole," *Life*, February 13, 1939, p. 58.

74. Westcott, *Exaltation of the Flag*, 146.

75. "Last Night's Meeting," *Manila Times*, August 24, 1907, quoted in Westcott, *Exaltation of the Flag*, 149.

76. Minerva Agnes Davis, "The Red, White and Blue," written in Manila, August 24, 1907; quoted in Westcott, *Exaltation of the Flag*, 152–54.

77. "Katipunan Emblem to Be Quietly Suppressed: Manila Police Receive Orders to Stop Indiscriminate Display of Society's Insignia," *Manila American*, August 23, 1907, quoted in Westcott, *Exaltation of the Flag*, 63–64.

78. "Captain of Police Removes Insurrecto Emblem from Street Parade," *Manila Times*, August 23, 1907, quoted in Baja, *Our Country's Flag and Anthem*, 103.

79. McCoy, *Policing America's Empire*, 72.

80. "Is it illegal to exhibit the badge of the Nationalista party?" *El Renacimiento*, August 23, 1907, quoted in Baja, *Our Country's Flag and Anthem*, 108.

81. "Beginning of an Era of Dangerous Political Reaction and Perhaps of Return to the Days of the Conquest: Words of a Respectful Protest," *El Renacimiento*, August 24, 1907; quoted in Baja, *Our Country's Flag and Anthem*, 132.

82. *The United States v. Juan Panganiban*, G.R. no. L-5584, October 29, 1910. Supreme Court of the Philippines.

83. *The United States v. Go*, G.R. no. 4963, September 15, 1909. Supreme Court of the Philippines.

84. Brands, *Bound to Empire*, 104–18.

85. *An Act to Declare the Purpose of the People of the United States as to the Future Political Status of the People of the Philippine Islands, and to Provide a More Autonomous Government for Those Islands*, Public Law 64–240, *U.S. Statutes at Large* 39 (1916): 545–56.

86. Manuel Quezon, October 16, 1919, quoted in Baja, *Our Country's Flag and Anthem*, 145.

87. The Philippine Flag," *El Ideal*, October 18, 1919, box 101, folder 526-16 to 62 Philippine Flag, BIA 1914–45, record group 350, Bureau of Insular Affairs (hereafter RG 350), US National Archives and Records Administration (hereafter NARA), College Park, MD.

88. Governor General Harrison message to the Fifth Legislature of the Philippines, October 16, 1919, quoted in Baja, *Our Country's Flag and Anthem*, 142.

89. Rafael Palma, quoted in Baja, *Our Country's Flag and Anthem*, 143.

90. Representative Jose Generoso, quoted in Baja, *Our Country's Flag and Anthem*, 148; Representative Recto, quoted in Baja, *Our Country's Flag and Anthem*, 151.

91. "Act No. 2871, s. 1919," *Philippine Gazette*, October 22, 1919.

92. "Under Two Flags," *Cablenews-American*, October 19, 1919, Box 101, Folder 526–16 to 62 Philippine Flag, BIA 1914–1945, RG 350, NARA, College Park, MD.

93. "Repealing the Flag Law," *Cablenews-American*, October 18, 1919, box 101, folder 526-16 to 62 Philippine Flag, BIA 1914–45, RG 350, NARA, College Park, MD.

94. W. G. Barker, teacher in school of Naga Camarines, P. I., to Senator Arthur Copper, October 27, 1919, box 101, folder 526-16 to 62 Philippine Flag, BIA 1914–45, RG 350, NARA, College Park, MD. Emphasis in original.

95. "The Philippine Flag:" *El Ideal*, October 18, 1919, box 101, folder 526-16 to 62 Philippine Flag, BIA 1914–45, RG 350, NARA, College Park, MD.

96. "General Aguinaldo on the Filipino Flag," *The Citizen*, October 23, 1919, quoted in Baja, *Our Country's Flag and Anthem*, 154.

97. "It Is a Right," *El Comercio*, October 29, 1919, box 101, folder 526-16 to 62 Philippine Flag, BIA 1914–45, RG 350, NARA, College Park, MD; "Aguinaldo Wants to Carry the Flag in Person: Says That This Pleasure Will Hasten His Recovery," *El Comercio*, October 28, 1919, box 101, folder 526-16 to 62 Philippine Flag, BIA 1914–45, RG 350, NARA, College Park, MD; "Expressive Letter from the Leader of the Revolution," *La Vanguardia*, November 5, 1919, box 101, folder 526-16 to 62 Philippine Flag, BIA 1914–45, RG 350, NARA, College Park, MD; General Aguinaldo letter to Senate President Quezon, written from the General Hospital, October 27, 1919, quoted in Baja, *Our Country's Flag and Anthem*, 172.

98. Extract from cable, October 31, 1919, box 101, folder 526-16 to 62 Philippine Flag, BIA 1914–45, RG 350, NARA, College Park, MD.

99. "Facing the Situation," *Philippine Review* 4, no. 10 (October 1919): 590.

100. Sergio Osmeña, October 30, 1919, quoted in Baja, *Our Country's Flag and Anthem*, 175–77.

101. Victor Mendoza, *Metroimperial Intimacies: Fantasy, Racial-Sexual Governance, and the Philippines in U.S. Imperialism, 1899–1913* (Durham, NC: Duke University Press, 2015).

102. "An Act to Adopt an Official Flag for the Government of the Philippine Islands, Prescribe Rules for Its Use, and Provide Penalties for the Violation of Said Rules," *Philippine Gazette*, March 26, 1920.

103. John W. Weeks, secretary of war, to secretary of state, September 7, 1921, box 101, folder 526-16 to 62 Philippine Flag, BIA 1914–45, RG 350, NARA, College Park, MD.

104. "Facing the Situation," *Philippine Review* 4, no. 10 (October 1919): 584.

105. "This Has Gone Far Enough," *Philippine Free Press*, January 18, 1941, quoted in Jung, *Menace to Empire*, 235.

106. Renato Constantino, *The Philippines: A Past Revisited: From the Spanish Colonization to the Second World War* (1975), 367–70; Jung, *Menace to Empire*, 268–72.

107. Pedro Albizu Campos, "Porto Rico and the War," *Harvard Crimson*, April 14, 1917.

108. Lillian Guerra, *Popular Expression and National Identity in Puerto Rico* (Gainesville: University Press of Florida, 1998), 23–37; José Trías Monge, *Puerto Rico: The Trials of the Oldest Colony in the World* (New Haven, CT: Yale University Press, 1997), 66.

109. President Wilson speech to Congress, December 5, 1916, *Presidential Messages and State Papers, Vol. X* (New York: Review of Reviews Company, 1917), 341.

110. For an overview of the historical debates on the extensions of US citizenship to Puerto Rico, see Charles Venator-Santiago, "Mapping the Contours of the History of Extension of U.S. Citizenship to Puerto Rico, 1898–Present," *CENTRO Journal* 29, no. 1 (Spring 2017): 38–55. See also Robert C. McGreevey, *Borderline Citizens: The United States, Puerto Rico, and the Politics of Colonial Migration* (Ithaca, NY: Cornell University Press, 2018); Sam Erman, *Almost Citizens: Puerto Rico, The U.S. Constitution, and Empire* (Cambridge, UK: Cambridge University Press, 2019).

111. President Wilson speech to Congress, December 2, 1913, *Presidential Messages and State Papers, Vol. X* (New York: Review of Reviews Company, 1917), 44; President Wilson speech to Congress, December 7, 1915, *Presidential Messages and State Papers, Vol. X* (New York: Review of Reviews Company, 1917), 145–46.

112. Bartholomew Sparrow and Jennifer Lamm, "Puerto Ricans and U.S. Citizenship in 1917: Imperatives of Security," *CENTRO Journal* 29, no. 1 (Spring 2017): 284–315.

113. William A. Jones to Governor Arthur Yager, March 24, 1914, quoted in Sparrow and Lamm, "Puerto Ricans and U.S. Citizenship in 1917," 299.

114. Pedro A. Cabán, *Constructing a Colonial People: Puerto Rico and the United States, 1898–1932* (Boulder, CO: Westview Press, 1999), 11.

115. *An Act to Provide a Civil Government for Porto Rico, and for Other Purposes*, Public Law 64-368, *U.S. Statutes at Large* 39 (1917): 951–69.

116. Trías Monge, *Puerto Rico*, 77–87.

117. *Conditions in the Philippine Islands: Report of the Special Mission to the Philippine Islands to the Secretary of War* (Washington: Government Printing Office, 1922), 45–46.

118. Letter from T. E. Mayhew to "Uncle Ed" (Governor Edward Dorn), October 21, 1919, box 2, folder 17, Governor Edward John Dorn Papers, Richard Flores Taitano Micronesian Area Research Center (hereafter MARC), University of Guam.

119. Executive Order from W. W. Gilmer, 1920, box 2, folder 20, Governor Edward John Dorn Papers, MARC, University of Guam.

120. "Safe for Democracy, Eh?" *Public Ledger: Philadelphia*, September 19, 1920, folder 3: Printed Articles on Guam, Helen L. Paul Collection, MARC, University of Guam.

121. Arthur Warner, "Thou Shalt Not Whistle in Guam," n.d., folder 5, Thomas E. Mayhew Papers, MARC, University of Guam.

122. Mayhew to Dorn, October 21, 1919.

123. *La Democracia*, August 1, 1921, quoted in Nancy Morris, *Puerto Rico: Culture, Politics, and Identity* (Westport, CT: Praeger, 1995), 34; "New Governor Takes Office in Porto Rico: E. Mont Reily Brings Cheer When He Says Old Glory Is Only Flag for Island," *New York Times*, July 31, 1921.

124. Elena Martínez, "¡Que Bonita Bandera! Place, Space, and Identity as Expressed with the Puerto Rican Flag," *Public Performance: Studies in the Carnivalesque and Ritualesque*, ed. Jack Santino (Logan: Utah State University Press, 2017), 118.

125. "Porto Ricans Urge Removal of Reily: Cable Long List of Charges to Resident Delegate Davila against Governor: Signed by 39 of Assembly: Declare, among Other Things, He Lacks 'Discretion'—Say He Called Their Flag 'Rag,'" *Washington Post*, November 23, 1921, p. 1.

126. Extension of Remarks of Hon. Felix Cordova Davila of Porto Rico, March 2, 1922, 67th Cong., 2nd sess., *Congressional Record* 62, pt. 4: H 3303.

127. "Porto Ricans Urge Removal of Reily," p. 1.

128. Extension of Remarks of Hon. Felix Cordova Davila of Porto Rico, March 2, 1922, 67th Cong., 2nd sess., *Congressional Record* 62, pt. 4: H 3303.

129. *Porto Rico Progress*, October, 1921, p. 19, quoted in Aída Negrón de Montilla, *Americanization in Puerto Rico and the Public School System 1900–1930* (Río Piedras, Puerto Rico: Editorial Edil, 1970), 180–81.

130. Negrón de Montilla, *Americanization in Puerto Rico*, 181–83.

131. "Superintendent McGuire, under Instruction Given by Juan B. Huyke, Moves the Police against the Students," *La Democracia*, June 28, 1922, p. 1, quoted in Negrón de Montilla, *Americanization in Puerto Rico*, 198.

132. Negrón de Montilla, *Americanization in Puerto Rico*, 198.

133. Extension of Remarks of Hon. Felix Cordova Davila of Porto Rico, March 2, 1922, 67th Cong., 2nd sess., *Congressional Record* 62, pt. 4: H 3301.

134. Hon. Felix Cordova Davila of Porto Rico, March 8, 1922, 67th Cong., 2nd sess., *Congressional Record* 62, pt. 4: H 3583–84.

135. Representative Philip Campbell, April 12, 1922, 67th Cong., 2nd sess., *Congressional Record* 62, pt. 5: H 5408.

136. *Porto Rico Progress*, February 10, 1923, p. 1, quoted in Negrón de Montilla, *Americaniza-tion in Puerto Rico*, 200.

137. Albizu told this story in a speech he gave on April 16, 1950, at the annual Nationalist celebration of the birthday of José de Diego. Item 22 (a, b): Memorandum for the chief of insular police, April 17, 1950, 4, box 21, series: Documentos Nacionalistas, fondo: Departamento de Jus-ticia, Archivo General de Puerto Rico, San Juan.

138. Power, "Nationalism in a Colonized Nation," 129–31.

139. Dávila, "Los bonos del Partido Nacionalista," 32–43; Power, "Nationalism in a Colonized Nation," 122–24.

140. Dávila, "Los bonos," 36; "$5,000,000 Bonds of Puerto Rican 'Republic' Launched by Junta Here; Capital Not Alarmed," *New York Times*, June 29, 1932, p. 1.

141. Dávila, "Los bonos," 38.

142. Carrión, "War of the Flags," 110–11; Bolívar Pagán, *Historia de los Partidos Políticos Puer-torriqueños (1898–1956) Tomo II* (San Juan: Librería Campos, 1959), 31.

143. Item 22 (a,b): Memorandum for the chief of insular police, April 17, 1950, 4, box 21, serie: Documentos Nacionalistas, Fondo: Departamento de Justicia, Archivo General de Puerto Rico, San Juan.

144. Carrión, "War of the Flags," 111; Pagán, *Historia de los Partidos Políticos*, 31.

145. Olga Jiménez de Wagenheim, *Nationalist Heroines: Puerto Rican Women History Forgot, 1930s–1950s* (Princeton, NJ: Markus Wiener Publishers, 2016), 36.

146. A. W. Maldonado, *Luis Muñoz Marín: Puerto Rico's Democratic Revolution* (San Juan: Editorial Universidad de Puerto Rico, 2006), 119–20.

147. Maldonado, *Luis Muñoz Marín*, 137.

148. Ruth M. Reynolds, *Campus in Bondage: A 1948 Microcosm of Puerto Rico in Bondage* (New York: Centro de Estudios Puertorriqueños, 1989), 16; Maldonado, *Luis Muñoz Marín*, 138.

149. Reynolds, *Campus in Bondage*, 17; Maldonado, *Luis Muñoz Marín*, 139.

150. Daniel Immerwahr, *How to Hide an Empire: A History of the Greater United States* (New York: Farrar, Straus and Giroux, 2019), 148.

151. Frank Otto Gatell, "Independence Rejected: Puerto Rico and the Tydings Bill of 1936," *Hispanic American Historical Review* 38, no. 1 (February 1958): 33.

152. The *New York Times* referred to Riggs as Tydings's "political protégé." "Freedom Bill Splits Puerto Rico: Senate Move Complicates Trial of Nationalists, Who Hold That the Island Is Already Legally Independent," *New York Times*, May 3, 1936, p. E6.

153. Resident Commissioner Santiago Iglesias, May 19, 1936, 74th Cong., 2nd sess., *Congres-sional Record* 80 pt. 7: H 7522.

154. "Ban Puerto Rican Flag for Public Buildings: Acting Governor and Police Chief Call Substitution Challenge to U.S. Sovereignty," *Baltimore Sun*, May 3, 1936, p. 14; "Puerto Rico Rules U.S. Flag Dominant: Acting Governor Bans Use of Nationalist Emblem over Public Buildings," *New York Times*, May 3, 1936.

155. "Troops Called Out as Students Riot: Young Puerto Rican Nationals Tear U.S. Flag to Shreds," *Washington Herald*, May 14, 1936; Thomas Mathews, *Puerto Rican Politics and the New Deal* (Gainesville: University of Florida Press, 1960), 261.

156. "Pictures of Roosevelt Displaced in San Juan," *Washington Post*, May 2, 1936, p. 5; "Puerto Rican Flag Hoisted at Ponce: Pictures of Roosevelt and Hoover Removed," *Daily Boston Globe*, May 2, 1936, p. 1.

157. "Puerto Rico Rules U.S. Flag Dominant," p. 39.

158. "Troops Called Out as Students Riot: Young Puerto Rican Nationals Tear U.S. Flag to Shreds," *Washington Herald*, May 14, 1936; "Zioncheck Offers to Clean Up Island: Congressman Asks President for Power to Straighten Out Puerto Rican Affairs," *New York Times*, May 14, 1936, p. 12; "San Juan Guard Mobilized as Students Strike: Zioncheck, Hurling Cocoanuts, Also Irks Capital; Marines Fly Him Away," *New York Herald Tribune*, May 14, 1936, p. 1A.

159. "Troops Called Out As Students Riot: Young Puerto Rican Nationals Tear U.S. Flag to Shreds," *Washington Herald*, May 14, 1936; "San Juan Guard Mobilized as Students Strike: Zioncheck, Hurling Cocoanuts, Also Irks Capital; Marines Fly Him Away," May 14, 1936, *New York Herald Tribune*, p. 1A; "Troops Called as Students Riot in Puerto Rico: Winship Closes All Schools as Youths Trample on American Flag," *Washington Post*, May 14, 1936, p. X11; "Gov. Winship Warns Island on 'Terrorism': Puerto Rico Officers Told to Act Sternly if Flag Is Desecrated," *Washington Post*, May 16, 1936.

160. "Puerto Rico Students in Riot: Police Ignore Governor's Order to Remove Nationalist Flags," *Washington Times*, May 14, 1936.

161. "Troops Called as Students Riot in Puerto Rico: Winship Closes All Schools as Youths Trample on American Flag," *Washington Post*, May 14, 1936, p. X11; "Troops Called Out as Students Riot: Young Puerto Rican Nationals Tear U.S. Flag to Shreds," *Washington Herald*, May 14, 1936.

162. W. F. O'Reilly, "Puerto Ricans Subside, but Not Zioncheck: San Juan Schools Are Reopened after Rioting by Students Opposing U.S.," *New York Herald Tribune*, May 15, 1936, p. 6.

163. "Zioncheck Offers to Clean Up Island," p. 12.

164. *El País*, quoted in O'Reilly, "Puerto Ricans Subside."

165. Córdova Dávila quoted in O'Reilly, "Puerto Ricans Subside."

166. "Moderation Urged on Puerto Ricans: Press and Some Leaders Ask People to Be Peaceful in Independence Campaign," *New York Times*, May 15, 1936, p. 11.

167. Harwood Hull, "Freedom Bill Splits Puerto Rico: Senate Move Complicates Trial of Nationalists, Who Hold That the Island Is Already Legally Independent," *New York Times*, May 3, 1936, p. E6.

168. "The Case for Puerto Rican Independence," *Listín Diario* (Dominican Republic), May 24, 1936, Box 864, 9–8-68 Government–Status–Independence–for–American Republics, Central Files Puerto Rico, RG 126, NARA, College Park.

169. Sr. Ramon Emilio Jimenez, "Puerto Rico at the Height of Its Duty and Rights," *Listín Diario*, May 25, 1936, box 864, 9-8-68 Government–Status–Independence–for–American Republics, Central Files Puerto Rico, RG 126, NARA, College Park, MD.

170. "Gov. Winship Warns Island on 'Terrorism': Puerto Rico Officers Told to Act Sternly if Flag Is Desecrated," *Washington Post*, May 16, 1936; "Warns Puerto Rico to Respect Flag: Governor Orders Prosecution of Persons Desecrating Stars and Stripes," *Baltimore Sun*, May 16, 1936, p. 2.

171. Blanton Winship to Ernest Gruening, director of Division of Territories and Insular Possessions (hereafter DTIP), dated June 26, 1936, but sent after July 4, box 1128, folder 9-8-108 Holidays, etc.–Fourth of July, Central Files Puerto Rico, RG 126, NARA, College Park, MD.

172. "La parada del cuatro de julio en San Juan," *El Mundo*, July 6, 1936.

173. Speech made by Hon. Blanton Winship, governor of Puerto Rico, July 4, 1936, box 1128, folder 9-8-108 Holidays, etc.–Fourth of July, Central Files Puerto, RG 126, NARA, College Park, MD.

174. "Hate under the Palms," *Ken Magazine*, December 1, 1938, box 952, folder 9-8-84 Publicity, Central Files Puerto Rico, RG 126, NARA, College Park, MD.

175. Winship to Gruening, box 1128, folder 9-8-108 Holidays, etc.–Fourth of July, RG 126–Central Files Puerto Rico, NARA, College Park, MD.

176. "Puerto Rico Is Held Free under the U.S.: Chief Justice Cheered When He Makes Statement at Fourth of July Celebration," *New York Times*, July 5, 1936.

177. Jiménez de Wagenheim, *Nationalist Heroines*, 38–41.

178. Jiménez de Wagenheim, *Nationalist Heroines*, 29, 42.

179. Box 934, folder 9-8-78 Law & Order–Nationalists–Ponce, Central Files Puerto Rico, RG 126, NARA, College Park, MD.

180. "Have We Forgotten 1776?" *New York Post*, March 27, 1937.

181. Secretary of Interior Harold Ickes believed the Ponce Massacre was clear evidence that Winship's "mailed fist" policy wasn't working. The Hays Commission found the same thing. And the ACLU argued that Winship had violated Puerto Ricans' civil rights. See Jorge Rodríguez Beruff, *Strategy as Politics: Puerto Rico on the Eve of the Second World War* (San Juan: La Editorial Universidad de Puerto Rico, 2007), 193–95.

182. "Killers Strike in Puerto Rico: Assassins Shoot Officer but Miss Gov. Winship," *Daily Boston Globe*, July 26, 1938, p. 1; "2 Held for Murder in Winship Attack: Governor of Puerto Rico Target of Assassins," *Baltimore Sun*, July 6, 1938, p. 1.

183. Rodríguez Beruff, *Strategy as Politics*, 162–65.

184. Harwood Hull, "Puerto Ricans Fire upon Gov. Winship: Two Slain as 15 Bullets Miss Official, Reviewing Parade before 40,000 at Ponce," *New York Times*, July 26, 1938, pp. 1, 11.

185. Hull, "Puerto Ricans Fire upon Gov. Winship." The Nationalist Party officially disavowed the attack: "Puerto Rico Shooting Disavowed by Party: Nationalists for Revolutionary Means, but Bar Single Acts," *New York Times*, August 1, 1938, p. 6.

186. Hull, "Puerto Ricans Fire upon Gov. Winship."

187. Proclamation by Governor: "National Flag Week," administrative bulletin no. 614, May 29, 1939, box 1128, folder 9-8-108, Holidays, Observances, Celebrations–General, Central Files Puerto Rico, RG 126, NARA, College Park, MD.

188. José M. Gallardo, commissioner of education, January 30, 1939, "2nd Endorsement Office of the Commissioner of Education, San Juan, P. R." box 850, folder 9-8-65, Education–General, Central Files Puerto Rico, RG 126, NARA, College Park; "Esa costumbre se suspendió cuando el espíritu anti-americano campeaba por su respeto en el Depto. de Instrucción," *El País*, October 9, 1940, English translation in box 850, folder 9-8-65, Education–General, Central Files Puerto Rico, RG 126, NARA, College Park, MD.

189. "Esa costumbre se suspendió cuando el espíritu anti-americano."

190. "Puerto Rico Celebrates: Island Pictured as 4th State in July 4 Festivities," *New York Times*, July 5, 1939, box 1128, folder 9-8-108 Holidays, etc.–Fourth of July, RG 126–Central Files Puerto Rico, NARA, College Park, MD.

191. Rodríguez Beruff, *Strategy as Politics*, 223–24.

192. Rodríguez Beruff, *Strategy as Politics*, 16, 124.

193. Rodríguez Beruff, *Strategy as Politics*, 114.

194. Rodríguez Beruff, *Strategy as Politics*, 111, ix.

195. Rodríguez Beruff, *Strategy as Politics*, ix, 195.

196. William Leahy diary, quoted in Rodríguez Beruff, *Strategy as Politics*, 331.

197. Ruby Black to Muna Lee, November 1938, quoted in Rodríguez Beruff, *Strategy as Politics*, 327.

198. Rodríguez Beruff, *Strategy as Politics*, 290, 327, 333.

199. *The Progressive Guide* 4, no. 24 (June 7, 1941), box 1274, folder 9–11–36 Publicity–Publications–"The Progressive Guide," Central Files Virgin Islands, RG 126, NARA, College Park, MD.

200. "Flag Day Celebrated by Guam Schools," *GTA Advocate*, no. 3 (February 15, 1939): 3, box 517, folder: Guam Bulletin, Central Files Guam, RG 126, NARA, College Park, MD.

201. Jung, *Menace to Empire*, 68–70, 79–104; Christopher Capozzola, *Bound by War: How the United States and the Philippines Built America's First Pacific Century* (New York: Basic Books, 2020), 71–74.

202. "Ignores American Flag: Japanese Ship at Manila Flies Its Own and Filipino Colors," *New York Times*, February 1, 1921, p. 10.

203. "Japanese Boats Hoist P.I. Flag under Nippon's: Replacement of American Standard, Use of Philippine Flag under Japanese Sun Denounced; Aldanese Acts," *Philippine Herald*, January 17, 1935, box 101, folder 526–16 to 62, Philippine Flag, RG 350 BIA 1914–45, NARA, College Park, MD.

204. "Kimura Warns Nationals to Observe Law on Flags," *Philippine Herald*, January 18, 1935, box 101, folder 526–16 to 62, Philippine Flag, RG 350 BIA 1914–45, NARA, College Park, MD.

205. "Japanese Boats Hoist P.I. Flag under Nippon's: Replacement of American Standard, Use of Philippine Flag under Japanese Sun Denounced; Aldanese Acts," *Philippine Herald*, January 17, 1935, box 101, folder 526–16 to 62, Philippine Flag, RG 350 BIA 1914–45, NARA, College Park, MD.

Chapter 4

1. W. B. Courtney, "Guam: Haunted Paradise," *Collier's*, April 1939, pp. 51, 57.

2. Courtney, "Guam: Haunted Paradise," 15, 50.

3. *Annual Report of the Governor of Guam for Fiscal Year Ending June 30, 1930*, 17; *Annual Report of the Governor of Guam for Fiscal Year Ending June 30, 1931*, 16; *Annual Report of the Governor of Guam for Fiscal Year Ending June 30, 1935*, 12; *Annual Report of the Governor of Guam for Fiscal Year Ending June 30, 1936*, 10, box 531, folder 9-3-18 Reports-Governor-Annual, Central Files-Guam, record group 126, Office of Territories (hereafter RG 126), US National Archives and Records Administration (hereafter NARA), College Park, MD; "Flag Day Celebrated by Guam Schools," *GTA Advocate*, no. 3 (February 15, 1939): 15, box 517, folder: Guam Bulletin, Central Files Guam, RG 126, NARA, College Park, MD.

4. Courtney, "Guam: Haunted Paradise," 59.

5. Courtney, "Guam: Haunted Paradise," 14.

6. Keith L. Camacho, *Cultures of Commemoration: The Politics of War, Memory, and History in the Mariana Islands* (Honolulu: University of Hawai'i Press, 2011), 21–38.

7. Courtney, "Guam: Haunted Paradise," 59.

8. The initial declaration that unincorporated territories were "foreign to the United States in a domestic sense" comes from *Downes v. Bidwell* 182, U.S. 222, at 341 (1901).

9. Courtney, "Guam: Haunted Paradise," 59.

10. Extension of Remarks of Hon. Michael J. Kirwan of Ohio, March 30, 1939, 76th Cong., 1st sess., *Congressional Record* 84, pt. 12: H 1229.

11. Camacho, *Cultures of Commemoration*, 39.

12. Jon Kamakawiwioʻole Osorio, "Memorializing Puʻuloa and Remembering Pearl Harbor," in *Militarized Currents: Toward a Decolonized Future in Asia and the Pacific*, ed. Setsu Shigematsu and Keith L. Camacho (Minneapolis: University of Minnesota Press, 2010), 8.

13. "Flag Day Celebrated by Guam Schools," *GTA Advocate*, no. 3 (February 15, 1939): 3, box 517, folder Guam Bulletin, Central Files Guam, RG 126, NARA, College Park, MD.

14. "Flag Day Celebrated by Guam Schools," *GTA Advocate*, no. 3, (February 15, 1939): 4, box 517, folder Guam Bulletin, Central Files Guam, RG 126, NARA, College Park, MD.

15. Camacho, *Cultures of Commemoration*, 3–7; Genevieve Clutario, "World War II and the Promise of Normalcy: Overlapping Empires and Everyday Lives in the Philippines," in *Crossing Empires: Taking U.S. History into Transimperial Terrain*, ed. Kristin Hoganson and Jay Sexton (Durham, NC: Duke University Press, 2020), 241; Daniel Immerwahr, *How to Hide an Empire: A History of the Greater United States* (New York: Farrar, Straus, and Giroux, 2019), 171–212; Jeremy A. Yellen, *The Greater East Asia Co-Prosperity Sphere: When Total Empire Met Total War* (Ithaca, NY: Cornell University Press, 2019), 21; Setsu Shigematsu and Keith L. Camacho, "Introduction: Militarized Currents, Decolonizing Futures," in *Militarized Currents: Toward a Decolonized Future in Asia and the Pacific*, ed. Setsu Shigematsu and Keith L. Camacho (Minneapolis: University of Minnesota Press, 2010), xvi–xxvi.

16. Clutario, "World War II and the Promise of Normalcy," 243.

17. Camacho, *Cultures of Commemoration*, 46. Toward the end of the war there was an uprising in Malesso. See Jose M. Torres, *The Massacre at Atåte* (Mangilao: Richard F. Taitano Micronesian Area Research Center, University of Guam, 2015).

18. Yellen, *Greater East Asia Co-Prosperity Sphere*, 4. On the term "Greater United States," see Immerwahr, *How to Hide an Empire*, 74–76.

19. Wakako Higuchi, "The Japanisation Policy for the Chamorros of Guam, 1941–1944," *Journal of Pacific History* 36, no. 1 (2001): 19–35.

20. Yellen, *Greater East Asia Co-Prosperity Sphere*, 4–6.

21. Jorge B. Vargas, "Executive Order No. 110 Changing the Names of Streets, Highways, Bridges, Towns, Parks, and Public Buildings in Various Chartered Cities and Provinces," *Official Journal of the Japanese Military Administration*, no. 8 (December 8, 1942): 27–32, serials, Filipinas Heritage Library (hereafter FHL), Ayala Museum, Manila; Yellen, *Greater East Asia Co-Prosperity Sphere*, 4–6.

22. Helen N. Mendoza, *Memories of the War Years: A Teenage Girl's Life in the Philippines under Japanese Rule* (Quezon City, Philippines: Pantas, 2016), 8.

23. Armando J. Malay, *Occupied Philippines: The Role of Jorge B. Vargas during the Japanese Occupation* (Manila: Filipiniana Book Guild, 1967), 98.

24. "Corregidor Is a Badly Battered Fortress," *Tribune* (Manila), May 10, 1942, p. 2.

25. Charles A. Willoughby and John Chamberlain, *MacArthur, 1941–1951* (New York: McGraw-Hill, 1954), 55–56.

26. Carlos P. Romulo, *I Saw the Fall of the Philippines* (Garden City, NY: Doubleday, Doran, & Company, 1943), 46; box 7, folder: Papers re Philippines, Scrapbook: Talks and Papers, 1930–1933, Walter W. Marquardt Papers, Bentley Historical Library, University of Michigan; Corban K. Alabado and Ceres S. C. Alabado, *Philippine World War II Stories for Children in Bilingual Text, English and Pilipino* (San Diego: University Readers, 2009).

27. *Guam Past & Present Part III: Under the Stars & Stripes*, 132, box 3, folder 6: Miscellaneous Publications, Governor Carlton S. Skinner Papers, MSS 2850, Richard F. Taitano Micronesian Area Research Center (hereafter MARC), University of Guam.

28. Commander in chief, Imperial Japanese Forces, "Military Ordinance No. 3. April 22, 1942: Ordinance Concerning Prohibition of the Use of the Philippine Flag," *Official Journal of the Japanese Military Administration* 3, serials, FHL. Japanese officials also routinely talked about the evils of

US colonial rule and how they were there to liberate Filipinos. Commander-in-chief of Japanese Expeditionary Forces to the Philippines, "Address to the Filipino People, July 31, 1942"; Major-General K. Sato, "Address to Constabulary Trainees, Delivered at Constabulary Training School, September 16, 1942"; "Address to the Public Officials and Inhabitants of the Visayan Provinces by the Director General of the Japanese Military Administration, April 26th, 18th Year of Syowa," monographs, American Historical Collection (hereafter AHC), Ateneo de Manila University, Manila.

29. Louise L. Charyauros, "Japs Ravaged Guam," box 7, folder: Personal Narratives of High School Students after World War II, Agueda Iglesias Johnston papers, MARC, University of Guam.

30. Tony Palomo, "Island in Agony: The War in Guam," in *Remembering the Pacific War*, ed. Geoffrey White (Honolulu: Center for Pacific Islands Studies, 1991), 139.

31. José Miguel C. Fernández, *Carmen & I: Life under Japanese Occupation in WWII; Memoirs of José Miguel C. Fernández* (Maria Lourdes F. Godinez, 2014), 135.

32. Wakako Higuchi, *The Japanese Administration of Guam, 1941–1944: A Study of Occupation and Integration Policies, with Japanese Oral Histories* (Jefferson, NC: McFarland & Company, 2013), 10.

33. Torres, *Massacre at Atåte*, 26.

34. Claro M. Recto, "Instruction No. 18, 28 April 1942 from the Commissioner of Education, Health, and Public Welfare," *Official Journal of the Japanese Military Administration* 3, 2–7, serials, FHL; "Orders and Instructions by the Commander-in-Chief and the Director General of the Military Administration: Instruction No. 27: Supplementary Readers to Be Used in Elementary Schools," *Philippine Gazette* 2, no. 3 (March 1943): 269–70.

35. Teodoro Agoncillo, *The Fateful Years: Japan's Adventure in the Philippines, 1941–1945, Vol. 1* (Quezon City: University of the Philippines Press, 2001), 440.

36. Brigadier General Carlos P. Romulo, "Address Delivered before the National Press Club by December 14, 1944," box 781, folder 9-7-42 Resident Commissioner, press release December 14, 1944, Central Files: Philippines, RG 126, NARA, College Park, MD.

37. "Oral Historiography of the Japanese Administration in Palau, October 1986," 126–27, 212, 243, 352, box 2, Mark R. Peattie papers, MARC, University of Guam.

38. *RealFACES: Guam's World War II Survivors* (Hagåtña, Guam: War Survivors Memorial Foundation, 2014), 8, 16.

39. Originally, Camp O'Donnell held Filipino and continental US American prisoners of war, but the continental US Americans were moved to different camps in June 1942. After that, O'Donnell became a "rehabilitation center for the Filipino prisoners of war." Office of the Provost Marshal General, "Report on American Prisoners of War Interned by the Japanese in the Philippines," November 19, 1945.

40. M. D. Nazario, "O'Donnell: Not a Prison Camp but a School," *Shin Seiki* 1, no. 5 (February 2603): 8, serials, Filipinas Heritage Library, Ayala Museum, Manila.

41. Malay, *Occupied Philippines*, 115.

42. Jorge B. Vargas, "Executive Order No. 150 Declaring Thursday Morning May 6, 1943 and Friday Afternoon May 7, 1943 Special Public Holidays," *Official Journal of the Japanese Military Administration* 12, Serials, FHL.

43. Appendix C, "*The People of the Philippines vs. Jorge B. Vargas*, Criminal Case No. 3520," in Malay, *Occupied Philippines*, 237, 243–44, 247–48, 254–55, 260.

44. Jose P. Laurel, "One Nation, One Heart, One Republic," speech delivered extemporaneously by Laurel, president of the Preparatory Commission for Philippine Independence, at the

special general assembly of the KALIBAPI, held at the Session Hall of the Legislative Building, Manila, September 7, 1943, *Official Journal of the Japanese Military Administration* 13:49, serials, FHL.

45. Camacho, *Cultures of Commemoration*, 46.

46. Camacho, *Cultures of Commemoration*, 47.

47. Joseph Santo Tomas, "Song of Hope, Song of Faith," in *Liberation: Guam Remembers; A Golden Salute for the 50th Anniversary of the Liberation of Guam* (Hagåtña, Guam: Golden Salute Committee, 1994), 26.

48. Roughly translated as "Great Shrine Island," "Shinto Shrine," or "Island of the Imperial Court." Torres, *Massacre at Atåte*, 24; Higuchi, *Japanese Administration of Guam*, 280.

49. Jorge B. Vargas, "Executive Order No. 41 Changing the Name of Dewey Boulevard to Heiwa Boulevard; Taft Avenue to Daitoa Avenue; Harrison Boulevard to Koa Boulevard; Jones Bridge to Banzai Bridge; Harrison Park to Rizal Park; and Wallace Field and Burnham Green to Plaza Bagong Filipinas," *Official Journal of the Japanese Military Administration* 4 (May 18, 1942): 33, serials, FHL.

50. Fernández, *Carmen & I*, 62.

51. "Program for Safekeeping of Currency, Bonds, and Treasury Checks Accepted for Safekeeping," 108, box 3, folder: 6th annual report of US High Commissioner to the Philippine Islands, July 1, 1941–June 1, 1942, library materials, record group 350, Bureau of Insular Affairs (hereafter RG 350), NARA, College Park, MD.

52. "Program for Safekeeping of Currency," 110.

53. "Program for Safekeeping of Currency," 111.

54. "Program for Safekeeping of Currency," 112.

55. "Program for Safekeeping of Currency," 117.

56. Paraphrase of Telegram received from US High Commissioner Philippines January 7, 1942, midnight, box 781, folder 9-7-43, Philippine Islands, Money, Deposits 1941–42, Central Files, Philippines, RG 126, NARA, College Park, MD.

57. "Program for Safekeeping of Currency," 118.

58. Cabot Coville, "Our Two Months on Corregidor," *Saturday Evening Post*, June 27, 1942, p. 99, box 722, folder 9-7-33, Publicity–Publications–Press Clippings, Central Files–Philippines, RG 126, NARA, College Park, MD.

59. Francis B. Sayre, *War Days on Corregidor*, reprinted from the April 20, 1942, issue of *Life* magazine, box 3, folder: 6th annual report of US high commissioner to the Philippine Islands, July 1, 1941–June 1, 1942, Library Materials, RG 350, NARA, College Park, MD.

60. Coville, "Our Two Months on Corregidor," 99.

61. Sayre, *War Days on Corregidor*.

62. Robert C. Sheats, *One Man's War: Diving as a Guest of the Emperor 1942* (Flagstaff, AZ: Best Publishing Company, 1998), 31.

63. Troy R. Cole, *The Silver Secret of Caballo Bay* (Trafford, 2011), 12–13.

64. Sheats, *One Man's War*, 34–35.

65. Alvita Akiboh, "Pocket-Sized Imperialism," *Diplomatic History* 41, no. 5 (November 2017): 894.

66. Akiboh "Pocket-Sized Imperialism," 897–98.

67. "Notification, February 23, 1942 from Commander in Chief," *Official Journal of the Japanese Military Administration* 1, no. 1: 47, serials, FHL.

68. Fernández, *Carmen & I*, 130.

69. Fernández, *Carmen & I*, 130.

70. "Instruction no. 4, February 21, 1942 Concerning the Reopening of Postal Administration in the Philippines," *Official Journal of the Japanese Military Administration* 1, no. 1: 31, serials, FHL; Enrique P. San Jose, "Stamps Are History: The Postal Issues and Events in the Philippines during the Japanese Occupation, 1942–1945," *Philippine Philately* 3, no. 1 (September-October 1950), National Postal Museum (hereafter NPM) Library, Smithsonian Institution, Washington.

71. *Stamps of the Philippines: Historical and Topical Collections, 1854–2004* (Pasay: Philippine Small and Medium Business Development Foundation, 2008), 48, Philippine National Library, Manila.

72. Enrique P. San Jose, "Stamps Are History: The Postal Issues and Events in the Philippines during the Japanese Occupation, 1942–1945," *Philippine Philately* 2, no. 4 (March-April 1950): 26, NPM Library.

73. San Jose, "Stamps are History," 28–29.

74. Fernández, *Carmen & I*, 126.

75. Speech read at meeting of Manila Rotary Club, September 14, 1950, where Dr. Perez was guest of honor and speaker, in Gilbert S. Perez, *The History of Money* (Manila: Philippine Numismatic and Antiquarian Society, 1950), 16, AHC.

76. "Lt. Col. Vicente T. Blaz, Interview by Maj. D. W. Brown, USMC, Head of the Writing and Graphics Section, Production Branch, Division of Information, Headquarters, Marine Corps. Tape Made on January 10, 1969," 12, folder 27: Oral History Lt. Col. Vicente T. Blaz, Thomas B. McGrath S. J. papers, MARC, University of Guam.

77. Paul V. McNutt, *Seventh and Final Report of the High Commissioner Paul V. McNutt to the Philippines, Covering the Period September 14, 1945 to July 4, 1946*, 21, box 5, folder: Seventh and Final Report of the High Commissioner Paul V. McNutt to the Philippines, covering the period September 14, 1945 to July 4, 1946, library materials, RG 350, NARA, College Park, MD.

78. John M. Hunt, "World War II Emergency Service Currency for Mountain Province," *Pesos Fuertes: Bank Note Society of the Philippines Journal* 1 (August 2005): 27.

79. Carlos P. Romulo, foreword to Neil Shafer, *Philippine Emergency Currency and Guerrilla Currency of World War II* (Racine, WI: Western, 1974), 9–10.

80. Paul V. McNutt, *Seventh and Final Report of the High Commissioner Paul V. McNutt to the Philippines, Covering the Period September 14, 1945 to July 4, 1946*, 21, box 5, folder: Seventh and Final Report of the High Commissioner Paul V. McNutt to the Philippines, covering the period September 14, 1945 to July 4, 1946, library materials, RG 350, NARA, College Park, MD.

81. Fernández, *Carmen & I*, 130.

82. Pura Villanueva Kalaw, *A Brief History of the Filipino Flag* (Manila: Bureau of Printing, 1947), 13.

83. Kalaw, *Brief History of the Filipino Flag*, 14.

84. Pedro A. Gagelonia, *The Philippine National Flag* (Caloocan City: Philippine Youth Supplier, 1967), Filipinas Heritage Library, Ayala Museum, Manila.

85. *La Vanguardia*, quoted in Kalaw, *Brief History of the Filipino Flag*, 15.

86. Kalaw, *Brief History of the Filipino Flag*, 15–16.

87. Laurel, "One Nation, One Heart, One Republic."

88. Manuel L. Quezon, "Report to the Filipino People, an Address by President of the Philippines, February 20, 1943, Broadcast via Short Wave from Washington, D.C.," box 7, folder: Reports of the President of the Philippines, 1936–1940, library materials, RG 350, NARA, College Park, MD.

89. Claro M. Recto to Takaji Wachi, June 15, 1944, quoted in Agoncillo, *The Fateful Years*, 417.

90. Enrique San Jose, "Commemorative Issues," *Philippine Philately* 2, no. 6 (July-August 1950): 35, NPM Library.

91. San Jose, "Commemorative Issues."

92. Japan did make official plans to invade Hawai'i. John J. Stephan, *Hawaii under the Rising Sun: Japan's Plans for Conquest after Pearl Harbor* (Honolulu: University of Hawaii Press, 1984).

93. George S. Waterhouse and E. W. Carden to Joseph Poindexter, February 6, 1942, box 724, folder 9-4-113, World War-Currency, Central Files, Hawaii, RG 126, NARA, College Park, MD.

94. J. H. Bowman to archivist Kathryn H. Stidham, August 1, 1946, folder 29.08 US Treasury Department, Foreign Funds Control, Ephemera, Hawaii War Records Depository, University of Hawai'i Manoa; Harold Ickes to Joseph B. Poindexter, March 9, 1942, box 724, folder 9-4-113, World War-Currency, Central Files, Hawaii, RG 126, NARA, College Park, MD.

95. Bowman to Stidham, August 1, 1946.

96. W. S. B. to Mr. Hall and Mr. William S. Broughton, June 8, 1942, box 1, folder: Currency, Printing of for Hawaii, series K currency, 53-87-101, Entry UD Circulation of Historical Value of US and Foreign Securities (Series "K") Currency, 1890–1942, record group 53, Bureau of Public Debt (hereafter RG 53), NARA, College Park, MD.

97. "Old Money Turned in for Hawaii Currency," *Honolulu Star Bulletin*, June 26, 1942, ox 689, folder 9-4-101, Money-General, Central Files, Hawaii, RG 126, NARA, College Park, MD.

98. Brigadier-General Thomas H. Green, "General Orders No. 118 from the Office of the Military Governor," June 2, 1942, box 1, folder: Currency, Printing of for Hawaii, Series K Currency 53-87-101, Entry UD Circulation of Historical Value of US and Foreign Securities (Series "K") Currency, 1890–1942, RG 53, NARA, College Park, MD.

99. "Old Money Turned in for Hawaii Currency."

100. "Public Documents Relating to Foreign Funds Control, Issued by the Office of the Governor of Hawaii," March 1, 1944, 2, Foreign Funds Control, ephemera, Hawaii War Records Depository, University of Hawai'i at Manoa.

101. Hanson W. Baldwin, "Hawaii's Tenth Month of War," *San Francisco Chronicle*, September 19, 1942, p. 10; box 15, folder 14: Descriptions & Accounts of Life in Hawaii, newspaper clippings, ephemera, Hawaii War Records Depository, University of Hawai'i at Manoa.

102. Governor of Hawaii, "Under the regulations every person renting a safe deposit box at a local bank or trust company must open it before October 1 in the presence of an official designated by the United States Treasury." Press release, June 25, 1942, box 724, folder 9-4-113, World War-Currency, Central Files, Hawaii, RG 126, NARA, College Park, MD.

103. For more on martial law in Hawai'i, see Harry N. Scheiber and Jane L. Scheiber, *Bayonets in Paradise: Martial Law in Hawai'i during World War II* (Honolulu: University of Hawai'i Press, 2016); Immerwahr, *How to Hide an Empire*, 174–78.

104. "Hawaii Currency Regulations Revoked by Governor Stainback," folder 29.08 US Treasury Department, Foreign Funds Control, ephemera, Hawaii War Records Depository, University of Hawai'i at Manoa; Treasury Department press release, October 21, 1944, box 1, folder: Currency, Printing of for Hawaii, Series K currency 53-87-101, entry UD Circulation of Historical Value of US and Foreign Securities (Series "K") Currency, 1890–1942, RG 53, NARA, College Park, MD.

105. "M'Arthur Appeals for Filipinos' Aid: Broadcasts Call to Rise and Strike Japanese as Lines of Battle Roll Forward," *New York Times*, October 21, 1944.

106. Pat Kelly, "Stamps as Psychological Warfare," *Philippine Philately* 5, no. 1 (September-October 1952): 32, NPM Library; Neil Shafer, *A Guide Book of Philippine Paper Money* (Racine, WI: Whitman, 1964), 55.

107. Memorandum of conversation. Subject: Monetary problems of reoccupation of the Philippines. Participants: Andre Soriano, secretary of finance of the Commonwealth of the Philippines; Mr. Foley of Philippine National Bank, New York; Mr. Hernandez, auditor general of the Commonwealth of the Philippines; and Mr. Luthringer; January 8, 1944, box 781, folder 9-7-43, Philippine Islands–Money–General–1941–1946, Central Files–Philippines, RG 126, NARA, College Park, MD.

108. Harold Ickes to Henry Stimson, July 8, 1944, box 781, folder 9-7-43, Philippine Islands–Money–General–1941–1946, Central Files–Philippines, RG 126, NARA, College Park, MD.

109. Acting secretary of war to Secretary of Interior Harold Ickes, July 15, 1944, box 781, folder 9-7-43, Philippine Islands–Money–General–1941–1946, Central Files–Philippines, RG 126, NARA, College Park, MD.

110. M. Hamlin Cannon, *Leyte: Return to the Philippines* (Washington: Center of Military History, 1993), 199.

111. Fernández, *Carmen & I*, 126.

112. Leaflet: "Overprinted Occupation Money," Psychological Warfare Branch, GHQ, APO 500, December 7, 1944, photo 5, envelope 29: Propaganda/Surrender/Liberation, Jim Black Collection Part V: Black, Carter, Dawson, Dwyre, Moore, and Wendover Collections, AHC; Shafer, *A Guide Book of Philippine Paper Money*, 53.

113. Paul V. McNutt, "Philippine Peso circulation after Liberation," *Seventh and Final Report of the High Commissioner Paul V. McNutt to the Philippines, Covering the Period September 14, 1945 to July 4, 1946*, box 5, folder: Seventh and Final Report of the High Commissioner Paul V. McNutt to the Philippines, Covering the Period September 14, 1945 to July 4, 1946, library materials, RG 350, NARA, College Park, MD.

114. McNutt, "Philippine Peso Circulation after Liberation"; Aldo P. Basso, "Overstamps on Japanese Invasion Money of the Philippines (JIM)," *Pesos Fuertes: Bank Note Society of the Philippines Journal* 1, no. 2 (May 1983): 4–5.

115. McNutt, "Philippine Peso Circulation after Liberation."

116. Cesar V. Callanta, "The Story of the 1935 Pictorial Stamps," *Philippine Journal of Philately* 5, no. 6 (July-August 1953): 8, NPM Library.

117. Jose Escuadra, "The Story Our Victory Stamps Tell," *Philippine Journal of Philately* 1, no. 2 (November-December 1948): 30, NPM Library.

118. Vicente M. Diaz, "Deliberating 'Liberation Day': Identity, History, Memory, and War in Guam," in *Perilous Memories: The Asia-Pacific Wars*, ed. T. Fujitanti, Geoffrey White, and L. Yoneyama (Durham, NC: Duke University Press, 1998), 160.

119. Philip A. Crowl, *Campaign in the Marianas* (Washington: Center of Military History, 1993), 382.

120. Lt. Col. Vicente T. Blaz interviewed by Maj. D. W. Brown USMC on January 10, 1969, 14, folder 27: Oral History Lt. Col. Vicente Blaz, Thomas B. McGrath S. J. Papers, MARC, University of Guam.

121. "A young Filipina brings a tattered U.S. flag out of hiding," Part I: General Collection, envelope 95: Liberation, 1945, Photograph Collection, AHC.

122. Evelyn Chapman Castillo, *And They Returned: Life in Leyte during World War II* (Houston: Bright Sky Press, 2015), 92–93.

123. "Japanese War Crime Trial: At Jap war crimes trial in Manila, Buenaventura Bello, former President of Northern College, Vigan, Northwestern Luzon (left) shows the American flag which he says Jap soldiers tore down from his office wall after shooting him through the side.

Holding the flag with him is prosecuting attorney Lt. Col. Kim of the Philippine Army," January 13, 1946, Getty Images.

124. Alice Byram Condict, *Old Glory and the Gospel in the Philippines: Notes Gathered during Professional and Missionary Work* (Chicago: Fleming H. Revell, 1902), 87.

125. The death toll comes from Ken De Bevoise, *Agents of the Apocalypse* (Princeton, NJ: Princeton University Press, 1995), 13.

126. Courtney, "Guam: Haunted Paradise," 15.

127. Executive Order from W. W. Gilmer, 1920, box 2, folder 20, Governor Edward John Dorn Papers, MARC, University of Guam.

128. Michael Lujan Bevacqua, "The Uprising at Atåte," in Torres, *Massacre at Atåte*, 127.

129. Christine DeLisle, "Navy Wives/Native Lives: The Cultural and Historical Relations between American Naval Wives and Chamorro Women in Guam, 1898–1945," (Ph.D. diss., University of Michigan, 2008), 163–169; Anita M. Elvidge, "The Guam Flag and Seal," MSS 650, Anita M. Elvidge papers, MARC, University of Guam.

130. Robert Underwood, "Red, Whitewash and Blue: Painting Over the Chamorro Experience," *Pacific Daily News*, July 17, 1977, 8. For more on World War II commemoration on Guam, see Camacho, *Cultures of Commemoration*.

131. Michael Lujan Bevacqua, "The Exceptional Life and Death of a Chamorro Soldier: Tracing the Militarization of Desire in Guam, ~~USA~~," in *Militarized Currents*, 48.

132. Michael Peter Perez, "The Dialectic of Indigenous Identity in the Wake of Colonialism: The Case of Chamorros of Guam," (Ph.D. diss., University of California Riverside, 1997), x–xi.

133. Rogers M. Smith, *Civic Ideals: Conflicting Visions of Citizenship in U.S. History* (New Haven, CT: Yale University Press, 1997), 15.

134. DeLisle, "'Guamanian-Chamorro by Birth but American Patriotic by Choice,'" 63.

135. Bevacqua, "The Uprising at Atåte," in Torres, *Massacre at Atåte*, 111.

136. Blaz interviewed by Brown on January 10, 1969.

137. "Old Glory Sways Proudly Once Again," in *Liberation: Guam Remembers; A Golden Salute for the 50th Anniversary of the Liberation of Guam* (Hagåtña, Guam: Golden Salute Committee, 1994), 80.

138. Dorothy E. Richard, *United States Naval Administration of the Trust Territory of the Pacific Islands, Volume I: The Wartime Military Government Period, 1942–1945* (Washington: Office of the Chief of Naval Operations, 1957), 123.

139. Richard, *United States Naval Administration of the Trust Territory of the Pacific Islands, Volume I*, 334, 342, 126, 627; Dorothy E. Richard, *United States Naval Administration of the Trust Territory of the Pacific Islands, Volume II: The Postwar Military Government Era, 1945–1947* (Washington: Office of the Chief of Naval Operations, 1957), 8, 21, 10, 13, 17, 19; Lt. Col. Robert D. Heinl Jr. and Lt. Col. John A. Crown, *The Marshalls: Increasing the Tempo* (Historical Branch, US Marine Corps, 1954), 135, 150–51, 154, 157–58.

140. Report of Reconnaissance of Wotho, Ujae and Lae Atolls, Chief of Civil Affairs Section, March 15, 1944, quoted in Heinl Jr. and Crown, *The Marshalls*, 153–54. On the religious aspect of these ceremonies, see Carleigh Beriont, "In Translation: Religious Freedom, Democracy, and US Empire from the Perspective of the Postwar Pacific Islands," *American Religion, Inside Out* (Feb 2021), https://www.american-religion.org/inside-out/beriont.

141. Richard, *United States Naval Administration of the Trust Territory of the Pacific Islands, Volume I*, 332.

142. Richard, *United States Naval Administration of the Trust Territory of the Pacific Islands, Volume I*, 332–34, 654, 670.

143. Dorothy E. Richard, *United States Naval Administration of the Trust Territory of the Pacific Islands, Volume III: The Trusteeship Period, 1947–1951* (Washington: Office of the Chief of Naval Operations, 1957), 1.

144. Richard, *United States Naval Administration of the Trust Territory of the Pacific Islands, Volume I*, 8, 46.

145. "Fais Islanders try out a new custom: saluting the American flag," January 1945, US Navy photo, University of Hawai'i at Manoa Library Digital Image Collections, https://digital.library .manoa.hawaii.edu/items/show/6711.

146. Weekly report no. 10, "Status of By Passed Islands in the Marshalls-Gilberts Area," week ending November 26, 1945, quoted in Richard, *United States Naval Administration of the Trust Territory of the Pacific Islands, Volume II*, 54.

147. Crowl, *Campaign in the Marianas*, 371.

148. Tony Palomo, "Island in Agony: The War in Guam," in *Remembering the Pacific War*, ed. Geoffrey White (Honolulu: Center for Pacific Islands Studies, 1991), 141.

149. *U.S. Navy Report on Guam, 1899–1950* (Washington: Department of the Navy, 1950), 8.

150. "Forgotten Guam," *New York Times*, February 20, 1946.

151. Lamont Lindstrom and Geoffrey M. White, *Island Encounters: Black and White Memories of the Pacific War* (Washington: Smithsonian Institution Press, 1990), 61.

152. "Forgotten Guam."

153. Richard, *United States Naval Administration of the Trust Territory of the Pacific Islands, Volume I*, 331.

154. Carleigh Beriont, "'For the Good of Mankind': Atomic Exceptionalism, Religion, and United States Empire in the Postwar Pacific," in *A Companion to American Religious History*, ed. Benjamin E. Park (Hoboken, NJ: Wiley, 2021), 287.

155. Jack Niedenthal, "A History of the People of Bikini Following Nuclear Weapons Testing in the Marshall Islands: With Recollections and Views of Elders of Bikini Atoll," *Health Physics* 73, no. 1 (July 1997): 29–31.

156. DeLisle, "'Guamanian-Chamorro by Birth but American Patriotic by Choice,'" 74.

157. Camacho, *Cultures of Commemoration*, 25–27.

158. There are counter narratives of Guam CHamorus who collaborated with the Japanese. See Diaz, "Deliberating 'Liberation Day,'" 159.

159. Draft of statement to be made by Secretary of the Interior Oscar L. Chapman at Guam hearings, May 20, 1947, box 512, folder 9-3-1, Guam Organic Act–General–Part 1, Central Files–Guam, RG 126, NARA, College Park, MD.

160. Ripley H. Allen, editor *Honolulu Star-Bulletin*, to James P. Davis, director Division of Territories and Island Possessions, March 23, 1949, box 512, folder 9-3-1, Guam Organic Act part 2, Central Files Guam, RG 126, NARA, College Park, MD; "Guam's 'Boston Tea-Party,'" *Honolulu Star-Bulletin*, March 29, 1949; "Guam Upper House Joins 'Strike' against Governor," *Washington Star*, March 13, 1949; "Navy Action Protested by Guam Assembly," *Washington Post*, March 5, 1949; "Revolt Spreads in Guam Legislature against Navy Rule: Solons Will Shun Special Session Today: Upper House of Isle Congress Backs Fight to Force Organic Act Approval by U.S." [newspaper title cut off], March 10, 1949.

161. Harold Ickes, "Man to Man," *Honolulu Star-Bulletin*, September 29, 1947, p. 8.

Chapter 5

1. Francis B. Sayre, quoted in *Blue Book of the First Year of the Republic* (Manila: Bureau of Printing, July 4, 1947), 21.

2. Ken'ichi Goto, *Tensions of Empire: Japan and Southeast Asia in the Colonial and Post Colonial World* (Athens: Ohio University Press, 2003); Christopher Bayly and Tim Harper, *Forgotten Armies: The Fall of British Asia, 1941–1945* (Cambridge, MA: Harvard University Press, 2006); Shohei Sato, "Britain's Decision to Withdraw from the Persian Gulf, 1964–68: A Pattern and a Puzzle," *Journal of Imperial and Commonwealth History* 37, no. 1 (2009): 99–117; Anthony Clayton, *The Wars of French Decolonization* (Harlow, UK: Longman, 1994); Frederick Cooper, *Citizenship between Empire and Nation: Remaking France and French Africa, 1945–1960* (Princeton, NJ: Princeton University Press, 2014); Simeon Man, *Soldiering through Empire: Race and the Making of the Decolonizing Pacific* (Berkeley: University of California Press, 2018), 5–10.

3. Gretchen Heefner, "A Symbol of the New Frontier," *Pacific Historical Review* 74, no. 4 (November 2005): 550–51.

4. On the myriad uses of the term "decolonization," see Eve Tuck and K. Wayne Yang, "Decolonization Is Not a Metaphor," *Decolonization: Indigeneity, Education & Society* 1, no. 1 (2012): 1–40.

5. David Cannadine, *Ornamentalism: How the British Saw Their Empire* (Oxford, UK: Oxford University Press, 2001), 161.

6. David Cannadine, "Introduction: Independence Day Ceremonials in Historical Perspective," *Round Table* 97, no. 398 (October 2008): 651. An edited collection with Cannadine and other British imperial historians centers the importance of independence day ceremonies. Robert Holland, Susan Williams, and Terry Barringer, eds., *The Iconography of Independence: 'Freedoms at Midnight'* (New York: Routledge, 2010).

7. Kwame Nkrumah, "Why the Queen's Head Is Coming Off Our Coins," *Daily Sketch*, June 20, 1957, 12; quoted in Harcourt Fuller, *Building the Ghanaian Nation-State: Kwame Nkrumah's Symbolic Nationalism* (New York: Palgrave Macmillan, 2014), 77.

8. Fuller, *Building the Ghanaian Nation-State*, 2.

9. For examples of this genre, see William Appleman Williams, *The Tragedy of American Diplomacy* (New York: W. W. Norton, 1959); William Appleman Williams, *Empire as a Way of Life: An Essay on the Causes and Character of America's Present Predicament along with a Few Thoughts about an Alternative* (Oxford, UK: Oxford University Press, 1980); Niall Ferguson, *Colossus: The Price of America's Empire* (New York: Penguin Press, 2004); Richard H. Immerman, *Empire for Liberty: A History of American Imperialism from Benjamin Franklin to Paul Wolfowitz* (Princeton, NJ: Princeton University Press, 2010); Charles S. Maier, *Among Empires: American Ascendancy and Its Predecessors* (Cambridge, MA: Harvard University Press, 2006); Noam Chomsky, *Hegemony or Survival: America's Quest for Global Dominance* (New York: Henry Holt, 2007); Noam Chomsky, *Making the Future: Occupations, Interventions, Empire, and Resistance* (New York: Penguin, 2012); Noam Chomsky, *Who Rules the World?* (New York: Metropolitan, 2016).

10. Haunani-Kay Trask, *From a Native Daughter: Colonialism and Sovereignty in Hawai'i* (Honolulu: University of Hawai'i Press, 1999), 29–30, 77, 235.

11. Daniel Immerwahr, "Philippine Independence in U.S. History: A Car, Not a Train," *Pacific Historical Review* 91, no. 2 (2022): 220–48.

12. Secretary of state to the ambassador in the United Kingdom (Winant), November 20, 1942, 9 p.m., in *Foreign Relations of the United States*, vol. 1, ed. G. Bernard Noble and E. R. Perkins (Washington: Government Printing Office, 1960), document 632.

13. Memorandum by the assistant secretary of state (Long), October 2, 1943, in *Foreign Relations of The United States*, vol. 3, ed. William M. Franklin and E. R. Perkins (Washington: Government Printing Office, 1963), document 979.

14. Secretary of state to the president, September 8, 1944, in *Foreign Relations of The United States*, ed. Richardson Dougall, Arthur G. Kogan, Richard S. Patterson, and Irving L. Thompson (Washington: Government Printing Office, 1972), document 165.

15. US high commissioner in the Philippines (McNutt) to Mr. Richard R. Ely, of the Office of the US High Commissioner, January 18, 1946, in *Foreign Relations of The United States*, ed. John G. Reid and Herbert A. Fine (Washington: Government Printing Office, 1971), document 651.

16. "Manila Is Making Plans for July 4: No Protocol Exists for Type of Ceremonies Involved in Launching Republic," *New York Times*, June 23, 1946, p. 22.

17. Pura Villanueva Kalaw, *A Brief History of the Filipino Flag* (Manila: Bureau of Printing, 1947), 19–20.

18. Kalaw, *Brief History*, 17.

19. Kalaw, *Brief History*, 18–19.

20. Kalaw, *Brief History*, 19.

21. Kalaw, *Brief History*, 19.

22. Kalaw, *Brief History*, 20.

23. History card no. 418A, PSPI 46: Filipina with Philippine Flag, series 1946, Bureau of Engraving and Printing Historical Resource Center, Washington.

24. Souvenir official program: *Proclamation and Inauguration of the Republic of the Philippines, Luneta, City of Manila, July 4, 1946* (Manila: Bureau of Printing, 1946), box 2, folder: Inauguration of the Philippine Republic, July 4, 1946, record group 59, State Department (hereafter RG 59), US National Archives and Records Administration (hereafter NARA), College Park, MD.

25. "Veterans of the Philippine Revolution, headed by Gen. Emilio Aguinaldo, president of the first Philippine Republic, joined the parade garbed in their own rayadillo uniform." Album: Republic Day, photo archive, Presidential Museum and Library of the Philippines, https://www.flickr.com/photos/govph/19410358446/in/album-72157654628088620/.

26. "Manila Is Making Plans for July 4: No Protocol Exists for Type of Ceremonies Involved in Launching Republic," *New York Times*, June 23, 1946, p. 22.

27. Souvenir official program: *Proclamation and Inauguration of the Republic of the Philippines*, box 2, folder: Inauguration of the Philippine Republic, July 4, 1946, RG 59, NARA, College Park, MD.

28. *Blue Book of the First Year of the Republic*, 5.

29. Manuel A. Roxas, "Inaugural Address of the President," in *Blue Book of the First Year of the Republic*, 218.

30. Roxas, "Inaugural Address," 218.

31. "Senator Millard Tydings Address July 4, 1946," in *Blue Book of the First Year of the Republic*, 230–31.

32. James Morgan, "New Glory for Old Glory: America's Unhappy Adventure in Imperialism to Have a Happy Ending This Fourth, When the Declaration of Independence Will Vindicate Itself Anew on Shore of Manila Bay," *Daily Boston Globe*, June 30, 1946, p. 2A.

33. Margaret Parton "City in a Turmoil," *New York Herald Tribune*, July 4, 1946, p. 4.

34. Souvenir Official Program: *Proclamation and Inauguration of the Republic of the Philippines*.

35. US State Department, "Confidential Release for Publication at 7:05 p.m., E.S.T., Wednesday July 3, 1946," 7, July 3, 1946, box 2, folder: Inauguration of the Philippine Republic, July 4, 1946, RG 59, NARA, College Park, MD.

36. The United States did continue to aid the Philippines until 1951 through the Philippine War Damage Commission, created by the Philippine Rehabilitation Act of 1946.

37. "Republic Is Born amid Rejoicing by Filipinos," *Chicago Daily Tribune*, July 4, 1946, p. 1.

38. US State Department, "Confidential Release for Publication at 7:05 p.m., E.S.T., Wednesday July 3, 1946," July 3, 1946, box 2, folder: Inauguration of the Philippine Republic, July 4, 1946, RG 59, NARA, College Park, MD.

39. Roxas, "Inaugural Address," *Blue Book of the First Year of the Republic*, 219.

40. "US Proclaims Independence for Philippines: Truman Acts 12 Hours after Event in Islands Owing to Time Difference," *New York Herald Tribune*, July 5, 1946, p. 4; "Kalayan! Is Cry as Philippines Receive Liberty: McNutt and MacArthur Attend Ceremony," *Chicago Daily Tribune*, July 5, 1946, p. 3.

41. "500 Filipinos Here Hail Independence: Messages from Roxas, Dewey, and O'Dwyer Read at Colorful Celebration," *New York Times*, July 4, 1946, p. 6; "Holiday Exodus from City Begins," *New York Times*, July 3, 1946, p. 23.

42. "City's Filipinos Raise Flag of New Republic," *Chicago Daily Tribune*, July 5, 1946, p. 3.

43. "Los Angeles Filipinos Hail Birth of Republic," *Los Angeles Times*, July 5, 1946, p. 5.

44. "Terms Philippines' Independence a 'Hoax,'" *Philadelphia Tribune*, July 6, 1946, p. 1; Margaret Parton "City in a Turmoil," *New York Herald Tribune*, July 4, 1946, p. 4.

45. "Chiang Praises U.S. for Freeing of Philippines," *Chicago Daily Tribune*, July 5, 1946, p. 3.

46. *Hindustan Times* quoted in "Indians Greet Filipinos," *New York Herald Tribune*, July 5, 1946, p. 4.

47. *Blue Book of the First Year of the Republic*, 14.

48. Celestino Iriarte, "Urges Removal of Tugwell: President of Union Republican Party Issues Statement," *World Journal*, July 1942, box 1128, folder 9-8-108, Holidays, etc.–Fourth of July, Central Files–Puerto Rico, record group 126, Office of Territories (hereafter RG 126), NARA, College Park, MD; Shannon Collins, "Puerto Ricans Represented Throughout U.S. Military History," *Department of Defense News*, October 14, 2016.

49. Ruth M. Reynolds, *Campus in Bondage: A 1948 Microcosm of Puerto Rico in Bondage* (New York: Centro de Estudios Puertorriqueños, 1989), 76.

50. Ivonne Acosta, *La Mordaza: Puerto Rico 1948–1957* (Rio Piedras, Puerto Rico: Editorial Edil, 1989), 21.

51. Acosta, *La Mordaza*, 29.

52. Press Survey no. 14, August 15, 1947, Office of Puerto Rico, "An Appeal from Puerto Rico," (editorial comment), *Enterprise* (Beaumont, TX), March 28, 1947, box 862, folder 9-8-68, Government-Status-General Part #5, Central Files: Puerto Rico 1907–1951, RG 126, NARA, College Park, MD.

53. Andrea Friedman, *Citizenship in Cold War America: The National Security State and the Possibilities of Dissent* (Amherst: University of Massachusetts Press, 2014), 121.

54. C R. Morales, summary/translation of *El Imparcial* article, box 861, folder 9-8-68, Government–Status–General, Central Files, Puerto Rico 1907–1951, RG 126, NARA, College Park, MD.

55. Box 861, folder 9-8-68, Government–Status–General, Central Files Puerto Rico 1907–1951, RG 126, NARA, College Park, MD.

56. New York College Teachers Union, Bernard F. Riess, president, and Joseph Bressler, secretary, July 1942, box 933, folder 9-8-78, Law & Order–Nationalists–Albizu et al., Misc. Protest, Central Files Puerto Rico 1951–1971, RG 126, NARA, College Park, MD.

57. "P.R. Status Seen as Test of Trusteeship," *Washington Post*, June 5, 1945, box 350, folder PR-Legal Status-1-Independence, Central Files Puerto Rico 1951–1971, RG 126, NARA, College Park, MD.

58. Jesus T. Piñero, letter to the editor, *New York Times*, March 12, 1946, box 861, folder 9-8-68, Government–Status–General, Central Files Puerto Rico 1907–1951, RG 126, NARA, College Park, MD.

59. Jack B. Fahy, special assistant to the secretary, "Balance Sheet of Interests," April 4, 1945, box 861, folder 9-8-68, Government–Status–General, Central Files Puerto Rico 1907–1951, RG 126, NARA, College Park, MD.

60. President Harry S. Truman, message to Congress regarding Puerto Rican political status, October 16, 1945, box 861, folder 9-8-68, Government-Status-General, Central Files Puerto Rico 1907–1951, RG 126, NARA, College Park, MD.

61. Reynolds, *Campus in Bondage*, 67.

62. Reynolds, *Campus in Bondage*, 33.

63. Reynolds, *Campus in Bondage*, 41.

64. Jaime Benítez, "Circular to University Administrators, Faculty, and Students (circular no. 511), March 24, 1947; quoted in Pablo Navarro-Rivera, "The ACLU and Civil Liberties in Puerto Rico," *Journal of Pedagogy, Pluralism, and Practice* 3, no. 3 (Summer 2006): 37.

65. *Civil Liberties in American Colonies* (New York: American Civil Liberties Union, 1939), 15, 17.

66. Reynolds, *Campus in Bondage*, 42–43.

67. Jaime Benítez, press statements by the rector of the University of Puerto Rico, December 15, 1947, quoted in Navarro-Rivera, "The ACLU and Civil Liberties in Puerto Rico," 35–36; Reynolds, *Campus in Bondage*, 68–69.

68. Reynolds, *Campus in Bondage*, 312.

69. Reynolds, *Campus in Bondage*, 82.

70. Statements by Carlos A. Patterne on the December 15, 1947, flag incident quoted in Navarro-Rivera, "The ACLU and Civil Liberties in Puerto Rico," 35.

71. Reynolds, *Campus in Bondage*, 74. Emphasis in original.

72. Navarro-Rivera, "ACLU and Civil Liberties in Puerto Rico," 39.

73. Reynolds, *Campus in Bondage*, 134–35.

74. Reynolds, *Campus in Bondage*, 134.

75. Letter to Clarence Picket, Executive Secretary of the American Friends Service Committee, from E. D. Stannard and L. F. Valentín, Cruzada Universitaria, May 14, 1948 quoted in Navarro-Rivera, "ACLU and Civil Liberties in Puerto Rico," 41.

76. Reynolds, *Campus in Bondage*, 138–49.

77. Public Law 53, quoted in Elena Martínez, "¡Que Bonita Bandera! Place, Space, and Identity as Expressed with the Puerto Rican Flag," in Jack Santino, ed., *Public Performance: Studies in the Carnivalesque and Ritualesque* (Logan: Utah State University Press, 2017), 119.

78. Martínez, "¡Que Bonita Bandera!" 119.

79. Item 8a: Memorandum for the chief of insular police, June 14, 1948, from Jorge Camacho Torres, squadron commandant for internal security, caja 21, tarea 90–29, serie: Nacionalistas, fondo: Departamento de Justicia, Archivo General de Puerto Rico (hereafter AGPR), San Juan, Puerto Rico.

80. Item 9a: Boletin Informativo no. 18: Actividades Nacionalistas y Comunistas, July 27, 1948; item 22 (a,b): address by Pedro Albizu Campos April 16, 1950–Natalicio de José de Diego, 6; item 23: address by Pedro Albizu Campos at Ponce, March 21, 1950, Plaza de Luis Muñoz Rivera; item 22 (a, b): memorandum for chief of police, April 17, 1950–Natalicio de José de Diego, caja 21, tarea 90-29, serie: Nacionalistas, fondo: Departamento de Justicia, AGPR.

81. Serie: Nacionalistas, fondo: Departamento de Justicia, AGPR.

82. Item 22 (a, b): address by Pedro Albizu Campos, April 16, 1950–Natalicio de José de Diego, 6, caja 21, tarea 90–29, serie: Nacionalistas, fondo: Departamento de Justicia, AGPR.

83. Item 23: address by Pedro Albizu Campos at Ponce, March 21, 1950, Plaza de Luis Muñoz Rivera, caja 21, tarea 90–29, serie: Nacionalistas, fondo: Departamento de Justicia, AGPR.

84. Text of address by Luis Muñoz Marín, president of the Senate of Puerto Rico, Sunday, July 4, 1948 (translated from "Muñoz Suggests Special Status for Puerto Rico," El Mundo July 5, 1948), box 862, folder 9-8-68 Government-Status-General Part #5, Central Files–Puerto Rico 1907–1951, RG 126, NARA, College Park, MD.

85. "Under Secretary Chapman Hails Puerto Rican Elected Governor Bill," press release, Department of the Interior, August 5, 1947, box 861, no folder, Central Files Puerto Rico 1907–1951, RG 126, NARA, College Park, MD.

86. J. Stanton Robbins, director of Office of Tourism in San Juan, to Postmaster George de Pass, August 23, 1948, box 953, folder 9-8-84, Puerto Rico–Publicity–Commemorative Stamps– 1935–1950, Central Files Puerto Rico 1951–1971, RG 126, NARA, College Park, MD.

87. Jesús T. Piñero, governor of Puerto Rico, to Irwin W. Silverman, acting director of the Division of Territories and Island Possessions (hereafter DTIP), September 8, 1948, box 953, folder 9-8-84, Puerto Rico–Publicity–Commemorative Stamps–1935–1950, Central Files Puerto Rico 1951–1971, RG 126, NARA, College Park, MD.

88. National Philatelic Museum: US Possessions Stamp Exhibition, stamp issue featuring first gubernatorial election in Puerto Rico. National Philatelic Museum, vol. 1, no. 2, box 953, folder 9-8-84, Puerto Rico-Publicity-Commemorative Stamps 1935–1950, Central Files Puerto Rico 1951–1971, RG 126, NARA, College Park, MD. On Delano's work with the Division of Cinema and Graphics, see Lloréns, Imaging the Great Puerto Rican Family, 93–95.

89. National Philatelic Museum: US Possessions Stamp Exhibition, stamp issue featuring first gubernatorial election in Puerto Rico.

90. Press Release, March 14, 1949, box 953, folder 9-8-84, Puerto Rico–Publicity– Commemorative Stamps–1935–1950, Central Files Puerto Rico 1951–1971, RG 126, NARA, College Park, MD. For more on the national symbolism of the jíbaro, see Lillian Guerra, Popular Expression and National Identity in Puerto Rico: The Struggle for Self, Community, and Nation (Gainesville: University Press of Florida, 1998).

91. National Philatelic Museum: US Possessions Stamp Exhibition, stamp issue featuring first gubernatorial election in Puerto Rico.

92. J. A. Krug to Sol Glass, August 15, 1949, box 953, folder 9-8-84, Puerto Rico–Publicity– Commemorative Stamps–1935–1950, Central Files Puerto Rico 1951–1971, RG 126, NARA, College Park, MD.

93. Fourth of July speech delivered by Senator Victor Gutierrez Franqui, floor leader of the Senate of Puerto Rico, July 4, 1949, box 1128, folder 9-8-108 Holidays, etc.–Fourth of July, Central Files Puerto Rico, RG 126, NARA, College Park, MD.

94. Jose Arvelo, veteran de la G.M. #1, to President Harry Truman, August 16, 1950, box 864, folder 9-8-68, Government–Status–Miscellaneous Inquiries, Central Files–Puerto Rico 1907–1951, RG 126, NARA, College Park, MD.

95. Luisa Santos de Muniz, Arecibo, Puerto Rico to President Truman, December 2, 1950, box 864, folder 9-8-68, Government–Status–Miscellaneous Inquiries, Central Files–Puerto Rico 1907–1951, RG 126, NARA, College Park, MD.

96. Letter of transmittal accompanying draft of a bill establishing the Commonwealth of Puerto Rico, box 861, folder 9-8-68, Government–Status–General, Central Files Puerto Rico 1907–1951, RG 126, NARA, College Park, MD.

97. Statement of Pedro Capo-Rodriguez before the House Committee on Insular Affairs on Senate Bill no. 1407, to amend the Organic Act of Puerto Rico, 78th Cong. 2nd Sess., Washington, March 29, 1944, box 859, folder 9-8-68, Government- Organic Act–Amendments–Advisory Committee to the President–General part 5, Central Files Puerto Rico 1907–1951, RG 126, NARA, College Park, MD.

98. "An Act to Provide for the Organization of a Constitutional Government by the People of Puerto Rico," Public Law 81–600, *U.S. Statutes at Large* 64 (1950): 319–20.

99. Acosta, *La Mordaza*, 115.

100. Olga Jiménez de Wagenheim, *Nationalist Heroines: Puerto Rican Women History Forgot, 1930s–1950s* (Princeton, NJ: Markus Wiener, 2016), 27–28; Acosta, *La Mordaza*, 114.

101. Miñi Seijo Bruno, *La Insurreción Nacionalista en Puerto Rico 1950* (Rio Piedras: Universidad de Puerto Rico, 1989), 83–87.

102. Jiménez de Wagenheim, *Nationalist Heroines*, 59.

103. Seijo Bruno, *La Insurreción Nacionalista en Puerto Rico 1950*, 91–109.

104. Seijo Bruno, *La Insurreción Nacionalista en Puerto Rico 1950*, 113–21.

105. Blanca Canales, quoted in Jiménez de Wagenheim, *Nationalist Heroines*, 61.

106. Jiménez de Wagenheim, *Nationalist Heroines*, 62.

107. "Insurrection," *Time*, November 13, 1950.

108. Friedman, *Citizenship in Cold War America*, 137; César J. Ayala and Rafael Bernabe, *Puerto Rico in the American Century: A History Since 1898* (Chapel Hill: University of North Carolina Press, 2007), 167.

109. "Muñoz Reports to Secretary Chapman," October 31, 1950, quoted in Acosta, *La Mordaza*, 116.

110. Department of State Outgoing Telegram, Nov 2, 1950, quoted in Acosta, *La Mordaza*, 116.

111. Acosta, *La Mordaza*, 117.

112. Friedman, *Citizenship in Cold War America*, 137.

113. Stephen Hunter and John Bainbridge, Jr., *American Gunfight: The Plot to Kill Harry Truman—and the Shoot-Out That Stopped It* (New York: Simon & Schuster, 2005), 242; Friedman, *Citizenship in Cold War America*, 137; Immerwahr, *How to Hide an Empire*, 254.

114. Oscar Callazo, quoted in Friedman, *Citizenship in Cold War America*, 138.

115. "President Says He's Sick over Death of Guard," *Times-Herald*, November 3, 1950, box 934, folder 9-8-79, Law & Order–Nationalist Party–Press Clippings, Central Files Puerto Rico 1907–1951, RG 126, NARA, College Park, MD.

116. "Trouble in Puerto Rico," *Washington Post*, November 1 1950; "1 Killed, 5 Shot in San Juan as Revolt Flares," *Washington Post*, November 1, 1950, box 934, folder 9-8-79 Law & Order–Nationalist Party–Press Clippings, Central Files Puerto Rico 1907–1951, RG 126, NARA, College Park, MD.

117. "U.S., World Leaders Shocked at Attempt on President's Life," *Washington Evening Star*, November 2, 1950, p. A4.

118. "Puerto Rico Police Round up 400 Nationalists, Communists," *Washington Post*, November 3, 1950, box 934, folder 9-8-79 Law & Order–Nationalist Party–Press Clippings, Central Files Puerto Rico 1907–1951, RG 126, NARA, College Park, MD.

119. Acosta, *La Mordaza*, 118.

120. Acosta, *La Mordaza*, 119.

121. Ayala and Bernabe, *Puerto Rico in the American Century*, 168.

122. "The Acting Secretary of the Interior (Vernon D. Northrop) to the Secretary of State, October 9, 1952," in *Foreign Relations of the United States*, 1952–1954, United Nations Affairs, Vol. 3, ed. Ralph Goodwin (Washington: Government Printing Office, 1979), document 902.

123. July 23, 1952 Draft Paper in Office of Territories from Mr. Cargo State Department, box 351, folder PR–Legal Status 9 (Part 1) Commonwealth of Puerto Rico, Central Files Puerto Rico 1951–1971, RG 126, NARA, College Park, MD.

124. Nancy Morris, *Puerto Rico: Culture, Politics, and Identity* (Westport, CT: Praeger, 1995), 50.

125. "Puerto Rico in Three-Day Fete," *New York Times*, July 24, 1952, p. 2.

126. Ayala and Bernabe, *Puerto Rico in the American Century*, 168.

127. "Puerto Rico Hoists Flag of Autonomy: Fiestas Mark Commonwealth's Birth of 54th Anniversary of American Landing," *New York Times*, July 26, 1952, p. 11.

128. "Discurso del Honorable Gobernador Luis Muñoz Marín," in *25 de Julio: Día del Estado Libre Asociado de Puerto Rico* (San Juan: Departamento de Instrucción Pública, 1959), 4.

129. "Discurso del Honorable Gobernador Luis Muñoz Marín," 4–6.

130. "Puerto Rico Hoists Flag of Autonomy: Fiestas Mark Commonwealth's Birth of 54th Anniversary of American Landing," *New York Times*, July 26, 1952, p. 11; "For Self-Rule: Puerto Rico Raises Flag, Celebrates," *Washington Post*, July 26, 1952, p. 7.

131. "Puerto Rico Hoists Flag of Autonomy."

132. Martínez, "¡Que Bonita Bandera!" 121.

133. "At Last Puerto Rico Has Ceased to Be a People without a Flag," *El Mundo*, quoted in Morris, *Puerto Rico*, 51.

134. Acosta, *La Mordaza*, 160.

135. *El Imparcial*, July 26, 1952, p. S-2, quoted in Acosta, *La Mordaza*, 160–61.

136. *El Imparcial*, July 28, 1952, p. 2, quoted in Acosta, *La Mordaza*, 161.

137. Item 6a: Juan Gonzalez Santa, internal security detective, Humacao zone, to the superintendent of internal security of San Juan, October 27, 1953, caja 21, tarea 90–29, serie: Nacionalistas, fondo: Departamento de Justicia, AGPR; item 9: March 21, 1953–Anniversary of Massacre de Ponce, caja 22, tarea 90–29, serie: Nacionalistas, fondo: Departamento de Justicia, AGPR; item 11: April 16, 1953–José de Diego, caja 22, tarea 90–29, serie: Nacionalistas, fondo: Departamento de Justicia, AGPR.

138. Miguel A. Franco Soto to Senator Joseph C O'Mahoney, chairman committee on insular affairs, September 7, 1952, box 351, folder PR–legal status 9 (part 1) Commonwealth of Puerto Rico, Central Files Puerto Rico 1951–1971, RG 126, NARA, College Park, MD.

139. Ignacio Guasp to Secretary of the Interior Fred A. Seaton, August 25, 1958, box 351, folder PR–Legal Status 9 (part 1), Commonwealth of Puerto Rico, Central Files Puerto Rico 1951–1971, RG 126, NARA, College Park, MD.

140. Luis Muñoz Marín, "A Brief Personal Statement on the Political Status Question," November 1949, given to Willard Thorp to give to DTIP, box 862, folder 9-8-68, Government–Status–General, part 5, Central Files, Puerto Rico 1907–1951, RG 126, NARA, College Park, MD.

141. Puerto Rican Independence Party: Puerto Rican Mission on Behalf of the Independence of Puerto Rico Submitted to the House of Representatives of the United States, Washington, box 350, folder PR–Legal Status-1–Independence, Central Files Puerto Rico 1951–1971, RG 126, NARA, College Park, MD.

142. "Puerto Rico Becomes a New U.S. State," *South China Morning Post* (Hong Kong), July 28, 1952, p, 6; Hon. Charles E. Bennett, "Puerto Rico Proves American Opposition to Colonialism," July 30, 1953, 83rd Cong., 1st sess., *Congressional Record* 99, pt. 12: A 4852.

143. Dan H. Wheeler, acting director of Office of Territories, to Charles B. Murray, assistant attorney general, Criminal Division, Department of Justice, August 15, 1952, box 351, folder PR–Legal Status 9 (part 1), Commonwealth of Puerto Rico, Central Files Puerto Rico 1951–1971, RG 126, NARA, College Park, MD.

144. James P. Davis, director of Office of Territories, to Governor Muñoz Marín, September 25, 1952, box 351, folder PR–Legal Status 9 (part 1), Commonwealth of Puerto Rico, Central Files Puerto Rico 1951–1971, RG 126, NARA, College Park, MD.

145. Luis Muñoz Marín to secretary of the interior, January 17, 1953, box 351, folder PR–Legal Status 9 (part 1), Commonwealth of Puerto Rico, Central Files Puerto Rico 1951–1971, RG 126, NARA, College Park, MD.

146. Kathleen McLaughlin, "India Disputes U.S. over Puerto Rico: Argues in U.N. That Territory Has Not Attained Status of Self-Government," *New York Times*, September 1, 1953, p. 7.

147. "The Secretary of State to the Embassy in Mexico," November 20, 1953, *Foreign Relations of the United States*, 1952–1954, United Nations Affairs, Volume 3, ed. Ralph Goodwin (Washington: Government Printing Office, 1979), document 924.

148. "The United States Representative at the United Nations (Lodge) to the Department of State," November 22, 1953, *Foreign Relations of the United States*, 1952–1954, United Nations Affairs, Volume 3, ed. Ralph Goodwin (Washington: Government Printing Office, 1979), document 925.

149. "The Secretary of State to the United States Representative at the United Nations (Lodge)," November 24, 1953, *Foreign Relations of the United States*, 1952–1954, United Nations Affairs, Volume 3, ed. Ralph Goodwin (Washington: Government Printing Office, 1979), document 927.

150. "The United States Representative at the United Nations (Lodge) to the Department of State," November 25, 1953, *Foreign Relations of the United States*, 1952–1954, United Nations Affairs, Volume 3, ed. Ralph Goodwin (Washington: Government Printing Office, 1979), document 929.

151. Lodge to Eisenhower, November 28, 1953, quoted in Friedman, *Citizenship in Cold War America*, 133.

152. McLaughlin, "India Disputes U.S. over Puerto Rico," *New York Times*, September 1, 1953, p. 7.

153. "Five Congressmen Shot in House by 3 Puerto Rican Nationalists: Bullets Spray from Gallery," *New York Times*, March 2, 1954, p. 1; Jiménez de Wagenheim, *Nationalist Heroines*, 259.

154. "Guns Frighten Two Witnesses: Lolita Makes Sure Puerto Rican Flag Isn't Misused," *Spokesman-Review* (Spokane), June 8, 1954, p. 2; "Hand-Made Flag Dips to Floor: Fiery Puerto Rican Protests," *Commercial Appeal* (Memphis), June 8, 1954, p. 1.

155. "Five Congressmen Shot in House by 3 Puerto Rican Nationalists."

156. Cancel Miranda, quoted in Friedman, *Citizenship in Cold War America*, 138.

157. For example: "Five Congressmen Shot in House by 3 Puerto Rican Nationalists"; "5 Congressmen Shot Down: Puerto Ricans Fire from House Gallery," *Chicago Daily Tribune*, March 2, 1954, p. 1; "Fanatics' Guns, Flag Shown after Sensational Shooting in House," *Wisconsin State Journal* (Madison), March 2, 1954, p. 2; "Terrorists Shoot Five Congressmen," *Philadelphia Inquirer*, March 2, 1954, p. 2; "Puerto Rican Flag Displayed," *Southern Illinoisan* (Carbondale), March 3, 1954, p. 16; "Four Puerto Rican Extremists Charged in Shooting of Solons," *Lubbock Morning Avalanche* (TX), March 2, 1954, p. 10; "5 Congressmen Wounded on House Floor by Fanatic Puerto Ricans," *Knoxville News-Sentinel*, March 2, 1954, p. 12; C. P. Trussell, "It Was Dull Day In House, until . . . ," *Dayton Daily News*, March 2, 1954, p. 14; *La Crosse Tribune* (WI), March 2, 1954, p. 2; "Police Say Three Admit Shooting 5 Congressmen," *San Angelo Standard-Times* (TX), March 2, 1954, p. 1; *Green Bay Press-Gazette* (WI), March 2, 1954, p. 26.

158. Duany, *Puerto Rican Nation on the Move*, 131.

159. Duany, *Puerto Rican Nation on the Move*, 123–24.

160. "Ridicules the Idea of Statehood for Hawaii: How the Eastern Press Looks upon This Insular Territory," *Honolulu Republican*, August 8, 1901; Roger Bell, *Last among Equals: Hawaiian Statehood and American Politics* (Honolulu: University of Hawai'i Press, 1984), 4.

161. Sarah Miller-Davenport, *Gateway State: Hawai'i and the Cultural Transformation of American Empire* (Princeton, NJ: Princeton University Press, 2019); Dean Itsuji Saranillio, *Unsustainable Empire: Alternative Histories of Hawai'i Statehood*, (Durham, NC: Duke University Press, 2018); Heefner, "A Symbol of the New Frontier," 545–74.

162. For more on the idea of "future wishing," see Saranillio, *Unsustainable Empire*, 11, 31–66.

163. Photo 126-HG-17-3, box 2, folder 126–HG–23: Statehood, Prints: Photographs of Hawaii, 1936–1957, Still Pictures, RG 126, NARA, College Park, MD.

164. Box 70, folder 9-0-2, Miscellaneous, Seals & Flags, General Central Files, 1927–1951, RG 126, NARA, College Park, MD.

165. Arthur Walter of Peckskill, New York, to President Truman, December 31, 1945, box 70, folder 9-0-2, Miscellaneous, Seals & Flags, General Central Files, 1927–1951, RG 126, NARA, College Park, MD.

166. Roman Smith of Youngstown, Ohio, to the president, January 28, 1946, box 70, folder 9-0-2, Miscellaneous, Seals & Flags, General Central Files, 1927–1951, RG 126, NARA, College Park, MD.

167. Louis R. Kelley of Philadelphia to Secretary Ickes, January 16, 1946, box 70, folder 9-0-2, Miscellaneous, Seals & Flags, General Central Files, 1927–1951, RG 126, NARA, College Park, MD.

168. Marjorie S. Lewis to Truman, February 4, 1948, box 70, folder 9-0-2, Miscellaneous, Seals & Flags, General Central Files, 1927–1951, RG 126, NARA, College Park, MD.

169. Letter from Ben Lobsinger, April 4, 1948; Melvin V. Olson (schoolboy, Wisconsin) to Truman, February 19, 1946, box 70, folder 9-0-2, Miscellaneous, Seals & Flags, General Central Files, 1927–1951, RG 126, NARA, College Park, MD.

170. Tomas Chavez Jr. of San Antonio, Texas, to Harry Truman, January 29, 1948, box 70, folder 9-0-2, Miscellaneous, Seals & Flags, General Central Files, 1927–1951, RG 126, NARA, College Park, MD.

171. Caroline Sarsen to President Truman, January 5, 1946, box 70, folder 9-0-2, Miscellaneous, Seals & Flags, General Central Files, 1927–1951, RG 126, NARA, College Park, MD.

172. Students at Beaver Creek School in Montana to President Truman, February 4, 1946, box 70, folder 9-0-2, Miscellaneous, Seals & Flags, General Central Files, 1927–1951, RG 126, NARA, College Park, MD.

173. Jack B. Fahy, acting director DTIP, to William D. Hassett, secretary to the president, March 4, 1946, box 70, folder 9-0-2, Miscellaneous, Seals & Flags, General Central Files, 1927–1951, RG 126, NARA, College Park, MD.

174. Press release from White House, October 16, 1958, box 150, folder: Legal Status 5, Seals, Flags, Coats of Arms Part 2, Central Files Alaska 1951–1971, RG 126, NARA, College Park, MD.

175. Marc Leepson, *Flag: An American Biography* (New York: Macmillan, 2007), 224–26.

176. Press release from Post Office Department, July 25, 1959, box 1, folder: Stamp Ceremony, Series 389: Records of the Hawaii Statehood Celebration Commission, Hawai'i State Archives, Honolulu.

177. Governor William F. Quinn to L. Rohe Walter, special assistant to postmaster general, July 30, 1959, box 1, folder: Stamp Ceremony, Series 389: Records of the Hawaii Statehood Celebration Commission, Hawai'i State Archives.

178. Address by Postmaster George T. Hara, representing Postmaster General Arthur E. Summerfield, at 7¢ Airmail Hawaii Commemorative Statehood Stamp Dedication Ceremony on Proclamation Day, August 21, 1959, box 1, folder: Stamp Ceremony, Series 389: Records of the Hawaii Statehood Celebration Commission, Hawai'i State Archives.

179. Jan Jabulka to Anthony Lausi, director DTIP, January 20, 1960, box 338, folder HA–legal status 5–Seals & Flags (part 2), Central Files Hawaii, RG 126, NARA, College Park, MD.

180. Jabulka to Lausi, January 20, 1960; P. Smith to Leo Pritchard, administrative director, April 16, 1960, box 1, folder: Flag Raising, July 4, 1960, series 389: Records of the Hawaii Statehood Celebration Commission, Hawai'i State Archives.

181. Press Release, Hawaii Statehood Celebration Committee, June 8, 1960, box 1, folder: Flag Raising, July 4, 1960, series 389: Records of the Hawaii Statehood Celebration Commission, Hawai'i State Archives.

182. James Cunningham, "10,000 See 50-Star Flag Wave," *Honolulu Advertiser*, July 5, 1960, p. 1.

183. Press Release from Hawaii Statehood Celebration Committee (undated), box 1, folder: Flag Raising, July 4, 1960, series 389: Records of the Hawaii Statehood Celebration Commission, Hawai'i State Archives.

184. "Wake Island First to Fly New Flag," *Honolulu Advertiser*, July 5, 1960, p. 2.

185. "Eastport Raises 50-Star Flag from Battery at 4:40," *Bangor Daily News*, July 5, 1960, p. 5.

186. "Fifty Star Flag Proudly Hailed from Maine To Hawaii," *Boston Globe*, July 4, 1960, p. 27; "50-Star Flag Marks Hawaii's Entry into Union," *Corsicana Daily Sun* (Corsicana, TX), July 4, 1960, p. 2.

187. Hiram Fong, quoted in William G. Weart, "Fifty-Star Flag Flies for the Fourth," *New York Times*, July 5, 1960.

188. James Cunningham, "10,000 See 50-Star Flag Wave," *Honolulu Advertiser*, July 5, 1960, p. 1.

189. "Complete Flag-Raising Ceremony Schedule," box 1, folder: Flag Raising, July 4, 1960, series 389: Records of the Hawaii Statehood Celebration Commission, Hawai'i State Archives.

On the essay contest, see box 1, folder: Essay Contest, series 389: Records of the Hawaii Statehood Celebration Commission, Hawai'i State Archives.

190. Notes on July 4 Planning Committee meeting, June 15, 1960, box 1, folder: Flag Raising, July 4, 1960, series 389: Records of the Hawaii Statehood Celebration Commission, Hawai'i State Archives.

191. "Armed Forces to Have Part in July 4 Flag Raising," press release, box 1, folder: Flag Raising, July 4, 1960, series 389: Records of the Hawaii Statehood Celebration Commission, Hawai'i State Archives.

192. "Text of Governor's Flag Speech," *Honolulu Advertiser*, July 5, 1960, p. A8.

193. "Text of Governor's Flag Speech," *Honolulu Advertiser*, July 5, 1960, p. A8.

194. Statehood dedication ceremony speech by William F. Quinn, governor of Hawaii, at Honolulu Stadium, November 29, 1959, box 1, folder: Admission Celebration November 1959, series 389: Records of the Hawaii Statehood Celebration Commission, Hawai'i State Archives.

195. "Remarks by Secretary of the Interior Fred A. Seaton at the Ceremony Marking the First Official Raising of the New 49-Star Flag, Fort McHenry National Monument, Baltimore, Maryland," press release, July 3, 1959, box 150, folder: Legal Status 5–Seals, Flags, Coats of Arms Part 2, Central Files Alaska 1951–1971, RG 126, NARA, College Park, MD.

196. "Independence a Goal of the Trusteeship System," minutes of the forty-fifth meeting of the US delegation, San Francisco, May 18, 1945, 9 a.m., in *Foreign Relations of The United States*: Diplomatic Papers, 1945, General: The United Nations, vol. 1, ed. Velma Hastings Cassidy, Ralph R. Goodwin, and George H. Dengler (Washington: Government Printing Office, 1967), document 239.

197. "The Deputy United States Representative at the United Nations (Wadsworth) to the Department of State," May 3, 1954, *Foreign Relations of the United States*, 1952–1954, United Nations Affairs, vol. 3, ed. Ralph R. Goodwin (Washington: Government Printing Office, 1979), document 932.

198. "Memorandum by the Director of the Office of Dependent Area Affairs (Gerig) to George C. Spiegel in the Office of the Secretary of State's Consultant for Atomic Energy Affairs," July 26, 1954, *Foreign Relations of the United States*, 1952–1954, United Nations Affairs, vol. 3, ed. Ralph R. Goodwin (Washington: Government Printing Office, 1979), document 953.

199. "Position Paper Prepared in the Department of State for the United States Delegation to the Ninth Regular Session of the General Assembly," September 7, 1954, *Foreign Relations of the United States*, 1952–1954, United Nations Affairs, vol. 3, ed. Ralph R. Goodwin (Washington: Government Printing Office, 1979), document 962.

200. "The Secretary of State to Certain Diplomatic Missions," August 25, 1954, *Foreign Relations of the United States*, 1952–1954, United Nations Affairs, vol. 3, ed. Ralph R. Goodwin (Washington: Government Printing Office, 1979), document 960.

201. Roger W. Gale, *The Americanization of Micronesia: A Study of the Consolidation of U.S. Rule in the Pacific* (Washington: University Press of America, 1979), 3.

Conclusion

1. "Text of Governor's Flag Speech," *Honolulu Advertiser*, July 5, 1960, p. A8.

2. Dean Itsuji Saranillio, *Unsustainable Empire: Alternative Histories of Hawai'i Statehood* (Durham, NC: Duke University Press, 2018), 2.

3. "Celebration of Hawaii's 50th Year of Statehood Is Muted," *Los Angeles Daily News*, August 21, 2009; Haunani-Kay Trask, "Speeches for the Centennial of the Overthrow, 'Iolani Palace 1993," in *Huihui: Navigating Art and Literature in the Pacific*, ed. Jeffrey Carroll, Brandy Nālani McDougall, and Georganne Nordstrom (Honolulu: University of Hawaiʻi Press, 2014), 99.

4. "Native Hawaiian Protestors End March, Burn 50th Star on U.S. Flag in Protest," *Honolulu Advertiser*, August 21, 2009.

5. "Celebration of Hawaii's 50th Year of Statehood Is Muted," *Los Angeles Daily News*, August 21, 2009.

6. Saranillio, *Unsustainable Empire*, 2–3.

7. An Act to Provide for a 10-Year Circulating Commemorative Coin Program to Commemorate Each of the 50 States, and for Other Purposes, Public Law 105–124, *U.S. Statutes at Large* 111 (1997): 2534–39.

8. Kenneth Bressett, "Statement of Kenneth Bressett, Member, Citizens Commemorative Coin Advisory Committee, and President, American Numismatic Association," in H.R. 3793, the 50-State Commemorative Coin Act: Hearing before the Subcommittee on Domestic and International Monetary Policy of the Committee on Banking and Financial Services, House of Representatives, One Hundred Fourth Congress, Second Session, July 31, 1996 (Washington, 1997), 5; Clifford Mishler, "Statement of Clifford Mishler, President, Krause Publications," hearing before the Subcommittee on Domestic and International Monetary Policy, 9; Floyd Flake, 50 States Commemorative Coin Program Act, 104 Cong. Rec. HH9982 (September 4, 1996).

9. Flake, 50 States Commemorative Coin Program Act, H9982.

10. H. R. 3673, 50 States Commemorative Coin Program Amendments Act of 1998, 105th Congress.

11. Kenneth McClintock-Hernandez, "Statement to the Subcommittee on Domestic and International Monetary Policy, Committee on Banking and Financial Services on H. R. 5010–District of Columbia and U.S. Territories Circulating Quarter Dollar Program Act," hearing, September 7, 2000, http://commdocs.house.gov/committees/bank/hba66816.000/hba66816_0 .HTM#10, p. 20.

12. Robert Underwood, "Statement to the Subcommittee on Domestic and International Monetary Policy," hearing, September 7, 2000, http://commdocs.house.gov/committees/bank /hba66816.000/hba66816_0.HTM#10, p. 13.

13. Underwood "Statement to the Subcommittee," 14.

14. Sec. 622 of Public Law 110–161. An Act Making Appropriations for the Department of State, Foreign Operations, and Related Programs for the Fiscal Year Ending September 30, 2008, and for Other Purposes, Public Law 110–161 (December 26, 2007): 2016.

15. Doug Mack, *The Not-Quite States of America: Dispatches from the Territories and Other Far-Flung Outposts of the USA* (New York: W. W. Norton, 2018), xvii.

16. Hawaiʻi was included in the initial state quarter program. Brandy Nālani McDougall, "'We Are Not American': Competing Rhetorical Archipelagos in Hawaiʻi," in *Archipelagic American Studies*, ed. Brian Russell Roberts and Michelle Ann Stephens (Durham, NC: Duke University Press, 2017), 270.

Bibliography

Archival Sources

American Samoa Historic Preservation Society, Pago Pago, American Samoa
American Historical Collection at Ateneo de Manila University, Quezon City, Philippines
Archivo General de Puerto Rico, San Juan
    Album de Puerto Rico
    Gertrude Baynham
    Departmento de Instrucción Pública
    Departmento de Justicia
    Fortaleza
    Guy V. Henry
    Instituto de Cultura Puertorriqueña
    Antonio Mirabal
    Tarjetas postales
Bentley Historical Library, University of Michigan, Ann Arbor
    Frederick Behner papers
    George E. Carrothers papers
    Harry Newton Cole papers
    Fred L. Crawford papers
    John C. Early papers
    Walter W. Marquardt papers
    Irene Murphy papers
    Bertha Schaffer papers
    Richard Schneidewind papers
    Dean C. Worcester papers
Bureau of Engraving and Printing Historical Resource Center, Washington
Feleti Barstow Library, Utulei, American Samoa
Filipinas Heritage Library, Ayala Museum, Makati, Philippines
Hawai'i State Archives, Honolulu
    Henry Ernest Cooper papers
    Sanford B. Dole papers
    Walter F. Frear papers

Government records
Hawaiian Archives Scrapbook
Hawaiian Statehood Celebration Commission records
Victor S. K. Houston collection
Liliuokalani collection
Lorrin Andrews Thurston papers
National Library of the Philippines, Manila
National Numismatic Collection, Smithsonian National Museum of American History,
    Washington
Manuscript Division, Library of Congress, Washington
    W. Cameron Forbes papers
Micronesian Area Research Center, University of Guam
    Edward John Dorn papers
    Anita M. Elvidge papers
    Agueda I. Johnston papers
    Bernice Bronson Lawrence papers
    Thomas E. Mayhew papers
    Thomas B. McGrath papers
    William Robert Norwood papers
    Helen L. Paul papers
    Carlton S. Skinner papers
Smithsonian National Postal Museum, Washington
    Records of the third assistant postmaster general
St. Croix Landmarks Society, St. Croix, US Virgin Islands
    Vertical file: Transfer Day, March 31, 1917
University of Hawai'i Archives
    Digital image collections
    Hawaii War Records Depository
    World War II manuscript collections
US National Archives and Records Administration, College Park, Maryland
    Bureau of Insular Affairs, record group 350
    Bureau of Public Debt, record group 53
    Office of Territories, record group 126

Government-Published Primary Sources

Annual Report of the Governor of Porto Rico for the Fiscal Year Ended June 30, 1908. Washington:
    Government Printing Office, 1909.
*Annual Reports of the Navy Department for the Year 1900: Report of the Secretary of the Navy:
    Miscellaneous Reports*. Washington: Government Printing Office, 1900.
Annual Reports of the Post-Office Department for the Fiscal Year Ended June 30, 1898. Washing-
    ton: Government Printing Office, 1898.
Annual Reports of the Post-Office Department for the Fiscal Year Ended June 30, 1899. Washing-
    ton: Government Printing Office, 1899.
Annual Reports of the Post-Office Department for the Fiscal Year Ended June 30, 1900. Washing-
    ton: Government Printing Office, 1900.

Annual Reports of the Post Office Department for the Fiscal Year Ended June 30, 1901. Washington: Government Printing Office, 1901.

Annual Reports of the Post-Office Department for the Fiscal Year Ended June 30, 1903. Washington: Government Printing Office, 1903.

Annual Reports of the War Department for the Fiscal Year Ended June 30, 1902, Volume X. Report of the Philippine Commission, Part 1. Washington: Government Printing Office, 1903.

Annual Reports of the War Department for the Fiscal Year Ended June 30, 1905, Volume XIII, Report of the Philippine Commission, Part 4. Washington: Government Printing Office, 1905.

Report of the Philippine Commission to the Secretary of War 1908, Part 2. Washington: Government Printing Office, 1909.

Blue Book of the First Year of the Republic. Manila: Bureau of Printing, July 4, 1947.

Bryan, Henry F. *American Samoa: A General Report by the Governor.* Washington: Government Printing Office, 1927.

Conditions in the Philippine Islands: Report of the Special Mission to the Philippine Islands to the Secretary of War. Washington: Government Printing Office, 1922.

Dougall, Richardson, Arthur G. Kogan, Richard S. Patterson, and Irving L. Thompson, eds. *Foreign Relations of The United States, Conference at Quebec, 1944.* Washington: Government Printing Office, 1972.

Edwards, Clarence R. *Memorandum for the Secretary of War on Currency and Exchange in the Philippines.* Washington: Government Printing Office, 1900.

First Annual Report of Charles H. Allen, Governor of Porto Rico Covering the Period from May 1, 1900 to May 1, 1901. Washington: Government Printing Office, 1901.

Fifth Annual Report of the Philippine Commission to the Secretary of War, 1904, Part 1. Washington: Government Printing Office, 1905.

Fifth Annual Report of the Philippine Commission to the Secretary of War, 1904, Part 3. Washington: Bureau of Insular Affairs, 1905.

Fourth Annual Report of the Philippine Commission 1903, Part 1. Washington: Government Printing Office, 1904.

Fourth Annual Report of the Philippine Commission 1903, Part 3. Washington: Government Printing Office, 1904.

Franklin, William M., and E. R. Perkins, eds. *Foreign Relations of The United States: Diplomatic Papers, 1943, The British Commonwealth, Eastern Europe, The Far East, Volume III.* Washington: Government Printing Office, 1963.

Ralph Goodwin, ed. *Foreign Relations of the United States, 1952–1954, United Nations Affairs, Volume III.* Washington: Government Printing Office, 1979.

Hanna, Hugh, Charles A. Conant, and Jeremiah W. Jenks. *Stability of International Exchange: Report on the Introduction of the Gold-Exchange Standard into China and Other Silver-Using Countries.* Washington: Government Printing Office, 1903.

Hawaiian Investigation Part 3. Exhibits, Memorials, Petitions, and Letters Presented to the Committee on Pacific Islands and Porto Rico, United States Senate. Washington: Government Printing Office, 1903.

Heinl, Lt. Col. Robert D., Jr., and Lt. Col. John A. Crown, *The Marshalls: Increasing the Tempo.* Historical Branch, US Marine Corps, 1954.

Ide, Henry C. *Second Annual Report of the Secretary of Finance and Justice to the Philippine Commission for the Period from September 30, 1902, to September 1, 1903.* Manila: Bureau of Public Printing, 1904.

Jenks, Jeremiah. *Report of the Commission on International Exchange on the Introduction of the Gold-Exchange Standard into China, the Philippine Islands, Panama, and Other Silver-Using Countries and on the Stability of Exchange.* Washington: Government Printing Office, 1904.

Kemmerer, Edwin Walter. *First Annual Report of the Chief of the Division of the Currency for the Philippine Islands to the Treasurer of the Philippine Islands for the Period from October 10, 1903 to September 1, 1904.* Manila: Bureau of Public Printing, 1905.

Lawler, Daniel J., and Erin R. Mahan, eds. *Foreign Relations of the United States, Diplomatic Papers, 1942, General; The British Commonwealth; The Far East, Volume I.* Washington: Government Printing Office, 2010.

Lawler, Daniel J., and Erin R. Mahan, eds. *Foreign Relations of the United States: Diplomatic Papers, 1943, The British Commonwealth, Eastern Europe, The Far East, Volume III.* Washington: Government Printing Office, 2010.

Lawler, Daniel J., and Erin R. Mahan, eds. *Foreign Relations of the United States, 1946, The Far East, Volume VIII.* Washington: Government Printing Office, 2010.

Laws, Ordinances, Decrees, and Military Orders Having the Force of Law, Effective in Porto Rico May 1, 1900, Part 4. Washington: Government Printing Office, 1909.

Minot, George, ed., *The Statutes at Large and Treaties of the United States of America, 1845 to 1851.* Boston: Little, Brown, and Company, 1862.

Noble, G. Bernard, and E. R. Perkins, eds. *Foreign Relations of the United States, Diplomatic Papers, 1942, General; The British Commonwealth; The Far East, Volume I.* Washington: Government Printing Office, 1960.

Pearson, Paul M. *Annual Report of the Governor of the Virgin Islands for the Fiscal Year Ended June 30, 1934.* Washington: Government Printing Office, 1934.

The Postal Laws and Regulations of the United States of America. Washington: Government Printing Office, 1887.

Post-Office Department Annual Reports for the Fiscal Year Ended June 30, 1905. Washington: Government Printing Office, 1905.

Reid, John G., and Herbert A. Fine, eds. *Foreign Relations of The United States, 1946, The Far East, Volume VIII.* Washington: Government Printing Office.

Report of the Commissioner of Education for Porto Rico. Washington: Government Printing Office, 1902.

The Report of the Hawaiian Commission. Washington: Government Printing Office, 1898.

Report of the Hawaiian Commission to the Committee on Foreign Relations. Washington: Government Printing Office, 1898.

Report of the Military Governor of Porto Rico on Civil Affairs, 1900, Part 13. Washington: Government Printing Office, 1902.

Report of the Philippine Commission to the Secretary of War, Vol. II: Testimony and Exhibits. Washington: Government Printing Office, 1900.

Report of the Philippine Commission to the Secretary of War, 1911. Washington: Government Printing Office, 1912.

Report of the United States Philippine Commission to the Secretary of War for the Period from December 1, 1900 to October 15, 1901, Part 1. Washington: Government Printing Office, 1901.

Reports of Henry K. Carroll Dec 30, 1898, and Oct 1899 and of U.S. Insular Commission May 1899. Washington: Government Printing Office, 1899.

Revised Laws of Hawaii: Comprising the Statues of the Territory, Consolidated, Revised and Annotated. Honolulu: Honolulu Star-Bulletin, 1915.

Richard, Dorothy E. *United States Naval Administration of the Trust Territory of the Pacific Islands, Volume I: The Wartime Military Government Period, 1942–1945.* Washington: Office of the Chief of Naval Operations, 1957.

Richard, Dorothy E. *United States Naval Administration of the Trust Territory of the Pacific Islands, Volume II: The Postwar Military Government Era, 1945–1947.* Washington: Office of the Chief of Naval Operations, 1957.

Richard, Dorothy E. *United States Naval Administration of the Trust Territory of the Pacific Islands, Volume III: The Trusteeship Period, 1947–1951.* Washington: Office of the Chief of Naval Operations, 1957.

Sixth Annual Report of the Philippine Commission to the Secretary of War, 1905, Part I. Washington: Government Printing Office, 1906.

The United States Official Postal Guide. Washington: Government Printing Office, 1899.

U.S. Navy Report on Guam, 1899–1950. Washington: Department of the Navy, 1950.

Virgin Islands: Report of the Joint Commission Appointed under the Authority of the Concurrent Resolution Passed by the Congress of the United States, January 1920. Washington: Government Printing Office, 1920.

Published Primary Sources

Albizu Campos, Pedro. "Porto Rico and the War," *Harvard Crimson*, April 14, 1917.

Blackwell, Edward Maurice. *Book Two: Memoirs of Edward Maurice Blackwell.* Richmond, VA: Old Dominion Press, 1948.

Castillo, Evelyn Chapman. *And They Returned: Life in Leyte during World War II.* Houston, TX: Bright Sky Press, 2015.

Civil Liberties in American Colonies. New York: American Civil Liberties Union, 1939.

Condict, Alice Byram. *Old Glory and the Gospel in the Philippines: Notes Gathered during Professional and Missionary Work.* Chicago: Fleming H. Revell Company, 1902.

Courtney, W. B. "Guam: Haunted Paradise." *Collier's*, April 1939, pp. 14–15, 50–59.

Davis, Oscar King. *Our Conquests in the Pacific.* New York: Frederick A. Stokes, 1899.

Dockery, A. M. "Domestic Rates and Conditions Applicable to Alaska, Hawaii, Porto Rico, and the Possessions of the United States," *Post Office Clerk* 15, no. 10 (1917).

Fee, Mary H. *A Woman's Impression of the Philippines.* Chicago: A. C. McClurg, 1910.

Fernández, José Miguel C. *Carmen & I: Life under Japanese Occupation in WWII: Memoirs of José Miguel C. Fernández.* Maria Lourdes F. Godinez, 2014.

Forbes, W. Cameron. *The Philippine Islands, Revised Edition.* Cambridge, MA: Harvard University Press, 1945.

Fowler, Charles N. *"The Fowler Financial and Currency Bill": Speech in the House of Representatives, June 26, 1902.* Washington: Government Printing Office, 1902.

Guevara, Sulpicio, ed. *The Laws of the First Philippine Republic (The Laws of Malolos), 1898–1899.* Manila: National Historical Commission, 1972.

History of the Gift of Six Hundred National Flags to the Schools of Porto Rico by Lafayette Post, No. 140 Department of New York Grand Army of the Republic 1898. New York: J. J. Little, 1899.

Jordan, David Starr. *Imperial Democracy: A Study of the Relation of Government by the People, Equality before the Law, and other Tenets of Democracy, to the Demands of a Vigorous Foreign Policy and other Demands of Imperial Dominion.* New York: D. Appleton, 1899.

Journal of the Thirty-Third National Encampment of the Grand Army of the Republic, Philadelphia, PA September 6–7, 1899. Philadelphia: Town Printing Company, 1899.

Journal of the Thirty-Fourth National Encampment of the Grand Army of the Republic, August 29–30, Chicago IL. Philadelphia: Town Printing Company, 1901.

Journal of the Thirty-Seventh National Encampment of the Grand Army of the Republic, San Francisco, August 20–21, 1903. Philadelphia: Town Printing Company, 1903.

Journal of the Thirty-Eighth National Encampment of the Grand Army of the Republic, Boston, Massachusetts, August 17th and 18th, 1904. Chicago: M. Umbdenstock & Co., 1904.

Journal of the Thirty-Ninth National Encampment of the Grand Army of the Republic, Denver, Colorado, September 7th and 8th, 1905. Boston: Griffith-Stillings Press, 1905.

Kalaw, Pura Villanueva. *A Brief History of the Filipino Flag.* Manila: Bureau of Printing, 1947.

Kenyon, Brewster C. *History of the Postal Issues of Hawaii: A List of the Adhesive Postage Stamps, Stamped Envelopes and Postal Cards of the Hawaiian Government.* Self-published, 1895.

Kemmerer, Edwin Walter. *Modern Currency Reforms: A History and Discussion of Recent Currency Reforms in India, Porto Rico, Philippine Islands, Straits Settlements, and Mexico.* New York: Macmillan, 1916.

Life and Speeches of Hon. Wm. Jennings Bryan. Baltimore: R. H. Woodward, 1900.

Mendoza, Helen N. *Memories of the War Years: A Teenage Girl's Life in the Philippines under Japanese Rule.* Quezon City, Philippines: Pantas, 2016.

Moss, James A. *The Spirit of the American Flag.* Washington: United States Flag Association, 1933.

Presidential Messages and State Papers, Vol. X. New York: Review of Reviews Company, 1917.

Romulo, Carlos P. *I Saw the Fall of the Philippines.* Garden City, NY: Doubleday, Doran, & Company, 1943.

Roosevelt, Theodore, Jr. *Colonial Policies of the United States.* Garden City, NY: Doubleday, Doran and Company, 1937.

Russell, Florence Kimball. *A Woman's Journey through the Philippines on a Cable Ship That Linked Together the Strange Lands Seen en Route.* Boston: L. Century Page, 1907.

Thurston, Lucy G. *The Life and Times of Lucy G. Thurston.* Ann Arbor, MI: S. C. Andrews, 1882.

Washburn, H. C. *Illustrated Case Descriptions from the Official Catalogue of the Trophy Flags of the United States Navy.* Baltimore: Lord Baltimore Press, 1913.

Westcott, Robert B. *The Exaltation of the Flag: Proceedings at the Patriotic Mass Meeting Held by the Americans of the Philippine Islands, Which Took Place in the City of Manila, P.I., on the Evening of Friday, August 23, 1907.* Manila: John R. Edgar, 1907.

White, Trumbull. *Our New Possessions: A Graphic Account, Descriptive and Historical, of the Tropic-Islands of the Sea That Have Fallen under Our Sway.* Chicago: National Educational Union, 1898.

Zabriskie, Luther K. *The Virgin Islands of the United States of America: Historical and Descriptive Commercial and Industrial Facts, Figures, and Resources.* New York: G. P. Putnam's Sons, 1918.

Secondary Sources

Acosta, Ivonne. *La Mordaza: Puerto Rico 1948–1957.* Rio Piedras, PR: Editorial Edil, 1989.

Adas, Michael. *Dominance by Design: Technological Imperatives and America's Civilizing Mission.* Cambridge, MA: Harvard University Press, 2009.

Agoncillo, Teodoro A. *The Fateful Years: Japan's Adventure in the Philippines, 1941–1945, Vol. 1.* Quezon City: University of the Philippines Press, 2001.

Agoncillo, Teodoro A. *The Revolt of the Masses: The Story of Bonifacio and the Katipunan.* Quezon City: University of the Philippines, 1956.

Akana, Elizabeth A. *Hawaiian Quilting as a Fine Art.* Honolulu: Hawaiian Mission Children's Society, 1986.

Akiboh, Alvita. "Pocket-Sized Imperialism: U.S. Designs on Colonial Currency." *Diplomatic History* 41 (2017): 874–902.

Alabado, Corban K., and Ceres S. C. Alabado. *Philippine World War II Stories for Children in Bilingual Text English and Pilipino.* San Diego: University Readers, 2009.

Anderson, Benedict. *Imagined Communities: Reflections on the Origin and Spread of Nationalism.* London: Verso, 2006.

Andrew, A. Piatt. "The End of the Mexican Dollar." *Quarterly Journal of Economics* 18, no. 3 (May 1904): 321–56.

Appadurai, Arjun, ed. *The Social Life of Things: Commodities in Cultural Perspective.* Cambridge, UK: Cambridge University Press, 1986.

Arvin, Maile. "Pacifically Possessed: Scientific Production and Native Hawaiian Critique of the 'Almost White' Polynesian Race." PhD diss., University of California San Diego, 2013.

Ayala, César, and Rafael Bernabe, *Puerto Rico in the American Century: A History since 1898.* Chapel Hill: University of North Carolina Press, 2007.

Baja, Emanuel A. *Our Country's Flag and Anthem.* Manila: Juan Fajardo Press, 1928.

Balogh, Brian. *A Government Out of Sight: The Mystery of National Authority in Nineteenth-Century America.* Cambridge, UK: Cambridge University Press, 2009.

Banerjee, Sukanya. *Becoming Imperial Citizens: Indians in the Late-Victorian Empire.* Durham, NC: Duke University Press, 2010.

Basso, Aldo P. *Coins, Medals, and Tokens of the Philippines.* Menlo Park, NJ: Chenby, 1968.

Bator, Stefanie. "Toward Filipino Self-Rule: American Reform Organizations and American Colonialism in the Philippines, 1898–1946." PhD diss., Northwestern University, 2012.

Bayly, Christopher, and Tim Harper. *Forgotten Armies: The Fall of British Asia, 1941–1945.* Cambridge, MA: Harvard University Press, 2006.

Bender, Daniel E., and Jana Liplan, eds. *Making the Empire Work: Labor and United States Imperialism.* New York: New York University Press, 2015.

Bellah, Robert. "Civil Religion in America," *Daedalus* 96, no. 1 (Winter 1967): 1–21.

Bemis, Samuel Flagg. *A Diplomatic History of the United States.* New York: Henry Holt, 1955).

Benson, Jane, and Nancy Olsen. *The Power of Cloth: Political Quilts, 1845–1986.* Cupertino, CA: De Anza College, 1987.

Beriont, Carleigh. "'For the Good of Mankind': Atomic Exceptionalism, Religion, and United States Empire in the Postwar Pacific." In *A Companion to American Religious History*, ed. Benjamin E. Park, 287–98. Hoboken, NJ: Wiley, 2021.

Beriont, Carleigh. "In Translation: Religious Freedom, Democracy, and US Empire from the Perspective of the Postwar Pacific Islands." *American Religion, Inside Out*, February 2021. https://www.american-religion.org/inside-out/beriont.

Bernstein, Robin. *Racial Innocence: Performing American Childhood from Slavery to Civil Rights.* New York: New York University Press, 2011.

Bevacqua, Michael Lujan. "Chamorros, Ghosts, Non-Voting Delegates: Guam! Where the Production of America's Sovereignty Begins." PhD diss., University of California San Diego, 2010.

Bevacqua, Michael Lujan. "Guam: Protests at the Tip of America's Spear," *South Atlantic Quarterly* 116, no. 1 (2017): 174–83.

Billig, Michael. *Banal Nationalism*. London: Sage Publications, 1995.

Blevins, Cameron. *Paper Trails: The US Post and State Power in the American West*. Oxford, UK: Oxford University Press, 2021.

Blight, David. *Race and Reunion: The Civil War in American Memory*. Cambridge, MA: Harvard University Press, 2002.

Bodnar, John. *Remaking America: Public Memory, Commemoration, and Patriotism in the Twentieth Century*. Princeton, NJ: Princeton University Press, 1992.

Bonilla, Yarimar, and Marisol Lebrón, eds, *Aftershocks of Disaster: Puerto Rico before and after the Storm*. Chicago: Haymarket Books, 2019.

Brandon, Reiko Mochinaga. *The Hawaiian Quilt*. Honolulu: Honolulu Academy of Arts.

Brands, H. W. *Bound to Empire: The United States and the Philippines*. Oxford, UK: Oxford University Press, 1992.

Brennan, Sheila A. *Stamping American Memory: Collectors, Citizens, and the Post*. Ann Arbor: University of Michigan Press, 2018.

Brigham, William T. *Ka Hana Kapa: The Making of Bark-Cloth in Hawaii*. Honolulu: Bishop Museum Press, 1911.

Brunn, Stanley D. "Stamps as Iconography: Celebrating the Independence of New European and Central Asian States." *GeoJournal* 52, no. 4 (2000): 316–17.

Brunn, Stanley D. "Stamps as Messengers of Political Transition." *Geographical Review* 101, no. 1 (January 2011): 19–36.

Cabán, Pedro A. *Constructing a Colonial People: Puerto Rico and the United States, 1898–1932*. Boulder, CO: Westview Press, 1999.

Camacho, Keith L. *Cultures of Commemoration: The Politics of War, Memory, and History in the Mariana Islands*. Honolulu: University of Hawaiʻi Press, 2011.

Cannadine, David. *Ornamentalism: How the British Saw Their Empire*. Oxford, UK: Oxford University Press, 2001.

Cannon, M. Hamlin. *Leyte: Return to the Philippines*. Washington: Center of Military History, 1993.

Capozzola, Christopher. *Bound by War: How the United States and the Philippines Built America's First Pacific Century*. New York: Basic Books, 2020.

Carrión, Juan Manuel. "The War of the Flags: Conflicting National Loyalties in a Modern Colonial Situation." *Centro Journal* (September 2006): 110–11.

Cerulo, Karen A. "Symbols and the World System: Nation Anthems and Flags." *Sociological Forum* 8, no. 2 (June 1993): 243–71.

Child, Jack. "The Politics and Semiotics of the Smallest Icons of Popular Culture: Latin American Postage Stamps." *Latin American Research Review* 40, no. 1 (2005): 108–37.

Chomsky, Noam. *Hegemony or Survival: America's Quest for Global Dominance*. New York: Henry Holt, 2007.

Chomsky, Noam. *Making the Future: Occupations, Interventions, Empire, and Resistance*. New York: Penguin Books, 2012.

Chomsky, Noam. *Who Rules the World?* New York: Metropolitan Books, 2016.

Clayton, Anthony. *The Wars of French Decolonization*. Harlow, UK: Longman, 1994.

Clutario, Genevieve A. "World War II and the Promise of Normalcy: Overlapping Empires and Everyday Lives in the Philippines," in *Crossing Empires: Taking U.S. History into Transimperial Terrain*, ed. Kristin Hoganson and Jay Sexton), 241–58. Durham, NC: Duke University Press, 2020.

Coffman, Tom. *Nation Within: The History of the American Occupation of Hawai'i*. Durham, NC: Duke University Press, 2016.

Cohen, Deborah. *Household Gods: The British and Their Possessions*. New Haven, CT: Yale University Press, 2006.

Cole, Troy R. *The Silver Secret of Caballo Bay*. Trafford Publishing, 2011.

Conklin, Alice L. *A Mission to Civilize: The Republican Idea of Empire in France and West Africa 1895–1930*. Stanford, CA: Stanford University Press, 1997.

Connelly, Matthew. *A Diplomatic Revolution: Algeria's Fight for Independence and the Origins of the Post–Cold War Era*. Oxford, UK : Oxford University Press, 2002.

Constantino, Renato. *Insight and Foresight*. Quezon City, Philippines: Foundation for Nationalist Studies, 1977.

Cook, Kealani. *Return to Kahiki: Native Hawaiians in Oceania*. Cambridge, UK: Cambridge University Press, 2018.

Cooper, Frederick. *Citizenship between Empire and Nation: Remaking France and French Africa, 1945–1960*. Princeton, NJ: Princeton University Press, 2014.

Cooper, Frederick, and Jane Burbank. *Empires in World History: Power and the Politics of Difference*. Princeton, NJ: Princeton University Press, 2010.

Corpuz, Onofre D. *The Roots of the Filipino Nation, Volume 2*. Quezon City, Philippines: Aklahi Foundation, 1989.

Crowl, Philip A. *Campaign in the Marianas*. Washington: Center of Military History, 1993.

Cruz, Romeo V. *America's Colonial Desk and the Philippines, 1898–1934*. Quezon City: University of the Philippines Press, 1974.

Csikszentmihalyi, Mihaly. "Why We Need Things." In *History from Things: Essays on Material Culture*, ed. Steven Lubar and W. David Kingery. Washington: Smithsonian Institution Press, 1993.

Csikszentmihalyi, Mihaly, and Eugene Rochberg-Halton, eds. *The Meaning of Things: Domestic Symbols and the Self*. Chicago: University of Chicago Press, 1981.

Cullinane, Michael Patrick. *Liberty and American Anti-Imperialism: 1898–1909*. New York: Palgrave Macmillan, 2012.

CuUnjieng Aboitiz, Nicole. *Asian Place, Filipino Nation: A Global Intellectual History of the Philippine Revolution, 1887–1912*. New York: Columbia University Press, 2020.

Dávila Dávila, Ovidio. "Los bonos del Partido Nacionalista para la reconstitución de la República de Puerto Rico," 1930. Reprinted in *Revista del Instituto de Cultura Puertorriqueña* 6, no. 11 (2005): 32–43.

De Bevoise, Ken *Agents of the Apocalypse*. Princeton, NJ: Princeton University Press, 1995.

De Grazia, Victoria. *Irresistible Empire: America's Advance through Twentieth Century Europe*. Cambridge, MA: Harvard University Press, 2005.

DeLisle, Christine. "Navy Wives/Native Lives: The Cultural and Historical Relations between American Naval Wives and Chamorro Women in Guam, 1898–1945." PhD diss., University of Michigan, 2008.

DeLisle, Christine Taitano. " 'Guamanian-Chamorro by Birth but American Patriotic by Choice': Subjectivity and Performance in the Life of Agueda Iglesias Johnston," *Amerasia Journal* 37, no. 3 (2011): 61–75.

Delmendo, Sharon. *The Star-Entangled Banner: One Hundred Years of America in the Philippines*. Quezon City: University of Philippines Press, 2005.

Del Moral, Solsiree. *Negotiating Empire: The Cultural Politics of Schools in Puerto Rico, 1898–1952.* Madison: University of Wisconsin Press, 2013.

Diaz, Vicente M. "Deliberating 'Liberation Day': Identity, History, Memory, and War in Guam," in *Perilous Memories: The Asia-Pacific Wars,* ed. T. Fujitanti, Geoffrey White, and L. Yoneyama (Durham, NC: Duke University Press, 1998), 155–80.

Diaz, Vicente M. *Repositioning the Missionary: Rewriting the Histories of Colonialism, Native Catholicism, and Indigeneity in Guam.* Honolulu: University of Hawaiʻi Press, 2010.

Di Venuti, Biago. *Money and Banking in Puerto Rico.* Río Piedras: University of Puerto Rico Press, 1950.

Domosh, Mona. *American Commodities in an Age of Empire.* New York: Routledge, 2007.

Driscoll, Joseph. *War Discovers Alaska.* Philadelphia: J. B. Lippincott, 1943.

Duany, Jorge. *The Puerto Rican Nation on the Move: Identities on the Island and in the United States.* Chapel Hill: University of North Carolina Press, 2002.

Dudley, Sandra H., ed. *Museum Materialities: Objects, Engagements, Interpretations.* London: Routledge, 2010.

Duffy Burnett, Christina. "*Untied* States: American Expansion and Territorial Deannexation." *University of Chicago Law Review* 72, no. 3 (Summer 2005): 797–879.

Duffy Burnett, Christina, and Burke Marshall, eds. *Foreign in a Domestic Sense: Puerto Rico, American Expansion, and the Constitution.* Durham, NC: Duke University Press, 2001.

Eriksen, Thomas Hylland, and Richard Jenkins, eds. *Flag, Nation, and Symbolism in Europe and America.* London: Routledge, 2007.

Erman, Sam. *Almost Citizens: Puerto Rico, The U.S. Constitution, and Empire.* Cambridge, UK: Cambridge University Press, 2019.

Eyerman, Ron. "False Consciousness and Ideology in Marxist Theory." *Acta Sociologica* 24, no. 1/2 (1981): 43–56.

Faaleva, Toetu. "*Fitafita*: Samoan Landsmen in the United States Navy, 1900–1951." Ph.D. diss., University of California, Berkeley, 2003.

Fanon, Franz. *The Wretched of the Earth.* New York: Grove Press, 1963.

Fast, Jonathan, and Jim Richardson. *Roots of Dependency: Political and Economic Revolution in the Nineteenth-Century Philippines.* Quezon City: Foundation for Nationalist Studies, 1979.

Ferguson, Niall. *Colossus: The Price of America's Empire.* New York: Penguin, 2004.

Flores, Alfred Peredo, Jr. "'Little Island into Mighty Base': Indigeneity, Race, and U.S. Empire in Guam, 1944–1962." PhD diss, University of California, Los Angeles, 2015.

Francia, Luis H. *A History of the Philippines from Indios Bravos to Filipinos.* New York: Overlook Press, 2010.

Franqui-Rivera, Harry. *Soldiers of the Nation: Military Service and Modern Puerto Rico, 1868–1952.* Lincoln: University of Nebraska Press, 2018).

Friedman, Andrea. *Citizenship in Cold War America: The National Security State and the Possibilities of Dissent.* Amherst: University of Massachusetts Press, 2014.

Friend, Theodore. *Between Two Empires: The Ordeal of the Philippines, 1929–1946.* New Haven, CT: Yale University Press, 1965.

Fuller, Harcourt. *Building the Ghanaian Nation-Sate: Kwame Nkrumah's Symbolic Nationalism.* New York: Palgrave Macmillan, 2014.

Fuller, Wayne E. *RFD: The Changing Face of Rural America.* Bloomington: Indiana University Press, 1964.

Gagelonia, Pedro A. *The Philippine National Flag*. Caloocan City: Philippine Youth Supplier, 1967.

Gale, Roger W. *The Americanization of Micronesia: A Study of the Consolidation of U.S. Rule in the Pacific*. Washington: University Press of America, 1979.

Gallagher, John, and Ronald Robinson. "The Imperialism of Free Trade." *Economic History Review* 6 (1953): 1–15.

Gatell, Frank Otto. "Independence Rejected: Puerto Rico and the Tydings Bill of 1936." *Hispanic American Historical Review* 38, no. 1 (February 1958): 33.

Go, Julian. *American Empire and the Politics of Meaning: Elite Political Cultures in the Philippines and Puerto Rico During U.S. Colonialism*. Durham, NC: Duke University Press, 2008.

Go, Julian. *Patterns of Empire: The British and American Empires, 1688 to the Present*. Cambridge, UK: Cambridge University Press, 2011.

Go, Julian, and Anne Foster, eds. *The American Colonial State in the Philippines: Global Perspectives*. Durham, NC: Duke University Press, 2003.

Goldstein, Alyosha, ed., *Formations of United States Colonialism*. Durham, NC: Duke University Press, 2014.

Goldstein, Donald M., and Katherine V. Dillon. *The Williwaw War: The Arkansas National Guard in the Aleutians in World War II*. Fayetteville: University of Arkansas Press, 1992.

Golodoff, Nick. *Attu Boy*. Anchorage, AK: National Park Service, 2012.

Gonzalez, Vernadette Vicuña. "Hawaiian Quilts, Global Domesticities, and Patterns of Counterhegemony." In *Transnational Crossroads: Remapping the Americas and the Pacific*, ed. Camilla Fojas and Rudy P. Guevarra Jr., 87–115. Lincoln: University of Nebraska Press, 2012.

Gonzalez, Vernadette Vicuña. *Securing Paradise: Tourism and Militarism in Hawai'i and the Philippines*. Durham, NC: Duke University Press, 2013.

Goodyear-Kaopua, Noelani, Ikaika Hussey, and Erin Kahunawaika'ala Wright, eds. *A Nation Rising: Hawaiian Movements for Life, Land, and Sovereignty*. Durham, NC: Duke University Press, 2014.

Goto, Ken'ichi. *Tensions of Empire: Japan and Southeast Asia in the Colonial and Postcolonial World*. Athens: Ohio University Press, 2003.

Gottmann, Jean. "The Political Partitioning of Our World: An Attempt at Analysis," *World Politics* 4, no. 4 (July 1952): 512–19.

Gowing, Peter Gordon. *Mandate in Moroland: The American Government of Muslim Filipinos, 1899–1920*. Quezon City, Philippines: New Day Publishers, 1983.

Gram, John R. *Education at the Edge of Empire: Negotiating Pueblo Identity in New Mexico's Indian Boarding Schools*. Seattle: University of Washington Press, 2015.

Greene, Julie. "Movable Empire: Labor, Migration, and U.S. Global Power during the Gilded Age and Progressive Era." *Journal of the Gilded Age and Progressive Era* 15 (2016): 4–20.

Grewal, David Singh. *Network Power: The Social Dynamics of Globalization*. New Haven, CT: Yale University Press, 2008.

Guerra, Lillian. *Popular Expression and National Identity in Puerto Rico*. Gainesville: University Press of Florida, 1998.

Hackler, Rhoda E. A., and Loretta G. H. Woodard. *The Queen's Quilt*. Honolulu: Friends of Iolani Palace, 2004.

Hammond, Joyce D. "Hawaiian Flag Quilts: Multivalent Symbols of a Hawaiian Quilt Tradition." *Hawaiian Journal of History* 27 (1993): 1–26.

Harding, Deborah. *Stars and Stripes: Patriotic Motifs in American Folk Art*. New York: Rizzoli, 2002.

Hardt, Michael, and Antonio Negri. *Empire*. Cambridge, MA: Harvard University Press, 2000.

Hattori, Anne Perez. *Colonial Dis-Ease: US Navy Health Policies and the Chamorros of Guam, 1898–1941*. Honolulu: University of Hawai'i Press, 2004.

Hattori, Anne Perez. "Navy Blues: US Naval Rule on Guam and the Rough Road to Assimilation." *Pacific Asia Inquiry* 5, no. 1 (Fall 2014): 13–30.

Hau'ofa, Epeli. "Our Sea of Islands." *Contemporary Pacific* 6, no. 1 (Spring 1994): 148–61.

Heefner, Gretchen. "A Symbol of the New Frontier." *Pacific Historical Review* 74, no. 4 (November 2005): 545–74.

Helleiner, Eric. *The Making of National Money: Territorial Currencies in Historical Perspective*. Ithaca, NY: Cornell University Press, 2003).

Henkin, M. David. *The Postal Age: The Emergence of Modern Communications in Nineteenth-Century America*. Chicago: University of Chicago Press, 2006.

Herlily-Mera, Jeffrey. *After American Studies: Rethinking the Legacies of Transnational Exceptionalism*. London: Routledge, 2018.

Higuchi, Wakako. *The Japanese Administration of Guam, 1941–1944: A Study of Occupation and Integration Policies, with Japanese Oral Histories*. Jefferson, NC: McFarland & Company, 2013.

Higuchi, Wakako. "The Japanisation Policy for the Chamorros of Guam, 1941–1944." *Journal of Pacific History* 36, no. 1 (2001): 19–35.

Hill, Valdemar A., Sr. *Rise to Recognition: An Account of Virgin Islanders from Slavery to Self-Government*. St. Thomas, VI: Valdemar A. Hill Sr., 1971.

Hoganson, Kristin L. *Fighting for American Manhood: How Gender Politics Provoked the Spanish-American War*. New Haven, CT: Yale University Press, 1998.

Holland, Robert, Susan Williams, and Terry Barringer. *The Iconography of Independence: "Freedoms at Midnight."* New York: Routledge, 2010.

Hopkins, Anthony. *American Empire: A Global History*. Princeton, NJ: Princeton University Press, 2018.

Hsu, Funie. "The Coloniality of Neoliberal English: The Enduring Structures of American Colonial English Instruction in the Philippines and Puerto Rico." *L2 Journal* 7 (2015): 123–45.

Hudson, Peter James. *Bankers and Empire: How Wall Street Colonized the Caribbean*. Chicago: University of Chicago Press, 2017.

Hunt, John M. "World War II Emergency Service Currency for Mountain Province." *Pesos Fuertes: Bank Note Society of the Philippines Journal* 1 (August 2005): 27.

Hunt, Michael H., and Steven I. Levine. *Arc of Empire: America's Wars in Asia from the Philippines to Vietnam*. Chapel Hill: University of North Carolina Press, 2012.

Hunter, Stephen, and John Bainbridge, Jr. *American Gunfight: The Plot to Kill Harry Truman—and the Shoot-Out That Stopped It*. New York: Simon & Schuster, 2005.

Iglesias Utset, Marial. *A Cultural History of Cuba During the U.S. Occupation, 1898–1902*. Trans. Russ Davidson. Chapel Hill: University of North Carolina Press, 2011.

Ileto, Reynaldo. *Knowing America's Colony: A Hundred Years from the Philippine War*. Honolulu: Center for Philippine Studies, 1999.

Ileto, Reynaldo C. *Pasyon and Revolution: Popular Movements in the Philippines, 1840–1910*. Quezon City, Philippines: Ateneo de Manila University Press, 1979.

Imada, Adria L. *Aloha America: Hula Circuits through the U.S. Empire*. Durham, NC: Duke University Press, 2012.

Immerman, Richard H. *Empire for Liberty: A History of American Imperialism from Benjamin Franklin to Paul Wolfowitz*. Princeton, NJ: Princeton University Press, 2010.

Immerwahr, Daniel. *How to Hide an Empire: A History of the Greater United States*. New York: Farrar, Straus and Giroux, 2019.

Immerwahr, Daniel. "Philippine Independence in U.S. History: A Car, Not a Train." *Pacific Historical Review* 91, no. 2 (2022): 220–48.

Irwin, Bernice Piilani. *I Knew Queen Liliuokalani*. Honolulu: South Sea Sales, 1960.

Jacobson, Matthew Frye. *Barbarian Virtues: The United States Encounters Foreign Peoples at Home and Abroad, 1876–1917*. New York: Hill and Wang, 2001.

Jiménez de Wagenheim, Olga. *Nationalist Heroines: Puerto Rican Women History Forgot, 1930s–1950s*. Princeton, NJ: Markus Wiener Publishers, 2016.

John, Richard R. *Spreading the News: The American Postal System from Franklin to Morse*. Cambridge, MA: Harvard University Press, 1995.

Jung, Moon-Ho. *Menace to Empire: Anticolonial Solidarities and the Transpacific Origins of the US Security State*. Berkeley: University of California Press, 2022.

Kamehiro, Stacy L. "Hawaiian Quilts: Chiefly Self-Representations in Nineteenth-Century Hawaiʻi." *Pacific Arts* 3/5 (2007): 24.

Kaplan, Amy. *The Anarchy of Empire and the Making of U.S. Culture*. Cambridge, MA: Harvard University Press, 2002.

Kaplan, Amy, and Donald Pease, eds. *Cultures of United States Imperialism*. Durham, NC: Duke University Press, 1993.

Karnow, Stanley. *In Our Image: America's Empire in the Philippines*. New York: Random House, 1989.

Kauanui, J. Kehaulani. *Hawaiian Blood: Colonialism and the Politics of Sovereignty and Indigeneity, Narrating Native Histories*. Durham, NC: Duke University Press, 2008.

Kerr, James A. *The Insular Cases: The Role of the Judiciary in American Expansionism*. Port Washington, NY: Kennikat Press, 1982.

Kent, Noel J. *Hawaii: Islands under the Influence*. Honolulu: University of Hawaiʻi Press, 1993.

Kevane, Michael. "Official Representations of the Nation: Comparing the Postage Stamps of Sudan and Burkina Faso." *African Studies Quarterly* 10, no. 1 (Spring 2008): 71–94.

Kinzer, Stephen. *The True Flag: Theodore Roosevelt, Mark Twain, and the Birth of American Empire*. New York: Henry Holt, 2017.

Kramer, Paul A. *The Blood of Government: Race, Empire, the United States, and the Philippines*. Chapel Hill: University of North Carolina Press, 2006.

Kramer, Paul A. "Power and Connection: Imperial Histories of the United States in the World." *American Historical Review* 116 (December 2011): 1348–91.

LaFeber, Walter. *The New Empire: An Interpretation of American Expansion, 1860–1898*. Ithaca, NY: Cornell University Press, 1963.

Leepson, Marc. *Flag: An American Biography*. New York: Macmillan, 2007.

Licuanan, Virginia Benitez. *Money in the Bank: The Story of Money and Banking in the Philippines and the PCIBank Story*. Manila: Philippine Commercial International Bank, 1985.

Lindstrom, Lamont, and Geoffrey M. White. *Island Encounters: Black and White Memories of the Pacific War*. Washington: Smithsonian Institution Press, 1990.

Lloréns, Hilda. *Imaging the Great Puerto Rican Family: Framing Nation, Race, and Gender during the American Century*. Lanham, MD: Lexington Books, 2014.

Lumba, Allan E. S. "Imperial Standards: Colonial Currencies, Racial Capacities, and Economic Knowledge during the Philippine-American War." *Diplomatic History* 39, no. 44 (September 2015): 603–28.

Lumba, Allan E. S. *Monetary Authorities: Capitalism and Decolonization in the American Colonial Philippines*. Durham, NC: Duke University Press, 2022.

Mack, Doug. *The Not-Quite States of America: Dispatches from the Territories and Other Far-Flung Outposts of the USA*. New York: W. W. Norton, 2018.

Maier, Charles S. *Among Empires: American Ascendancy and Its Predecessors*. Cambridge, MA: Harvard University Press, 2006.

Majul, Cesar Adib. *The Political and Constitutional Ideas of the Philippine Revolution*. New York: Oriole Editions, 1967.

Malay, Armando J. *Occupied Philippines: The Role of Jorge B. Vargas during the Japanese Occupation*. Manila: Filipiniana Book Guild, 1967.

Maldonado, A. W. *Luis Muñoz Marín: Puerto Rico's Democratic Revolution*. San Juan: Editorial Universidad de Puerto Rico, 2006.

Man, Simeon. *Soldiering through Empire: Race and the Making of the Decolonizing Pacific*. Berkeley: University of California Press, 2018.

Martin, David A. "The Changing Role of Foreign Money in the United States, 1782–1857." *Journal of Economic History* 37, no. 4 (December 1977): 1009–27.

Martín-Aceña, Pablo, and Inés Roldán de Montaud. "A Colonial Bank under Spanish and American Sovereignty: The Banco Español de Puerto Rico, 1888–1913." *Caribbean Studies* 41, no. 1 (July-December 2013): 163–207.

Martínez, Elena. "¡Que Bonita Bandera!: Place, Space, and Identity as Expressed with the Puerto Rican Flag." In *Public Performance: Studies in the Carnivalesque and Ritualesque*, ed. Jack Santino, 113–32. Logan: Utah State University Press.

Mathews, Thomas. *Puerto Rican Politics and the New Deal*. Gainesville: University of Florida Press, 1960.

May, Glenn Anthony. *Battle for Batangas: A Philippine Province at War*. New Haven, CT: Yale University Press, 1991.

May, Glenn Anthony. *Social Engineering in the Philippines: The Aims, Execution, and Impact of American Colonial Policy, 1900–1913*. Westport, CT: Greenwood Press, 1980.

McClintock, Anne. "Family Feuds: Gender, Nationalism and the Family." *Feminist Review*, no. 44 (Summer 1993): 61–80.

McCormick, Thomas J. *China Market: America's Quest for Informal Empire 1893–1901*. Chicago: Quadrangle Books, 1967.

McCoy, Alfred W. *Policing America's Empire: The United States, the Philippines, and the Rise of the Surveillance State*. Madison: University of Wisconsin Press, 2009.

McCoy, Alfred W., and Francisco Scarano, eds. *Colonial Crucible: Empire in the Making of the Modern American State*. Madison: University of Wisconsin Press, 2009.

McGreevey, Robert C. *Borderline Citizens: The United States, Puerto Rico, and the Politics of Colonial Migration*. Ithaca, NY: Cornell University Press, 2018.

Mendoza, Victor. *Metroimperial Intimacies: Fantasy, Racial-Sexual Governance, and the Philippines in U.S. Imperialism, 1899–1913*. Durham, NC: Duke University Press, 2015.

Merleaux, April. *Sugar and Civilization: American Empire and the Cultural Politics of Sweetness*. Chapel Hill: University of North Carolina Press, 2015.

Mihm, Stephen. *A Nation of Counterfeiters: Capitalists, Con Men, and the Making of the United States*. Cambridge, MA: Harvard University Press, 2007.

Miller, Stuart Creighton. *"Benevolent Assimilation": The American Conquest of the Philippines, 1899–1903*. New Haven, CT: Yale University Press, 1982.

Miller-Davenport, Sarah. *Gateway State: Hawai'i and the Cultural Transformation of American Empire*. Princeton, NJ: Princeton University Press, 2019.

Moore, Colin D. *American Imperialism and the State, 1893–1921*. Cambridge, UK: Cambridge University Press, 2017.

Moore, Colin D. "State Building through Partnership: Delegation, Public-Private Partnerships, and the Political Development of American Imperialism, 1898–1916." *Studies in American Political Development* 25 (April 2011): 27–55.

Morris, Nancy. *Puerto Rico: Culture, Politics, and Identity*. Westport, CT: Praeger, 1995.

Morton, Louis. *The Fall of the Philippines*. Washington: Center of Military History, 1993.

Motyl, Alexander J. "Review: Empire Falls: Washington May Be Imperious, but It Is Not Imperial." *Foreign Affairs* 85, no. 4 (July-August 2006): 190–94.

Nagano, Yoshiko. *State and Finance in the Philippines, 1898–1941: The Mismanagement of an American Colony*. Singapore: National University of Singapore Press, 2015.

Navarro, José-Manuel. *Creating Tropical Yankees: Social Science Textbooks and U.S. Ideological Control in Puerto Rico, 1898–1908*. New York: Routledge, 2002.

Navarro-Rivera, Pablo. "The ACLU and Civil Liberties in Puerto Rico." *Journal of Pedagogy, Pluralism, and Practice* 3, no. 3 (Summer 2006): 34–70.

Negrón de Montilla, Aída. *Americanization in Puerto Rico and the Public School System 1900–1930*. Río Piedras, PR: Editorial Edil, 1970.

Neuman, Gerald L., and Tomiko Brown-Nagin, eds. *Reconsidering the Insular Cases: The Past and Future of the American Empire*. Cambridge, MA: Harvard University Press, 2015.

Niedenthal, Jack. "A History of the People of Bikini following Nuclear Weapons Testing in the Marshall Islands: With Recollections and Views of Elders of Bikini Atoll." *Health Physics* 73, no. 1 (July 1997): 28–36.

O'Neill, Edward A. *Rape of the American Virgins*. New York: Praeger Publishers, 1972.

Orquiza, Jr., René Alexander Disini. *Taste of Control: Food and the Filipino Colonial Mentality under American Rule*. New Brunswick, NJ: Rutgers University Press, 2020.

Ozouf, Mona. *Festivals and the French Revolution*. Cambridge, MA: Harvard University Press, 1988.

Pagán, Bolívar. *Historia de los Partidos Políticos Puertorriqueños (1898–1956), Tomo II*. San Juan, PR: Librería Campos, 1959.

Palomo, Tony. "Island in Agony: The War in Guam." In *Remembering the Pacific War*, ed. Geoffrey White. Honolulu: Center for Pacific Islands Studies, 1991. 133–44.

Parket, Roszika. *The Subversive Stitch: Embroidery and the Making of the Feminine*. London: J. B. Tauris, 2010.

Pearsall, Sarah M. S. "Madame Sacho: How One Iroquois Woman Survived the American Revolution." *Humanities* 36, no. 3 (May/June 2015).

Perez, Michael P. "Colonialism, Americanization, and Indigenous Identity: A Research Note on Chamorro Identity in Guam," *Sociological Spectrum* 25, no. 5: 571–91.

Perez, Michael Peter. "The Dialectic of Indigenous Identity in the Wake of Colonialism: The Case of Chamorros of Guam." PhD diss., University of California, Riverside, 1997.

Pierce, Todd. "Philatelic Propaganda: Stamps in Territorial Disputes." *IBRU Boundary and Security Bulletin* 4, no. 2 (1996): 62–64.

Pinch, Trevor, and Wiebe Bijker. "Social Construction of Facts and Artifacts." In *Social Construction of Technological Systems: New Directions in the Sociology and History of Technology*, ed. Wiebe Bijker, Thomas Hughes, and Trevor Pinch, 17–50. Cambridge, MA: MIT Press, 1987.

Poblete, JoAnna. *Islanders in the Empire: Filipino and Puerto Rican Laborers in the Empire*. Urbana: University of Illinois Press, 2014.

Power, Margaret. "Nationalism in a Colonized Nation: The Nationalist Party and Puerto Rico." *Memorias: Revista digital de historia y arqueología desde el Caribe Colombiano* 10, no. 20 (May-August 2013): 119–37.

Pratt, Julius W. *America's Colonial Experiment: How the United States Gained, Governed, and in Part Gave Away a Colonial Empire*. New York: Prentice-Hall, 1951.

Preble, Geo. Henry. *Origin and History of the American Flag, Vol. II*. Philadelphia: Nicholas L. Brown, 1917.

Rafael, Vicente L. *White Love and Other Events in Filipino History*. Durham, NC: Duke University Press, 2000.

Raustalia, Kal. *Does the Constitution Follow the Flag? The Evolution of Territoriality in American Law*. Oxford, UK: Oxford University Press, 2009.

RealFACES: Guam's World War II Survivors. Hagåtña, Guam: War Survivors Memorial Foundation, 2014.

Reeves, Richard. *Infamy: The Shocking Story of the Japanese American Internment in World War II*. New York: Henry Holt, 2015.

Renda, Mary. *Taking Haiti: Military Occupation and the Culture of U.S. Imperialism, 1915–1940*. Chapel Hill: University of North Carolina Press, 2004.

Reports of General MacArthur: The Campaigns of MacArthur in the Pacific, Vol. 1. Washington: Center for Military History, 1994.

Reynolds, Ruth M. *Campus in Bondage: A 1948 Microcosm of Puerto Rico in Bondage*. New York: Centro de Estudios Puertorriqueños, 1989.

Riddell, J. L. *A Monograph of the Silver Dollar: Good and Bad*. New Orleans: Norman, 1845.

Roberts, Brian Russel, and Michelle Ann Stephens, eds. *Archipelagic American Studies*. Durham, NC: Duke University Press, 2017.

Rodríguez Beruff, Jorge. *Strategy as Politics: Puerto Rico on the Eve of the Second World War*. San Juan, PR: Editorial Universidad de Puerto Rico, 2007.

Rodríguez Vázquez, Eduardo. *The Notes of the Island of Puerto Rico: The Humberto Costa Collection*. Mayagüez, PR: Westernbank, 2007.

Root, Elizabeth. *Menehune Quilts: the Hawaiian Way*. Kailua, HI: Erdhi Publishing, 2001.

Rosario Natal, Carmelo, ed. *Escudo, Himno y Bandera: Origen e Historia de los Símbolos de Puerto Rico*. Rio Piedras, PR: Editorial Edil, 1989.

Rose, Roger G. *Hawai'i, The Royal Isles, Bernice P. Bishop Museum Special Publication 67*. Honolulu: Bishop Museum Press, 1980.

Rosenberg, Emily S. *Financial Missionaries to the World: The Politics and Culture of Dollar Diplomacy, 1900–1930*. Cambridge, MA: Harvard University Press, 1999.

Rush, Anne. *Bonds of Empire: West Indians and Britishness from Victoria to Decolonization*. Oxford, UK: Oxford University Press, 2011.

Sailiata, Kirisitina. "The Samoan Cause: Colonialism, Culture, and the Rule of Law." PhD diss., University of Michigan, 2014.

Saranillio, Dean Itsuji. *Unsustainable Empire: Alternative Histories of Hawai'i Statehood*. Durham, NC: Duke University Press, 2018.

Sato, Shohei. "Britain's Decision to Withdraw from the Persian Gulf, 1964–68: A Pattern and a Puzzle." *Journal of Imperial and Commonwealth History* 37, no. 1 (2009): 99–117.

Scheele, Carl H., and Constance Minkin. *Neither Snow, Nor Rain . . . : The Story of the United States Mails*. Washington: Smithsonian, 1970.

Scheiber, Harry N., and Jane L. Scheiber. *Bayonets in Paradise: Martial Law in Hawai'i during World War II*. Honolulu: University of Hawai'i Press, 2016.

Schumacher, John N. *Revolutionary Clergy: The Filipino Clergy and the Nationalist Movement, 1850–1903*. Manila: Ateneo de Manila University Press, 1981.

Seijo Bruno, Miñi. *La Insurreción Nacionalista en Puerto Rico 1950*. Rio Piedras: Universidad de Puerto Rico, 1989.

Serrao, Poakalani, John Serrao, Raelene Correia, and Cissy Serrao. *The Hawaiian Quilt: The Tradition Continues*. Honolulu: Mutual, 2007.

Shafer, Neil. *A Guide Book of Philippine Paper Money*. Racine, WI: Whitman, 1964.

Shafer, Neil. *Philippine Emergency Currency and Guerrilla Currency of World War II*. Racine, WI: Western Publishing, 1974.

Shaw, Angel Velasco, and Luis H. Francia, eds. *Vestiges of War: The Philippine-American War and the Aftermath of an Imperial Dream*. New York: New York University Press, 2002.

Shaw, Robert. *Hawaiian Quilt Masterpieces*. Fairfield, CT: Hugh Lauter Levin Associates, 1996.

Sheats, Robert C. *One Man's War: Diving as a Guest of the Emperor 1942*. Flagstaff, AZ: Best Publishing, 1998.

Shigematsu, Setsu, and Keith L. Camacho, eds. *Militarized Currents: Toward a Decolonized Future in Asia and the Pacific*. Minneapolis: University of Minnesota Press, 2010.

Silbey, David J. *A War of Frontier and Empire: The Philippine-American War, 1899–1902*. New York: Hill and Wang, 2007.

Silva, Noenoe K. *Aloha Betrayed: Native Hawaiian Resistance to American Colonialism*. Durham, NC: Duke University Press, 2004.

Sinha, Mrinalini. *Specters of Mother India: The Global Restructuring of an Empire*. Durham, NC: Duke University Press, 2006.

Skocpol, Theda. "The Tocqueville Problem: Civic Engagement in American Democracy." *Social Science History* 21 (Winter 1997): 455–79.

Smith, Neil. *American Empire: Roosevelt's Geographer and the Prelude to Globalization*. Berkeley: University of California Press, 2003.

Smith, Rogers M. *Civic Ideals: Conflicting Visions of Citizenship in U.S. History*. New Haven, CT: Yale University Press, 1997.

Snow, Richard. *A Guide Book of Flying Eagle and Indian Head Cents: Complete Source for History, Grading, and Prices*. Atlanta: Whitman, 2009.

Sotomayor, Antonio. *The Sovereign Colony: Olympic Sport, National Identity, and International Politics in Puerto Rico*. Lincoln: University of Nebraska Press, 2016.

Sparrow, Bartholomew. *The Insular Cases and the Emergence of American Empire*. Lawrence: Kansas University Press, 2006.

Sparrow, Bartholomew, and Jennifer Lamm. "Puerto Ricans and U.S. Citizenship in 1917: Imperatives of Security." *CENTRO Journal* 29, no. 1 (Spring 2017): 284–315.

Spyer, Patricia, ed. *Border Fetishisms: Material Objects in Unstable Spaces*. New York: Routledge, 1998.

Stamps of the Philippines: Historical and Topical Collections, 1854–2004. Pasay: Philippine Small and Medium Business Development Foundation, 2008.

Steinbock-Pratt, Sarah. *Educating the Empire: American Teachers and Contested Colonization in the Philippines*. Cambridge, UK: Cambridge University Press, 2019.

Stephan, John J. *Hawaii under the Rising Sun: Japan's Plans for Conquest after Pearl Harbor*. Honolulu: University of Hawaii Press, 1984.

Stephanson, Anders. *Manifest Destiny, American Expansion and the Empire of Right*. New York: Hill and Wang, 1995.

Stoler, Ann Laura. *Along the Archival Grain: Epistemic Anxieties and Colonial Common Sense*. Princeton, NJ: Princeton University Press, 2009.

Stoler, Ann Laura. *Carnal Knowledge and Imperial Power: Race and the Intimate in Colonial Rule*. Berkeley: University of California Press, 2002.

Stoler, Ann Laura. "On Degrees of Imperial Sovereignty." *Public Culture* 18 (Winter 2006): 125–46.

Stoler, Ann Laura, ed. *Haunted by Empire: Geographies of Intimacy in North American History*. Durham, NC: Duke University Press, 2006.

Stuart, Peter C. *Isles of Empire: The United States and Its Overseas Possessions*. Lanham, MD: University Press of America, 1999.

Sturtevant, David R. *Popular Uprisings in the Philippines 1840–1940*. Ithaca, NY: Cornell University Press, 1976.

Tabrah, Ruth M. *Hawaii: A History*. New York: W. W. Norton, 1984.

Testi, Arnaldo. *Capture the Flag: The Stars and Stripes in American History*. New York: New York University Press, 2010.

Thompson, Lanny. *Imperial Archipelago: Representation and Rule in the Insular Territories under U.S. Dominion after 1898*. Honolulu: University of Hawai'i Press, 2010.

Tinio McKenna, Rebecca. *American Imperial Pastoral: The Architecture of US Colonialism in the Philippines*. Chicago: University of Chicago Press, 2017.

Tomas, Joseph Santo. "Song of Hope, Song of Faith." In *Liberation—Guam Remembers: A Golden Salute for the 50th Anniversary of the Liberation of Guam*. Hagåtña, Guam: Golden Salute Committee, 1994.

Tompkins, E. Berkeley. *Anti-Imperialism in the United States; The Great Debate, 1890–1920*. Philadelphia: University of Pennsylvania Press, 1970.

Torres, Jose M. *The Massacre at Atåte*. Richard F. Taitano Micronesian Area Research Center, University of Guam, 2015.

Trask, Haunani-Kay. *From a Native Daughter: Colonialism and Sovereignty in Hawai'i*. Honoulu: University of Hawai'i Press, 1999.

Trask, Haunani-Kay. "Speeches for the Centennial of the Overthrow, 'Iolani Palace 1993." In *Huihui: Navigating Art and Literature in the Pacific*, ed. Jeffrey Carroll, Brandy Nālani McDougall, and Georganne Nordstrom, 99–114. Honolulu: University of Hawai'i Press, 2014.

Trías Monge, José. *Puerto Rico: The Trials of the Oldest Colony in the World*. New Haven, CT: Yale University Press, 1997.

Tuck, Eve, and K. Wayne Yang. "Decolonization Is Not a Metaphor." *Decolonization: Indigeneity, Education & Society* 1, no. 1 (2012): 1–40.

Underwood, Robert. "Red, Whitewash and Blue: Painting Over the Chamorro Experience." *Pacific Daily News*, July 17, 1977, p. 8.

Venator-Santiago, Charles. "Mapping the Contours of the History of Extension of U.S. Citizenship to Puerto Rico, 1898-Present." *CENTRO Journal* 29, no. 1 (Spring 2017): 38–55.

Viernes, James Perez. "Negotiating Manhood: Chamorro Masculinities and U.S. Military Colonialism in Guam, 1898–1941." PhD diss., University of Hawai'i at Manoa, 2015.

Wexler, Laura. *Tender Violence: Domestic Visions in an Age of U.S. Imperialism.* Chapel Hill: University of North Carolina Press, 2000.

White, Richard. *"It's Your Misfortune and None of My Own": A New History of the American West.* Norman: University of Oklahoma Press, 1991.

Wilder, Gary. *The French Imperial Nation-State: Negritude and Colonial Humanism between the Two World Wars.* Chicago: University of Chicago Press, 2005.

Williams, Edith B. *Ka Hae Hawaii: The Story of the Hawaiian Flag.* Honolulu: South Sea Sales, 1963.

Williams, William Appleman. *Empire as a Way of Life: An Essay on the Causes and Character of America's Present Predicament along with a Few Thoughts about an Alternative.* Oxford, UK: Oxford University Press, 1980.

Williams, William Appleman. *The Tragedy of American Diplomacy.* New York: W. W. Norton, 1959.

Willocks, Harold W. L. *The Umbilical Cord: The History of the United States Virgin Islands from Pre-Columbian Era to the Present.* St. Croix, VI: Harold W. L. Willocks, 1995.

Willoughby Charles A., and John Chamberlain. *MacArthur, 1941–1951.* New York: McGraw-Hill, 1954.

Wilson, James G. *The Imperial Republic: A Structural History of American Constitutionalism from the Colonial Era to the Beginning of the Twentieth Century.* Burlington, VT: Ashgate, 2002.

Winner, Langdon. *The Whale and the Reactor: A Search for Limits in an Age of High Technology.* Chicago: University of Chicago Press, 1986.

Woodard, Loretta, G. H. "Communities of Quilters: Hawaiian Pattern Collecting, 1900–1959." *Uncoverings* 27 (2006): 1–27.

Yellen, Jeremy A. *The Greater East Asia Co-Prosperity Sphere: When Total Empire Met Total War.* Ithaca, NY: Cornell University Press, 2019.

Zaide, Gregorio F. *The Philippine Revolution.* Manila: Modern Book Company, 1954.

Index

Page numbers in italics refer to figures.